John Marsden has written more than 40 books, mostly for teenagers and children, including *Tomorrow When the War Began*, *So Much to Tell You* and *Letters from the Inside*. He has sold over five million books worldwide, and has won every major award in Australia for young people's fiction. *South of Darkness*, written for adults, won the Christina Stead Award for Best Novel of 2015.

John's passionate interest in education led him to start two schools: Candlebark, on a vast forested estate near Romsey Victoria, and Alice Miller, at Macedon, a Year 7–12 school with a particular emphasis on the creative arts.

Also by John Marsden

The Tomorrow Series
Tomorrow, When the War Began
The Dead of the Night
The Third Day, The Frost
Darkness, Be My Friend
Burning for Revenge
The Night is for Hunting
The Other Side of Dawn

The Ellie Chronicles
While I Live
Incurable
Circle of Flight

Fiction
South of Darkness
The Journey
The Great Gatenby
Out of Time
Letters from the Inside
Take My Word for It
Checkers
Staying Alive in Year 5
Looking for Trouble
Cool School
Creep Street
Dear Miffy
Winter
Millie
The Year My Life Broke

Non-fiction
For Weddings and a Funeral
Everything I Know About Writing
Secret Men's Business
Marsden on Marsden
The Head Book
The Boy You Brought Home

The

ART

of

GROWING

UP

JOHN
MARSDEN

MACMILLAN
Pan Macmillan Australia

First published 2019 in by Pan Macmillan Australia Pty Ltd
1 Market Street, Sydney, New South Wales, Australia, 2000

 A catalogue record for this
book is available from the
National Library of Australia

Typeset in 12/16 pt Bembo by Post Pre-press
Printed by McPherson's Printing Group

Extract pp. 18 reproduced from Reading and Loving (RLE, Literacy), 1st Edition by Leila Berg, published by Routledge. © Leila Berg 1977, reproduced by arrangement with Taylor & Francis Books UK.

Extract pp. 30 from Denise Levertov, *New Selected Poems* (Bloodaxe Books, 2003). www.bloodaxebooks.com

Extract pp. 38–39 from GUESS WHO'S COMING TO DINNER © 1967, renewed 1995 Columbia Pictures Industries, Inc. All Rights Reserved. Courtesy of Columbia Pictures.

Extract pp. 106 from 'Stamps' reprinted with permission of Siv Widerberg.

Extract pp. 154 from 'Introduction; Myths of Protection, Acts of Exposure; Home Alone with the Adorable Child' in *Erotic Innocence*, James Kincaid, pp. 13. Copyright, 1998, Duke University Press. All rights reserved. Republished by permission of the copyright holder. www.dukeupress.edu

Extract pp. 239 from 'Valediction' from *Collected Poems* © Estate of Louis MacNeice, reprinted by permission of David Higham.

Extract pp. 329–330 reprinted with permission from *The Hate Race* by Maxine Beneba Clarke, Hachette Australia, 2016.

Extract on pp. 330–332, 'I'm not that special', reprinted by permission of Niamh Choesang (formerly Niamh Scally).

The author and the publisher have made every effort to contact copyright holders for material used in this book. Any person or organisation that may have been overlooked should contact the publisher.

Aboriginal and Torres Strait Islander people should be aware that this book may contain images or names of people now deceased.

 The paper in this book is FSC® certified.
FSC® promotes environmentally responsible,
socially beneficial and economically viable
management of the world's forests.

For Kris,
my partner in this noble and ridiculous world

This book draws upon my experience of teaching over 40 years, but where necessary (including for privacy reasons), details have been changed. For similar reasons, while based on actual correspondence, letters purporting to be from parents have been created by me.

CONTENTS

PREFACE

Your parents and your school. Does anything else matter?

Well yes, probably. The question is not entirely serious, but these two forces are enormously powerful. They can be compared perhaps to the effect of sun and rain upon the earth. The sun's rays sculpt the earth, as does rain's relentless impact. The results can be beautiful, stirring to the soul, or they can be as mud, attractive to some but not to others. The earth can become a pile of dust, blown away by the wind, to become grit in the eyes of passing creatures. It can become a desert of dunes, forever changing in form and size, glaring at the thirsty traveller, or softly, richly beautiful. Or an infinite number of variations on those extremes.

Adults have for the most part physically left school and left the parental home. However, they are forever shaped by those two influences. The impacts of parents and school on them are so vast and far reaching that I cannot think of any person I've known in my life who has been able to completely reverse those effects: in other words, to profoundly change their personality, to redesign or reinvent the inner person.

Children, however, are still in the early stages of formation. They are somewhat akin to the early studies for a piece that a painter hopes ultimately to finish. So this book is really about future adults, the next generation – the one for which current adults are now responsible. It must also be about the past and the present, because every adult who comes into contact with children and adolescents brings with them their own experiences as children and adolescents. These adults still have many choices in their lives – thousands of them, every day. They can, on each occasion, replicate the words, behaviour and values of the parents and teachers who cared for them when they were young, or they can decide on different paths. The parent who was savagely criticised as a child, or who was made to feel that his worth could be measured as the sum of his tangible achievements, or who was treated as a starlet fit for diamonds and gold, or who was taught that the world is a cruel and untrustworthy place, may come to understand that these behaviours by parents and teachers were ugly, damaging and unhelpful. He or she might find the strength to bring different attitudes to their own parenting.

The person who grew up in a home established by a parent or parents with good values, emotional intelligence, and a healthy liking for children and adolescents, and who went to a school staffed by wise, thoughtful, mature teachers, may replicate the attitudes and behaviours of those adults when they themselves become responsible for children or adolescents. Or, they may not.

I am grateful to those who showed me kindness when I was a child. I have not found it easy to navigate childhood, adolescence and adulthood, but I've worked at it. As a person, as a parent, as a teacher, as a principal, I've learned a bit. There are times when a GPS system, a compass, a map are useful, but much more is needed. A deep and profound insight to ourselves, to others, and to relationships has to underpin our lives if our journey is to have meaning and value. My goal is to gain as much of that insight as possible.

In *The Art of Growing Up* I've written about some of the truths which I believe we need to confront, explore and understand as much as possible. Comprehension of those truths can be helpful in our own lives, and can change the lives of the young people with whom we interact.

John Marsden

I

THE PEOPLE WHO MATTER MOST: PARENTS

It can be difficult for us to confront an obvious truth: that one consequence of toxic parenting is uncountable numbers of people in our world who suffer from mental health problems. These people include many psychopaths and sociopaths, some of whom are assassins, terrorists, serial rapists and serial killers. We exclaim over the conspicuous lack of empathy so easily noted in cold-blooded murderers, wondering how they commit their atrocities with no apparent emotion, no empathy for either their victims or the people who loved them.

Every person's situation is different, every life story unique. But common to most deeply troubled individuals is the simple reality that their parents, through what we could call over-loving or under-loving, or a distorted understanding of children and their needs, damaged their capacity to feel. Violent criminals, whom we commonly term as evil, are people who in many cases discovered at an early age that feelings were dangerous, because feelings were penalised, sentimental-ised, used to entrap, treated with scorn or contempt, ignored, denied.

Key figures in the early lives of many psychopaths proved they could not be trusted: relationships were unstable and betrayals common-place. Emotional abuse was the default setting for their childhoods. They were often abused in other ways too, but it is impossible to have physical and/or sexual abuse without emotional abuse being part of the mixture.

Emotional abuse is still underrated in our society, partly because it is nebulous, abstract. Physical abuse is easier to diagnose: bruises, scars, cigarette burns, broken bones and internal injuries tell their terrible stories to anyone whose eyes and minds are open enough to read them. A child who suffers 'only' emotional abuse can be an elusive figure when visiting for play dates or occupying a space in a classroom or hanging out in the school yard at lunchtimes.

As a result of abuse by toxic parents, we have huge numbers of people around the world with addictive behaviours and problems associated with addiction. The United Nations Office on Drugs and Crime estimates that 27 million people in the world are 'problem drug users', and about half of this number are injecting drugs. These figures do not include addictions to food, exercise, pornography, 'screens', gambling and other potentially addictive activities.[1] The American National Council on Alcoholism and Drug Dependence reports that in the United States approximately 17.6 million people, 5.4% of the population, suffer from alcohol abuse or dependence, along with several million more who engage in risky, binge-drinking patterns.[2]

Addicts are people with a great emptiness at the centre of their being, an emptiness that so often comes from parents who for various reasons were unable to meet their early emotional needs. Sometimes those reasons are related to the parents' own needs and addictions. They were unable to give parenting the priority it demands.

Inadequate parenting is a huge factor in the lives of hundreds of millions of people around the world who suffer from psychiatric illnesses, including depression, anxiety, separation disorders, personality

---

1   United Nations Office on Drugs and Crime, 'Status and trend analysis of illicit drug markets', *World Drug Report 2015*, UNODC, Vienna, 2015, pp. 1, 4, unodc.org/documents/wdr2015/World_Drug_Report_2015.pdf, accessed 13 March 2019.
2   National Council on Alcoholism and Drug Dependence, 'Facts about Alcohol', Facing Addiction with NCADD, facingaddiction.org/resources/facts-about-alcohol, accessed 13 March 2019.

disorders and anger management issues. The Australian Bureau of Statistics reports that about one in four young Australians currently has a mental health condition.[3] Many more young Australians die by suicide than by car accident (324 to 198, in 2012).[4]

Comedian and actor Robin Williams committed suicide in 2014. His father had been a General Motors senior executive, and his mother a fashion model. Robin was raised in isolation in his parents' mansion, and from an early age was dressed in a suit and tie, as if mimicking his father's role in the corporate world. He later described the family maid as his best friend. The success, fame and wealth he acquired in adulthood were never enough to compensate for the emotional emptiness of his childhood. The comedy skills that entertained the world were developed, as he told television host James Lipton in 2001, as a way of getting his mother's attention. In trying to explain 'how his mind worked', Williams told Lipton, in one of his trademark stream-of-consciousness rants, delivered in a flat robotic voice: 'It comes from a deep part inside myself that was actually looking for my mother but then I saw that moment when she looked up there and I went "Okay, I'll be funny for her" but that . . . Okay, that's fine, work that way, come back out from that, but then realise after a while that I want to be accepted: "You like me, you really like me," no, it's not that, no, it's not that; I can be trained, I can actually show you how intelligent I am; I can use a word like "delicatessen" and know what it means . . .'[5]

He got a big laugh from the audience for the comment about 'delicatessen', which seemed to trigger another torrent of language, pursuing the theme of using long words and thereby getting away, one can reasonably assume, from his painful and honest thoughts about his

---

3   Australian Bureau of Statistics, 'Summary of Findings', 4326.0 – *National Survey of Mental Health and Wellbeing: Summary of Results*, 2007, ABS, Canberra, 2008, abs.gov.au/ausstats/abs@.nsf/ Latestproducts/4326.0Main Features32007, accessed 13 March 2019.

4   See youthbeyondblue.com/footer/stats-and-facts, attributed by way of footnote to 3303.0 ABS Causes of Death, Australia, 2012 (2014), accessed 13 March 2019. Underlying causes of death (Australia) Table 1.3.

5   Inside the Actors Studio, *Bravo*, Season 7, Episode 14, 10 June 2001.

mother: his relationship with her and, especially, the tactics of comedy and intellectual achievement he used in childhood to try to engage her interest.

As a result of toxic parenting, we have domestic violence, claiming, in four years from July 2010 to June 2014, the lives of 121 women in Australia alone – about 30 women a year.[6] It is estimated that 70 per cent of women worldwide will experience physical or sexual abuse at the hands of an intimate partner.[7] Worldwide, men who were exposed to domestic violence as children are three to four times more likely to perpetrate intimate partner violence as adults than men who did not experience domestic abuse as children.[8]

Men who feel rage as a result of the failure of their mothers to effectively manage the inevitable eventual separation between mothers and their sons – the transition from what is arguably the most intimate relationship known to males to a relationship that must perforce be of a very different nature – are highly likely to project that rage onto future intimate partners, and often all women. Men's hatred of women, which often coexists confusingly with an authentic love of women, is manifested in jokes, vicious comments and trolling on social media, domestic violence, maltreatment of women who are successful in public life, and other more mundane quotidian encounters between the sexes.

In Queensland, Australia, in 2017, a man employed by a university as an advisor, to help and counsel students, was convicted of a serious sexual assault on a young woman – one of the very students he had been hired to support. Affected by alcohol, she was unable to resist his

---

6   'Australian Domestic and Family Violence Data Report 2018', *Australian Domestic and Family Violence Death Review Network*, 31 May 2018, coronerscourt.vic.gov.au/sites/default/files/2018–11/website%2Bversion%2B-%2Badfvdrn_data_report_2018_.pdf, accessed 13 March 2019.

7   WHO, 'Violence and Injury Prevention: 16 Days of Activism against Gender Violence: Physical and/or Sexual Violence by an Intimate Partner', World Health Organization, n.d., who.int/violence_injury_prevention/violence/global_campaign/16_days/en, accessed 13 March 2019.

8   WHO, 'Violence and Injury Prevention: 16 Days of Activism against Gender Violence: The Link between Child Maltreatment and Intimate Partner Violence', World Health Organization, n.d., who.int/violence_injury_prevention/violence/global_campaign/16_days/en/index7.html, accessed 13 March 2019.

attack. He pleaded guilty to the charge and received a two-year jail sentence.[9]

In his profile on a dating site, he had described himself in these terms: 'Single dad – three kids :) Looking to make new friends. Enjoy my coffee, eating, having intellectual discussions, feminism, welfare, big daring ideas, strategic ideas to fix societal problems. I consider myself on the left of politics . . .'[10]

Understandably, much media attention was paid to the offender's claimed appreciation of the principles of feminism. But those who work closely and empathetically with damaged men would have little difficulty recognising the dichotomy at work here: a man who can hold liberal, progressive and feminist ideas whilst simultaneously sexually assaulting a semiconscious, powerless and vulnerable young woman.

As a result of toxic parenting, we have greed, selfishness, cruelty and other perversions of behaviour, from people either replicating their parents' values and attitudes, or people who as children were over-indulged to the point where they could not bear to be denied their most trivial requests, or people consumed by negativity arising from the rage they feel at unfulfilled needs from their early years, or people whose parents denied their children's true selves.

Children's needs – to be held closely skin to skin, to be kept safe, to be fed when hungry, to be smiled at and talked to, to be enjoyed, to be exercised in every sense of the word – are not optional extras, to be made available or withheld at will by parents. But many parents, weakened emotionally by the poor parenting they themselves received, are unable to perform these essential tasks, or are unaware of their vital importance, and so the next generation of the ongoing family is weakened emotionally in its turn. Consequently, sexism, racism, homophobia, misogyny, xenophobia, road rage, mistreatment

9   Nina Funnell, 'Exclusive: James Cook University adviser Douglas Steele promoted after raping student', *news.com.au*, 20 January 2017, news.com.au/lifestyle/real-life/news-life/exclusive-james-cook-university-adviser-douglas-steele-was-promoted-after-pleading-guilty-to-raping-a-student/news-story/fd0b00c9aa8eb528e1f43c3a5ac9c223, accessed 13 March 2019.
10 Ibid.

of animals, reckless driving, paedophilia and other distortions of sexual attraction (the list is endless) develop all too easily.

Children breathe in their parents' attitudes in the same way they breathe in microbes. As the children grow up, the vast majority will perpetuate these attitudes with the next generation, helpless to change what are often long-established familial patterns.

As a result of toxic parenting, we have prisons. People who grew up in happy, well-balanced families, with good-natured parents who knew when and where to set limits, could tolerate their children's less attractive behaviours, and consequently were able to raise mentally healthy and emotionally stable children, do not commit crimes. They feel no compulsion to steal, to behave violently, to abuse others, to set fires, to rape, to murder. They do not become uncontrollably enraged when they experience disappointment or frustration.

FROM PROBLEM PARENTS TO PROBLEM CHILD

A.S. Neill, founder of the famous Summerhill school in England, wrote in his book *Summerhill: A Radical Approach to Child Rearing*, 'There is never a problem child; there are only problem parents.' Neill went on to say: 'Perhaps it would be better to say that *there is only a problem humanity*. That is why the atomic bomb is so sinister, for it is under the control of people who are anti-life – for what person whose arms were tied in the cradle is not anti-life?'[11]

A problem humanity, yes. But every society and every culture is a collection of individuals. The values and practices of the society are a magnification of the values and practices of the individuals, and the bigger the society, the more difficult this becomes. Humanity becomes enmeshed in a struggle to accommodate a wide variety of viewpoints, behaviours, traditions, beliefs.

As a result of toxic parents who tie their babies to the cradle, either literally or metaphorically or both, we have had wars and we continue

11   A.S. Neill, *Summerhill: A Radical Approach to Child Rearing*, Victor Gollancz, London, 1960, p. 103.

to have wars. We have had Napoleon Bonaparte, Adolf Hitler, Joseph Stalin, Mao Zedong, Saddam Hussein, Genghis Khan, Idi Amin . . .

Napoleon's father was a drinker and gambler; Napoleon's mother was an extremely religious woman who slapped her child's face if he did not attend Mass and who used her son to spy on his father and report on his misdeeds. Hitler's strict and rigid father hated his child's interest in art. Stalin's father was a violently abusive alcoholic who opposed the idea of his son being educated. Mao's father was a disciplinarian who beat his son, was unable to show affection, and was furious whenever he caught the boy reading books. Saddam Hussein's father abandoned the family before Saddam was born, and his depressed mother gave him to an uncle when the child was three. Later Saddam's mother reclaimed him, but he then found himself at the mercy of an abusive stepfather.

Genghis Khan's father delivered him to a faraway tribe when the child was nine, as part of the preparations for an arranged marriage. The father was murdered on his way back to his home. When the little boy learned about the murder, he returned to his tribe, but he and his family were abandoned by them and had to live off the land for several years, engaged in a bitter and relentless struggle for survival. At the age of fourteen, Genghis Khan realised that his older half-brother Begter planned to seduce the boy's mother (Begter's stepmother). Angered by this, and by an unfair division of food, Genghis Khan murdered Begter.

Idi Amin's father deserted him and the family when the child was very young. We know little about his childhood, but we can surmise a great deal from his behaviour as an adult. For example, one of his sons tells of his first meeting with his father, which did not take place until the little boy was four years old. Idi, red-faced and sweating, was eating from a bowl of chicken. He gave some to the child and told him to try it. Moments later the boy was writhing in agony, clutching his throat and gasping, burnt by the hot chilli used in the dish. Idi found this vastly amusing, and laughed uproariously. Among his other practical jokes was throwing spears at people in such a way that it seemed the spears would kill them, but instead he aimed them to land at the feet of his victims. A regular amusement was to drive an amphibious car filled with concubines and girlfriends into a lake, provoking screams and panic from the women, who, unaware of the vehicle's capabilities, believed they were about to die.[12]

Swiss author and psychotherapist Alice Miller writes, in her book *The Untouched Key*:

> When someone has been exposed throughout childhood to nothing but harshness, coldness, coercion, and the rigid wielding of power, as Hitler and his closest followers were, when any sign of softness, tenderness, creativity, or vitality is scorned, then the person against whom that violence is directed accepts it as perfectly justified. Children believe they deserve the blows they are given, idealize their persecutors, and later search out objects for projection, seeking release by displacing their supposed guilt onto other individuals or even a whole people. And in this way they become guilty themselves.[13]

When Miller researched senior members of the Nazi hierarchy, she was unable to find one who had not been raised in a strictly disciplined and regimented household.

The elusive quest for world peace would end happily and quickly if we could somehow stop sociopaths from gaining power, but the grim lessons of history and indeed of current events tell us that not only do sociopaths gain power, they are assisted and abetted in the process by close associates who share their psychopathology; by a coterie of passive-aggressive sycophants who believe they can acquire power for themselves by worming their way into the inner circle; and by the

---

12 Adam Luck, 'Mad Ugandan dictator's son reveals all about his "Big Daddy"', *Daily Mail*, 13 January 2007, dailymail.co.uk/news/article-428628/Mad-Ugandan-dictators-son-reveals-Big-Daddy.html, accessed 13 March 2019.

13 Alice Miller, *The Untouched Key: Tracing Childhood Trauma in Creativity and Destructiveness*, trans. Hildegarde & Hunter Hannum, Anchor Books, New York, 1991, pp. 52–53.

great mass of the population who are overwhelmed, tricked, manipulated or frightened into becoming complicit or passive supporters, or, at best, ineffectual opponents.

If we seek to blame someone for wars, genocides, murders and assaults, then rather than accuse Hitler, Stalin, Josef Mengele, Jack the Ripper, Andrei Chikatilo (the 'Butcher of Rostov') and other psychopaths and sociopaths, including the current ones, we should look to their parents, and perhaps beyond them to their parents' parents, and further, through centuries lost in the shadows of time. Yet these forebears too should be considered victims: victims who grew up and, with a dreadful inevitability, became perpetrators.

We recognise the process in mistreated puppies: we are not surprised at their becoming dogs that are savage or terrified, or both at the same time. But we struggle sometimes to accept the same proposition in relation to humans.

In our society, many of us purport to have all the sympathy in the world for abused children. We weep at their loss of innocence. We understand how it is that many (in some cases all) of the foundations of their lives were ripped from under them by a destructive human bulldozer. We support them with counselling and care. We are horrified as we read stories in the media of children abused by trusted adults.

That's how it's supposed to work anyway.

Almost in the same breath we denounce child abusers. We call them 'scum', 'filth', 'animals', 'monsters'. We want them to be castrated, locked up for life, executed. 'If I could get my hands on those mongrels,' we say fiercely.

Television news programs bring us scenes of sullen adults outside a courthouse, surrounding a police wagon containing a child molester and rocking it backwards and forwards, or a crowd raining spit on a child molester as he is led from court, or a mob throwing rocks at the house of a child molester who has been released from prison. Furious adults expressed their loathing of Australian religious leader Cardinal George Pell in 2018 and 2019, as he went in and out of a courtroom during his trials for sexual offences against children.

One of the ways we justify this rage is to tell ourselves and each other that we are showing our solidarity and sympathy with the abused children, and protecting our own children, even though they are presumably not threatened by people who have already been arrested. 'Think of the children!' as Helen Lovejoy cries at regular intervals in *The Simpsons*, flapping her arms in helpless anguish. 'Won't somebody please think of the children?'

However, wherever there is great rage, something interesting is always happening. I'm attracted to the thick black smoke of communal rage, because I know that if I can get to the truth within, I'll understand a little more about humanity.

One of the truths about the complex issue of child abuse is that the child for whom we show such support, and the abuser for whom we show such contempt, are the same person. We claim to feel love for the abused child, but when some abused children grow up and start acting out the consequences of their abuse, we react to them with fury and hatred.

That abused child who had the foundations of his life so devastatingly damaged will, without support and understanding, grow up continuing to feel frightened and lost. To allay these feelings he may try to recreate a situation in which he felt 'held', and this may include encounters where he was literally held, whilst being beaten, or being seduced into a sexual encounter.

At those times the adult created a little world inhabited by just the two of them, a world where all other concerns ceased to exist, and where the child, no matter how grotesquely, felt something morbidly akin to security. If, as an adult, that same child finds himself in a world that is frightening and insecure, a world in which he has no real connections with others, he may try to recreate those moments of illusionary security.

It's a difficult process to understand, especially for those of us who have not had these experiences. And it's not an inevitable process. Many, perhaps most, people who were abused as children go on to lead secure and well-balanced lives as adults, often because the abuse took place out of context. If they lived in positive effective families where the supports were strong, the destruction of some of the foundations by the abuser does not destroy the child, because so many supports are left standing. If, as is highly likely, the abuse is perpetrated by a parent or another close family member, the other parent or a close family member can still save the child from psychic ruin.

In her book *Banished Knowledge*, Alice Miller referred to a survey of American prisoners, which showed that about 90 per cent had been abused as children. She commented that the other 10 per cent would have been abused too; it was just that they had not yet been able to admit it.[14] The prisons of Australia are likewise full of people who were abused in their formative years. The Victorian Youth Parole Board's Annual Report for 2015–16 includes the following characteristics of young offenders held in the system, on a randomly chosen date in 2015:

- 167 were male and nine female
- 45 per cent had been subject to a previous child protection order
- 19 per cent were subject to a current child protection order
- 63 per cent were victims of abuse, trauma or neglect
- 62 per cent had previously been suspended or expelled from school
- 30 per cent presented with mental health issues
- 18 per cent had a history of self-harm or suicidal ideation
- 24 per cent presented with issues concerning their intellectual functioning
- 10 per cent had a history of alcohol misuse
- 16 per cent had a history of drug misuse
- 66 per cent had a history of both alcohol and drug misuse
- 12 per cent had offended while under the influence of alcohol but not drugs

---

14 Alice Miller, *Banished Knowledge: Facing Childhood Injuries*, trans. Leila Vennewitz, Virago, London, 1990, revised 1997, p. 24.

- 20 per cent had offended while under the influence of drugs but not alcohol
- 58 per cent had offended while under the influence of alcohol, and also while under the influence of drugs
- 12 per cent were parents
- 38 per cent had a family history of parental or sibling imprisonment
- 10 per cent were homeless with no fixed address, or residing in insecure housing before custody.[15]

There was an increase in the percentages in almost every category from 2014 to 2015.

In keeping with Alice Miller's assertion in *Banished Knowledge*, I would argue that the Victorian figure of 63 per cent for victims of abuse, trauma or neglect is likely to be massively understated. Through 2015 and 2016, Professor Carol Bower led a West Australian team studying young people held in youth detention centres. The researchers found that 89 per cent of the offenders had a severe cognitive impairment and 36 per cent had foetal alcohol spectrum disorder, but Professor Bower suspected that the latter figure might have been understated, because it had not proved possible to obtain the necessary information from some parents.[16]

When it comes to managing these young offenders, society's best answer is often to lock them up. These are the same children we professed to care about when they were five or ten, but whom we stop caring about when they are sixteen or eighteen. Our support ends when they cross the line between victim and perpetrator, and suddenly we howl for whips, elastrators and the gallows.

---

15 Youth Parole Board, *Youth Parole Board Annual Report 2015–16*, State of Victoria, Department of Justice and Regulation, September 2017, justice.vic.gov.au/sites/default/files/embridge_cache/emshare/original/public/2018/08/2f/7a73bdaeb/youth_parole_board_annual_report_2016–17.pdf, accessed 13 March 2019.
16 'Nine out of ten young people in detention found to have severe neuro-disability', Telethon Kids Institute, 13 February 2018, telethonkids.org.au/news--events/news-and-events-nav/2018/february/young-people-in-detention-neuro-disability, accessed 13 March 2019.

In 2018, a nineteen-year-old man entered the Florida high school from which he had been expelled as a student a year earlier, opened fire with a semiautomatic weapon, and killed seventeen people. At the first court hearing, his lawyer briefly outlined his background: he had been adopted at birth, but both his adoptive parents died, one of a heart attack and one of pneumonia, leaving him orphaned. He was then looked after by 'friends of the family'. His lawyer said of him that he was 'a broken human being'.[17]

All crime is illness. All who commit serious crimes are ill. The more horrifying the crime, the greater the illness of the perpetrator. It is impossible for a loved, secure person to commit a serious crime. In Law School I learned the Latin expression 'res ipsa loquitor': 'The thing speaks for itself.' The commission of the crime is sufficient proof of the illness. We need no further evidence that the person is ill. Politicians who use 'getting tough on law and order' as an election slogan are exploiting those who were abused as children, in order to gain power for themselves.

Some criminals may be so badly damaged by the psychic injuries they have suffered in childhood that they are unable to control themselves, and therefore cannot be allowed back into the community. I feel sad for these people. But I don't call them monsters.

We say we care about abused children, but it's clear that as a society we only care about them up to a point. If we truly cared for them, we would continue to do so when they become adults, even if they are confused and mentally ill adults. We should be grateful to the few people who are able to show such understanding and to act on it. Years ago I read of an American woman who in childhood had been sexually abused by her father. As an adult, she travelled from one side of the continent to the other to find her father, to tell him that she understood how, in sexually abusing her, he must have damaged himself terribly . . . as he had damaged her. Such wisdom and understanding is rare.

---

17 'Nikolas Cruz: Depressed loner "crazy about guns"', *BBC News*, 16 February 2018, bbc.com/news/world-us-canada-43067530, accessed 13 March 2019.

The leading cause of death in the world is not heart disease or cancer or influenza. It is the nature of individual humans: a person's personality. People smoke, drink too much, eat too much, and/or consume drugs because their personalities predispose them to these behaviours. Much heart disease is caused or exacerbated by factors like obesity, lack of exercise and stress – which in turn are outcomes of aspects of personality. Stroke is often related to stress. Victims of murders are often people who, tragically, are attracted to relationships with violent abusers, as a result of the abuse they themselves suffered in childhood from parents or parent substitutes. A great number of people who die in 'accidents' do so because they or someone else behaved recklessly, dangerously, negligently – which should lead us to ask why the person who caused the death was failing to take proper care of themselves or others. And so, we have endlessly repeated scenarios: the drunk driver in an out-of-control car speeding through a red light, the gun owner wrongly assuming a firearm is unloaded, the farmer riding a quad bike across a steep slope . . .

Well-balanced people, those who are mature in the best sense of the word, do not swim in billabongs where saltwater crocodiles are known to lurk; do not go bodysurfing after consuming half a bottle of vodka; do not drive at 160 kilometres an hour in a car with bald tyres; do not commit suicide when a relationship fails or they lose their life savings.

Although it is argued by some that certain personality types are more prone to particular types of cancer than are other people, the evidence for this is not convincing.[18] Exacerbating the mortality rates of cancer, however, are people who leave it too long to have disturbing symptoms investigated. Why are some people afraid to go to a doctor? Why are some people careless about their health, perhaps even callously indifferent to their own welfare?

---

18 M. Jokela, G.D. Batty, T. Hinsta, et al., 'Is personality associated with cancer incidence and mortality? An individual-participant meta-analysis of 2156 incident cancer cases among 42 843 men and women', *British Journal of Cancer*, 2014, vol. 110, 1820–1824, ncbi.nlm.nih.gov/pmc/articles/PMC3974080/, accessed 10 April 2019.

TOXIC PARENTING

For nearly all of us, the strongest influence in forming our personalities is the behaviour of our parents. Toxic parenting results in distorted personalities, people who struggle to function effectively in human society. Truly has it been said that in the lost boyhood of Judas, Jesus was betrayed.

We are seeing an epidemic of damaging parenting at the moment. The familiar benign (and often malign) neglect of decades past continues, but the phenomenon of educated middle-class parents who don't just love their children but are in love with them has reached a critical level. Such parents agonise over every disappointment their child suffers, lavish them with praise when they manage to eat a green bean ('We are so proud of you'), record every moment of their children's lives on camera, encourage them to parrot adult phrases at each other ('Dougie, you hurt my feelings when you said I was stupid'), manipulate their friendships and encourage their feuds, subvert schools by listening avidly to any criticisms of teachers and believing every story of injustice their child brings home – and then appear at school clothed in righteous indignation to advocate for their child, only to find that they are missing vital information ('Oh! She bit Maggie? Are you sure? No, she didn't mention that actually . . .').

In short, they minimise their child's transgressions, have no regard for those who are hurt by their child's narcissism, block any attempts to create a culture with consistent and easily understood values, and blame others for the child's aberrant behaviour. They are doing irreparable damage to their kids.

In our wildest fantasies we cannot imagine a time when every parent or pair of parents might be raising children in a healthy, positive, creative and successful way, walking the line between freedom and limit-setting. Were that to eventuate, we would know that the evolution of humanity was essentially complete, and we would indeed have a world of 'golden beings'.

In her 1977 book *Reading and Loving*, British writer Leila Berg wrote about expectant mothers' encounters with the British public health system:

> No-one looking at most future mothers – who have in any case had little nutritious food, or rest, or space to explore or relax in, or time to spare – sitting on the rows of straight-back seats in the ante-natal clinic where they are regularly surrounded by reminders of catastrophe and evidence of touchy staff hierarchies, afraid to put a foot wrong or speak out of turn, waiting literally for hours for their name to be called from an impersonal pile of cards, sometimes with another child that they had to bring with them whom somehow they must keep quiet, still, and frustrated for these same hours on end, would claim this periodic experience gives the mother a sense of glowing and exciting well-being. No-one, listening to young mothers recently home from hospital, where they had been given drugs (even when they'd asked not to be given them) and forceps deliveries and caesareans and inductions, could claim they got exhilarating self-confidence from their cooperation at birth with their baby, or a proud delight in the capability, strength, tenderness, and achievement of their own body that would last through this baby's childhood.[19]

This is not the place for an extensive discussion of how best to deliver babies, but nevertheless, when Berg contrasts the apparently typical experiences of British mothers in the 1970s with the birth of her own grandson, Kit, it is difficult not to be struck by the likely results of Kit's first experiences with the world. Kit was born in a very small natural-childbirth maternity home, where, Berg says:

> I know that a baby born here will be laid on his mother's naked, exultant body, still himself naked, slimy and bloody, the umbilical cord still pulsating and uncut between them, and that as he draws in his first air and shouts with life his mother will hold him, skin

19 Leila Berg, *Reading and Loving*, Routledge & Kegan Paul Ltd, London p. 51.

to skin, heart to heart, half-crying perhaps with the overwhelming joy of hard achievement. I know that the father may have actively helped with the delivery so that her achievement – and the baby's – was also his, and riding through difficulties and effort and pain into triumphant vitality and tenderness has been inextricably interlinked for all three of them. And there has been nothing academic or clinical about this; real bodies have worked and sweated at it, and held each other. So from the very outset, at such a birth sound goes with vitality, with discovery, with exaltation, with the deeply-felt and hotly physical experience of private individuals.[20]

Kit and his mother stayed in the maternity home for three weeks. The woman who ran the home believed that it took three weeks for the mother to become aware of the baby's sleep rhythm. During this time, Berg says, 'Kit's crying was listened to, and the different meanings behind it discovered, which meant too that for Kit *communication early became successful* because what was said was understood and truly responded to; he was not filled with milk when he was speaking of something else until he finally became confused *himself* about what he was communicating. During their three-week stay, the three of them received belief in themselves, joy in each other, and a confidence in dialogue.'[21]

'As the twig is bent . . .' From the germination of the seed, when that first tiny bud tremulously pushes its way through the seed coat, the influence of the immediate environment shapes the direction and strength of the plant's progress. Some believe the influence begins even earlier: Sir George Sitwell, father of three famous children, Edith, Osbert and Sacheverell, approached his role in the conception of his children with what Sacheverell's biographer called 'ritual deliberation'. 'Sir George would prepare himself for his act of dynastic responsibility by immersing himself in suitable books and works of art. He would

---

20 Berg, *Reading and Loving*, p. 15.
21 Berg, *Reading and Loving*, p. 16.

then announce, "Ida, I am ready!" and the procreation of another Sitwell genius would take place.'[22]

It seems that Sir George was more effective at conceiving than at parenting. He was an eccentric man who spent most of his time in his library, allowing entry to no one and eating alone. All three of his children were scathing in their assessments of him as a father. Their mother was equally ineffectual and uninterested; her passions were for shopping, playing bridge and reading in bed. In 1915 she was sent to jail for fraud.

Only one of the Sitwell offspring, Sacheverell, had children: two sons, both of whom described him, in a 1994 newspaper interview, as an unhappy man. 'There was a dark side to his nature,' said one. 'I was terrified of him.'[23]

One imagines that Berg's grandson Kit had better prospects than did the Sitwell children. Contrast Kit's early life with the experiences of babies described by Sheila McAllister, in a self-published book called *My Life in Three Continents*. McAllister worked as a nurse in Fremantle Hospital, beginning in 1956, when she was seventeen years old. Assigned to the children's ward, she found that visiting was only allowed on Wednesday and Sunday afternoons. 'We hated being on at those times. Such a weeping and wailing when the parents left as it must have seemed a very long time until they could see each other again. The children were much harder to settle on those days and, in our ignorance, we concluded that visiting was not necessarily a good thing, as it only upset the children.'[24]

Many of the patients were babies less than twelve months old.

Contrast too Berg's account of children's needs with the tone of this letter to an Australian tabloid newspaper by a man named Ivan Hoy, from Kambah, ACT. The letter, in its entirety, reads:

---

22 Sarah Bradford, *Sacheverell Sitwell: Splendours and Miseries*, Sinclair-Stevenson, 1993, p. 9.

23 Vicky Ward, 'Life after Osbert, Edith and Sachie', *The Independent*, 18 October 1994, independent.co.uk/life-style/life-after-osbert-edith-and-sachie-vicky-ward-spoke-to-the-sons-of-sacheverell-sachie-sitwell-about-1443627.html, accessed 13 March 2019.

24 Sheila McAllister, *My Life in Three Continents*, self-published, Melbourne, 2008.

When I was a child, I was smacked by my parents when I misbehaved. In school, I was caned by the teacher when I acted up or didn't do my homework. I would now like to thank these people who cared enough for me, about me, to teach me that bad behaviour would result in punishment and some pain. Otherwise, I could have finished up like some of the ignoramuses I see around today.

Perhaps Mr Hoy was a product of the regimen described by Sheila McAllister, or the British public health system described by Leila Berg. It seems likely, from the last sentence of his letter, that he is perpetuating the attitudes, values and behaviour of his parents and teachers. Of course virtually all people either perpetuate, or react against, the behaviours of their own parents towards them. Just as teachers placed under pressure by students tend to reflexively revert to the teaching styles adopted by the teachers they experienced when young, so adults under pressure revert to the language and behaviours of their parents. Or, filled with anger at the way they were raised, they determine to do anything rather than imitate their parents. In comprehensively disposing of the bathwater with stubborn passive rage, they usually throw away the baby: in other words, the child's best interests. Reacting to their authoritarian and repressive parents, they veer too far towards freedom, imagining that any restriction on their children is an intolerable curtailment of individual rights.

We can reasonably assume that a parent who does not say 'no' at least once a day to their child is failing as a parent. 'He has never heard the word "no",' some parents boast, when I interview them before enrolment at my schools. I feel sorry for them, as their children's behaviour is invariably awful, and the parents do not look as though they are enjoying child-raising. Later, when the children are teenagers, many of those same parents tell me: 'I wish we'd been more old-fashioned when she was young, and laid down some rules. We were too idealistic, and now it seems like it's too late to do anything about it. We try, but she won't listen.'

Other parents are rigid and authoritarian in their approach. They believe they can keep themselves safe only by controlling the area around them. Any disruption within that territory is seen as a threat. For most people like this, home is the one area they can realistically hope to control. We're all familiar with the clichéd battles between parents and teenagers over bedrooms: 'It's my house and I'm telling you to clean your room, *now*!' to which the teenager almost inevitably retorts: 'It's my bedroom, and I'll keep it any way I like!' Both are right – and both are determined to maintain a zone that is entirely theirs to command. In extreme cases this can result in tyrannical behaviour, with family members or other victims imprisoned like animals in a ghastly zoo.

Some authoritarian adults extend their territory to infringe on the houses or apartments that surround them. In Melbourne, in 2016, an 83-year-old man died after an altercation with his 90-year-old neighbour. He had accused the neighbour of poisoning his rose-bushes. The two had been feuding for 47 years.[25] Such tensions, over noise, pets, overhanging branches, rubbish bins, children's balls landing on neighbours' lawns, car parking, locations of boundaries, are common.

Some authoritarian adults extend their territory even further, to the workplace, to a train carriage in which they are riding, to a soccer pitch, to a public car park. Some go further still, hence 'Fuck off we're full' messages are superimposed on maps of Australia and displayed on the back of cars, and large numbers of people support political movements based on xenophobia and meaningless talk of 'old-fashioned values', which is code for 'I want the world to accord exactly with my opinions and beliefs, and I'm very unhappy when it doesn't'.

Some authoritarian adults know no limits. Dictators like Hitler, Stalin, Kim Jong-il and Pol Pot were unable to feel safe, no matter how vast their reach. They seemed to want to control the entire planet, and,

---

25 Stephanie Anderson, 'Reservoir man's death after argument with 90yo neighbour deemed not suspicious', *ABC News*, 29 November 2016, abc.net.au/news/2016–11–29/mans-death-not-suspicious-despite-decades-long-feud/8076336, accessed 13 March 2019.

had they been successful, would no doubt have aspired to extend their reach to the furthest corners of the universe.

Megalomaniacs believe they must deal with any hint of indifference, disagreement or defiance, real or imagined, immediately and brutally. These extreme insecure narcissists need reassurance every hour of every day that they are adored, and, further, that no one is threatening them. Kim Jong-un allegedly executed a high-ranking functionary of the North Korean Communist Party for falling asleep during one of Kim's speeches.[26] The devastation wrought by Hitler is too well known to need further detailing here. An article by Ian Johnson in the *New York Review of Books* assesses the death toll attributable to Mao as between 25 million and 45 million people.[27] Typical of the operations of Stalin's Russia was this NKVD operative order 00593, from 1937: 'All people who have ever worked in Chinese territory are to be arrested.' As a result of this order 46,317 arrests were made and 30,992 of the people arrested were executed. It is generally estimated that Stalin caused the death of between 20 million and 40 million people.[28] The possibility that a few members of a group might be disloyal meant that the whole group had to be liquidated, so that the head upon which the crown rested so uneasily could sleep a fraction more safely, for one more night.

The world has paid a high price for the parenting failures of Besarion Jughashvili and Ketevan Geladze (parents of Stalin), of Alois Hitler and Klara Pölzl (parents of Hitler), of Mao Yichang and Wen Qimei (parents of Mao).

26 AFP, 'North Korea's Vice-Premier Executed for Sleeping during Speech', *The Australian*, 1 September 2016, theaustralian.com.au/news/world/north-koreas-vicepremier-executed-for-sleeping-during-speech/news-story/85b8342f9acf870892746bfd37bc63aa, accessed 13 March 2019.
27 Ian Johnson, 'Who Killed More: Hitler, Stalin or Mao?', *New York Review of Books*, 5 February 2018.
28 Dmitri Volkogonov, *Autopsy for an Empire: The Seven Leaders Who Built the Soviet Regime*, trans. Harold Shukman, The Free Press, New York, 1998, p. 139.

2

WINDSCREEN WIPERS DON'T STEER THE CAR: SOME APPROACHES TO PARENTING

It is the personalities of the children we are raising with which we must be most concerned. The role of adults is to help children develop an open, generous, thoughtful approach to life.

The biggest difficulty for schools in the 21st century is parents who have mental health issues. Their confused, depressed and/or distorted ways of viewing the world often make them impervious to reason. They can be suspicious, resistant and hostile in their dealings with schools, teachers and others, including their extended families, at whose hands they have suffered in the past, although it is likely that neither they nor their families will be able to confront these anguished histories in a meaningful way. Their mental health issues are commonly visited upon their children, who are simultaneously the people most precious to them, but also the people upon whom they can most easily vent their frustrations, fears, dark impulses, anxieties, rage and desires.

Many people parent beautifully. And many don't. Here are some examples of common ineffectual approaches to child-raising that I have encountered.

'MY CHILD IS MY HERO'

When I look back at the most difficult and troubled kids I have encountered in classrooms, two elements stand out. Firstly, a majority are boys, and secondly, they often have mothers or fathers who indulged them no matter what they did. In many cases, the mothers in particular had an excessively adoring approach towards their children. They showed a stubborn blindness to the aspects of the child that others found unpalatable or that made others feel uncomfortable.

CAMILLO

Camillo seemed to have big issues with power, seeking power both overtly and covertly. He had spectacular tantrums when he did not get his own way. He hit and kicked other children, grabbed some around the throat, and attacked teachers on occasion. We came to realise that Camillo always kept a knife secreted on his body. When we put a stop to that, Camillo turned up the next day with a needle in his pocket. On the same day, he grabbed a boy around the neck and lifted him from behind in a dangerous manoeuvre that scared the other boy. An hour later he played stick wars (a kind of sword-fighting game) with a boy from the Foundation[29] class, but Camillo got a huge piece of wood and repeatedly hit the younger child's small stick with disproportionate force, scaring that boy too.

The mother's response to our concerns was to blame other children for bullying her son, but this was clearly not happening. Interestingly, the mother never expressed any concern for the children or teachers her son had attacked, and never enquired about their welfare. She did tell me, however, that I should believe her younger child's account of Camillo's school life rather than our own observations, because the younger sister, at the age of six, was, in her words, 'the most honest child I have ever known'.

---

29 Also known as 'Prep' and 'Kindergarten', depending where you live; for convenience I'll refer to all first-year classes as 'Foundation'.

BRENDAN

Brendan, whilst still in Foundation, threatened to knife and kill other children. He was filled with contempt for girls in particular. He talked of wanting to cut off his penis and to kill his father. He started a fire at school early one morning, at a sleepover. During one meeting with his parents, as the father lavishly praised Brendan to me, a teacher came in to report that Brendan was jumping all over the bonnet and roof of his father's car. We unofficially consulted no fewer than four child psychiatrists and/or psychotherapists about Brendan, and they were unanimous in their views that he was so deeply disturbed that he needed urgent and immediate intervention. The father began his next meeting with us by shouting three words: 'BRENDAN IS AWESOME.' The father seemed to be the president of the Brendan Fan Club; the stepmother was passive but complicit.

The father always insisted to us that Brendan had been very popular at preschool: 'He was the leader of all the games. Everyone loved him.'

We had a meeting with the preschool, where a somewhat different picture emerged. The teacher reported that in Brendan's first year he was 'pretty wild': 'We had to draw boundaries, to ensure that other kids were safe.' In his second year at preschool the staff had a special meeting to ask what they could do about Brendan. They felt they had exhausted every strategy. The teacher described 'games' where Brendan would box other kids into corners, or create a jail in which he imprisoned them, but he never seemed to notice that the other children were not enjoying the games. 'Nothing you've told me surprises me,' the teacher said.

Brendan only stayed a couple of terms at Candlebark before his father, apparently not happy with our attempts to set limits for his son, withdrew him.

PHILIPPE

Philippe constantly stole, lied, hurt other children, and displayed narcissistic tendencies. 'We have never set limits for him,' his mother told me one day. Like a number of these children, Philippe seemed highly sexualised from an early age, with knowledge that was inappropriate for a young child, and sexualised behaviour (including exposing himself) towards girls. A concerned close relative told us that Philippe often sat up late watching inappropriate movies with his father. 'They don't seem to care what he watches,' the person said.

Philippe's mother gushed to me: 'I tell him every day that he has special qualities, special qualities that other children don't have.'

His 'special qualities' included sticking his middle finger down at kids instead of up and then telling the teacher that it was okay, because he was not 'giving them the rude finger'.

Philippe seemed able to manipulate with great skill his parents' responses to problems at school. For example, when he had been in trouble during the day, Philippe invariably got off the bus looking downcast. His mother would ask: 'What's wrong?', leading Philippe to confess his sins, between contrite sobs. The mother would then contact us, usually by email, to say that Philippe had told them about 'today's incident', so they had 'had a long talk' with him about how to treat others with respect and consideration, and he now 'seemed to understand'.

Gradually this pattern became monotonous to us, especially as the long talks at home effected no apparent improvement in Philippe's behaviour.

After a series of disruptive and troubling episodes, his mother described him to me in an email thus:

> He is a wonderful child, who enjoys life to the hilt. He throws himself into everything in a way that I find absolutely exhilarating. Sure, he has his moments when he forgets to consider the other child's point of view, but so do all kids, surely? Overall he is beautifully kind and sympathetic, and he has great integrity. He has taught us so much already.

They then withdrew him from the school.

I don't think that the many children hurt by Philippe whilst he was with us would have recognised him as 'beautifully kind and sympathetic'.

VICTOR

On his first day at the school where I knew him, Victor sexually abused (verbally) a girl. I contacted his parents that evening. They told me he had no idea of the meaning of the word he used and was very embarrassed when he found it out. This seemed unlikely, given I already knew that staff at his previous school had held special meetings with his parents to discuss his obscene language. His mother, in an email, described him to me in these words: 'He is a delightful child, who is not being allowed to express himself creatively in his current school. If there's one thing I can say about Victor with confidence, it is that everyone he meets quickly comes to adore him. There is nothing he cannot do.'

His previous principal described him as dishonest '100 per cent of the time'. Whenever possible, the principal sat with him at the start of recess and lunchbreak to coach him about his behaviour with other kids. Victor threatened children, swore at them, and had to be restricted to limited areas of the playground.

We found Victor to be spectacularly vicious in his sly comments to other children, which included racist and homophobic remarks, and his particular specialty: making horrible comments to children about their parents. At the same time he worked hard to ingratiate himself with staff. We were not taken in by his double dealing, and failed to identify the qualities that might justify the mother's comment that he had the ability to win the adoration of everyone he met. However, over a considerable period of time we were delighted to witness a huge improvement in Victor's behaviour and attitudes.

One thing that I can say with confidence presages great difficulties for children is the inversion of the parent–child relationship, so that the parent develops an excessive admiration for the child. Some celebrities are fond of statements like 'I am in awe of my children' or 'My son/daughter is my hero'. I feel slightly ill when I read these remarks. When Philippe's mother wrote 'He has taught us so much already', I was troubled by doubts about their parenting style. Philippe was less than ten years old when this comment was made. Of course, we can learn from children, given their fresh, vivid and direct view of the world. But that really goes without saying, and should be incidental in a healthy parent–child relationship. Children need to know that their parents have a good understanding of the way the world works, that their parents are able to guide them, mentor them, lead them, nurture and nourish them, and keep them safe. If parents are gazing at their child in a gooey-eyed reverie of adoration, the child's situation is dangerous, for the parents are at risk of confusion, losing sight of their essential roles in the child's life, and becoming blind to the child's 'less attractive' features. It is too easy for children to manipulate parents who have idealised them; it is rather like a young guru in a cult manipulating credulous members of their community.

Often, it seems to me, parents who adore their children are themselves suffering from narcissism. Perhaps they imagine that the fruit of their loins must be superior to every other child who has walked the earth, and can hardly believe they have produced something so pure, so beautiful, so perfect. This may well be the greatest achievement of their lives. Understandably, they look at their child in wonder: 'Did he/she really come from me, from us? Did I create this wondrous creature?'

In recent years it has become unusual for me to get an application for a Foundation enrolment from a parent who does not describe their child as gifted, imaginative and/or creative. This leads me to assume that it's hard nowadays to find any children who are average, let alone below average – which makes for a difficult mathematical paradox. Given that these applications are made when children are four years old, or younger, I believe the assessments must commonly be based upon the child's use of language, and probably upon the child's attempts to compensate for (naturally enough) inadequate vocabularies by 'grabbing' words from one category and applying them to another. A child who has not yet learned the word 'rainbow' may well say, 'Look, Mummy, there's a giant lollipop in the sky.' Or, upon seeing her first helicopter coming to earth, she may ask, 'Did that big wasp eat those people?'

I suspect that naïve parents seize ecstatically upon these undeniably charming moments as evidence that their child is an incipient genius, when in fact they merely reflect the child's groping for words that will enable them to communicate effectively, despite their limited knowledge of language.

A friend of mine told the story of driving along a country road one day with her little son, when he remarked: 'Look at the beautiful tree, Mummy.' She replied: 'Yes, it's a manna gum.' There was a long silence from the back seat, broken at last by her child asking: 'So is there a name for everything, then?'

There isn't, of course, but there are names for many things. As we grow older, we learn more and more names for the concrete and abstract 'things' around us. The more of these words we learn, the less we need to improvise. Hence, when it comes to language at least, most children become less and less creative, more and more precise, so that British writer Jane Gardam can rightly say: 'Every child is a poet until she's eight years old.'[30] Only a few slip through the net, and they become our Seamus Heaneys, our Miroslav Holubs, our Emily Dickinsons, our Denise Levertovs:

> *He told me of journeys,*
> *of where sun and moon go while we stand in dark,*
> *of an earth-journey he dreamed he would take some day*
> *deeper than roots . . .*
> *He told of the dreams of man, wars, passions, griefs,*
> *and I, a tree, understood words — ah, it seemed*
> *my thick bark would split like a sapling's that*
> *grew too fast in the spring*
> *when a late frost wounds it.*[31]

---

30 Jane Gardam speaking at the Adelaide Writers Festival in 1996.
31 Denise Levertov, *A Tree Telling of Orpheus*, Black Sparrow Press, Los Angeles, 1968.

Criticism of their children cannot be borne by narcissistic parents, because it casts doubt upon their ongoing need for the child to be exceptional, and may even force them to look more closely at their child's true nature, which they are afraid to do. Such parents respond with angry defensiveness to criticism, and quickly look around to see who can be blamed for whatever incident has occurred. Their targets are often the school, or a teacher, or other students, or all three. In the face of our ongoing concern about Camillo's behaviour, his parents withdrew both their children from that particular school. His mother then sent an email to other parents, saying: 'When a school that purports to be kind and caring excludes a boy like Camillo, just because he doesn't conform to the way other kids behave, then I feel despair for the future of our country.'

We did not exclude Camillo. We did not want him to leave, as we felt we were making good progress with his issues. But we had difficulty accepting his right to half-strangle other children. We also felt sorry for his sibling, who was suddenly uprooted from her school, and marched away into an unknown future because her parents were unwilling or unable to confront her brother's problems.

'MY CHILD IS EXTRAORDINARY'

This may not seem, on the face of it, to be very different from 'My child is my hero'. I think that both often spring from the parents' narcissism, but they also spring from the parents' sense of failure in their adult lives. As Alice Miller says, grandiosity and depression are two sides of the same coin.[32]

KEITH

This boy wreaked havoc with his bullying behaviour. His parents told me during one interview that they were shocked and bewildered by our reports, as there had never been problems at his last school. 'You'd

---

32 Alice Miller, *The Drama of Being a Child: the Search for the True Self*, trans. Ruth Ward, Virago, London, 2005 (also known as *The Drama of the Gifted Child*), pp. 38–46.

better be able to substantiate these allegations,' Keith's father told me, in a tense meeting. 'They are very serious charges.'

A colleague who was with me, a woman of great experience, said quietly, 'I can substantiate the allegations, because I've frequently been a victim of his bullying.'

The principal of Keith's previous school had a somewhat different story from the one promulgated by the parents. He said the parents had 'set a record' for the number of times they had been summoned to the school for discussions about Keith's destructive and disruptive behaviour. I asked if meetings between the parents and teachers/principal had been as frequent as once a week. 'No,' he replied, 'more like every other day.' In Keith's first term at school there were fifteen meetings between the principal and one or both of the parents. The principal had told the mother that Keith's behaviour was abnormal, and that he was the pupil who caused staff the greatest concern. However, the parents refused to accept that Keith was capable of bad behaviour, and implied that the principal was unfairly targeting their son. In an email to me, they accused the previous school of 'being unable to confront the truth: that the school was the problem, not Keith'.

The principal described Keith jumping on other children, making sexualised attacks on them, ruining games, screwing up other children's work, kicking children in the face, and throwing other children's toys away.

The behaviour that we saw was consistent with the reports from his previous school. He deliberately distracted other students, tried to sabotage lessons, and was disruptive, destructive and inappropriate. One of my notes about him reads as follows:

Keith was in a friendly water fight when he made as if to throw water at Bobby, who was passing on a bike. Bobby told Keith that he, Bobby, was not in the water fight, and not to throw water at him. This was a convention understood and respected by all the children. Keith threw the entire bucket at Bobby, hitting him in the chest and hurting him.

Other episodes included pulling down his own pants and those of another boy, swearing at teachers, and taking other children's toys.

On one occasion Keith hit another boy in the stomach, then said, 'I did that deliberately, to wind you.' Keith explained to me that he hit the boy because children were gloating when Keith got out in a game, even though hilarious gloating was part of the culture of that particular game on that particular day, as Keith readily admitted to me. Keith had joyously participated in the gloating when other kids got out.

On another occasion, he pushed a Grade 1 girl onto rocks, causing her to scrape her knee badly. When asked to apologise to the girl, he replied, 'I like to apologise when I'm ready.' The teacher explained that the girl needed the apology now, pointing out that she could have been seriously injured, and adding, 'You would have felt responsible and sad if your actions had intentionally caused someone a bad injury.' Keith's reply was, 'I would if I was a different kind of person, but I'm not that kind of person.'

Keith seemed to believe he could manipulate situations at school. It was noticeable that when he was caught behaving badly he would cry loudly and ostentatiously if a teacher was anywhere near, but would stop as soon as the teacher moved out of range.

In an interview with a teacher, Keith's mother said: 'All day I wait for him to come home so I can tell him how much I love him . . . I just want him to get off the bus so I can hear him say, "I love you, Mummy."' She recounted to me how she frequently told Keith that he had 'qualities, special talents, gifts' that other children did not have. She did not specify the nature of his special talents/qualities/gifts, and they remained obscure to me.

A driver should not imagine that operating the windscreen wipers is the way to steer the car. Keith's mother wanted her son to be special, and could not countenance any other possibility. Parenting, like driving a car, is a complex matter, requiring the synthesis of many functions. Programming the child to believe he is uniquely gifted, and giving him a script for communication with his parents, does not achieve much. Keith did not stay long at the school where I worked, and when last heard of was at his fourth school, whilst still in Grade 3.

MALCOLM

Malcolm was a young man whose behaviour was wild and out of control on many occasions. His outbursts, which could be verbal or physical, were often in response to minimal or even imagined provocation. His mother went to considerable lengths to hide his diagnoses of autism spectrum disorder (ASD) and attention deficit hyperactivity disorder (ADHD) from us as she went through the enrolment process, and as, it later emerged, she had done at his previous school.

Within a few weeks of his commencement with us, his mother wrote to a teacher:

> We, Mal's parents, have always been committed to support him in his many endeavours. So when there are situations at school that cause him distress, we do our very best to find solutions. At the moment, Mal is having trouble with a number of children, including one called Harold. Harold obviously has made something of a specialty of tormenting Mal, and when Mal gets upset, as anyone would, other kids join in and turn the whole thing into a bit of a circus.
>
> We are of course well aware that Mal has a lot to learn yet about social interactions – that's hardly surprising, given his age. But what are you doing to teach the other kids in the class that not everybody thinks and behaves the same way? What are you doing to teach them that life can be harder for some people – including Mal?

When the author of this letter dropped the adolescent Malcolm off for a camp, she unfurled a home-made banner with the message 'I'll miss you, Malcolm' and held it up as the bus departed, for all Malcolm's classmates to see. As this brief incident indicates, with its lack of sensitivity and understanding, and its contribution to Malcolm's difficulties with 'social interactions', Malcolm's mother's was a significant factor in the problems Malcolm was experiencing.

I was struck, though, by her comment that other children needed to be made aware that life was harder for people like Malcolm, with the implication that this would make them more sympathetic to him. If other students should be expected to understand the difficulties Malcolm faced, shouldn't it logically follow that his mother needed to make an effort to ascertain whether his alleged tormentor, Harold, also found life difficult, and whether he perhaps faced particular problems of his own?

And that was in fact the case. Harold was either on the autism spectrum or had post-traumatic stress disorder (PTSD), or both – the symptoms are often very similar for children – and had extreme difficulties in social relationships and in his management of frustration or exclusion. It would have greatly helped if Malcolm's mother had been honest about her child's difficulties when she enrolled him. I understand the desire of parents not to 'blacken their child's reputation' at a new school, but there has to be some openness in the transaction, as much is at stake.

Malcolm's mother's sympathy with her son, so evident in the letter, was not always apparent in other situations. One afternoon, in the car park at school, she raged at her son for losing his rain jacket and then lying about losing it. A teacher, shocked by the extent of her fury, intervened, saying, 'We all make mistakes.'

'Yes,' the mother snapped back, in front of her son. 'Mine was giving birth.'

The teacher showed her horror at this remark, upon which the mother explained, 'I'm a Buddhist, and to us lying is the worst sin. It's absolutely unforgivable.'

MAUREEN

Maureen was unusual to me in that she was one of the few really violent girls I have ever taught. She attacked both teachers and students. A report by one teacher describes a typical incident: 'Maureen punched both my chest and stomach quite forcefully. Maureen may have hit me around about fifteen times; she also dug her nails into my arm. She tore at my jacket (which I removed) and she also pulled on the scarf I was wearing. I then told the other children to leave class early and wait for their next teacher. Maureen began to throw my books.'

On one memorable day, Maureen hit two boys in the face, then hit a girl, then physically attacked another teacher.

The mother, in a conversation with me, said: 'I don't like my kids to fail at anything . . . I set Billie [Maureen's older sister] up to succeed in everything she did, so that she wouldn't experience failure. I haven't really done that so much with Maureen, so to some extent Maureen has had to live in the shadow of Billie.'

The parents were perfectionists. They were from another country, and one year held a celebration for a sporting event associated with that country. I was stunned by the amount of preparation that had been invested in the party. The whole house had been redecorated for the occasion – from top to bottom, from back to front. The well-groomed children met guests in the driveway as they arrived, showed them where to park, then escorted them into the house before rushing outside to greet the next arrivals.

The major leisure-time pursuit for the parents and children in this family revolved around a highly demanding activity involving animals, in which the animals were required to show a level of obedience that could only be achieved after years of rigorous training. Billie excelled in this. This was a family where shadows were not allowed to exist; they could not be tolerated; there was no room for them in such a carefully managed household. They were buried somewhere way out back, in a paddock.

We arranged for a counsellor to come to the school for regular appointments with Maureen. Tellingly, her parents did not bother to meet with the counsellor before the start of the therapy. The therapy was very helpful and we saw significant improvements in Maureen's behaviour. The counsellor reported that much of Maureen's rage seemed to be directed at Billie, which helped us make sense of the fact that she often attacked young female teachers.

However, after some months, the parents asked for their first meeting with the counsellor, at which I was present. During the meeting, they thanked the counsellor for her work but told her they were terminating her services, effective immediately. I spoke to Maureen's father that evening, pointing out that they had wilfully and with no warning put a stop to the only successful strategy we had found for helping their daughter. The next day Maureen attacked another boy, from behind, hitting him a number of times, as hard as she could. In view of the fact that the parents were sabotaging our attempts to support Maureen, we reluctantly ended her enrolment at the school.

In his innermost being, Keith would have known that he was flawed, like everyone else. But he had to conceal this knowledge from his parents, because he would also have known that flaws were unacceptable to them. Keith's behaviour at school was often narcissistic, when he acted like 'the chosen one': a young princeling. But when thwarted or frustrated he became angry and destructive. Then came denial, or other responses indicating confusion and frustration at his parents' high expectations and his inability to live up to them, as well as his inability to understand why he was treated differently at school from the way he was treated at home.

Training Keith to say 'I love you, Mummy' every afternoon when he got off the bus illustrates another misunderstanding parents often have about children. One of the many inadequacies of the English language is that it only provides us with the one word, 'love', to describe so many different relationships. The word 'love' is expected to cover my relationship with my wife, my feelings about our children, my relationship with ice cream, my attitude to spectacular sunsets, my responses to my favourite songs, books, movies, TV programs . . . I love my wife Kris, I love our boys, I love playing Scrabble, I love *The Simpsons*, I love words, I love my Toyota LandCruiser, I love chocolate, I love Bob Dylan, even though I've never met him . . .

There should be one word for the love parents have for their children and another for the love children have for their parents, because they are so different in their nature. Children will never, can never, should never, love their parents in the same way that parents love their children. Of course, children will obligingly parrot phrases like 'I love you, Mummy' or 'You're the best Daddy in the world' when taught to do so. Equally, a cockatoo can be trained to say 'Polly wants a cracker'. But many parents labour under the misapprehension that all they have to do is love their children and the love will automatically be returned . . . in the same manner and form.

Parents love their children because it is deep in the human psyche, as it is in the psyche of many other life forms, to nurture, nourish, protect and care for their offspring. In the old movie *Guess Who's Coming to Dinner*, Roy Glenn, who plays the father of the young Dr John Prentice, tries some emotional blackmail to get his son to obey his will, citing the sacrifices the parents have made in order for John to go to college and obtain a medical degree. Sidney Poitier, playing Dr Prentice, launches a blistering attack in reply, telling his father, who had been a mailman:

> You say you don't want to tell me how to live my life? What do you
> think you've been doing? You tell me what rights I've got or haven't
> got . . . and what I owe to you for what you've done for me. Let me
> tell you something. I owe you nothing. If you carried that [mail]
> bag a million miles you did what you were supposed to do, because
> you brought me into this world . . . and from that day you owed me
> everything you could ever do for me, like I will owe my son . . . if
> I ever have one. But you don't own me. You can't tell me when or
> where I'm out of line . . . or try to get me to live my life according
> to your rules. You don't even know what I am, Dad. You don't know
> who I am, how I feel, what I think. And if I tried to explain it the
> rest of your life, you would never understand. You are years older
> than I am. You and your whole lousy generation . . . believes the way
> it was for you is the way it's got to be! And not until your whole

generation has lain down and died . . . will the deadweight of you be off our backs! You understand? You've got to get off my back, Dad. You're my father. I'm your son. I love you. I always have and I always will. But you think of yourself as a coloured man. I think of myself as a man.[33]

Children love their parents because of the deep primal connections formed before and after birth, and because they (should) feel safe and protected whilst under the 'umbrella' of their parents' care. This protection is vital if the child is to survive, and grow healthily. They are ducklings, not fingerlings; they will probably die if not carefully guarded by their parents. At a deep level, the child knows this: he or she may not survive unless the mother, or mother-substitute, is functioning at a high level of efficiency. When the mother (or primary caregiver) is sick, her child will perform all kinds of touching services for her. But this care and attention is driven by self-need: the child urgently needs the mother to be well again, so that Mummy can continue to look after the child.

Children also know, at some level, that no one has a more valid and vital interest in them than their parents. Parents, and other close relatives, like grandparents, are usually the only adults who can be reliably expected to set aside their own egos (something which the child cannot yet do) to be caught up in the drama of the child's loose tooth, new Lego construction, performance in the 50 metre sprint at the school sports, drawing of an elephant, or grievance with the kid next door. This gratifies the young child's powerful need to be the centre of the universe. The young child is compellingly fascinated by himself or herself, and the only people prepared to share any significant part of this fascination are, most likely, the parents and perhaps some other family members. The good parent, the one who can function as an adult in the relationship, understands this need of the child, and is happy to gratify the child's ego (whilst being genuinely thrilled at

33 *Guess Who's Coming to Dinner*, motion picture, Columbia Pictures, 1967.

the child's growth and development) but at the same time is able to constantly bring to the child's attention the feelings, needs and rights of others. They teach the child perspective, a sense of proportion. They help the child understand relativity, and so gradually lead the child towards such abstract concepts as compassion, selflessness and empathy.

Here is a conversation I overheard recently at a restaurant between a mother and an eight-year-old, after a fruit platter had been placed on the table and the child started to help herself to fruit.

Mother: That's enough mango, darling. Other people might want some too.

(Child continues to take pieces of mango.)

Mother: Harriet! No more mango for you. Other people want some too.
Child: But Mummy, I like mango.
Mother: But so do the other people. Isn't it fairer if everyone has five pieces each instead of you having ten pieces and someone else not having any?

(Child subsides and reluctantly stops taking mango.)

This is good parenting in action. It might seem simple but it's really quite complex. It required three elements from the parent. She was observant – she noticed that Harriet was shovelling up mango with excessive enthusiasm. She was firm: she maintained her authority and did not give in to her daughter's wishes, recognising that Harriet, at her stage of ego development, was unable to regulate herself. Finally, she taught her daughter an important lesson about sharing and empathy, by using basic maths to make a concrete point in a way that her daughter was able to understand and could not refute.

Parents don't need to love their children, but if they don't love them, they have to be able to fake it. This is not so difficult, because children take it for granted that their parents love them, unless given cause to doubt the love – and when that happens the child is in big trouble. Children will desperately make up all sorts of explanations to cover their unconscious knowledge that a parent does not love them in the way they expect to be loved, deserve to be loved, and are entitled to be loved. A Grade 3 boy told me that the reason he had not seen his father for eighteen months was that 'he hasn't got enough money to buy food and stuff for me. That's why I can't go there'. Yet minutes earlier in the conversation he had boasted about all the wonderful times he spent with his father, including trips to the movies and to football grand finals. He told another member of staff about his father's magnificent Ferrari/Lamborghini/Maserati – I forget which it was.

I knew enough about this boy's life to be well aware that he was trying to invent a magical, perfect father to replace his real father, whom he understood at some level was uninterested in him.

More important than the parents loving the child is the need for parents to like the child. If the parent genuinely enjoys the son or daughter's company because of the child's good nature, positive energy, awareness of the world, sense of humour, and willingness to be involved in activities that are important to the parent, then the relationship should prosper. This makes it all the more extraordinary that many parents tolerate unlikeable behaviours in their children. If a child has too many unlikeable behaviours, or too few likeable ones, the child will of course be inherently unlikeable. Yet I have known many families where parents seem to feel that they have to benignly tolerate awful behaviour by their children.

Why do they do this? The test for evaluating a child's behaviour is easy: 'Would this same behaviour, in an adult, be viewed as attractive or unattractive?' If the answer is that the behaviour, when practised by an adult, would be unattractive, then the next step is logical and natural. The main function of parents and teachers, apart from looking after children's immediate needs, is to prepare them to operate effectively as adults. They have to teach children how the world works. Thus, when Grade 2 child Penelope derived great amusement from running up behind people and slapping them hard on the bum, then dancing around giggling with glee, our duty as teachers was clear. If Penelope at the age of 25, 35, 45 still found this amusing, she would have no friends. In fact, she might end up in the dock of a courtroom, defending a charge of assault. We had to put a stop to her unpleasant behaviour, and we did, by immediately intervening every time she slapped someone, and telling her to quit this unattractive habit.

On her birthday, six-year-old Marlene woke her parents at 4 am, demanding that the celebrations begin. Wearily the parents got out of bed, fetched the presents and the cake, and indulged Marlene with a round of 'Happy Birthday'.

What kind of adult will Marlene become?

It's not uncommon at schools to see a parent deep in conversation with another parent, only to have a child rush up, grab one of the adults by an arm and haul her or him away. Almost invariably, the parent allows herself to be hauled, whilst at the same time rolling her eyes at other adults in the vicinity, as if to say, 'Isn't he awful? Oh my God, the things I have to put up with!'

The parent may think she is putting up with a lot when a child does this, but it is nothing to what she will have to endure when that child becomes an adolescent and then an adult. And it is nothing compared to the problems other people will encounter in dealing with that adult who has never learned that such behaviours are unlikeable and selfish.

Children who interrupt adults' conversations regularly, as a matter of right, need to be taught new behaviours. Many children believe that the words 'Excuse me' are magic, and the simple utterance of them gives the child licence to gatecrash whatever the adults are doing or saying. The words are not magic; they carry no special power, and children who have not learned this early in their lives are at grave risk of becoming unlikeable adults.

Equally, many children believe that the word 'Sorry' is magic, and its simple utterance fixes all problems and absolves perpetrators of all blame. Quickly they start to use the word robotically, meaninglessly, and the important adults in their lives have to teach them that repentance, contrition and penance involve much more than a casual 'Sorry'. As a wise person once said, 'The only true apology is changed behaviour.'

Parents' love for their children should be viewed through the lens of the knowledge that sooner or later the child must metaphorically kill his or her parents (especially the same-sex parent, in situations where a man and a woman are both engaged in raising the child). Dr John Prentice does this to his father in the scene described earlier in *Guess Who's Coming to Dinner*. But if the parent has laid good foundations early in the child's life, the relationship will transcend the 'killing' and evolve into a new, mature one – a process that we can see beginning already in the closing stages of Dr Prentice's speech. 'You're my father. I'm your son. I love you. I always have and I always will.'

In the French movie *La Famille Bélier*, a seventeen-year-old daughter 'kills' her parents by expressing her determination to go to Paris for a singing audition that may lead to her moving permanently away from their rural town. The parents, particularly the mother, are distraught. They are both profoundly deaf, and cannot understand the concept of singing, but more importantly they need their daughter to translate for them in their contacts with the hearing community, and to help keep the farm going. After much vacillating and agonising, the daughter goes to Paris. The parents follow, to watch the audition, and are won over to support their daughter's ambition.[34] The movie ends at that point, but we can be confident about the future relationship between parents and daughter, because it has been rebuilt, upon new foundations. The essential ingredient in the story though, as in every parent–child story with a happy

---

34 *La Famille Bélier*, motion picture, Palace Films 2014.

ending, is that those new foundations contain many solid stones from the old ones.

Recently my wife and I had dinner with a family I would call extremely successful in terms of their relationships with each other. The family consists of a father, mother and three daughters, aged thirteen, eleven and seven. We adults talked; the girls came and went, grabbing biscuits and cheese from a platter on the table, doing gymnastics on the lawn outside, bouncing on the trampoline, watching part of a movie on TV, chasing the family cat, interacting all the time with each other, their parents and us.

It was a warm night, so we ate outside. As the father carried a bowl of salad out to the table, he said casually to the seven-year-old, who was swinging on an old tyre suspended from a tree branch, 'God, you're ugly.'

'Yeah, I get it from you,' she replied, without missing a beat.

Later we were admiring a calligraphy set one of the girls received for her birthday. The child showed us a piece of paper where the father had demonstrated his calligraphic skills, which were of a high order. In elaborate, formal letters he had written: 'Dear Sir or Madam, thank you for your correspondence of 12 December. It gives me pleasure to advise you, on behalf of the company, to fuck off. Yours faithfully, etc . . .'

Both parents swore from time to time during the evening, without appearing to notice or care whether their children heard. At one point I asked the five of them whether the girls swore at school. They all looked surprised, and the girls said, 'No, we're not that stupid.' It struck me later that throughout the years I'd known them, I'd never heard any of the children swear.

These parents might appear to be spectacularly defying 21st-century middle-class Western parenting values, yet the girls are cheerful, fun, well mannered, lively, intelligent and articulate. They are immensely likeable. And no one sister dominates the others. Each has her separate identity, voice, personality. I did not feel the presence of shadows hidden under beds or locked in the attic.

How can this be?

I think the answers are found in the two incidents I have described from our evening together. When the father said to the seven-year-old 'God, you're ugly', it was in the context of seven years of positive, sincere, cheerful parenting. She, like her sisters, was in no doubt that her parents loved her wholeheartedly. She also knew that the family culture included constant joking and teasing. She understood that this banter had no sinister undertones. She was able to reply immediately, 'Yeah, I get it from you,' because she had learned the language of the family and enjoyed participating in the repartee.

More than this, though, her father was doing her a favour. He was preparing her for the big rough world that awaits her. A world where she will often enough encounter people who are cruel, malicious, hurtful. I believe that she will handle that world with skill and resilience. If as an adult she has an emotionally abusive boyfriend who yells at her, 'You're an ugly bitch,' I think there's a good chance she will be able to laugh and say, 'Ugly! You've got a face like a wombat's bum.'

But I imagine that, recognising the difference between the way this hypothetical boyfriend speaks to her, and the way her father spoke to her, she will be sensible enough to quickly and decisively end the relationship with the boyfriend.

Each family has its own language, and the girls in this family understood that their parents swore quite often, but that swearing was adult language, and furthermore was private or semi-private, only to be used at home. Their parents did not patronise the daughters by changing their vocabulary or the tone of their voices when the kids were around. Instead, the children were given a sophisticated understanding of the way language works. They had probably never sat down and had a family meeting about it, but nevertheless, the parents had conveyed important understandings, both subtly and effectively.

'I BELIEVE IN FREE-RANGE FARMING . . . AND PARENTING'

Perhaps Candlebark and Alice Miller are more prone than other schools to attract a number of parents who operate according to a free-range philosophy. However, many people who function this way don't do so because of deeply held philosophical beliefs. Rather, they have found looking after children too difficult (sometimes it seems they did not want children in the first place) and so they avoid the tough decisions that are inherent in good parenting.

But we also see a number of families where the parents float around in a haze of brightly coloured hemp and honey-almond candles, a copy of a self-help book tucked under an arm, and a Dalai Lama keyring for their four-wheel-drive clutched in their hand.

Then there are the families who give their children everything, possibly because they themselves were deprived of life's luxuries when young, possibly because they think it's good parenting, possibly because it's a way of showing off their wealth. Melania Trump may fall into one or more of these categories. Her son Barron, as a young child, was apparently given plenty of licence. Melania told *Parenting* magazine, 'He draws on the wall of his playroom . . . He is very creative. If you say to a child, no, no, no, where does the creativity go?'[35]

Where indeed? I look forward to Barron's career as an innovative artist. I'm surprised the Director of the Metropolitan Museum of Art hasn't invited him in, issued him with a large box of permanent markers, and told him, 'Go for it, Barron.'

SAVANNAH

Savannah came to us at the start of Year 9, and seemed to flourish. Her parents clearly loved the school, and were delighted to have found a place that so suited their daughter. They were supportive of us in all kinds of ways, both practical and abstract. I was taken aback then to

---

35 Sabrina James, 'Melania Trump juggles motherhood, marriage, and a career just like us', *Parenting*, n.d., parenting.com/blogs/hip-mama/melania-trump-shares-her-1-parenting-tip-and-secrets-lasting-marriage, accessed 13 March 2019.

receive this email from her mother after just five months: 'I'm writing on behalf of Savannah because she wanted me to tell you that she is thinking of quitting your school and going to XXXX College. She wants to do this only because she believes she will have new friendship groups to choose from. We have set things up during the vacation so that she has the time and opportunities to decide about making this change.'

It later emerged that Savannah was spending her holidays in Scandinavia, at what her parents described as 'a course where teenagers are taught to recognise and respond to what their emotions are telling them'. Having worked through her feelings, Savannah confirmed that she did wish to leave the school. Her parents told us they were utterly devastated – to the point of tears – by her decision, but they felt they could not stand in their daughter's way … even though they were well aware that the school Savannah had chosen was notorious for its toxic culture, easy availability of drugs and poor academic standards.

It was concerning that Savannah was considered mature enough to make the decision to switch schools but was apparently not mature enough to communicate with us directly, instead getting the mother to do this on her behalf. It might be argued that either she was mature enough to do both or that she was too immature to do either.

It is not uncommon for parents of four-year-olds to tell us proudly that they are allowing their child to choose their own school, as if four-year-olds have an intimate knowledge of educational philosophy, curriculum, teaching standards and pedagogical styles. Four days before beginning the editing of this book, I had an email from the parent of a prospective student, a boy aged five. The parent wrote: 'Much as we love everything we've seen and heard about your school, Scotty has decided it's not for him. It is our belief that he should be the one who decides, as children have an instinct for what suits them.'

I'm afraid my own belief is that young children are more likely to base their decisions on the gradients of the slippery dips. Offer them a choc-chip biscuit and they will sign up on the spot.

Two days before beginning the edit, I had an email from the parents of a Grade 6 girl who wished to come to Candlebark – at the end of Term 1. They wrote: 'We know that many people would say this is not a good time to be changing schools, but we have always left it to her to choose her school.'

TRIXIE

Trixie's mother came to see me about her older daughter, but soon started talking about Trixie, her three-year-old, whom she described as 'impossible'. The conversation became all about Trixie, with the mother citing endless examples of Trixie's powerful personality.

'Does she know who's the boss in the family?' I eventually interrupted, to ask.

'Oh yes, she knows who the boss is. She's the boss.'

The mother said that every car trip was a nightmare, because Trixie refused to be buckled into the child seat. 'I spend fifteen minutes negotiating with her and explaining how we can't go anywhere until she's buckled in and finally I tell her that I'm just going to have to buckle her in by force, but when I do, she's furious with me.'

'How about telling her in advance: "We're leaving in five minutes, I'll be buckling you into your car seat, and then we're going to the deli and the butcher's?"'

'Oh, I do that.'

'Well, if the outcome is the same no matter what approach you take, you might as well skip the fifteen minutes' negotiation and use force from the start. Sounds like the negotiation is a waste of time. Three-year-olds don't negotiate very well anyway.'

'Yes . . . okay . . . I might try that.'

Trixie's parents were lovely people who just wanted to do 'the right thing' by their children. But nature abhors a vacuum, and so do children. Vacuums make everyone uncomfortable. If children sense a vacuum in the family they will rush to fill it. To prevent this happening, the adults often need to take up more space. It's the same for teachers. If students sense that the teacher is not confident or competent, that there's a vacuum, they will test the teacher every day until he or she proves to be capable of doing the job properly. Once the class knows that the teacher is capable, the kids relax, and never feel the need to test the teacher again. All good teachers give subtle signals as they walk in and put down their bag that they are in command and are comfortable with that role. The class settles, knowing they are in safe hands.

> . . . any serious cricketer gets a good idea of what a batsman's like simply by the way he comes in, takes guard, checks the field placements, settles himself for the first ball . . . you just know right away whether he is going to be a tough nut or a pushover, or somewhere in between. By now I'd played so much cricket that I arrived at the crease like I was coming home. I felt confident in that little rectangle . . .[36]

That's Josh, a twelve-year-old cricketer, in my book *The Year My Life Broke*. His description of a batsman arriving at the crease could serve as an analogy for the way an effective teacher enters a classroom.

If the teacher leaves a vacuum, it won't be filled by the nice, diligent, responsible student in the front row. It will be filled by the loudest, most aggressive, most unpleasant kid – the one with the worst values, the worst manners and the worst attitudes. American diplomat and presidential advisor Dennis Ross said on Melbourne radio in mid-2017: 'Every time we see a vacuum occur, we see the worst forces fill it.'[37] He was speaking of international politics, but unsurprisingly the same principle applies in classrooms and families.

Many teachers new to Candlebark or Alice Miller schools, particularly young and inexperienced ones, make the mistake of thinking that because the students are 'so nice and friendly', the teachers can be nice and friendly too, from day one. Despite the low frequency

---

36 John Marsden, *The Year My Life Broke*, Pan Australia, Sydney, 2013, pp. 47–48.
37 *The Conversation Hour,* John Faine on ABC Radio 774 Melbourne, 4 July 2017.

of behaviour problems at the two schools, students and classes will behave poorly if they sense a teacher, to borrow from the traditional chant of schoolkids everywhere, 'can't control us'. It can be a long hard slog for a teacher who loses the respect of kids in the early stages of the relationship. In his autobiography, Sir James Darling, long-time Headmaster of Geelong Grammar School, wrote of his first year of teaching: 'By the end of the [first] three days I had taught them everything which I knew and they had achieved the mastery, a position which I never redressed, at least that year. It did not surprise me that at the end of the first year the headmaster sent for me and told me that were it not for the fact that he was a friend of my father's he would have felt forced to dispense with my services.'[38]

Darling went on to become a man described by journalist Keith Dunstan in his autobiography as 'one of the great headmasters in the history of Australian education'.[39]

It seems very difficult for some teachers to understand that being respected is infinitely more important than being liked. Being liked is usually a by-product of being respected.

The current fashion in education is to downgrade the role of the teacher, relegating him or her to a place on the sidelines in a classroom that is child-centred, features experiential learning, and has students determining the curriculum. The teacher becomes just another resource.

That is not the way I run my schools. Candlebark and Alice Miller schools are not particularly democratic. The teachers I hire have experiences far beyond those of the students, have knowledge far beyond that possessed by the students (including highly specialised and sometimes arcane knowledge in their particular subject areas), and have the wisdom that comes from combining life experience and skills with perspective and a worldview. I expect the teachers, as the 'elders' in our community, to pass on their knowledge and wisdom

---

38 Sir James Darling, *Richly Rewarding*, Hill of Content, Melbourne, 1978, p. 72.
39 Keith Dunstan, *No Brains At All*, Viking/Penguin, Ringwood, 1990, p. 58.

to their young charges, in the way human societies have functioned for countless thousands of years. When I teach writing, I do so from a background of 50 years of passionate involvement and intensive study, 50 years of honing my skills and constantly seeking to improve my practice. Part of my library is a collection of more than 500 books about writing. I have browsed through or read them all. My students have never read a single book about writing.

My teachers and I each have at least four years' tertiary education in pedagogical practices, so that we know how to communicate effectively, transmit information, and help students advance in their life and in their learning journeys.

The other day a middle-aged woman told me with shining eyes of the 'best teacher I ever had. She was inspirational'.

'What did she do?' I asked.

'Do you know, on the first day of the year she walked in – she was about the size of a sparrow – and she stood on the stage at the front of the room, told us her name, and then said, "You're not going to like me but you are going to respect me, and you will do what I say." And we all just went "O-kayyy", and from that moment on she had us in the palm of her hand.'

Of course a fascist teacher might adopt this approach in an unhealthy way, but I was interested that this teacher was remembered with such love and admiration. It seems very likely that her opening remarks to the class were designed to enable learning to take place in an optimal atmosphere.

Teachers and parents who allow children to dominate situations – whether the family, the classroom or elsewhere – need more self-respect. They are selling themselves short. In a discussion on social media in early 2017, one contributor wrote: 'Parenting is having your eyelids prised open at 6 am on a Sunday by someone demanding Weet-Bix.'[40] Well, yes, that is a cute sentence and an amusing image.

---

40 Jordan Baker, 'Rachael Finch, I did not misquote you. Stop dancing around the truth', *Daily Telegraph*, 8 January 2017.

(We can safely assume that a child is doing the prising of the eyelids, not an escaped convict from a maximum-security prison, or a demented grandfather.)

But parenting is also saying 'Go back to bed' or 'Go read a book – we'll tell you when it's time for breakfast' or 'This is Mummy and Daddy time, not kid time' or 'Get your own Weet-Bix, but be quiet about it, and make sure you put the milk away after you've finished'.

Parenting means teaching children to get their own Weet-Bix. We at Candlebark know, with absolute certainty, that every four-year-old who is not seriously disabled can make a sandwich or a wrap, can cut up their own apple, can pour a glass of milk. We know this because we have 25 or so kids from this age group in our year-long Foundation orientation program, and we quickly train them to do all these things. It's not difficult.

I am dissembling a little, though, because there is one problem with our teaching children to make their own lunches. The problem is that their parents won't let them. Many parents find it impossible to stand back and let the child do the work. They are at his or her side: 'Would you like jam or Vegemite?' 'Would you like your apple peeled or unpeeled?' 'Here, let Daddy do that for you.' 'Here, let Mummy do that, darling.' 'Would you like your sandwich cut in halves or quarters?' 'Is that enough mayonnaise or would you like some more? Or has Mummy put too much on? Oh, all right, look, I'll scrape some off. See, I'm scraping it off . . .' 'I'll just cut the crusts off your bread for you.' We've had four-year-olds who refuse to eat a sandwich that has not had the crusts amputated, or an apple that has not been peeled and cut into slices.

We at the school gnash our teeth in frustration at this. Fortunately, our teeth, strengthened by biting into apples and eating bread crusts when we were young, are able to survive. But parents who behave like this are determinedly continuing the learned helplessness they have been successfully inculcating in their children for at least three years. It starts with the parent intervening to get the rattle or toy for the child who is stretching out his little fingers to grasp it. It continues with parents hand-feeding infants for much longer than necessary, unwrapping presents for their children, attaching one Duplo piece to another, picking up toys after the children have lost interest and wandered away.

The parents may believe that this is good parenting, that they are showing their devotion to their children by such excessive attention, and that some highly critical observer (probably the parents' own father or mother) is watching and judging (whether physically present or not), and any neglect of these tasks means that they are incompetent and will be savagely told so. I wonder if Trixie's mother ever used a loud angry voice to say to her daughter: 'Get in the car! Now!' I'd say not, because she would believe this was bad parenting and might inflict lifelong scars on Trixie. Sadly, her parenting style might well inflict lifelong scars on Trixie, but scars that are less obvious and not so easily understood.

Sooner or later – generally sooner – we start ushering the parents of the four-year-olds in the Candlebark orientation program out the door and away from their kids. But often we have to be quite forceful: 'It's time for you to go now. She won't do it by herself while you're standing there.'

Unless checked at an early age, the excessive attention paid by some parents to their children will go on forever. For those who have not seen it, the old black-and-white mother-and-son routine performed by comedians Mike Nichols and Elaine May is timelessly funny and a salutary lesson in the dangers of over-involved parenting.[41] The unrelenting emotional blackmail from the possessive and dominating mother, played by Elaine May, causes the son, played by Mike Nichols, to regress to helpless infancy by the end of the phone call, in a manner that is exquisitely and horrifyingly true to life.

In John Steinbeck's *Travels with Charley*, published in 1962, Steinbeck recalls his observations of a mother–child interaction

---

41 'Nichols _ May classic _Mother and Son_ skit', YouTube, youtube.com/watch?v=lKL1tNv__kU.

from years earlier, during a visit he and his wife paid to their boys at summer camp:

> When we were about to depart, a lady parent told us she had to leave quickly to keep her child from going into hysterics. And with brave but trembling lips she fled blindly, masking her feeling to save her child. The boy watched her go and then with infinite relief went back to his gang and his business, knowing that he too had played the game.[42]

We see this little drama played out by quite a few parents and kids on a daily basis. Nothing has changed since Steinbeck's time, except that the scenes now seem even more intense, and the acting even more emotionally charged. It is an everyday event for parents to say to us 'I can't leave, because he won't let me' or 'Maybe if I sneak away she won't notice'. They go to children, who may be as young as four or five or six, and say: 'Is it all right if Mummy leaves now?' 'Can Daddy leave now?' *They have to seek their children's permission before they can go on with their lives!* They negotiate complex treaties: 'Daddy has to go now, but I'll be back at the start of clean-up, and I'll bring the puppy, and we'll come and find you then. And on the way home we'll get an ice cream. Is that all right?' These treaties frequently include the teacher's services traded away gratis, without reference to the teacher: 'I have to go now but Olive [teacher] will hold your hand when you go on the walk.' 'I have to go now but you can sit with Olive to do your drawing.' 'I have to go now but Olive will help you make your lunch.'

The parents seem unaware that Olive has fifteen other children to look after, and some might have needs more pressing and demanding than those of their little prince or princess. Or Olive might actually know that it's not in the child's best interests to be indulged with slavish attention on a 24/7 basis.

---

42 John Steinbeck, *Travels with Charley: In Search of America*, Bantam, New York, 1963, p. 124.

One day I saw the parents of a Grade 6 girl sitting wearily on a bench near the school tennis court. It was 11 am, and classes had been in session for two hours. It was the child's first day at our school but she had previously enjoyed two trial days with us.

'You're still here?' I asked, although the question was somewhat redundant.

'Oh yes,' they sighed.

'I think she'd actually be better off if you left. I'm sure she'll be fine.'

They rolled their eyes. 'Oh yes, we think so too. And we've told her that as soon as they go on the excursion, we're out of here.'

The excursion left shortly afterwards, but I noticed that the parents returned at the same time as the bus − 45 minutes before school ended. I remembered then that during the child's trial days the parents had remained with us for the entire school day.

It is now absolutely normal for parents to stay with their children when the kids go to another child's birthday party. Once the invitation is issued, it's taken for granted that the hosts will cater for adults as well as children. To make things worse, the adults scoff all the fairy bread before the kids get near it.

When we send students on trips, a number of mothers (or, much less frequently, fathers) compete with each other on social media to claim the title of 'Most Bereft Parent', with heartrending sob-soaked accounts of the days and nights of torment they endure as they wait for their child to return to the sanctuary of home. Some, for example, go online every day to check the weather in the location where the kids are staying. The parents' lives apparently are put on hold as they sit staring at a clock or calendar or computer, unable to function until their fifteen-year-old walks through the doorway again. Except that the parent won't have to wait quite so long – she'll be at the airport three hours before the plane lands, anxiously watching the Arrivals board.

MARGUERITE AND JANE

Marguerite's mother, Roslyn, had a close friendship with Jane's mother, Sybil, and the two girls were also very close. Marguerite had been two years at a school where I was teaching before Sybil approached us and asked if Jane could enrol at the same school. I checked with Roslyn to see whether this would be in Marguerite's best interests. She said that she was concerned that the relationship of the two girls was not particularly healthy, that they followed each other too closely, and it might be better if they had more time apart. Nevertheless, after telling me this, she surprised me by concluding that it would be fine for the girls to attend the same school. On the basis of this conversation, the school agreed to enrol Jane.

Within a few terms the behaviour of both girls began to deteriorate, and about a year later both started lobbying their parents to be allowed to go together to a different school . . . one that had a similarly poor reputation to the one newly chosen by Savannah.

Whilst this drama was slowly unfolding, I got an email from Roslyn, from which these passages have been extracted:

> Looking back over my years as a parent, I can see now that I
> have switched from one style to another, especially in the last
> 12 months or so. But somehow, nothing seems to be working very
> well – whether it's me standing back and trusting her to make
> good choices and letting her cop the consequences when things go
> wrong, whether it's me being bossy and telling her how things have
> to be done (and punishing her when she disobeys), whether I use
> the "we're both adults" style and try to have open conversations with
> her, or whether I just try to keep out of her way and wait for her to
> approach me . . .
>
> I know yours is the best school for her. By a long way. She went
> to two schools before yours, and they were both horrible. But now
> she's got it into her head that she wants to leave and go to a big
> high school near us. I think she feels that this will give her a more
> "normal" experience! She is getting more and more determined

about it, and it's breaking my heart, as I think your school is fantastic – the teachers are so dedicated and so inspiring and it seems terrible that Marguerite is willing to throw such a unique experience away so easily. But I guess that's just the stage she's at. I should warn you too that if I give in to her and let her leave, I think Jane is probably heading the same way. I wish they hadn't both gone to your school, even though I encouraged you to accept Jane. Unfortunately, though, I think Jane is a bit of a shadow to Marguerite, and it's not good for either girl . . .

I appreciated and respected the sincerity of this email, the deep feelings underlying it, and the authenticity of Roslyn's efforts to find the best outcome for her daughter. Unfortunately, however, it was evident from the email, and my other interactions with her, that Roslyn's parenting lacked strength and consistency. Although she was doubtful of the influence of Jane on Marguerite, and constantly expressed the need for her and Marguerite to separate from Jane and Sybil, the two women developed a plan to move closer to each other, where they and the girls would be in frequent contact. Roslyn was pregnant when Marguerite left us; she had a baby daughter whom she named, to my astonishment, Janet, despite her frequently expressed concerns about the families being too close. Whilst the moving plan was still under consideration both girls did leave us. They enrolled at the same high school, ignoring Roslyn's express desire that this not happen.

I had the strong feeling in conversations with Jane and Marguerite that they knew they would be kept safe at our school, but this, understandably enough, was exactly what they did not want. They wanted excitement, they wanted to live on the edge. It was as though they had seen too many bad American movies about teenagers, and were keen to imitate the girls in those films. Sure enough, at their new school their attendance became irregular and infrequent, they got involved in the local drug culture, and made some dangerous choices of boyfriends.

Jane had not been at our school long before her mother Sybil was sending me emails about courses, workshops, books and other material that reflected her approach to life. These courses offered such topics as Deep Nature Connection, which was described on its website in these terms: 'Deep Nature Connection produces powerful Creativity. We leverage a process called Renewal of Creative Path that brings out the brightest light in individuals, communities, collaborators, and organizations.'[43]

I wrote back that language like this set my teeth on edge (which would have made it more difficult for me to eat unpeeled apples), so fortunately Sybil dropped me from her list of sympathisers.

Many parents (not Roslyn and Sybil, however) who at first sight appear permissive, are controlling to the point of fascism with their children. The only difference between them and aggressive, materialistic, authoritarian parents is that their authoritarianism is disguised with soft language and gentle voices.

SIMONE

Simone's parents were very 'new age' and no doubt would have been enthusiastic embracers of courses like the Deep Nature Connection mentioned above. At age fourteen, Simone came back one Friday afternoon from a five-day school hike, looking forward to a normal weekend with her mother, who lived close by. She was devastated to find that her mother had plans for herself for the weekend, with her new partner, and to facilitate those plans had arranged for her ex-husband, Simone's father, to come from his distant town, pick Simone up, and take her back to his house.

As soon as she heard this, Simone rang her father and told him not to come. He replied that the weekend plans were not negotiable. I had a lot of sympathy with Simone when I heard this, as she was physically and emotionally exhausted by the hike, in a way that the

---

43 *BioSpiritual Permaculture*, 4 December 2011, http://biospiritualpermaculture.tumblr.com/post/13741379323/8-shields-philosophy, accessed 18 April.

parents might not have understood, so I rang the father. However, the stepmother answered the phone and explained that I was too late: the father was already on his way.

Simone talked to a girlfriend then rang her father again, on his mobile, and told him to turn around and go back, as she was not going to his place; she had just arranged to stay with her girlfriend for the weekend. The father said he was still coming and that they would 'sort it out when he got there'. I then rang both the father and the mother, putting it to them that their arrangements were unfair to Simone, but neither would yield.

By now it was about 4.45 pm, and the school day had been over for an hour or more, but Simone was in a state of such anxiety and distress that I thought I had better wait with her until her father arrived. When he appeared, Simone became so agitated that I deliberately sat within hearing distance, pretending to mark essays, to give her a sense of security. Simone insisted to her father that the arrangements made by her parents were unfair, and that she was not going with him. The quiet, calm, gentle father, who worked in the arts, quietly, calmly, gently, relentlessly told her that she was going with him, to get in the car, and that 'you're just tired; everything will work out fine'. Not once did he raise his voice, not once did he show anger, not once did he listen to his daughter, not once did he attempt any compromise or negotiation. The tone of his voice disguised the implacability of his attitude. He was simply going to wear his daughter down until she did what he wanted. He knew the movements he wanted for his dance and he was going to get them.

Eventually the tension reached such a level that I felt I had to intervene. I walked over and asked Simone if I could have a chat with her father, just the two of us. With evident relief she scuttled off and sat with her girlfriend, some distance away. I said to the father, 'I appreciate that you've had a long drive, but you're now in a lose–lose situation. You can of course force her to get into the car, but you'll have a horrible weekend, because she'll be so angry that she'll give you hell right through until Monday morning, and possibly beyond.

Your relationship with her could be damaged for a long time. Or you can back down, which means you've had a long trip for nothing, and you'll be deprived of your daughter's company for the weekend. You may also feel that if you back down you will lose some of your authority as a parent. But on the other hand, Simone may appreciate that you have listened to her, shown respect for her point of view, and agreed to her wishes. After all, her position is not unreasonable – she's exhausted, and had no knowledge that these plans had been made by you and your ex-wife.' I pointed out too that Simone was four-teen years old and should be allowed some input into arrangements like these.

Painted into a corner, he reluctantly conceded, and told Simone she could stay with her girlfriend. But the interesting thing to me was Simone's reaction after her father drove away. She was relatively new to the school, and before this episode had been quite negative about us. Now she was utterly exhilarated, but at the same time tearful and inarticulate in expressing her joy. Her girlfriend spoke for her, telling me: 'This is the first time anyone has stood up for her. This is the first time she has ever gotten her own way with either of her parents. This is the first time either of them has listened to her.'

The afternoon with Simone and her father had not surprised me. Time and again we see parents who present as libertarian but who become steely-eyed when their control of their children is threatened. Worse, they can become venomous. Frequently, food is the vehicle by which this desire for control is most visibly expressed. In recent years we've seen a dramatic growth in the number of parents who are obsessed with the food their children eat. For example, I remember the woman who would not allow her children any sugar – but the children told me how their mother had her own secret stashes of lollies around the house and in the car, which the kids frequently raided. At school, the children were notorious for surreptitiously feeding them-selves large quantities of sugar directly from the bag in the pantry.

I remember a woman who wrote to me saying that her son had eaten some strawberries at school and as a consequence had been 'defiant and naughty that evening, and also wet his bed'. I remember the interview with parents who told me that their child was gluten-intolerant. 'What happens if he eats food containing gluten?' I asked. 'We don't know,' they replied. 'We've never given him any. We just feel that he probably wouldn't react well to it.'

These parents sometimes give the impression that they are hovering over their children like ominous hawks, ready to swoop if they see their child eat a fragment that's on their proscribed list. They throw the word 'allergic' around as loosely as a toddler throws Duplo pieces. In doing so, they jeopardise the wellbeing of those children who have genuine food allergies or intolerances. They frequently hold a view, so popular in recent times, that the body is 'full of toxins' and must be frequently flushed or purged or starved or purified. They believe their own bodies are forever working against them, trying to poison them. But it seems more likely that they fear their child developing a taste for a forbidden fruit, which will somehow make the parents feel that their control is threatened.

'HE/SHE IS MY CHILD, AND HE/SHE WILL DO WHAT I SAY'

Some adults are overtly controlling, and have no compunction about articulating and exercising their 'rights' as parents. Of course, every parent has not just a right, but an obligation to set limits, establish rules, draw boundary lines. There are disastrous consequences for children when parents fail to do this. But the parents who strut around their tiny kingdoms shouting at or punishing a child who breaks the rules (even relatively insignificant ones), or defies them, are destructive adults who will cause lasting damage to their child.

Authoritarian parents frequently attempt to bully teachers, but they pick their targets, concentrating on younger, less experienced teachers, and on women. If a school does not strongly resist such bullying, its employees can be traumatised and its culture damaged.

There are limits to a parent's authority over a child. A child is not an object or a possession. They are not like Pinocchio, carved by Geppetto from a block of wood because he wanted a beautiful puppet who could dance, fence and turn somersaults – so that Geppetto could earn money from him. Just as men in many cultures over thousands of years have regarded and continue to regard women as possessions, objects that they own, so do many parents think of children as 'theirs', and brook no challenge to their 'ownership'.

Here's a description of bad parenting, an episode as inconsequential and trivial as the mango incident described earlier – and yet equally telling, because it can safely be assumed that it was part of a pattern. I was sitting at a car dealership, waiting to collect my car after its regular service. Near me, in the waiting room, was a roped-off play area for children, where a little girl was absorbed in constructing a building with blocks. Her mother was perched at the edge of the play area, doing something with her phone. So far, so good. It's absolutely not necessary for parents to join in children's games: in fact, it's counterproductive to do it too much, partly because adults can never play in the same way children do, no matter how much they might like to delude themselves into thinking they are so 'young in heart' that they can meet the child on equal terms. But more importantly, children have to be allowed time and space to exercise their imagination by playing on their own.

After about five minutes, the father strode in. It appeared that the car was now available for collection, so he was ready to go. He resembled a busy and important corporate CEO. As he walked towards his wife and child he called out brusquely: 'Come on, let's get out of here.'

The child looked up, and appeared disconcerted that her game was about to end so suddenly. Before she had time to process what was happening, her father grabbed her under the armpits and lifted her out of the enclosure. She looked aghast, and then, as he pulled her along, she started crying. Impatiently, he took her up, and carried her outside to the car.

The mother also looked disconcerted. At that point, the cashier signalled to me that my car was ready. As I left the area, my last view was of the mother quickly packing up the blocks and putting them neatly back in their allocated places. I had the feeling that as well as seeing the parenting practices of this family, I was seeing gender politics at work.

The father's treatment of his wife and child seemed to be no different in substance from his treatment of his car. He apparently required objects to be available at his convenience. He no doubt needed his phone in his pocket so he could make phone calls whenever he wished and from wherever he wanted. Ergo, the phone must be fully charged, 24/7. He needed his car. When the time came that day for him to leave the dealership, his wife and daughter had to be as available as the car. I suspect that if the child proved tardy in any aspect of the family's life, the father would simply pick her up and carry her away.

The practice of picking children up and physically moving them, to suit the parents' convenience, might be justifiable at times, but should never be a pattern of parenting. If it's done habitually, it teaches the child that 'might is right', that physical strength trumps all other considerations. It's important to recognise the difference between conversation and negotiation: a parent shouldn't negotiate every situation with children, but in most situations they should extend the courtesy of a conversation. The father at the car dealership did not need to sit down with his daughter and say, 'Darling, Daddy would like to go soon, so how much longer do you think you might want to play with the blocks?' But he could say, 'Darling, the car's finally ready, but now we're running late, so I need you to leave the blocks right away and hurry out to the car with me.' Or: 'Sorry folks, we have to go soon, so this is a three-minute warning.' Or even: 'How exciting, the car's ready, let's go and have a look?' He could also have joined his wife in packing up the blocks – and insisted on the child's involvement in that task.

There are limitations to a parent's authority. One of the more abstract limitations is this: a parent has no right to keep a child in ignorance. Schools must actively oppose parents who seek to do so.

Young people have an absolute right to know about puberty, about sex, about politics, about human behaviour, about money, about history, about important global issues. To deliberately block the access of children and teenagers to such essential information is a form of child abuse.

It is particularly difficult to deal with parents who are certain they know the truth, because their certainty often leads them to believe that their truth should be everyone's truth, is the only truth, and that any other position is impossible because it must be untrue. This can then result in an authoritarian style of parenting. The view that 'the colour of truth is always grey' is not well understood or received by such people. British Prime Minister William Lamb supposedly said of the historian Thomas Macaulay, 'I wish I were as cocksure of anything as Tom Macaulay is of everything.'[44] For myself, I've always felt that I belong with Edna Everage's mother in the 'Home for the Perpetually Bewildered'. Life is complex, profound, nuanced and multifaceted.

The sad and traumatising consequences of keeping children in ignorance is illustrated by this story, told by a contributor on an internet forum. It will resonate with many women, even young 21st-century women:

My family (mom, dad, brother, and myself) were packing one morning to go on a week-long camping trip to the lake with some family friends. The family friends were a family of five, one of them being my little brother's best friend. I was 11. As we were about to leave my mom tells everyone to go to the bathroom before the drive, so I do. Turns out I had just started my first period and was covered in blood. I start crying, because at this point I hadn't gone through sex ed yet and my mother had never warned me about any of this. I had no idea what was going on.

So I go to the stairs and yell down to my mom from the upstairs landing that something is wrong with me and I need her to come up so I can talk to her. Instead she keeps yelling at me to just tell her

---

44   William Lamb, 2nd Viscount Melbourne, *The Spectator*, 30 November 1889.

what it is, but my brother, his friend, and my dad are all down there with her so I'm too embarrassed to say anything. At this point my mom is pissed because she's stressed from packing and I'm crying hysterically because I think something is really wrong. Finally I get it out that I'm bleeding and she screams 'Well take care of it and let's go,' throws me a pad from the bathroom, and continues packing. I spent the next week at the lake. Didn't know what tampons were, so I wore jeans on the boat. I was too afraid to lay down at night because of the mess, so I slept sitting up on the floor.[45]

As a general principle, adults should not lie to children, and schools should not be complicit in the lies some parents tell their children. Popular cultural myths involving rabbits that bring chocolate eggs, fairies that leave money in exchange for teeth, and overweight men in red suits who bring presents in late December pose some difficulties for schools, but it would be a brave principal who disillusioned kids about these mythical visitors. For my part, I try to walk the delicate line by describing these festive events as games: 'Yes, we could well be playing the Easter Bunny game again soon.'

It's rather odd that followers of many organised religions support the Easter Bunny and Santa Claus myths, because when children learn the truth about these miraculous beings they often assume that the divine figures whom they have been taught to worship are in the same category. They too can then be relegated to the status of silly childhood beliefs that kids feel mortified to have held. Turning water into wine? Flying around the world with reindeer? Raising people from the dead? Giving presents to every child in the world? Feeding a huge crowd with just a few loaves of bread and a couple of fish? Squeezing down chimneys? Walking across water? Really?

The biggest difficulty with Santa and his stablemates, however, is that they involve parents cold-bloodedly lying to their children. When

---

45   Answer from 'ascanner', 'What was your most awkward "puberty" moment', Reddit, 19 August 2010, reddit.com/r/AskReddit/comments/d2sff/what_was_your_most_awkward_puberty_moment, accessed 10 April 2014.

Indigenous Australians told creation myths to their children, when Irish grandmothers told stories about leprechauns, when Iroquois elders described the creation of the world by the Sky Woman and the water animals working together, they were not lying, because they believed in the myths themselves. When modern parents look their kids straight in the eye and say 'Yes, Santa is real', they are lying, and they know it. The consequences can be awful. I would estimate, from conversations with teenagers over the last 40 years, that 30 per cent of kids are seriously distressed when they find out the truth about Santa. They are not necessarily distressed because they learn that Santa is a myth; they are only a little distressed by the realisation that they may not get as many presents in future; but they are devastated by the knowledge that their parents lied to them. Many adults reading this will no doubt recall similar feelings when they found out the truth about the pantheon of childhood fantasy figures, but when children grow up to become parents a strange amnesia often comes into operation, and they repress intense emotional memories from their own childhoods.

In his autobiography, *My Lives and Loves*, writer Frank Harris tells of the pain he felt when sent to an English boarding school, thereby losing contact with the folktales of Ireland: 'I missed the kindliness of boy to boy and of the masters to the boys; above all [I missed] the imaginative fantasies of fairies and "the little people" which had been taught us by our nurses and though only half believed in; yet enriched and glorified life – all this was lost to me.'[46]

'Though only half believed in.' That is the critical phrase. Many of us only half-believe in Santa through our childhoods, once we have left infancy. It's likely that some Irish grandmothers only half-believed in the 'little people'. But the half-belief is important; it nourishes our need for contact with the romantic world of the magical and fantastical. Parents need to support that half-belief without going so far as to lie to children to convert the half-belief into a full one.

---

46 Frank Harris, *My Life and Loves*, Corgi, London, 1973, p. 36.

Maxim Gorky's relationship with his grandmother, solidly founded on her wonderful and seemingly endless telling of stories, was a rich and vital part of his development. In his autobiography, *My Childhood*, he describes life with her:

> After a pinch of snuff she would begin her wonderful stories about good robbers, saints, and all kinds of wild animals and evil spirits.
>
> She would tell these stories in a soft, mysterious voice, her face turned towards me. Her wide-open eyes would stare into mine as if she were pouring strength straight into my heart, which uplifted me.
>
> She seemed to sing the stories to me, and the longer she went on, the more harmonious and flowing the words became. Listening to her was the most marvellous experience. I would sit there, and then ask her: 'More!'
>
> 'It was like this: an old goblin was sitting by the fire when he got a splinter of vermicelli in his hand. He rocked to and fro with pain and whined: "Oh, little mice, I can't stand the pain!"' She would lift her leg up high, grip it and shake it, comically wrinkling up her face as if she were in pain herself.
>
> Some bearded sailors were standing by us. All of them looked very kind and they applauded and laughed as they listened to Grandmother's stories.
>
> 'Now, Grandma, let's have some more,' they kept on asking.
>
> Then they said: 'Come and have a bite with us.'[47]

Even the adult sailors were an appreciative audience, and at some level were no doubt aware of the contribution of such stories to the development and strengthening of a unique Russian culture.

It's interesting that the young criminals educated by the extraordinary Russian teacher Anton Makarenko in the 1920s loved Gorky's memoirs above all other books. According to biographer Valentin Kumarin: 'They listened to them with bated breath forgetting about everything else as they did so. Makarenko told his charges the story

---

47   Maxim Gorky, *My Childhood*, trans. by Ronal Wilks, Penguin, Harmondsworth, 1966, p. 21.

of Gorky's life. At first they could not believe what they heard but then exclaimed joyfully: "So that means Gorky is like one of us?"[48] Makarenko wrote in his famous work *The Road to Life*: 'Maxim Gorky's life seemed to become part of our life. Various episodes in it provided us with . . . a scale for the measurement of human values.'[49]

There is a similarity between the reactions of the 'juvenile delinquents' to Gorky, and the reaction of junior high school Afro-American students in Boston in 1964 to the poetry of Langston Hughes. Teacher Jonathan Kozol describes, in his book *Death at an Early Age*, the astonished response of the students to the revelation that a 'coloured' person not only wrote poems but had them published, and was honoured for it. When Kozol read to a Grade 4 class a Langston Hughes poem that criticised greedy, corrupt landlords and the American judicial system, he was sacked, and subsequently told in writing that 'a measure of control over the course of study is essential to protect the 94,000 Boston schoolchildren from ideologies and concepts not acceptable to our way of life. Without any restrictions, what guarantees would parents have that their children were not being taught that Adolf Hitler and Nazism were right for Germany and beneficial to mankind?'[50]

After an outcry, a young white attorney was appointed by the Boston Public Schools Committee to investigate whether Kozol's dismissal was justified. The man found that it was justified, and said in his report: 'Mr Kozol, or anyone else who lacks the personal discipline to abide by rules and regulations, as we all must in a civilised society, is obviously unsuited for the highly responsible profession of teaching.'

Years later the young white attorney who wrote those words was suspended indefinitely from practising law because he had misappropriated client funds for his own use. His words again: 'Anyone else

---

48 Valentin Kumarin, *Anton Makarenko: His Life and Work in Education*.
49 Anton Makarenko, *The Road to Life*, quoted in Kumarin, *Anton Makarenko*.
50 Jonathan Kozol, *Death at an Early Age: The Destruction of the Hearts and Minds of Negro Children in the Boston Public Schools*, Penguin, New York, 1967 and 1985, p. 226 (first published 1967).

who lacks the personal discipline to abide by rules and regulations, as we all must in a civilised society, is obviously unsuited for the highly responsible profession of teaching.'[51]

Realism and fantasy mingle and mix in fiction and poetry. So I'm not suggesting that children should grow up on a diet of all fantasy. But paradoxically, one of the great values of fantasy is that it gives us the courage to face reality, to bear the truth, and to develop the insight to understand truth.

In Western society we have developed a fear of children encountering truth, just as we have a fear of encountering the truth about children. In 1923 a massive earthquake in Japan, followed by horrific fires, destroyed Yokohama and three-fifths of Tokyo, and killed nearly 150,000 people. It still ranks as one of the worst natural disasters in human history. The legendary film-maker Akira Kurosawa (*Rashomon*, *Seven Samurai*) was a boy of thirteen at the time. Seventy years later he spoke of his experiences on the day after the disaster:

> My brother once forced me to spend a day wandering through Tokyo looking at the victims ... Corpses piled on bridges, corpses blocking off a whole street at the intersection, corpses displaying every manner of death possible to human beings. When I involuntarily looked away, my brother scolded me, 'Akira, look carefully now.' ... When that night I asked my brother why he made me look at those terrible sights, he replied: 'If you shut your eyes to a frightening sight, you end up being frightened. If you look at everything straight on, there is nothing to be afraid of.'[52]

When Candlebark parent Richard Lobb lost a leg in a motorcycle accident I asked him to come into the school shortly afterwards to talk to the kids about it, and about the way his life had changed. After Richard finished his frank and memorable address, he took questions from the

51 Ibid.
52 *Akira Kurosawa/Interviews*, ed. B. Cardullo, University Press of Mississippi, 2008.

audience. One of the first questions was 'Can we see your leg?'

The stump was still wrapped in bandages. Richard looked at me and said, 'It actually is not a pretty sight. I don't think it would be a good idea . . . but it's your call.'

Remembering the Kurosawa story, which had greatly impacted on me, I gulped and said, 'Well, if you don't show them, they'll use their imaginations to guess what it looks like, so it's probably better for them to see the reality.'

He unwound the bandage. His stump was crisscrossed with recent scars, but nothing about it appalled or horrified the kids, who crowded around, full of questions. They were fascinated. I'm confident in saying that it didn't traumatise anyone, although it did make a big impact. And years later Richard told me that the meeting had been a deeply significant event for him, and had helped him emotionally.

Many parents have a superficial philosophy of parenting that can be summed up as: 'There are so many horrible things in the world, and I will protect my child from them.' This approach often consists of hiding the so-called 'ugly realities'. It can quickly turn into bullying those who believe it more helpful to bring children face to face with the truth in ways that will help them understand the mysteries of life and hence lead more successful, rewarding and productive lives themselves.

A school has a moral obligation to stand firm against parents who try to bully it into helping them 'protect' their children in unhealthy ways.

Another father came to a school meeting one morning to talk about his occupation, which was to train police in the use of firearms. He brought various props, including a dummy revolver, and needless to say was a big hit with his young audience. One parent, however, was furious, and stormed out of the meeting. He complained to a teacher, loudly, that the presentation was inappropriate. It was strangely paradoxical that he used a string of swearwords during his tirade, indifferent to the fact that a number of very young children could hear him complaining about someone else being inappropriate. But what was the problem? Training police in the use of firearms is a legitimate occupation, and one of value to the community. Kids are aware from an early age that cops have guns, and I imagine it would be reassuring for them to know that the men and women using weapons are given extensive training.

The most common types of school-bullying I've seen from parents are by fathers who sometimes seem to be demonstrating a need to dominate and control others (their children, their partners and the school), and by mothers who sometimes seem to see their children as so precious and perfect that contact with children whom they have not carefully selected will involve exposure to toxic influences.

CLINT

Clint and his young half-siblings lived with Clint's mother and step-father. They had been at the school only a couple of terms and seemed to be travelling well, until one day the cook came to me and said that the stepfather had rung her to ask what was on the menu for lunch. Something in his tone caused her to feel uneasy, so she said she would ring him back.

I offered to call him on her behalf, and did so. He launched into a remarkable speech. 'Everyone knows the food is fantastic,' he said, 'but you promised you would have food to suit everybody. And it doesn't suit my children.'

'In what way?' I asked.

'Well, my stepdaughter doesn't like raspberry jam. She likes straw-berry, and she's asked repeatedly for it, but it's always raspberry – or blackberry. And Clint loves the scones, but he wants them with dates in, like he gets at home.'

I went through a detailed list of the food available each day for lunch, which totalled around 60 or 70 options. But my refusal to buckle under his pressure and guarantee the immediate introduction of strawberry jam and scones with dates seemed to enrage him. Half an hour later he rang back to say he was coming to pick up his kids and take them home while he and his wife thought about the situation.

'No problem,' I said, although my private thoughts were somewhat different.

I was teaching when they arrived, so I didn't see them. Their children were in classes, mid-lesson, but the parents pulled them out, bundled the bewildered kids into the car, and drove away. We never saw them again. Five days later the father informed me that he was withdrawing them from the school.

He was a man whose profession required the highest standards of self-discipline and skill. I assume there must have been bigger issues involved in his withdrawing the children, issues he was unable to talk about.

GRAEME

We had little warning of what we were in for with Graeme. The parents told us they had been homeschooling him, which we later found was untrue, but it's possible that they were keen to conceal his previous school record.

On the opening day of the school year, Graeme became very agitated when he realised that a much younger child was enjoying a second helping of spaghetti bolognese before Graeme had received his first helping. We don't have any highly regulated system for morning tea or lunch: food is available throughout the free time the children have, and they can come and get it when they're ready. But Graeme's reaction was extreme. He backed the small child into a corner, took his plate from him, and told him he'd 'break his arm if he ever tried a stunt like that again'.

I was 'fortunate' enough to hear that comment, and intervened, but I was staggered by his behaviour and also by his choice of words, which sounded incongruous for a twelve-year-old in the 21st century.

In the next few weeks, there were further threats, and complaints by younger children that Graeme had hit, pinched or kicked them. As well, I had to deal with three instances of Graeme stealing items: a bracelet from a girl, a calculator from a teacher, and a chess piece from a beautiful hand-carved set that a child had brought into school to show her classmates. These were thefts that suggested psychological difficulties in Graeme, rather than any real need for the possessions.

When Graeme, in a fit of rage, pushed a boy down a hill, causing him to hit the edge of a barbecue and cut his hand open – which in turn caused us to take him to a doctor, where his hand had to be stitched – I rang Graeme's parents, Cecilia and Joe, and asked them to come in for a meeting with me. I'd previously met twice with Cecilia, but this was the first time Joe came as well. Graeme was present for the conversation, and I ran through a list of situations in which he had been involved. Suddenly, Joe took over – he stood up and started bellowing at Graeme. I felt like I had been transported to the set of an Ealing comedy from the 1950s, with a red-faced Sergeant Major telling British Army recruits that they were 'orrible little men. I felt that it was important for Graeme to see that his father could not intimidate everybody, so I said to the father, 'You might do better if you sat down, spoke at a normal volume, and stopped treating your son like he is on a parade ground.'

Joe appeared completely flabbergasted by my comment, and wound the meeting up almost immediately. They left my office and, like Clint and his half-siblings, I never saw them again. Joe and his wife emailed me to say that they 'were very unsatisfied at the way in which you addressed us and our son. It's not your place to speak like that. Your comments were definitely inappropriate and you obviously need to learn your place as principal. It's not your job to tell us how to raise our child.'

They said that they were withdrawing Graeme from the school for a number of reasons, including the fact that Graeme had reported to them that quite a few kids used hammers and saws at lunchtimes, creating objects from offcuts of wood. As is typical of parents in these situations, they at no stage showed any interest in or concern for the welfare of the children Graeme had attacked or hurt.

Speaking the way I did in my office that day was a spur-of-the-moment decision. Would I do it again? Probably. It was a shame that Graeme was taken out of a school he was thoroughly enjoying, and where I think we could have helped him, but it wasn't just that I wanted to show him that his father could not bully everyone; I also wanted him to know that he was being subjected to bad parenting.

ELOISE

Eloise's home situation was one of conflict, including some domestic violence and emotional abuse perpetrated by her father.

When we organised a major excursion for Eloise's class, the father strongly objected to some of the terms and conditions of the excursion, which included no communication with parents during the kids' time away. He wrote a series of emails with statements like these:

> I don't know what kind of operation you think you're running there, and I don't know how you get away with it. What the hell are the people in education doing to allow a hillbilly school like this that just does what it likes and ignores all the rules? . . . Your teachers may be all right in the classroom and I suppose they have got all the right university degrees and that crap but they think they are experts in everything especially the way teenagers think and why they do what they do and I don't know what qualifications they think they've got to make all those kinds of assertions . . . I demand from you full details of this excursion. No one's told us something about it except Eloise and I don't know what the hell you think you're doing running a school like that. You haven't even bothered to meet me so Who Do You Think You Are??? . . . If Eloise goes on this trip then we will call her whenever we feel like it and whenever we think it's right and she will call us whenever we tell her to so don't you try and tell us things like that or else she will not be going and you will have to tell her why she will not be going.

Unimpressed by my responses to his emails, the father threatened to go to the opinion columns of the local newspapers, to have our policies debated publicly.

He requested a meeting, which both parents attended, although the mother hardly spoke – the father purported to speak for them both. He said that parents have an inalienable right to communicate with their children. We pointed out that as the organisers of the trip it was for us to stipulate the terms and conditions, and parents could then decide whether they wished their child to participate. The father claimed that no school anywhere would seek to impose a condition of no communication between parents and children for the duration of the activity such as the one we proposed. In response, I said that it was not so extraordinary. Various well-known educational institutions, such as Wesley College, MLC Melbourne, Lauriston, and the Victorian government's Alpine Schools, have similar if not identical policies. I described the operations of Geelong Grammar School Timbertop, where Year 9 students were not allowed contact with their parents during term time for a whole year, except by writing letters (and two visits a year that parents were allowed to make).

However, because we had not communicated our position regarding parent–student contact on this particular trip clearly and explicitly enough, we were happy to compromise on the issue. (In an attempt to minimise conflict with the father I had already agreed to this in a telephone conversation with Eloise's mother.)

My colleague who attended the meeting asked Eloise's father what kind of school he had imagined it to be when he and his wife enrolled their daughter. He replied, 'Well, we didn't know that we were enrolling her in a cult.' During the later stages of the interview it was unclear whether the father was addressing his wife or us, as his body language suggested the former. He appeared to be having a private conversation with her, which included comments that they were wasting their time talking to us. He ended the interview by stating, without reference to his wife, that it was the opinion of both that they had wasted their time. He suggested that we – i.e. my colleague and I – were 'so satisfied that [we're] doing a great job' that we're not able to have an open conversation, or 'listen to any suggestions or advice'. I responded by saying that it was difficult to accept advice from people who had gratuitously insulted us by calling us a cult. He denied emphatically that he had called us a cult ('at no point did

I say that you were a cult') and when challenged on this, embarked upon an exercise of hair-splitting so subtle that I could not follow his argument.

On the day the students returned from the trip, Eloise's parents were waiting, as were all the parents. Eloise's father told other parents that 'Eloise was in big trouble', because she had failed to follow instructions by making phone calls to them as per the father's schedule. As soon as Eloise arrived, she was spoken to sharply, then hurried away by her parents, leaving other parents and children to mingle and talk excitedly about their experiences.

Staff who had been on the trip reported how much Eloise had enjoyed her time away, and how frightened she had been of returning home.

ROLF

Rolf lived with his mother and younger siblings. His father was a professional man who didn't live close to Rolf, and Rolf had experienced only minimal contact with him over many years. As Rolf entered adolescence he became increasingly angry at his mother and absent father, and a number of times the mother called police to the house to deal with Rolf's violent behaviour towards her, his younger siblings and the house itself. As it happened, I knew the police officer who attended on most of these occasions, and he said to me, rolling his eyes, 'If only she would lighten up a bit with him!'

Many of the arguments occurred because of the mother's black-and-white approach to her son. For example, Rolf would be told to 'bring in the firewood when you get home from school'. If Rolf did his homework or watched TV or mooched around for a while before bringing in the firewood, this was interpreted by his mother as disobedience, and conflict quickly ensued. More and more holes appeared in the house as Rolf punched walls in frustration and anger.

I became seriously concerned about Rolf's emotional wellbeing, so I decided to track down his father and ring him, even though I thought I was probably exceeding my authority by doing so.

I began the conversation by introducing myself as being from Rolf's school, to which the father immediately replied, 'If this is an attempt to get money out of me, sir, I can tell you now, you're wasting your time.'

I replied: 'No, this has got nothing to do with money.' (We had in fact not been charging Rolf's mother any school fees for some time, as it was obvious that she had no money.) 'It's to do with your son's emotional health, as I'm concerned about his state of mind. He seems troubled and unhappy.'

'Well, sir,' replied the gentleman, with the air of an Old Testament prophet, 'in life, as I have frequently said to his mother, one reaps as one sows, and in regard to Rolf, she is now reaping what she has sown.'

He went on to list his grievances with his ex-wife.

He said that Rolf had stayed with him and his new partner for a few weeks 'a couple of years ago' but he 'just moped around and looked unhappy all the time'. The father appeared to have no interest in or insight into the causes of Rolf's unhappiness, nor did he accept any responsibility for his son's current situation.

Our conversation did not progress much further.

We were able, with his mother's agreement, to arrange accommodation for Rolf in a wonderful family that was able to give him the support he needed at that point of his life. Later, we paid his fees at an excellent private school, where he spent the next three years. We also paid for him to board with a family who lived close to the school. Rolf had shown an interest in music and an aptitude for it, and this was fostered at his new school. The story has a happy ending: Rolf is now a cheerful, idiosyncratic young man who enjoys good relationships with others, has travelled the world extensively, and has carved out an interesting and successful career as a musician.

Teaching is in some ways not a particularly high-status profession in Australia, and educated middle-class parents can hold (usually unconsciously) a view that teachers are their intellectual inferiors. High-achieving parents often believe that we can be bluffed or intimidated. It's important sometimes to remind them of the essentials, unglamorous though they may be. I was once approached by a parent who could be deemed a celebrity. He did a lot of corporate work, had written books and was a media favourite. 'What can I do to help you all?' he asked earnestly.

'Get your kids to school on time,' I replied.

Apparently he found this vastly entertaining, and told the story at dinner parties for years afterwards. However, he still didn't get his children to school on time.

An anonymous contributor to an internet forum tells this story:

> Told a lady at work about an interesting app that allows you to lock your child's phone anytime you want and the only option it gives them is to call the preset (parent's) number. The lady who designed it was pissed because she would call or text her children and they wouldn't answer, so it allowed her to lock their phones until they called and checked in. My co-worker immediately downloaded the app and now if she calls or texts her kids and they don't respond within two minutes, she locks their phones.[53]

Of course it is not just over-controlling parents who rob children of autonomy, of the opportunity to learn, of the opportunity to have adventures. A popular device in England is the Walkodile, which is the proud invention of a British teacher. It retails for £89.99.[54] It seems grimly ironic that it is named punningly after a creature notorious for capturing and consuming humans. Its function is to lock up to six children into a rigid frame, so that they can be led from place to place like a pack of obedient dogs. Given that the streets of Western cities are among the safer places on earth, this invention seems to pander to

53 'Teachers/Counsellors of Reddit – what's the worst case of "helicopter parenting" you've ever encountered?', Reddit, 17 August 2014, reddit.com/r/AskReddit/comments/2dq1lj/teacherscounsellors_of_reddit_whats_the_worst, accessed 13 March 2019.
54 'Walkodile® Classic', Wakodile: Walk. Learn. Safe, walkodile.com/product/2/walkodile/fcf78f819e72006825b9a6f644e8e235, accessed 13 March 2019

insecurities and fears that are irrational and cannot be justified. Even worse, the greatest danger to children on a footpath is probably from an out-of-control car, which, if it careers towards a Walkodile, is more likely to mow down six children than one or two.

I've seen a photo which is meant to show the virtues of the Walkodile. The picture shows four adults, in their hi-vis vests, leading twelve harnessed children along a narrow pathway protected by stone walls on either side. From what dangers are these children being saved?

Perhaps these kiddies will grow up to become bureaucrats in the Department of Education.

'I'M TOO BUSY SAVING THE WORLD; I DON'T HAVE TIME FOR MY CHILD'

Charles Dickens was onto this. In *Bleak House* he describes Mrs Jellyby, introducing her to the reader as a lady 'of very remarkable strength of character, who devotes herself entirely to the public . . . at present (until something else attracts her) . . . the subject of Africa; with a view to the general cultivation of the coffee berry – *and* the natives . . .'

The narrator, Esther Summerson, is conveyed to the Jellyby home, only to find that one of the Jellyby children has managed to get his head stuck between the street railings:

I made my way to the poor child, who was one of the dirtiest little
unfortunates I ever saw, and found him very hot and frightened,
and crying loudly, fixed by the neck between two iron railings,
while a milkman and a beadle, with the kindest intentions possible,
were endeavouring to drag him back by the legs, under a general
impression that his skull was compressible by those means. As I
found (after pacifying him), that he was a little boy, with a naturally
large head, I thought that, perhaps, where his head could go, his
body could follow, and mentioned that the best mode of extraction
might be to push him forward . . . At last he was happily got down

without any accident, and then he began to beat Mr Guppy with a hoop-stick in quite a frantic manner.

Nobody had appeared belonging to the house except a person in pattens, who had been poking at the child from below with a broom; I don't know with what object, and I don't think she did. I therefore supposed that Mrs Jellyby was not at home; and was quite surprised when the person appeared in the passage without the pattens, and going up to the back room on the first floor, before Ada and me, announced us as, 'Them two young ladies, Missis Jellyby!' We passed several more children on the way up, whom it was difficult to avoid treading on in the dark; and as we came into Mrs Jellyby's presence, one of the poor little things fell downstairs – down a whole flight (as it sounded to me), with a great noise.

Mrs Jellyby, whose face reflected none of the uneasiness which we could not help showing in our own faces, as the dear child's head recorded its passage with a bump on every stair – Richard afterwards said he counted seven, besides one for the landing – received us with perfect equanimity. She was a pretty, very diminutive, plump woman of from forty to fifty, with handsome eyes, though they had a curious habit of seeming to look a long way off. As if – I am quoting Richard again – they could see nothing nearer than Africa! . . .

But what principally struck us was a jaded and unhealthy-looking, though by no means plain girl, at the writing-table, who sat biting the feather of her pen, and staring at us. I suppose nobody ever was in such a state of ink. And from her tumbled hair to her pretty feet, which were disfigured with frayed and broken satin slippers trodden down at heel, she really seemed to have no article of dress upon her, from a pin upwards, that was in its proper condition or its right place.

'You find me, my dears,' said Mrs Jellyby . . . 'as usual, very busy; but that you will excuse. The African project at present employs my whole time. It involves me in correspondence with public bodies, and with private individuals anxious for the welfare of their species all over the country. I am happy to say it is advancing. We hope by this time next year to have from a hundred and fifty to two hundred healthy families cultivating coffee and educating the natives of Borrioboola-Gha, on the left bank of the Niger.'

As Ada said nothing, but looked at me, I said it must be very gratifying.

'It *is* gratifying,' said Mrs Jellyby. 'It involves the devotion of all my energies . . .'[55]

The jaded, unhealthy-looking and shabbily dressed girl at the writing table is Mrs Jellyby's oldest daughter, to whom Mrs Jellyby dictates the letters about Africa, although at times she is inconveniently interrupted by one of her other children:

"'And begs,'" said Mrs Jellyby, dictating, "'to inform him, in reference to his letter of inquiry on the African project —" No, Peepy! Not on any account!'

Peepy (so self-named) was the unfortunate child who had fallen downstairs, who now interrupted the correspondence by presenting himself with a strip of plaster on his forehead, to exhibit his wounded knees, in which Ada and I did not know which to pity most – the bruises or the dirt. Mrs Jellyby merely added, with the serene composure with which she said everything, 'Go along, you naughty Peepy!' and fixed her fine eyes on Africa again.

However, as she at once proceeded with her dictation, and as I interrupted nothing by doing it, I ventured quietly to stop poor Peepy as he was going out, and to take him up to nurse. He looked very much astonished at it, and at Ada's kissing him; but soon fell fast asleep in my arms, sobbing at longer and longer intervals, until he was quiet. I was so occupied with Peepy that I lost the letter in detail, though I derived such a general impression from it of the momentous importance of Africa, and the utter insignificance of all other places and things, that I felt quite ashamed to have thought so little about it.[56]

---

55   Charles Dickens, *Bleak House*, Penguin, London, 1985, pp. 84–86 (first published 1853).
56   Dickens, *Bleak House*, pp. 86–87.

HELEN

Helen had siblings who were notorious in the district for their wild and undisciplined behaviour. All the children lived with their mother, and had little contact with their father. Helen's mother worked as a volunteer every day at a city hospital, assisting families and young people who arrived there and were often filled, no doubt, with apprehension at the ordeal ahead of them.

As Helen approached adolescence she seemed increasingly rudderless, and appeared ardent to be taken under the wing of a mature woman. There was something lost and yearning about her, evidenced by the forlorn way she attached herself to various women staff members at the school.

From an early age, Helen sought romantic contact with boys. It was always difficult to track down her mother about Helen's issues, or to get a response from her, but after the fourth time Helen was found in a potentially compromising position with a boy, I insisted that the mother come in for an interview, instead of the telephone conversations that were all she would allow on previous occasions. In the interview, I outlined the episodes where Helen had been in breach of school rules, and emphasised that she seemed to be a child at risk, and, furthermore, that we as a school had to put a stop to these behaviours. The mother demanded to know if I was dealing with the boy in the same way that I was dealing with Helen. I explained (not for the first time) that there had been four different boys; the common factor in the situation was Helen, so therefore I was taking a somewhat different approach to the boys who had offended. The mother seemed unconvinced, and withdrew Helen from the school shortly afterwards. Helen's attendance at her next school was intermittent, and, like her older siblings, she quit at around Year 9 or 10 level. The last time I saw her was in a shoe shop, where she had obtained a job.

It seemed unfortunate to me that her mother's early morning departure for the hospital each day, and her late return home, suggested that families elsewhere were being helped, whilst her own was receiving little attention.

RALPH

The principal of Ralph's previous school said that Ralph and his mother were 'both difficult', and that Ralph's mother, unbeknown to her husband, had started a Facebook page to criticise the school and a particular teacher. He described Ralph as being nasty to other kids, defiant with teachers, underhanded and a bully.

Ralph's mother had graduated from university with an outstanding list of achievements, and now worked for an international human rights organisation. She spoke to me passionately about issues of justice and equality, and her desire to work for world peace.

To me, Ralph resembled a 'failure to thrive' child: thin, pasty appearance, head always down, often 'lost' inside a big hoodie. He reminded me of the 'jaded, unhealthy-looking and shabbily dressed girl' described by Dickens in *Bleak House*. Ralph would not make eye contact with teachers and would not respond to 'hellos' or 'good mornings'.

Ralph's relationships with his peers were difficult, but over the years he spent with us, he gradually improved. We saw animation in his face, more physical energy and activity, and heard him laughing more often. He got into a friendship group with two other boys; both well-balanced, cheerful, good-natured children, although the mother of one of the boys expressed grave concerns about her son's friendship with Ralph, describing him as having unhealthy attitudes and behaviours, knowing far too much about sex, and having a precocious interest in it.

Ralph spent a lot of time at home on his own, and spent much of this time on screens, where he accessed material that was unsuitable for his age. At the age of eight, Ralph told me that he had 'more screen time than other kids my age, probably too much'. He told me that he played first-person shooter computer games exclusively, and did so for an hour every morning before coming to school (he had told me on a previous occasion that he got up at 5.30 am on school days). When he was five he played a game, 'which I probably shouldn't have played', that gave him a nightmare. He said he had fights with his mother when his father was away, because she asked him to do chores all the time and because she believed he had too much screen time.

Among our parent body, we have had environmental activists, human rights advocates, animal rights lobbyists, and passionate defenders of numerous worthy causes. In some cases, crusading parents have neglected their own children, apparently finding the glamour and excitement of distant or global issues more interesting than mundane matters like applying Band-Aids, showing enthusiasm for clumsily executed artworks, playing UNO, or taking their child to a local playground.

'MY CHILD AND I ARE, LIKE, BEST FRIENDS?'

A common parental approach that has been around since the 1960s is the one characterised by earnest little monologues like this: 'I've told him, if you're going to do drugs, and I know you will, then do them at home. I don't mind if you bring your friends and have your party here. At least that way I know you're safe . . .' and so on.

Unfortunately, the child in this family is not safe. He or she is at grave risk, from a parent who has no idea of the job requirements for parenting. The child needs to see responsible adult behaviour modelled by the most important adult in his or her life. The child needs a parent, not a playmate.

Dave Eggers was 21 years old when he accepted the responsibility of raising his eight-year-old brother after both their parents died of cancer within a couple of months of each other. In his memoir *A Heartbreaking Work of Staggering Genius* (which is, incidentally, a heartbreaking work of staggering genius), Dave tells of an encounter with a mother as they waited in the school parking lot to pick up kids after an excursion. The mother is talking about how she manages her young son's marijuana smoking:

> 'I figure if he's gonna smoke, he's gonna smoke.' She shrugs
> elaborately. 'So I let him fire up at home. At least I know where he
> is, what he's doing, that he's not driving around or something.'

Though she is talking to another parent, she is glancing my way. I have the feeling she expects me, because I am closer to her high schooler's age than she is, and, because I have creative facial hair, to be sympathetic to her point of view.

But I'm too stunned to speak. She should be jailed. And I should raise her children.[57]

As Eggers, in his early twenties, is already aware, some libertarian parents abdicate their responsibilities. Others are no different from authoritarian parents in their determination to keep controlling their children ad infinitum. They want to know every aspect of their children's adolescent experiences, including the salacious ones, which raises the possibility that they are deriving vicarious titillation from the exchanges. Rather than respond wisely and with maturity to the child, they want to join the child in the shadow world where every young person (and every adult) lingers at times.

In her *Diary*, in 1944, fourteen-year-old Anne Frank wrote:

I've suddenly realised what's wrong with her [Anne's mother]. Mother has said that she sees us more as friends than as daughters. That's all very nice, of course, except that a friend can't take the place of a mother.[58]

Australian psychologist Michael Carr-Gregg remarked in a newspaper article in 2017 that he had never known a fifteen-year-old who wanted one of his or her parents as a best friend.

DONALD

Twelve years old when I met him, Donald was accompanied by his mother, Marnie. During our initial interview, Marnie made jokes about Donald's recent arrival at puberty, and the frequency of his

---

57   Dave Eggers, *A Heartbreaking Work of Staggering Genius*, Picador, London, 2000, p. 301.
58   Anne Frank, *Diary*, trans. Susan Massotty, Doubleday, New York, 1995, p. 160.

erections. He grinned through gritted teeth. She told me that at his current school he spent more time out of class than in class, because teachers kept sending him out for misbehaviour. 'But,' she said, laughing merrily, 'I tell him: you have more fun out of class than you do in class anyway. That's what it was like for me when I was at school!'

We had frequent problems with Donald and his siblings, all of whom needed professional counselling at one time or another. Donald had bouts of depression, leading, when he was older and at another school, to concerns about his being at risk of suicide. One of his siblings developed an eating disorder.

I think their behavioural difficulties stemmed from both the mother's immaturity and the disintegrating marriage of the parents. At one stage Marnie came in to see me about problems one of her daughters was having with another girl, Dolly. Like a number of immature mothers, Marnie seemed as involved in the melodrama of the adolescent girls' friendships as was her daughter – if not more so. During the interview she told me that Dolly was taking too much cake during morning tea time at school. This was presumably one of her daughter's complaints about Dolly, as Marnie could have had no first-hand knowledge of Dolly's cake consumption. It was not clear how Dolly's alleged fondness for cake impacted on Marnie, or her daughter for that matter.

Marnie also complained about Dolly hitting her daughter. She did not mention that Donald had punched a girl in the face at a youth group function: I heard about it from the mother of Donald's victim.

Marnie specifically forbade me to bring Dolly and her daughter together for a conversation about their friendship difficulties, which made our interview ultimately futile, as I had no other strategies for a short-term resolution of the tension between them (although time, the great healer, eventually took care of the problem).

During Marnie's children's time at our school I had to expel a student for a number of serious offences, which I was not able to discuss with anyone except the police and several senior staff members.

Marnie's response was to write to me that 'We don't know what's going on at school at the moment with Hamish leaving. Jennifer and Elsie [two students] have given us a very different story to what you wrote in the email to parents. We are at a loss to know what to say to our kids, because we don't know the truth.' Shortly afterwards she wrote to me again, telling me she had been speaking with a number of the students:

> because there are so many rumours going around that I thought the best thing was for me to get the story straight from them. They all say they really miss Hamish and they don't understand why he had to leave. I can tell you that they think making Hamish leave was overly severe, and very unfair – but of course the full story is a mystery to me.

Responses like this from parents leave me looking for the nearest oxygen mask. Marnie's statement 'but of course the full story is a mystery to me' should have been the beginning and end of her commentary. Any mature adult would understand that matters involving children, adolescents and parents are almost always complex, needing delicate handling and requiring strict confidentiality. In this particular case, I had, however, made all parents aware that there was police involvement in the matter.

On another occasion, I painstakingly investigated a serious brawl between two kids, obtaining written statements from them and all witnesses, and interviewing most of them. I then wrote to the parents of the two boys in the fight. One, a lawyer, replied: 'After receiving your email I talked to Kenny about what had transpired with the other boy and it seems that your account is quite an accurate one.'

'Go fuck yourself,' I thought. 'I wasn't inviting you to hold an in-house enquiry where you call one witness, your son, and then pass judgement on my investigations. I was actually inviting you to contemplate your son's disturbing behaviour and maybe even do something about it.'

The principal of an exclusive Sydney private school told me that in dealing with the children of lawyers I could expect the parents to be more concerned with process than substance. 'Rather than look at their child's problems,' he said, 'they'll attack you for "not contacting them earlier" or for "suspending them when they've got exams next week". They'll ask to see the school's discipline policy, so they can catch you out.'

He proved to be absolutely correct.

Kenny was not with us long (we were his sixth school) and was in a psychiatric ward by the age of seventeen, in a psychotic state after using crystal meth and other drugs.

Marnie's real issue was that she wanted to be 'in the know' about everything that was happening at the school. She was forever wanting personal reports from me on any stories the children brought home. Discretion was not part of her make-up. But as well, Marnie did not trust the school. In dealing with her over the years I had the feeling that she did not trust adults.

If parents reach a point where they have lost trust and confidence in their children's school, and its leadership, they really only have two choices: to start working for change, or to transfer to a different school.

RHIANNA

Rhianna's mother was a highly successful professional woman who, like Marnie, seemed to relish the politics of her adolescent daughter's relationships. The parents of another girl in her daughter's friendship group came to see me, furious about the behaviour of Rhianna's mother. They wanted her contact details so that they could sue her for defamation, because of the way they believed she had spoken about their daughter. They felt that Rhianna's mother was deliberately manipulating the friendship group, inviting the girls, one or two at a time, to come and stay at weekends, and working on them to develop an alliance that would pit Rhianna and the others against their daughter.

Their daughter was never invited to Rhianna's place.

This was consistent with my observations of Rhianna's mother. In one interview with me she called the other girl, who was fourteen years old at the time, a 'psychopath'. I said that I regretted her use of that word to describe a fourteen-year-old who was obviously struggling with some emotional and social issues. Rhianna's mother looked slightly abashed, then grumbled, 'Well, you have to allow me a certain licence for being angry.' I didn't feel that such a licence should be allowed, not only because she was the adult, but also because no one was quicker to complain if a child called any of her children a name she didn't like. If Rhianna's mother was entitled to the 'licence', then surely everyone was.

I heard on many occasions her lavish praise of her own children, whom she described as perfect and the best children in the school. To us, they appeared passive and insipid, overshadowed by their powerful parents.

Her husband and she had a rude shock when they wanted a meeting so they could voice bitter anger about a girl's negative behaviour towards their son. They learned at the meeting that the girl's attitude was a result of their son using Facebook to label the girl a slut. The boy shamefacedly admitted this in front of his parents. Having come to see me to complain about the girl, both Rhianna's parents were disconcerted to find that it was their son and not the girl who was the problem.

Their children had been to many schools. Their enrolment at our school was abruptly ended when the parents took exception to a trip we had planned, which they considered dangerous. At their request we had two meetings with them, laying out the details of the trip so that they could see the level of complexity and sophistication that had gone into its organisation, including of course the safety features. They were still not satisfied, and requested a third meeting. I refused, pointing out that the excursion was organised by professionals, that they themselves had no professional expertise in the activities being undertaken, that we had done many such trips in the past without problems, that we had given them all the information they could possibly require, and that no point would be served by yet another meeting. The father, who was a powerful figure in the corporate world, seemed incredulous at my refusal of his request. They withdrew their children the same day.

A Swedish lady told me that in Sweden they have a name for a certain kind of parent. They call them curling mums or dads. Curling is that extraordinary sport where people slide large chunks of polished granite on ice towards a place called 'home'. Part of curling is controlling the trajectory of the boulder by assiduously sweeping all impediments out of its way, to ensure its smooth path to its destination.

I hardly need to spell out the analogy. I've heard plenty of similar expressions though, such as snowploughs, lawnmowers, tiger mothers and, of course, the most common, helicopter parents. In China, they're called dinosaur parents, because they're seen as out of date, old-fashioned.

For some people, however, the term 'helicopter parent' is a badge of pride – except that it is apparently inadequate. In 2016, the American National Education Association invited readers of its magazine *Today* to 'meet Shani Weber', whom they described as an articulate former teacher with master's degrees in early childhood development and special education, a County Council PTA representative and room mother for the classes of her two children.[59]

Shani happily shared her views on schooling with the magazine's readers. 'My involvement level is high ... and because of my educational background, I'm a teacher's worst nightmare. I'm an Apache helicopter.'

The teachers of Shani's children might not have been aware that an Apache helicopter is, according to Wikipedia, armed with a '30 mm M230E1 Chain Gun, and typically a mixture of AGM-114 Hellfire anti-tank missiles, and Hydra 70 general-purpose unguided 70 mm

---

59 'The "helicopter" parent', *Today* magazine, National Education Association, September 2007, nea.org/archive/16289.htm, accessed 13 March 2019.

rockets. One eighteen-aircraft Apache battalion equipped with Hellfire missiles is capable of destroying 288 tanks. Since 2005, the Hellfire missile is sometimes outfitted with a thermobaric warhead . . .'[60]

Today went on to describe how, 'When Weber's son started kindergarten, she met with the principal and his teacher to let them know that she'd tested him with the appropriate developmental protocols and determined that he was gifted.' No surprise there. 'She asked how the school accommodated exceptional kindergartners. "They acted as if I was exaggerating Alec's abilities," she says. "They encounter lots of parents who don't see their kids in an accurate light, and they thought I was one of them."'

Silly old principal and teacher! What would they know?! According to Shani, her son did indeed prove to be brilliant at reading and maths, but the school – surprise, surprise – failed to cater adequately for him, until Shani, armed with her general-purpose unguided 70 mm rockets and Hellfire anti-tank missiles, intervened.

The magazine appears to have made no attempt to verify the claims of the child's academic brilliance, nor to assess the helpfulness or otherwise of Shani's parenting or the value of her involvement with the school.

'As a parent,' Weber told the magazine, 'I play an integral role. All parents do.'

In many forums and media articles, the 21st-century rhetoric surrounding parents' involvement in schools speaks of parents as a generic group. There is an assumption that all parents think the same way and feel the same way. Specifically, that all parents have their children's best interests at heart, know their children better than anyone else does, and are wise and thoughtful in supporting their children on their educational journey. When Weber says that 'all parents play an integral role in their children's lives', she's right – not counting the parents who have disappeared or died before the child's birth. But

---

60 'Boeing AH-64 Apache', Wikipedia, en.wikipedia.org/wiki/Boeing_AH-64_Apache, accessed 13 March 2019.

Weber is implying that all parents are involved in their children's lives in a positive way. Because she is a former teacher with qualifications in early childhood development and special education, she perhaps assumes that all parents have a similar background, or, at the very least, an enlightened attitude to their children's life at school.

Many parents interested in enrolling their children at Candlebark or Alice Miller schools ask, 'Does the school encourage parental involvement?' It seems, from their expectant faces and the optimistic tone of their voices, that they expect the usual bland answer: 'Oh yes, we are very committed to parental involvement . . .'

In reply, I don't say that. I say something like 'Well, we have parents out there with apprehended violence orders against them.'

We have had parents whom, we believe and hope, do not know that their child is at our school, and we are under police instructions to lock the school down and call 000 should such parents appear on the campus. We have had a parent under a court order not to enter the state of Victoria without special permission. We have had another who made death threats against the children's guardian and was similarly banned from entering Victoria, but the person entered Victoria anyway and became the subject of an intense police search.

'Do you think we should encourage parents with AVOs against them to be actively involved in the school?' I ask the questioners.

I would hope that anyone reading the case histories I have outlined above would recognise that the biological ability of most adults to have children does not necessarily make them fit and responsible parents. We sometimes cannot do much about toxic parents' destructive impact on their own sons and daughters, but we can at least keep them as far away from other children as possible.

As a result of unrelenting pressure from curling parents, schools all around the country try to jump simultaneously through two hoops that may be a long way apart: one hoop that leads to the parents' ambitions for their child, and another hoop that leads to a meaningful education. A meaningful education seeks to develop students creatively, intellectually, academically, socially, psychologically, emotionally, spiritually and physically, and recognises that the getting of wisdom is as worthwhile and important as the acquisition of knowledge. In the book *Mister God, This Is Anna*, a character called Old Woody tells Anna:

> They . . . will tell you and encourage you to develop your brain
> and your five senses. But that's only the half of it, that's only
> being half a human. The other half is to develop the heart and the
> wits . . . There's common wit, there's imagination, there's fantasy,
> there's estimation, and there's memory . . . Never let anyone rob you
> of your right to be complete.[61]

Happy the child where the two hoops coincide! But so often, schools are distracted, led down false trails, by parents' beliefs as to what will most benefit their children. For example, schools nowadays frequently offer programs for gifted and talented children, and these are seen as an essential part of marketing. I have watched the growth of these programs with some scepticism, and believe I can speak with some authority about gifted and talented children, both as an author/ teacher and an ex-child.

As an author/teacher, I am frequently asked to take weekend workshops for the gifted and talented. I usually accept, because I enjoy teaching, and because the gigs are well paid. For quite some time I arrived at these workshops full of ambitious ideas, challenging activities and intellectually stimulating exercises. On every occasion, I found I had to quickly drop the level down, down, down, until I was doing exactly the same sort of stuff that I'd do with any class, anywhere. Each group had a few kids who were precocious users of language, but that did not mean that they were intellectually superior. The great majority of the students were incredibly average, and there were usually a few who were well below average.

As a child, I tested out with an IQ of 151, which meant that when we (my family) moved to Sydney from Tasmania, I was shoehorned

---

61 Fynn, *Mister God, This is Anna*, Collins, London, 1974, pp. 164–165.

into a Grade 5 'Opportunity Class' for advanced children, even though the class was already at capacity. I stayed a year. None of my classmates struck me as exceptionally brilliant; the curriculum and teaching were not extraordinarily stimulating; and the whole experience was largely forgettable, although I did enjoy the excursion to the Coca-Cola factory.

In Grade 6 I went to a private school, and during the course of the year assessors from the Department of Education arrived to evaluate our reading skills. I had the embarrassing but gratifying experience of recording the highest score ever achieved in New South Wales, becoming the first student to finish a test that was designed to be unfinishable within the designated time. This meant I registered a reading speed of infinity. The assessors were incredulous and I learned a few months later that the test had to be redesigned as a result.

So on those few criteria I guess I would have been classified as a 'gifted and talented student'. Apart from my year in the Opportunity Class, no special provisions were made for me by anyone, through primary or secondary school. I spent a great deal of my time in class feeling utterly bored. Nowadays this would be viewed by advocates of programs for gifted children as a disgrace, an educational scandal. But what did I do during those thousands of hours? I spent a lot of time reading books – I became pretty skilful at having a book in my lap under my desk, or hidden behind textbooks on my desk. I also designed, wrote and 'published' endless newspapers, magazines and books for my classmates . . . including a daily newspaper, a rock music magazine, and a series of novels featuring a hero named Gibbings. As far as I know, no teacher was ever aware of my clandestine publishing operations.

And the other thing I did was daydream. With more vigilant teachers, who caught me when I tried to read books illicitly, I had no choice but to daydream. My Grade 3 teacher, who was obsessively, pathologically, vigilant, wrote on my school report: 'He should do very well, if he overcomes the tendency towards daydreaming.' I guess it was similar to the school report received by the parents of actor and writer Peter Ustinov, which spoke of his 'great originality, [which] must be curbed at all costs'.[62]

Luckily, I didn't overcome my tendency towards daydreaming any more than Ustinov managed to curb his originality. As an adult, I have daydreamed my way into writing 42 books and devising new English lessons and approaches to schooling.

More than 40 years after I left Devonport Primary School, I had a reunion with my Grade 4 teacher, who told me that the headmaster, Mr Ferguson, on his frequent visits to observe the class, would notice that I was not paying attention, and would pounce on me, asking: 'What did Mrs Scott just say, John?'

'And do you know?' she said to me, in 1999, 'you were always able to give him a perfect answer. He never caught you out once. Eventually he gave up asking you.'

I had only a dim recollection of those encounters, but I wasn't particularly surprised. I guess as a survival skill in school I'd developed the ability to read a book with my eyes whilst simultaneously listening to a conversation with my ears.

The preceding paragraphs are pretty wanky. But I believe it's important to acknowledge that benign neglect is often an appropriate approach for parents and teachers to adopt. Paediatrician Donald Winnicott's notion of the 'good enough mother'[63] can be extended to virtually all interactions with children. If we provide a reasonably safe place in which the child can play, and we answer her or his questions honestly and thoughtfully, then we won't be doing too much wrong. We don't need to be frenetic in the way we parent or teach. One of my most unpleasant placements as a student teacher was at a primary school in Adelaide, in an exclusive and expensive suburb, where the students seemed so overstimulated by the endless classroom games and activities that they were like rabbits on a rifle range during happy hour.

---

62 *Could Do Better, School Reports of the Great and Good*, ed. Catherine Hurley, Pocket Books, London, 2002.

63 D. Winnicott, 'Transitional Objects and Transitional Phenomena', *International Journal of Psychoanalysis*, 1953, vol. 34, pp. 89–97.

We shouldn't be afraid of boredom, for out of boredom comes creativity. An Australian chess grandmaster was quoted in Melbourne newspaper *The Age* as crediting his short time at Ivanhoe Grammar School for providing the impetus for his becoming a serious chess player. 'I went there for one year and was really incredibly bored and that's when I took up chess seriously because there was absolutely nothing to do. I had a few chess books confiscated for reading them in class and I thought this is the thing for me and that was the year I started playing my first tournaments.'[64]

Gifted and talented children will educate themselves. All the parent or teacher needs to do, pretty much, is leave stuff lying around that they might find interesting or engaging or challenging or amusing. Bright children do not have to be accelerated, restructured or reprogrammed. I know from English classes that I don't need to give brilliant writers much specific feedback, because they work it out for themselves, in their own good time. If they write a piece that doesn't quite succeed, or if their style is awkward at times, they'll be aware that something is not working, and they'll keep experimenting until they get it right. As Gertrude Stein said, 'No artist needs criticism, he only needs appreciation. If he needs criticism, he is no artist.'[65] On the rare occasions when I've been lucky enough to teach a genius, I find myself responding to their work with feedback like 'Fantastic! Great stuff. Keep it going. I'd love to read more. Wonderful!' I strongly believe that for such students, appreciation is sufficient.

Curling parents are more likely to obsess over small and unimportant details, to insist on conformity, to be pedantic. They don't appreciate that genius often looks unconventional, unorthodox. James Joyce's English teacher may not have valued his student's early work. The great golfer Jordan Spieth has an unusual grip and swing that enabled him to win a US Masters, a US Open and two Australian

---

64 Graham Reilly, 'Australia's own chess knight rides high', *The Age*, 3 August 1985.
65 Gertrude Stein, *The Autobiography of Alice B. Toklas*, The Continental Book Company, Stockholm, 1947, p. 240.

Opens before he was 22 years old.[66] Pablo Picasso's early schooling experiences are instructive – he was obsessed with drawing, and ignored most other lessons, preferring to doodle in his sketchbook. In his own words, 'For being a bad student I was banished to the calaboose, a bare cell with whitewashed walls and a bench to sit on. I liked it there because I took along a sketchpad and drew incessantly . . . I could have stayed there forever, drawing without stopping.'[67]

It reminded me of the hours I'd spent in Grade 3, when Mrs Lawrence sent me into a cavity behind the blackboard as punishment. Despite the cobwebs, I found it a peaceful and refreshing place, and highly conducive to daydreaming. No doubt Picasso's calaboose was designed to be so spartan that it would motivate students to behave better in class, to avoid being exiled. Like the blackboard cavity and me, the calaboose did not seem to do much harm to Picasso.

Pablo was fourteen when the family moved to Barcelona, and although he gained a place at the School of Fine Arts, he found it monotonous and uninspiring, and spent most of his time skipping class to explore the life of the streets. Two years later, in 1897, he went to Madrid, to the prestigious Royal Academy of San Fernando, but found it no more inspiring than the School of Fine Arts in Barcelona. 'They just go on and on about the same old stuff,'[68] he complained to a friend, Joaquim Boas, in a letter. Once again he spent much of his time on the streets – anywhere but in school.

Ideas like these are anathema to curling parents; their worst nightmare. Such parents don't realise that their insistence on rules and conventions holds children back, in all kinds of ways, both tangible and abstract.

The satirical online newsletter *The Onion* announced recently that Ritalin had cured the next Picasso. They reported that:

---

66 *USA Today*, 11 January 2016.

67 'Pablo Picasso Biography', biography.com/people/pablo-picasso-9440021, accessed 13 March 2019.

68 John Richardson and Marilyn McCully, *A Life of Picasso Volume I: 1881–1906*, Random House, New York, 1991, p. 92.

7-year-old Douglas Castellano's unbridled energy and creativity are no longer a problem thanks to Ritalin, doctors for the child announced Monday. 'After years of failed attempts to stop Douglas' uncontrollable bouts of self-expression, we have finally found success with Ritalin,' Dr. Erwin Schraeger said. 'For the first time in his life, Douglas can actually sit down and not think about lots of things at once.' Castellano's parents reported that the cured child no longer tries to draw on everything in sight, calming down enough to show an interest in television.[69]

So, apart from the administration of Ritalin, what does curling/snow-ploughing/helicopter parenting look like in practice? Well, in the area where I live, it looks like weekend tennis competitions between teams of kids.

The kids turn up every Saturday and play matches. Most are watched by their parents, point after point, game after game. When the children come off the court they go straight to their parents. They sit with them until they are called for their next set. Games are umpired by adults until the players have reached B grade, by which stage they might be twelve years old, or older.

The result is that the kids don't talk to each other. They don't talk to each other when they're on court, because the presence of the adult umpire, who stands at the end of the net, is intimidating. They don't talk to each other when they're off the court. Most of them don't even talk to their partners. It's not that the parents are aggressive or even overenthusiastic. They're mostly pretty nice. But their presence completely changes the dynamic between the children.

If children umpired their own games, with no adults within cooee, they would work things out. Most of the kids who play tennis for the local clubs seem like well-mannered, middle-class young people. Occasionally you see the spoiled brat syndrome in evidence, but it's

---

69 'Ritalin cures next Picasso', *The Onion*, 4 August 1999, theonion.com/ritalin-cures-next-picasso-1819565246, accessed 13 March 2019.

rare. And even with those problem children, the others *would work it out* – as long as there's no adult in sight. If an adult is in the vicinity, the kids will look to them to solve any problems – and the adult, whether invited or not, will be unable to resist stepping forward as a mediator or authority figure.

One morning I was watching one of our sons play in a competition game (yes, I'm as guilty as everyone else!). The game on the nearest court finished, but the game on the middle court was still in progress. The kids on the nearest court, with nothing to do but wait for the others, started fooling around, hitting incredibly high lobs and smashing the ball backwards and forwards.

I thought it was great to see young players interacting for once, and having fun, but not everyone felt the same way. It took only a few minutes for one parent to become enraged. Suddenly she stood up and shouted angrily: 'If you're not going to play properly, get off the court!'

'Why should they?' I wondered, as the kids slunk away. It was as much 'their' court as anyone else's. And what does 'play properly' mean, anyway? And what right did this mother have to determine how these four children should use the court? It seemed to me that she wanted to manage all the territory around her, in the way I described earlier in this book. But curling parenting is like that. It is controlling, arrogant, lacking in reflection or understanding.

The over-involvement of parents in junior sport leads to endless problems. For a time I did some voluntary work with a junior football club in a pleasant country town. Sadly, even in that apparently idyllic setting, the club had to send a letter to the parents of under-11 players, saying:

> We all love our football. We have a great club, and lots of people put
> many hours into helping it be better. For nearly 20 years Judy and
> I have enjoyed and appreciated the enthusiasm of all you parents
> who turn up to cheer your kids on, and to do all the thankless jobs
> like putting out the markers, running the sausage stall, cutting up

the oranges, doing the scoreboard and timing clock. We have a good reputation right through the region, I think I'm safe in saying. But in recent weeks there's been some really ugly stuff happening, with parents of our players on the sidelines yelling insults at the referees and the people from other clubs. Even our coaches have been spoken to pretty nastily, by our own supporters. I don't want to see our club getting a bad name, but we will if this keeps up. In fact, it's already happening. I know some of the referees aren't too good, but some of them are just starting out. We had a fifteen-year-old refereeing the other day, and the way he got yelled at was a shame to see. As a result he's told the Referees' Association that he doesn't want to do it anymore ...

Surrogate parents can also play the curling game. A British newspaper ran this article in 1988. The entire story is reprinted here:

Prince Harry's team of bodyguards jumped fully clothed into a swimming pool today to rescue him from a fight with another child. A report in the *Daily Express* said the four-year-old cried in pain as he was kicked in the face by the other boy. The fight took place in the pool at the exclusive Craigendarroch hotel, a few kilometres from Balmoral Castle.

An unnamed witness said: 'It all happened so quickly. The pool was crowded because the word went around the royal children were visiting. Harry and William looked wonderful in their trunks and were laughing and splashing each other. Then William swam off and Harry began playing with another little boy,' the witness said. 'The next thing we heard was a shout and Harry was crying and holding his face. It seems the other boy's father tried to separate the two when the splashing got vigorous. But as he pulled his son away the boy was still kicking and he kicked Harry in the face,' the witness said.

Prince Harry's Scotland Yard bodyguards, three armed SAS trained members of the Royal Protection Squad, leapt into action. As Prince William, six, looked on anxiously, the security guards picked up his weeping brother and carried him to the side of the pool.

Prince Harry was ushered into the changing rooms by a royal nanny, then taken back to Balmoral Castle, where the youngsters are staying with Prince Charles while Princess Diana attends official functions in London.

During the incident, Prince Charles had been fishing for salmon at a nearby river.

I like the last sentence, carrying just a hint that Prince Charles was neglecting his paternal duties and therefore could be held responsible for the life-threatening situation in which his son was placed.

Curling parenting looks like Paul's mother . . .

PAUL

Paul, in Grade 5, had a mild health complaint. The school files contained a letter from his cardiologist stating that Paul could take part in 'all normal school activities'. However, Paul's mother insisted on carrying her son's school bag from the car into the classroom for him. Every single day of the year, Paul and his mother arrived late to school. I would be teaching, we would be ten, fifteen, twenty minutes into the first lesson of the day, the door would open, and Paul's mother's cheerful face would peer in. After surveying the room she would turn around and whisper loudly to her son: 'Shhh! They've already started. Be very quiet!' She would then tiptoe melodramatically to Paul's desk and unpack his bag, making extravagant gestures throughout the process, to convey various pieces of information to the helpless, hapless Paul. Eventually, reluctantly, she would tiptoe out again, in the same exaggerated fashion, taking care to wave goodbye to Paul and to me, as she closed the door with a final theatrical flourish.

In Grade 4 Paul had somehow missed the information that the school athletic sports would be held on a particular day, and so when the sports began, at lunchtime, he was ill-prepared. Undaunted he ran in the 100 metre sprint in his school uniform, and to the astonishment of everyone, won the race easily. No one had any idea that he could run, as his mother kept him away from all sporting activity. However, the child's triumph was short-lived. The following year Paul's mother made sure to find out the date of the sports well in advance. She kept Paul at home that day.

Curling parenting looks like those people who complain to the school when their child is not picked for a team or concert or special privilege; in other words, when other children are considered to be ahead of their child in any area. Curling parenting looks like parents who ring teachers in the evenings or at weekends with routine or trivial enquiries or grievances. (If you feel there is a slightly bitter tone to that sentence, you are correct.) It looks like parents who search their kids' bedrooms, or scrutinise their phone to see who they're calling, or go through their Facebook messages to check for scandals. It looks like parents who conscientiously read every book set for their daughter or son for English classes, so they can have lots of lovely literary chats with their kids – but also so that they can assess the books for suitability. It looks like parents who cut the crusts off their four-year-old's sandwiches.

In one school in which I taught we had an email from a parent objecting to an English novel set for Year 9 students. One of the characters in the novel commits suicide, although suicide is not a major theme of the book. The email concluded with the words: 'This whole topic stinks of negativity. The book is negative. What happens if one of your students kills themselves after reading it?'

The truth about novels written for young people is that they are almost always about the overcoming of problems. It's extremely rare to read one in which the protagonist is overwhelmed by his or her problems, capitulates to them, is defeated by them. The email from the parent was written from the perspective of a middle-aged adult, which, more often than not, is different from the perspective of a teenager. Apart from the shallowness of the suggestion that reading a book about someone with psychological problems must perforce be a negative experience and not an uplifting one, the idea that a young person would commit suicide as a result of reading one book, and the school would then be responsible, sounded like emotional blackmail to me. Well-balanced people whose lives are built upon strong foundations do not commit suicide as the result of reading one book.

Many schools now become the accomplices of curling parents by implementing software that enables immediate communication between school and home when there is any glitch in the student's behaviour or work patterns. If the student is late with an assignment or skips a class or says something inappropriate, the parent gets a text or email. This constant tailing of kids, this obsessive over-interest in them, leads to frustration and anger for the young person – as it would for any adult were he or she to be treated that way. We would not tolerate this in our workplaces or homes or when we go shopping. And anyway, rebellious behaviour, like skipping a class or taking a day off school, is part of the adventure of adolescence. By tying teenagers around and around with double-braided nylon rope, we merely create other problems. As educator Kurt Hahn said in a 1960 address to the Outward Bound Trust organisation: 'Now many a youngster refuses to wilt, many of them grow to be lawless, those who wilt are the listless. I personally prefer the law breaker.'[70]

Young people now travel the world like never before. This might – and should – be a wonderful opportunity for them to become more independent and self-reliant. Landing in a city or country where they know no one might and should encourage them to reach out and initiate connections in a way that improves their confidence and social abilities. However, what do they do instead? They Skype their parents. Many spend an hour or more every day chatting on electronic devices with family members on the other side of the world. Not only does this mitigate against the likelihood of their making new friends, and weaken their sense that they have embarked upon a great adventure, it also means that they have no stories to tell when they

---

70 Dr. K Hahn, 'Outward Bound', Address by Dr. Kurt Hahn at the Annual Meeting of the Outward Bound Trust, 20 July 1960, outwardbounds50thanniversary.weebly.com/uploads/1/1/1/5/11151005/obt1960.pdf, accessed 13 March 2019.

return – they have already told them, in excruciating detail, to their loved ones back home.

RAWDON

Rawdon, aged twelve, was on a school camp, two hours from home, when he was stung several times by European wasps. Knowing Rawdon's mother's excessive anxiety about her son, I took him to a medical centre before calling her, figuring I would ring her after an expert verified that there was no real problem. The nurse checked Rawdon out, and advised that there were no issues: Rawdon could finish the camp without any fears.

Rawdon had been calm throughout the process. With him beside me, I rang his mother, went through the story and explained that everything was fine. She too seemed calm about the stings. I then handed the phone to Rawdon.

After a few moments, during which I could hear the mother's words, which to me sounded composed and unruffled, Rawdon began to weep. 'I know that voice!' he sobbed into the phone. 'I know when you use that voice. It means you're really upset. I know you're upset and trying not to show it.'

As his outburst continued, and he became quite hysterical, I managed to get the phone back. I reassured Rawdon's mother that he really was all right and would no doubt recover his composure once the call was over. She agreed, readily accepted that she would see him when we got home the next day, and after exchanging a few pleasantries we ended the call.

An hour and a half later my phone rang. It was Rawdon's mother. She was twenty minutes away from our campsite and wanted directions for finding us. As soon as she had hung up from the previous call she must have run to her car and driven at maximum speed to rescue Rawdon.

The excessive attachment between Rawdon and his mother meant that in my view Rawdon was so emotionally damaged by the age of twelve that his ability to relate to future partners in loving relationships was at serious risk. His mother was a social worker. From his first years at school we had observed that Rawdon was constantly burdened with emotional baggage from the mother's personal and professional life. It was evident from his conversations at school that from an early age his mother discussed her patients with him in a way that required sophisticated emotional understanding at a level no child could achieve. She had superimposed her shadow on him.

Rawdon's parents were excessively involved in his homework tasks, as well as any other school activities in which they could intervene. They successfully defied our best strategies to prevent this. Time and again, Rawdon presented projects and models that could have been done by a university graduate – and clearly were. When left to himself, Rawdon's own work was at a level well below that of his classmates.

CARL

Carl was the father of three young children: two girls and a boy. Despite his own rather rotund shape, Carl was obsessive about the food his children ate, and appeared to monitor every mouthful. His wife fully supported this intense scrutiny. At the martial arts classes the two girls attended after school a line was painted on the floor, with a sign saying 'No parents past this point'. Carl ignored the sign, and alone among the parents stood close by the girls for their training and bouts. The instructors had to tell him repeatedly and forcefully to desist, before he gave up this practice.

Carl arrived at school one day with some kind of device that purported to measure electromagnetic radiation. He walked around the grounds taking readings, and then reported to me that we had dangerously high levels of radiation. I thought this unlikely, given that there were only a couple of spots on the campus where we could get a mobile phone signal. I wished him luck in finding a school with lower levels than ours.

When one of Carl's daughters got 19/20 for a test, the teacher got an email from the child's mother: 'It was a great disappointment to me that she did not achieve a perfect score. We had done a lot of work to get her ready for this test. Where did she make a mistake?'

The words 'we had done a lot of work to get her ready', with the implication that the mother was way over-involved, bothered me. The child was in Grade 2 at the time.

Staff members found it disturbing that on outings Carl insisted on accompanying his daughters into toilet cubicles – not just the buildings but the actual cubicles – when they needed to use these facilities. This continued well beyond an age where it might have been considered appropriate.

Curling parenting is nicely exemplified in this pithy poem by Siv Widerberg:

I collected stamps
Papa gave me a big bagful
I didn't collect stamps anymore.[71]

I have heard of an American college student who was forced by her parents to turn on Skype before she went to sleep each night, so that they could be sure she was sleeping alone. It may be an urban legend, but most teachers would have no trouble believing it to be true.

71 Siv Widerberg, 'Stamps', *I'm Like Me*, trans. Verne Moberg, The Feminist Press, New York.

3

THE 21ST CENTURY JOURNEY: FROM ANGELS TO SULLEN ADOLESCENTS

Our first task, if we are to create a healthy climate for the raising of children, is to deconstruct and reconstruct the way we understand childhood and adolescence.

We're all familiar with the term 'Madonna/whore complex' as a description of societal attitudes towards women. Although Freud defined the Madonna/whore complex in terms of its effect on the sexual relationships between men and women, it has gradually become understood in a wider sense, as an impediment to, among other things, equity, justice and male–female interactions.

We're perhaps not so familiar with the angel/brat complex that applies to children. Nevertheless, this paradox in the way we regard and treat children is very real, and causes difficulties for them, just as the Madonna/whore complex does for women.

THE 'ANGEL/BRAT' COMPLEX

The term 'angel/brat complex' expresses the idea that children are expected to be pure and innocent, and if they deviate from this expectation, as they always must, they are then portrayed as vicious, evil and nasty. This view is elegantly depicted in one of the most important archetypal stories of our culture: the Adam and Eve allegory.

The King James Bible tells the Adam and Eve story thus:

And the Lord God took the man, and put him into the garden of Eden to dress it and to keep it. And the Lord God commanded the man, saying, Of every tree of the garden thou mayest freely eat: But of the tree of the knowledge of good and evil, thou shalt not eat of it: for in the day that thou eatest thereof thou shalt surely die.

And the Lord God said, It is not good that the man should be alone; I will make him an help meet for him. And out of the ground the Lord God formed every beast of the field, and every fowl of the air; and brought them unto Adam to see what he would call them: and whatsoever Adam called every living creature, that was the name thereof. And Adam gave names to all cattle, and to the fowl of the air, and to every beast of the field; but for Adam there was not found an help meet for him.

And the Lord God caused a deep sleep to fall upon Adam, and he slept: and he took one of his ribs, and closed up the flesh instead thereof; And the rib, which the Lord God had taken from man, made he a woman, and brought her unto the man. And Adam said, This is now bone of my bones, and flesh of my flesh: she shall be called Woman, because she was taken out of Man. Therefore shall a man leave his father and his mother, and shall cleave unto his wife: and they shall be one flesh.

And they were both naked, the man and his wife, and were not ashamed.

Now the serpent was more subtle than any beast of the field which the Lord God had made. And he said unto the woman, Yea, hath God said, Ye shall not eat of every tree of the garden?

And the woman said unto the serpent, We may eat of the fruit of the trees of the garden: But of the fruit of the tree which is in the midst of the garden, God hath said, Ye shall not eat of it, neither shall ye touch it, lest ye die.

And the serpent said unto the woman, Ye shall not surely die: For

God doth know that in the day ye eat thereof, then your eyes shall be opened, and ye shall be as gods, knowing good and evil.

And when the woman saw that the tree was good for food, and that it was pleasant to the eyes, and a tree to be desired to make one wise, she took of the fruit thereof, and did eat, and gave also unto her husband with her; and he did eat.

And the eyes of them both were opened, and they knew that they were naked; and they sewed fig leaves together, and made themselves aprons. And they heard the voice of the Lord God walking in the garden in the cool of the day: and Adam and his wife hid themselves from the presence of the Lord God amongst the trees of the garden. And the Lord God called unto Adam, and said unto him, Where art thou?

And he said, I heard thy voice in the garden, and I was afraid, because I was naked; and I hid myself.

And he said, Who told thee that thou wast naked? Hast thou eaten of the tree, whereof I commanded thee that thou shouldest not eat?

And the man said, The woman whom thou gavest to be with me, she gave me of the tree, and I did eat.

And the Lord God said unto the woman, What is this that thou hast done? And the woman said, The serpent beguiled me, and I did eat.

And the Lord God said unto the serpent, Because thou hast done this, thou art cursed above all cattle, and above every beast of the field; upon thy belly shalt thou go, and dust shalt thou eat all the days of thy life. And I will put enmity between thee and the woman, and between thy seed and her seed; it shall bruise thy head, and thou shalt bruise his heel.

Unto the woman he said, I will greatly multiply thy sorrow and thy conception; in sorrow thou shalt bring forth children; and thy desire shall be to thy husband, and he shall rule over thee.

And unto Adam he said, Because thou hast hearkened unto the voice of thy wife, and hast eaten of the tree, of which I commanded thee, saying, Thou shalt not eat of it: cursed is the ground for thy sake; in sorrow shalt thou eat of it all the days of thy life; Thorns also and thistles shall it bring forth to thee; and thou shalt eat the herb of the field; In the sweat of thy face shalt thou eat bread, till thou return unto the ground; for out of it wast thou taken: for dust thou art, and unto dust shalt thou return.

And Adam called his wife's name Eve; because she was the mother of all living.

Unto Adam also and to his wife did the Lord God make coats of skins, and clothed them.

And the Lord God said, Behold, the man is become as one of us, to know good and evil: and now, lest he put forth his hand, and take also of the tree of life, and eat, and live for ever: Therefore the Lord God sent him forth from the garden of Eden, to till the ground from whence he was taken.

So he drove out the man; and he placed at the east of the garden of Eden Cherubims, and a flaming sword which turned every way, to keep the way of the tree of life.[72]

Putting aside the possibility that the story is literally true, I suggest that it has arisen out of the individual and collective unconscious of our ancestors, and illustrates the three stages of life that many people simplistically believe we experience. First comes the purity of childhood, then the unhealthy, unattractive rebelliousness of adolescence, and then the burden of adulthood. Adam and Eve are created, asexually, as the epitome of child-like innocence. They are naked and unselfconscious, because, like young children (or, at least, children as viewed by the originators of the story), they have no understanding of sexual attraction, no awareness that one day their bodies will be sexually interesting to each other. Eventually however, the serpent, easily understood as a phallic symbol, tempts Eve and evokes in her the stirrings of sexual interest. This is consistent with the reality that girls mature sexually at an earlier age than boys, but has of course traditionally been used to cast women in the role of temptresses,

---

72 Genesis 2:15–3:22, *The Holy Bible, King James Version*. Cambridge Edition: 1769; *King James Bible Online*, 2019, kingjamesbibleonline.org.

seductresses, who can be conveniently blamed for the supposed lustful thoughts and behaviours of men.

Both Eve and Adam eat from the Tree of Knowledge, despite God's stern injunction against doing so. In tempting Eve to eat the fruit, the serpent explicitly told her: 'Ye shall be as gods, knowing good and evil.' Sex is clearly the evil of which they become aware.

This development in their lives is synonymous with the universal experience of puberty and adolescence. Adam and Eve have learned that their bodies are sexually powerful. It happens in just a few moments in the story, and, indeed, the dawning of sexuality for young people can seem like a sudden event – teenagers have been known to use expressions like 'the world got turned upside-down' or 'it just came out of the blue' to describe it.

With Adam and Eve's realisation comes self-consciousness and shame. Their discovery of sex enrages God, in the same way that a parent in our culture might react to the discovery that the son or daughter whom they imagined to be chaste actually has a sexual identity and is engaging in sexual activity. Adam and Eve are expelled from the place of perfect innocence. They and their descendants are cursed. They lose the possibility of living forever; Adam is told he can eat dirt and will eventually become dust himself. Eve must suffer pain in childbirth and be subservient to her husband; and even the snake is condemned to a miserable existence henceforth and forever more.

As God says, this is because 'the man is become as one of us'. He is no longer a child; he has passed through adolescence and by so doing has become an adult; he has become a fully mature sexual being.

The equation is clear: to be asexual is good; to be sexual is bad. Worse than bad: immoral, foul, and meriting violent and extreme punishment. This attitude is not unique to Judaism or Christianity but is, for example, echoed in the so-called 'honour killings' of girls in some areas of countries like Pakistan.

If we consider the significance of the Adam and Eve story, we see that it serves as an allegory for our perspective on children and adolescents. Tortured by our own dark anxieties about adulthood and sex, and associating the lives of adults with corruption, we long for the comfort that would come, we believe, from encounters with worlds where all is innocent, where the snake is dormant. Many people construct Nature as such a world, ignoring the stalking, hunting, killing and (frequently) savage sexual encounters that dominate the lives of so many animals, birds, reptiles, sea-dwellers and insects.

Alternatively, many people hope that an ashram or place of worship or remote country or even a place close to home can replicate Eden for them. Hanging out with Indigenous elders in Outback Australia, with Sherpas in Nepal, with gurus in India, with natural healing centre personal coaches at Byron Bay, with Native Americans in the United States, with the congregation at the Hillsong Church . . . such experiences give some Westerners hope of filling an emptiness they feel but often cannot easily articulate. They eagerly devour any evidence that a sense of inner peace can be gained from these sources. In other words, they seek to escape from the adult lives depicted in the Adam and Eve story as comprising pain and sorrow. They look for a Garden of Eden, in the hope that they can sneak past the allegorical cherubim and flaming sword and get back into that place of perfection.

Frequently they revere fantasy worlds, such as Camelot, Rivendell, Hogwarts, Shangri-La. Sometimes fantasy and reality coalesce – for example, the name Camelot was colloquially applied to John Kennedy's White House despite the far-from-perfect behaviour of some of its residents. Lobsang Rampa's *The Third Eye* and other books were thought by millions of Western readers to be the authentic experiences of a Tibetan lama, and caused many people to develop an interest in Tibetan Buddhism, but were actually written by a British plumber who had never been to Tibet.

Many people look to the past in their search for a utopia, invoking the 1950s, the 1960s, the 1970s, the decade of their childhoods, engaging in nostalgic reminiscences about playing unsupervised for hours on end, roaming on foot or on bikes, swimming in the river or in a dam . . .

There may be truthful aspects to these attractive images, but they conveniently overlook harsher realities of the golden past: the contemptuous treatment of women, the overuse of corporal punishment, the frequency of sexual abuse, the number of people injured or killed in accidents, the levels of alcoholism and nicotine addiction, and the emotional poverty experienced by many.

INNOCENCE VERSUS EVIL

We are surrounded by simplistic images redolent of purity and innocence. Forrest Gump, Mr Chips, George Bailey (*It's a Wonderful Life*), Dorothy (*The Wizard of Oz*), Anne of Green Gables are fantasy creations, but are among the most beloved iconic figures of the last hundred years. Children's picture books, TV advertisements and saccharine movies frequently feature cuddly grandparents, cuddly koalas, cuddly stockmen in Driza-bones, cuddly nuns singing sweet songs in the Austrian Alps. On TV ads, houses are overwhelmingly white, gleaming so brightly that I assume every wall and every item must be brand new and scrupulously polished. Clean-cut well-scrubbed families engage warmly with each other, usually in the white-walled kitchen with its white benches, or around a white table where they eat together in a glow of mutual affection. Difficult moments with potentially rebellious teenagers are dealt with swiftly and surely by decisive yet good-humoured mothers. Great mates play funny pranks on each other, causing everyone to chuckle heartily.

Norman Rockwell's paintings of warm-hearted American people in idyllic scenarios resonate with Australians as much as they do with Americans. And in contemporary picture books there's a closely related, ideologically correct world. Fathers knit and do laundry, look after children and play non-violent games with them (kite-flying is popular). Mothers drive bulldozers and lift weights. Wise Aboriginal people squat under trees telling wise stories as they munch on yummy shellfish and bush tucker. Everybody cares about the environment.

Many adults are powerfully and neurotically attracted to these worlds. We know the attraction is powerful because these images are so often promulgated by advertisers: the people in our culture who are among the most skilled at manipulating the popular psyche. Some of the images are used even more often than sexual ones to sell products – notably banking services, telephones, and, rather oddly, alcohol and gambling.

We can say the attraction is neurotic when such images are used frequently, obsessively or addictively by people who can't cope with reality. Upset and confused by the complexity of modern life, they slip away into a world that not only is unreal but has never been real. The almost pre-lapsarian world of picturesque stockmen, omniscient parents and anthropomorphic animals, for instance, is a lie. Not always a bad lie, but always a lie.

The strength of the need to believe in the lie can also be seen in public attitudes to figures who, for various reasons, must be viewed as perfect – Diana Spencer, because she was the archetypal fairytale princess; Mother Theresa, another incarnation of that impossible paradigm, the perfect virgin-mother; American presidents, the omnipotent father figures. On the day of President Bill Clinton's inauguration, a middle-aged male American was shown on a television vox pop with tears in his eyes, shaking his head and saying with deep emotion, 'I love Bill Clinton; (pause) I just love him.'

Enid Blyton, like many writers for children, was often made to fit the archetype of the wise, gentle storyteller. In the Melbourne *Age* on 20 January 1992, a photo of Blyton with her two daughters was captioned 'Enid Blyton in 1949 with two of her greatest fans, daughters Gillian, left, and Imogen'.[73]

A different perspective can be found in Imogen's autobiography, *A Childhood at Green Hedges*. Her memories show vividly the startling discrepancies that can exist in our society between illusion and reality, image and substance:

---

73 'A Young Reader's Guide to the Best Books', *The Age*, 20 January 1992.

On Saturday mornings, my sister and I would go down to the lounge to collect our pocket money, sometimes augmented by pay for small gardening jobs such as weeding. It was on one of these occasions, when I was on my way to collect my sixpence, that I came upon a new piece of knowledge. Something that one of the staff said to me made me realize that this woman with dark, curly hair and brown eyes, so different from my own mouse-like appearance, who paid me just as she paid the staff, who was in fact the absolute ruler of our household, was also my mother. By this time I had met mothers in stories that were read to me, Enid Blyton stories included, and I knew that a mother bore a special relationship to her child, from which others were excluded. In my case the pieces of the puzzle failed to fit together. There was no special relationship. There was scarcely a relationship at all.[74]

Public adoration of these humans falsely cast as mythical heroes and gods is matched only by public fury when it is discovered that they are normal humans after all. The savagery with which the public turned on Princess Diana when her marriage to Prince Charles began to fail has now been conveniently forgotten, but it was virulent. In 2016 an attractive young Australian woman who had falsely claimed to have cancer was pursued relentlessly by the media without regard to her emotional health, which one might reasonably assume was fragile. Politicians, upon being elected to high office, often with messianic fervour by their supporters, frequently enjoy a 'honeymoon period' with huge approval ratings in the polls, but truly is it said, 'Pity the man cheered by the crowd, for if he lives long enough he will hear the same crowd booing him.'

Particularly powerful to many people is the notion, the lie, of childhood innocence. Children as a generic group are not innocent. On the other hand, it's true that some children are innocent, as are some adults. I had a grandmother who was 'an innocent', to use an

---

74   Imogen Smallwood, *A Childhood at Green Hedges*, Methuen, London, 1989, p. 35.

old-fashioned expression. Her delightful nature seemed unaffected by the many difficulties with which she had been confronted. Awful experiences had not embittered her.

All children can be kind, generous, loving, selfless, self-disciplined, imaginative, honest, trusting and brave. Some of these qualities are popularly understood to be manifestations of innocence. But as anyone who knows children (powerful word that, *knows*) can testify, they can also be manipulative, dishonest, sexual, selfish, jealous, destructive, malicious, sly, greedy, cynical. Just like adults.

In May 2017, a pop concert in Manchester England was targeted by a suicide bomber, who killed 22 people, including an eight-year-old girl. In response, *The Sun* newspaper in Britain split its entire front page into two columns. One, headed 'PURE' was a photo of the child; the other headed 'EVIL' was a photo of the suicide bomber.[75] The Australian Prime Minister at the time, Malcolm Turnbull, responded in Parliament to this awful event by saying, 'This is an attack on innocence. Surely, there is no crime more reprehensible than the murder of children.'[76]

Words like 'pure', 'innocence' and 'evil' need to be considered thoughtfully. It should be recognised that powerful and wealthy countries around the world, including Russia, the United States, the United Kingdom and Australia, have, through ill-considered invasions of dubious morality, caused havoc in many countries in recent decades, and have directly and indirectly caused the deaths of many people, including children, and the displacement of millions more. These tragedies are not generally acknowledged by world leaders, including Australian Prime Ministers Rudd, Gillard, Abbott, Turnbull and Morrison.

It's perhaps also worth noting that the lives of men are often considered, by implication, as having less value than the lives of women and children. Hence, many newspaper articles contain sentences such as: '15 people were killed, including seven women and children'. If we

---

75 *The Sun*, 24 May 2017.
76 Australia, House of Representatives 2017, *Debates,* 23 May 2017, p. 4827.

do the mathematics, we realise that the other eight people killed were men, whose deaths apparently do not need to be highlighted.

Even lower on the scale are soldiers, leading to media references to 'innocent civilians'; for example, 'Many innocent civilians were among the casualties.' The remaining casualties are, by implication, guilty people; viz. soldiers.

I'm not sure who examines the life of each civilian to establish whether she or he could be fairly described as innocent, or the life of each soldier to establish whether he or she should be described as guilty. The premature death of any person, soldier or civilian, man or woman or child, is likely to bring grief to someone, and should leave us all with a sense of loss: a life unlived, possibilities unrealised, potential unfulfilled. Truly did John Donne write: 'Therefore, never send to know for whom the bell tolls; it tolls for thee.'[77]

Every day in the United States an average of seven teenagers and children are killed by guns. The writer Gary Younge chose a random day when ten young people were killed by guns, and in his remarkable book *Another Day in the Death of America* examined, one by one, the stories of these ten youngsters. He reflects on the culture that allows this seemingly-without-end slaughter, and goes on to make a point that cannot be emphasised too frequently or too strongly. For countless centuries countless people, including but not limited to warmongers, demagogues, religious leaders and so-called 'ordinary' people, have been all too ready to rank wounded and dead people according to criteria like age and gender:

> But dwelling on children can be calculated. In not only emphasising their vulnerability but also declaring their inherent innocence and insisting on their angelic nature, one moves them from a 'protected' to an elevated category: it shifts the emphasis from the availability of guns to the moral purity of those they might be used to kill.[78]

---

77 John Donne, *Devotions upon Emergent Occasions*, Meditation 17 (first published 1624).
78 Gary Younge, *Another Day in the Death of America*, Guardian Books and Faber, London, 2016, p. 57.

Younge reminds readers of the death in 1955 of fourteen-year-old African-American boy Emmett Till, savagely murdered by two white men because he had supposedly acted in a cheekily flirtatious way towards a 21-year-old white shopowner, whilst in her store. The two white men were acquitted by an all-white jury. Younge points out that an article in *Life* magazine attempted to condemn Emmett's murder by emphasising the moral purity of Emmett's father, Louis Till, saying that the man 'had died in the military during the Second World War'. The magazine went on to say that Emmett's father was 'killed in France fighting for the American proposition that all men are equal'.[79] However, the death of Louis was not that of a wartime hero. He was executed during the war – in Italy, not France – for murder and rape. Younge rightly says that this has no bearing on the death of the fourteen-year-old Emmett. 'No child should have been so brutally slain whether his or her father was a pimp or a priest.'[80]

The assumed 'purity' of children is contradicted by this story, told by an adult reminiscing in a Sydney newspaper: 'And I remember my eighth birthday. There was one girl I just left off the invitation list, but Mum invited her. So I stood waiting at the front gate, and when she arrived I took the present and told her to go home. She went off crying.' It is also contradicted by poet Eric Rolls, when he wrote in his book *Celebration of the Senses*: 'I was astonished to learn when our children were all under seven that they had named the Dorset Horn rams according to their sexual capacities. There were Greedy, Clumsy, Shy, Big Balls, Weary, Slowcoach, Jealous – several more.'[81]

Over the years I've been told many stories by kids, including a boy who reminisced how in Grade 1 he regularly pretended that he'd wet his pants so he could get out of boring classwork; a girl in Grade 4 who paid blackmail money to two classmates so they wouldn't tell others that she'd started menstruating; a boy who for

---

79 *Life* magazine quoted in Gary Younge, *Another Day in the Death of America*, Guardian Books and Faber, London, 2016, p. 57.
80 Younge, *Another Day in the Death of America*, p. 58.
81 Eric Rolls, *Celebration of the Senses,* Penguin, Melbourne, 1985, p. 3.

his birthday was tied to a tree by his friends, who then climbed the tree and, despite the boy's pleas, sat there for twenty minutes dropping raw eggs on his head. The eggs cut his head so badly that he needed eight stitches.

Whether these are learned behaviours, or whether they indicate some kind of innate corruption, is irrelevant. The important thing is that this is the way children are. And these behaviours are incompatible with our notions of purity and innocence.

INNOCENCE VERSUS IGNORANCE

The mistake many people make, I think, is to confuse innocence with ignorance. All children are ignorant – relative to most adults, anyway. But there's a complex dialectic at work here, and by understanding it we will understand a good deal more about children, the issues in their lives, and the passion with which people debate these issues.

The dialectic is this: that the people who desperately believe in and proclaim the doctrine of childhood innocence are, at the same time, contemptuous of children's ignorance and exult in the power their 'knowing' gives them over children.

Consider these four stories:

1 A Grade 1 child in Show and Tell: 'Dad and Uncle Jack got a new car last night, and they were in the garage all night painting it a different colour, and they even put new number plates on it.'
2 A four-year-old, when her parents went next door for a few minutes, decided she would help them by cleaning the sitting room. To do the job quickly she went outside and got the garden sprinkler, brought it in and turned it on.
3 A four-year-old asked his pregnant mother, 'Mummy, when the baby's born, does it come out naked?'
4 A child in Longreach, Queensland, years ago, upon hearing of the first Sputnik flight, asked, 'Mummy, does Sputnik go below heaven or above it?'

These stories have a number of things in common. One is that adults can be relied on to laugh at all of them. And underpinning their laughter is always this awareness: 'We're smarter than they are! We know and they don't!'

So we're laughing at their mistakes. We're laughing at their ignorance. We're laughing with the pleasure that comes from this proof of our greater status and power; the comfort that this gives us.

Much – perhaps most – laughter in our society has this mocking edge. In each of these stories the children are simply trying to get it right. They're experimenting with language and concepts. They're trying to figure out why Dad and Uncle Jack were behaving so mysteriously, how to clean a house like the adults do, the manner in which babies are born. They're trying to understand abstract concepts like God and heaven.

Laughing at children who are trying to figure it all out is one of our most widespread and damaging cultural traits, and the more contempt adults have for children, the louder they laugh. The laughter is not well received by children. The very tone such adults use when addressing children is always patronising: 'You are ignorant but I may let you have another jewel from my treasury of knowledge.'

If we accept that children are not automatically innocent and angelic, that they are complex, subtle humans who are trying to overcome their ignorance, trying to acquire knowledge so that they can move to the positions of strength that the knowing adults seemingly occupy, then we can get a clearer idea of the difficulties they face in our culture.

The unconscious thought processes in many adults operate like this: 'The world seems so dark and difficult. It frightens me. It's some comfort to imagine that there are pure, innocent places – the country-side [hence the attraction of James Herriot's Yorkshire, and 'Banjo' Paterson and Ian McNamara's outback Australia], sweet Fairyland [Enid Blyton's Toyland, James Barrie's Neverland, May Gibbs' bush], beautiful Camelot [Buckingham Palace, John Kennedy's White House] – and the innocent world of childhood.'

But they go further: 'My children – and by extension, all children – are still living in childhood's pure world. I must keep them in it. To let them out is to let myself out. *I will use my power to lock them in there and hide the key.* And I will oppose any adult who tries to give children the key.

'By doing this I ensure that, though I must stay in this dark troubling world, part of me at least will (vicariously) be safe in the secret garden.'

I read somewhere that 'protection is the oldest form of sexism'. It's a wise statement, encapsulating the way men justify their oppression of women by pretending to themselves and others that they are protecting women – usually to stop them having sexual experiences, which, in such situations, men want to monopolise for themselves. But protection is more than that: it's the oldest form of repression. Adults frequently excuse their repression of children by claiming that they're protecting them. The adults are not mature enough, or brave enough, to confront the real reasons. And they're reinforced by neurotic media monster stories about paedophiles, kidnappers and murderers ('A depraved beast is stalking the streets of Sydney . . .'), which they read anxiously and avidly, to reassure themselves that their repression of their children is legitimate, ignoring the unchallengeable fact that if children are going to be abused or assaulted, it will almost always be by a close family member or friend.

A big problem for our society, for all of us, is that we believe children can will bad habits out of themselves. We believe it about ourselves too. The message from religions, from parents, from teachers, has always been that if we try a little harder, work at it a little more, put in that extra bit of effort, we can erase our envy, lust, greed, laziness and other nasty habits. They will cease to be a problem for us. We can get them right out of our system.

Children are constantly being told: 'Stop being so selfish!' 'Don't be greedy.' 'You're very lazy sometimes.' 'It's time you started thinking more of others.' 'You could do better if you tried.'

Ah yes, we could all do better if we tried. I remember watching a principal at a school assembly in Gippsland as he shouted at the

Year 12 students: 'Not one of you is working to your full potential.' He was right, but then neither was the principal working to his full potential. Neither was I. Nor were any of the teachers present. Nor is anyone in the world.

In their attempts to excise their 'bad' bits, people sometimes go to extremes of self-criticism: abstract representations of the hair shirts, self-flagellation and physical mutilation practised in earlier times. And when we fail, and when children fail, as everyone inevitably does, to fix matters, it means that we just haven't tried hard enough, that we are in fact failures. Somewhere out there are the good boys and girls and men and women, and further out still are the saints.

Graham Greene, in *The Power and the Glory*, created the memorable character of the whisky priest, who at the end of the book is shown to be on the path to veneration and perhaps even canonisation, despite his alcohol problem and the fact that he has fathered a baby. The story could be seen as showing that canonisation is a deeply flawed process, or, as I prefer to see it, that even a man so deeply flawed has saintly qualities. I think the whisky priest is one of the saintliest figures I've encountered in fiction.

Robin Klein, in *Hating Alison Ashley*, gives us a young heroine who seems perfect, but late in the book we find out the truth about the saintly Alison Ashley: she is a deeply unhappy child, whose goodness is a desperate attempt to control her surroundings and please an unpleasable and uninterested mother. The more controlled someone is on the outside, the more out of control they're likely to be on the inside: hence Lisa in my books *So Much to Tell You* and *Take My Word for It*, described by her friends as the ice-woman, is at grave risk . . . as we eventually learn.

In schools we constantly give children the message that it is awful to be selfish or cruel or vulgar or dishonest or covetous. We ignore the truth, which is that all human beings, including us, the teachers and parents, have these aspects, no matter how much we try to deny them. I remember a school staff meeting during which someone began the familiar chant about the problem of students arriving late for assemblies and for classes. Other teachers joined in, I suspect because that's always a comfortable, easy and satisfying thing to do in these situations, to complain about the bad habits of young people. There was a problem, however, on the occasion of that staff meeting, which I eventually pointed out: more than half the teachers had been late for the meeting.

Some adults deny supposed negative aspects of themselves by becoming unnaturally sweet – in middle age they may still be speaking in sugary little voices, being super-helpful, filling their houses with potpourri or fragrant oils, sending loving messages to friends on Facebook. I have to say, I find people who assume an unremittingly sweet and beautiful façade almost as disturbing as people who appear to be unremittingly violent and appalling, because neither has been able to reconcile the paradoxes within them. In general, I find the first group more difficult to deal with, as all too frequently they become vicious when they don't get what they want, but they won't acknowledge that they are angry. Members of the second group do not dissemble as much.

Some people deny their 'darker' qualities by furiously criticising the manifestations of these in others. Children are especially good targets for these people, because children appear to be still malleable, not yet set in their evil ways, and because children, by virtue of their size and relative helplessness, make good targets. Hence schools are bombarded daily by people with agendas about which they feel passionate. When you want to change the world, and no one seems to be listening, where do you go? Why, to schools of course. Many people see schools as amorphous masses of pliant children waiting to be shaped and sculpted into devout believers in the causes espoused by evangelising adults. I am subjected every day to emails and other approaches from groups and individuals who want to come into the schools and give fervent presentations about cyberbullying, schoolyard bullying, eating disorders, transcendental meditation, yoga, feminism, the environment, bowel cancer, Cambodian orphanages . . .

In 2016 I received an email from a fifteen-year-old Australian girl who explained that she was currently in Cambodia with a group from her private school, so they could carry out Good Works with underprivileged Cambodian children. She was seeking the support of Candlebark for this cause. She described how one of her assigned tasks in Cambodia was to teach young kids about issues like stranger danger, abuse and rape. She said that some of the children were victims of these phenomena, but were not aware of it, and added that she felt she was 'very lucky' to be able to teach these subjects.

I responded:

> I appreciate your good intentions with the Cambodian project, but I must say I was taken aback at the idea of 15-year-old Australians, presumably with no teacher training or qualifications in psychology, teaching children in a third world country about issues like rape. I wouldn't welcome 15-year-old Cambodians coming into Candlebark to teach our Grade 3 or 4 children, for instance, about health, sexual abuse, and rape. It would seem startlingly inappropriate to me.

I never heard back from her.

WE ARE OUR GOOD PARTS *AND* OUR FLAWS

Adults, including mini-adults like my correspondent, would be better off working on themselves than frantically projecting onto children. They don't help children by traipsing off to Third World countries on missions of mercy that seem to be more about giving themselves a short-term warm glow. They don't help children by preaching the message that it's awful to be selfish, dishonest, cruel, vulgar, covetous – because that's giving them the message that it's awful to be who they are.

Rather, we ought to teach children that all feelings are as much a part of being human as having two ears, a nose and a pair of eyes. And we need to accept these feelings in children just as we accept them in ourselves. In fact, we won't be able to accept them in children until we can accept them in ourselves. The challenge for human beings is to accommodate and manage our darker aspects in ways that will bring as little grief as possible to ourselves and to other people.

4

PARENTING THE WRONG CHILD

These thoughts about the supposed purity and evil in children, the light and darkness, lead me to think that the biggest single problem for well-meaning parents in Western society in the 21st century is the same problem such parents have had for many generations past. They are parenting the wrong child. They think they are raising the three-dimensional, solid, tangible child who stands before them. This is the child who must be fed, clothed, toileted, washed and dried, put to sleep, taught reading 'riting 'rithmetic, entertained, taken to dance classes/swimming classes/martial arts classes/football training/tennis lessons, be rewarded for losing a tooth and given presents on birthdays and other festive occasions. This child has infinite needs, and many parents are massively involved, to the point of exhaustion at times, in meeting as many of these needs as possible.

But children have other needs as well as all these obvious ones, needs that we can perhaps characterise as 'invisible'. Parents must tend not just to the outer child but to the inner one. I'm not referring to the contents of the stomach, so much as emotions, intellect, spirit, strength of character, social intelligence . . . Children, like adults, dwell in both the conscious and the unconscious.

RAISING THE INNER CHILD

A man who was himself badly damaged, author James Barrie, gave us, from the depths of his pain, one of the most important texts we have for understanding the psychic needs of children. That book was *Peter Pan*. For those who have not read *Peter Pan* since childhood, or have been exposed only to sanitised movies that rob the book of its powerful hidden meanings, it's worth reading again, from an adult perspective.

In the first three chapters, we learn the following:

- Some parents are unable to bear the notion that their children will grow up. Children divine from a young age that growing up is an inevitable process. Many observant parents and teachers will be able to recall episodes where very young children are encountered in a state of grief and terror, and when asked the reason for their distress (which can reach a level of hysteria), are shocked to hear the child sob, 'I don't want to get old and die.' Adults are often rendered mute at such moments, understandably, for there is no meaningful comfort that can be offered to the terrified child, except, for some people, a religious one.

- For boys at least, the complexity of women is simultaneously fascinating and frustrating, for no matter how much one plumbs female depths, one never arrives at an ultimate understanding of the opposite gender. Barrie says of Mrs Darling: 'Her romantic mind was like the tiny boxes, one within the other, that come from the puzzling East, however many you discover there is always one more; and her sweet mocking mouth had one kiss on it that Wendy could never get, though there it was, perfectly conspicuous in the right-hand corner.' Although Barrie is writing from the perspective of a little girl at this point in the story, it is really the lost little boy, James himself, who is, like all little boys, expressing his frustration at being unable to attain ultimate access to the mother, because that privilege is reserved exclusively for the father – or at least, so the little boy believes. (In using the term 'ultimate access' I am of course including, among others, romantic and sexual access.) In the novel, Barrie shows his awareness that the father too does not have ultimate access to the mother, but we can reasonably assume that the few sentences disclosing this are written from the perspective of the knowing adult author.

- The father represents authority, rationality, the cold logic of the brain, whilst the mother represents emotion, love, the warm feelings of the heart. Readers may remember that when Wendy was born, her parents were conflicted: Mr Darling sat on the edge of his wife's bed, as she held their baby. He involved himself in intricate financial calculations to see whether they could afford to keep the child, 'while she [the mother] looked at him imploringly'. There is a passing reference to a £1 note that Mrs Darling impulsively lent to a man who came to the door: a tramp? This is further evidence of her irresponsible irrationality, and, possibly, her unconscious attraction to a man of a very different type to her husband. We know that had Mr Darling answered the door to the man, he would have done his sums and then sent the supplicant away empty-handed.

- It is important, according to many devotees of the Western model of parenting, that the child has no secrets from the mother, and further, that the mother occupies and colonises the child's mind so that the child can be 'properly' programmed for his or her role as an effectively functioning adult. A vital part of this colonisation is that thoughts, feelings, ideas or experiences which are considered, in Barrie's words, naughty or evil, must be 'stowed out of sight'. The mother is unable to bear the knowledge that her child has such thoughts, feelings, ideas or experiences. They must be repressed, sent to the basement of the mind, and the door firmly closed on them, so that only 'pretty thoughts' (again, using Barrie's words) are allowed.

Barrie gives us one of the most remarkably poetic descriptions of a child's mind that has ever been penned. He uses the metaphor of an island:

> [It] is not only confused, but keeps going round all the time. There are zigzag lines on it, just like your temperature on a card, and these are probably roads in the island, for the Neverland is always more or less an island, with astonishing splashes of colour here and there, and coral reefs and rakish-looking craft in the offing, and savages and lonely lairs, and gnomes who are mostly tailors, and caves through which a river runs, and princes with six elder brothers, and a hut fast going to decay, and one very small old lady with a hooked nose. It would be an easy map if that were all, but there is also first day at school, religion, fathers, the round pond, needle-work, murders, hangings, verbs that take the dative, chocolate pudding day, getting into braces, say ninety-nine, three-pence for pulling out your tooth yourself, and so on, and either these are part of the island or they are another map showing through, and it is all rather confusing, especially as nothing will stand still.
>
> Of course the Neverlands vary a good deal. John's, for instance, had a lagoon with flamingos flying over it at which John was shooting, while Michael, who was very small, had a flamingo with lagoons flying over it. John lived in a boat turned upside down on the sands, Michael in a wigwam, Wendy in a house of leaves deftly sewn together. John had no friends, Michael had friends at night, Wendy had a pet wolf forsaken by its parents, but on the whole the Neverlands have a family resemblance, and if they stood still in a row you could say of them that they have each other's nose, and so forth. On these magic shores children at play are for ever pitching their coracles. We too have been there; we can still hear the sound of the surf, though we shall land no more.
>
> Of all delectable islands the Neverland is the snuggest and most compact, not large and is sprawly, you know, with tedious distances between one adventure and another, but nicely crammed. When you play at it by day with the chairs and table-cloth, it is not in the least

alarming, but in the two minutes before you go to sleep it becomes very real. That is why there are night-lights.[82]

With the phrase '*or they are another map showing through*' Barrie captures in half a dozen words the place of the unconscious mind; a concept of which he had some instinctual understanding, though not a scholarly one. And his reference to the value of night-lights shows his fear of this unmapped, unmappable world, which operated so powerfully for him throughout his writing career, in more works than just *Peter Pan*. The play *Mary Rose,* for example, is the story of a girl who is, metaphorically speaking, frozen in time.

Intimations of sexuality make their presence felt in the early years of childhood. As Mrs Darling trawls through the unconscious mind of her young daughter she finds a peter, which for a long time was a popular euphemism for a penis. The peter is described several times as cocky:

> Occasionally in her travels through her children's minds Mrs Darling found things she could not understand, and of these quite the most perplexing was the word Peter. She knew of no Peter, and yet he was here and there in John and Michael's minds, while Wendy's began to be scrawled all over with him. The name stood out in bolder letters than any of the other words, and as Mrs Darling gazed she felt it had an oddly cocky appearance.
> 'Yes, he is rather cocky,' Wendy admitted with regret . . .[83]

The peter (I am using lowercase deliberately for the word, although Barrie of course uses uppercase for the first letter) already occupies a prominent place in her daughter's unconscious, more so than in the boys', no doubt because Wendy is closer to puberty than they are. Wendy has, however, already learned that it is not good to be thinking of a cocky peter. Mrs Darling knows of no peter because

---

82 J.M. Barrie, *Peter Pan and Wendy*, Puffin, England, 1967 pp. 19–20 (first published 1911).
83 Barrie, *Peter Pan and Wendy*, p. 20.

in Barrie's mind a mother should be pure, and know nothing of sex.

The peter is unruly and cannot be easily fitted into a neat, organ-ised, conscious understanding of the world. The peter visits Wendy at nights, and plays upon his pipes, leaving fragments of his clothing on the floor as he comes and goes. The mother is very disturbed by evidence that her daughter is consorting with the peter, and does her best to eliminate his presence. When Mrs Darling falls asleep and dreams of the peter, she 'thought she had seen him before in the faces of many women who have no children' and perhaps in the faces of some mothers also. At this moment in the text, Peter/the peter seems to represent a yearning for love and sexual fulfilment, and the natural outcome of sex: children.

When Peter Pan does appear to Mrs Darling, he closely resembles the god Pan from Greek mythology, not least in his paradoxically innocent yet sexualised appearance and behaviour. It's a reminder of just how sexual, how raunchy, Pan was, in the gallery of gods. Barrie was apparently unhappy with the famous statue of Peter Pan in Kensington Gardens, London, by Sir George Frampton, commenting that 'it doesn't show the devil in Peter'.[84]

Barrie describes his Peter Pan thus:'He was very like Mrs Darling's kiss. He was a lovely boy, clad in skeleton leaves and the juices that ooze out of trees but the most entrancing thing about him was that he had all his first teeth.'[85]

Of course the significance of a child having all his first teeth is that he is very much a child; he has not yet embarked upon the next period of his growth. On a Waldorf Steiner website, in 2011, a mother wrote of her deep emotions when her child lost his first tooth. She described how she tiptoed into his room when he was asleep, to leave money in exchange for the tooth, and then we have this: '"Goodbye, little one," I whispered as a tear slipped down my cheek.'[86]

84 Knowledge of London, knowledgeoflondon.com/writers/jmbarrie.html, accessed 1 April 2019.
85 Barrie, *Peter Pan and Wendy*, p. 24.
86 Arianne,'Waldorf and losing that first tooth', 6 January 2011, *The Magic Onions*, themagiconions. com/2011/01/discovering-waldorf-waldorf-and-losing.html.

Rationally, it makes no sense that Peter still has all his first teeth, as this would mean he is only five or six years old, at most, and yet throughout the rest of the book he is more like a ten- or eleven-year-old, at the very least. In the film versions he is often even older. But it was apparently important to Barrie to emphasise that Peter was a child in every sense, and therefore could be treated, at a conscious level, as innocent. Barrie's fury at his own mother, who essentially abandoned him when his older brother died, is evident in the last sentence of the chapter: 'When he saw that she was a grown-up, he gnashed the little pearls [his teeth] at her.'[87]

All of this, and more, is found in the first chapter of *Peter Pan*. But we have only begun to touch upon the meaning offered to us by this book. In the second chapter, we see what happens to children when the parents have interfered excessively with the unconscious mind. Peter, after his expression of rage at the woman who represents his mother, flees the Darling house (for it can be terrifying for the child to express fury at the mother), and in doing so loses his shadow. It is snapped off when the window is slammed shut as he races to escape. Mrs Darling is now in full possession of the shadow, the tangible representation of Peter Pan's unconscious self, but it makes her uncomfortable: for one thing, it will 'lower the whole tone of the house'. She rolls it up and puts it away carefully in a drawer – out of sight and, hopefully, in her view at least, out of mind. Mr Darling shares the disquiet that the shadow causes his wife: when she shows it to him, he says, 'It is nobody I know, but it does look a scoundrel.'[88]

We learn that Wendy, John and Michael have disappeared, and we are given the back story of the circumstances. It is an odd story indeed. It appears that the children's disappearance is a consequence of the irresponsibility, immaturity and inadequacy of the parents. On the last night the family is together, the parents go out to a party. It is already bad enough that the children's upbringing is largely entrusted to a

---

87 Barrie, *Peter Pan and Wendy*, p. 24.
88 Barrie, *Peter Pan and Wendy*, p. 31.

dog, but this night, thanks to a childish tantrum of Mr Darling's, even the dog is not on duty. Mr Darling, in trying to persuade Michael to take some medicine, has boasted about his own mature ability to take his medicine without complaint. The children immediately put him to the test, but when presented with his medicine, Mr Darling becomes increasingly infantile ('So are you a cowardy custard,' the father retorts, to his son) and the little boy becomes increasingly parental ('"Father, I am waiting," said Michael coldly.').[89]

Rather than take his medicine, Mr Darling resorts to an immature act of dishonesty, but is caught out by the children. His loss of status cannot be borne; he responds furiously by exiling the dog to the yard, in a meaningless act of revenge. The dog is chained up, and hence can no longer guard the household. The parents ignore the dog's attempts to warn them that the children are in danger; they go to their party, leaving the house protected only by a maid, who appears to be no older than ten. As an unknowing child, the maid cannot prevent the intrusion of the sexual energy represented by Peter Pan.

The Darlings are punished for their irresponsibility by the loss of the children. Peter arrives, with the fairy Tinkerbell, who is also shown in a sexualised light: described as 'exquisitely gowned in a skeleton leaf, cut low and square, through which her figure could be seen to the best advantage. She was slightly inclined to embonpoint . . .'[90] Barrie's use of the word 'embonpoint' is clearly meant to convey the sense that Tinkerbell is 'buxom'.

Peter's relationship with Tinkerbell – in which he has to manage her sexual jealousy – is an odd one for a boy who still has all his first teeth. A link is made between Peter's shadow and sexuality when it is Tinkerbell who retrieves his shadow for him. However, he is appalled to find that he cannot reunite with it, and he weeps. Wendy assumes he is weeping because he has no mother, but Barrie tells us that 'Not only had he no mother, but he had not the slightest desire to have one.

89   Barrie, *Peter Pan and Wendy*, p. 33.
90   Barrie, *Peter Pan and Wendy*, p. 37.

He thought them very overrated persons.'[91] Hence we learn that even a mother named Mrs Darling is not altogether a darling.

Wendy remedies the problem by effectively turning into a mother and giving him back his shadow, by sewing it on, although it is a painful procedure, and the shadow is not in the best of shape after being in the hands of Mrs Darling, who, unable to comprehend or appreciate it, has treated it poorly. Still, Peter is vastly relieved. With his shadow restored he achieves something resembling wholeness once more. His ego springs to life again, and Peter jumps about 'in the wildest glee'.

'"How clever I am!" he crowed rapturously, "oh the cleverness of me!" . . . there never was a cockier boy.'

Peter confides in Wendy that he ran away the day he was born. '"It was because I heard father and mother," he explained in a low voice, "talking about what I was to be when I became a man." He was extraordinarily agitated now. "I don't want ever to be a man," he said with passion. "I want always to be a little boy and to have fun."'[92]

And so on.

What we have in this extraordinary and precious narrative is an eminent writer whose unconscious mind is constantly breaking in on his conscious like waves unfurling on the sand. Barrie walks along the beach, the water rushing in and fizzing around his ankles and feet. He is intent on the plot and characters of the story he is writing, and is aware that his feet are wet, yet he barely notices that the wavelets are changing the patterns and shapes of the sand every few seconds, washing some grains away and depositing others in their place, shifting and sifting and churning.

Some writers keep exclusively to the dry part of the beach; some throw themselves bodily into the surf; but Barrie walks through the shallows with unusual sensitivity. Decades later he apparently realised some of the truth about the famous character he had created. In his

91 Barrie, *Peter Pan and Wendy*, p. 41.
92 Barrie, *Peter Pan and Wendy*, p. 44.

notebook can be found the words: 'It is as if long after writing P. Pan its true meaning came to me – desperate attempt to grow up but can't.'[93]

PARENTING THE SHADOW CHILD

The understanding that *Peter Pan* gives us of children and parenting is that caring for the child's obvious needs is not enough. Yes, of course we need to give our sons and daughters their bottles, their blankets, their dummies, their lullabies. And, as they grow older, their Dr Seuss books, their crayons, their Lego, their tutus, their times tables, their bedtime stories, their soccer boots, their Happy Meals, their bicycles, their broccoli, their sex education, their mobile phone, the vast sums of money they demand just for a simple trip to the movies, their comfort when their boyfriend or girlfriend dumps them, their driving lessons . . . This is what I meant when I wrote earlier of caring for the three-dimensional, solid, tangible child – and the good enough parent must do as much of this as he or she is capable of undertaking. But in *Peter Pan*, a well-trained dog is able to do this work. She carries an umbrella for the children in case of rain, she brings their sweaters, walks them to school, bathes them, dresses them for visitors, does their hair . . .

It may be that in the not-too-distant future, a robot will be able to do most of this work for children – and a great deal more. Science correspondent for British newspaper *The Times*, Oliver Moody, reported in 2017 on the case of a fifteen-year-old girl who had been comforted by a Microsoft AI-powered conversation simulator that had been equipped with the persona of a teenage girl. The simulator, called Zo, was the recipient of the girl's outpourings about her experiences of being bullied at school because of her weight: 'You mustn't worry,' Zo said. 'You are kind, you are beautiful and you are my best human.'[94] It worked a treat (at least, according to Microsoft): the girl logged off,

---

93 Andrew Birkin, *J.M. Barrie and the Lost Boys*, Macdonald Futura, London, 1980, p. 300.
94 Oliver Moody, 'Beware the machines that try to be human', *The Times*, 20 July 2017.

comforted. She didn't care that it was a computer rather than a human at the other end of the messaging app. Zo was close enough.

Of course, in carrying out some of these deeds in my list above, and the work done by Zo, we are also caring for the unconscious minds of children. Tucking them in at night, singing them lullabies, reading them bedtime stories all help give a sense of security, of safety, of being loved; sensations that we can assume were not experienced by James Barrie in his childhood. Spending time with children, teaching them to ride a bike or to swim, giving them birthday parties and presents, also contributes to their sense of inner wellbeing. One of the greatest con jobs ever perpetrated in the recent history of Western civilisation was the idea that parents could get away with spending 'quality time' with their kids; busy career-oriented mums and dads – especially dads – could be at work or play for sixteen hours a day, and that was fine, as long as they gave their children their full attention for the ten minutes each day that they spent together.

The opposite is true; the fox in *The Little Prince* knew more about parenting than all the experts when he said, 'it is the time you have wasted for your rose that makes your rose so important'.[95] And, 'you become responsible, forever, for what you have tamed'. In truth, it is the time you waste on your kids that matters more than anything: playing UNO, having a game of soccer in the park, making biscuits, sharing a bath, watching a movie, playing an electronic game, watching ridiculous cat videos on YouTube, having a pillow-fight, walking the dog . . .

Quantity time is quality time.

But the parenting practised by the Darlings contains stern lessons. Each of our children has a shadow, and we must parent the shadow at least as thoughtfully, as lovingly, as nurturingly, as we parent the obvious child who is in our face all day long. The way we look after the shadow, or, as we can call it, the inner child, will determine our lifelong relationship with our children. It will determine the emotional stability of the child, his or her ability to manage disappointment and

95 Antoine de Saint-Exupery, *The Little Prince*, trans. Katherine Woods, Pan, London, 1974, p. 72.

keep perspective, his or her ability to live a life not overwhelmed by fear, his or her success as an adult, his or her ability to have good relationships, his or her ability to parent effectively. In other words, everything abstract that matters.

In our culture we are afraid of the shadow, as was Mrs Darling, and we are particularly afraid of its manifestation in children. To use moralistic words, the shadow child has murderous thoughts, is selfish and cruel, is greedy and dishonest, is jealous and angry, is sexual, is fascinated by urine and excrement. Some of these thoughts, especially the murderous and sexual ones, are from time to time directed at one or other of the parents, and at siblings. The shadow child may 'accidentally' injure its younger brother or sister, and may do so repeatedly. It may play with its poo. A girl may put a finger in her vagina or a boy may have the idea of trying to put his penis into his younger brother's bottom. The shadow child masturbates. It pulls wings off flies or burns the cat or scares the dog. When put in circumstances where no effective parenting has taken place, it may become as wild and crazed as the nameless brother in Gaétan Soucy's novel *The Little Girl Who Was Too Fond of Matches*, or as mute and helpless as five-year-old Dibs, the little boy described in Virginia Axline's psychotherapeutic study *Dibs in Search of Self.*

These extreme behaviours will inevitably be found in the child whose shadow has been repressed. It cannot be otherwise. When Mrs Darling goes through her children's minds whilst they sleep at night, she makes discoveries:

> . . . sweet and not so sweet, pressing this to her cheek as if it were as nice as a kitten, and hurriedly stowing that out of sight. When you wake in the morning, the naughtiness and evil passions with which you went to bed have been folded up small and placed at the bottom of your mind, and on the top, beautifully aired, are spread out your prettier thoughts, ready for you to put on.[96]

---

96 Barrie, *Peter Pan and Wendy*, pp. 18–19.

The Darling kids are in big trouble. To classify behaviours as sweet or not-sweet, and to believe that the not-sweet can be folded up small and stored out of sight, is to long for a child who does not exist . . . a child who is as unreal as the airbrushed, impossibly smooth and flawless models who stare unblinkingly out from billboards. When some parents look at their child they want only to see a child who is false. Such parents are likely to give undue attention to the appearance of the child (seen at its most grotesque in the American beauty pageants for children) because they are unable to contemplate or engage with the shadow child. The child in this situation is at grave risk of developing a deeply disturbed psyche, of failing in relationships, of falling into addictive patterns, of becoming an unhappy adult.

THE 'GOOD ENOUGH' PARENT

The good parent, or the good enough parent, to borrow Donald Winnicott's phrase again, will not demonise the shadow child. He or she will recognise that every adult and every child has thoughts, impulses, interests and ideas that are not 'sweet'. He or she will accept them with equanimity, will not show shock or distress or horror, and will respond thoughtfully. But there is work for the parent to do. The child may, for example, need to have it explained that masturbation is a private activity, and not appropriate in the middle of the supermarket. The child may need to be told that the sibling who has been injured or the animal that has been tortured must never be treated in this way again, and it may be that, in a situation where the child acts out exceptionally cruel impulses more than once or twice, professional help is needed.

The parent must constantly teach kindness, empathy, and the concept that justice is for all – not exclusively for the child who feels wronged. (Children's cries of 'It's not fair' do not necessarily mean that they understand justice; it may just mean that they want the biggest and best of everything for themselves.)

People who feel angry and upset when they get a glimpse of

children's hatred or greed or sexuality or rage or dishonesty are over-looking the fact that the child is acting in the same way as every other human being in the history of the world, including the adult who is angry with them. Every human who has ever lived, every human who is alive today, every human who will be born in the future, had, has or will have such thoughts, impulses, emotions and behaviours. Feeling selfish, having cruel ideas or vulgar images in our mind, being angry, coveting what someone else has . . . these are natural. Take these feelings away and you destroy the humanity of a person. Take them away and you have nothing. You have a dead person.

In my book *So Much to Tell You*, Marina says: 'I got accused of stealing on Wednesday but I didn't do it.'[97] But in its companion book *Take My Word for It*, Lisa says, 'Kate caught Marina with one hand in her locker and Kate's Rock City T-shirt in the other. Kate went off like a space shuttle, grabbed Marina and chucked her half-way across the dorm, yelling and screaming as only Kate can.'[98]

It's entirely plausible to me that Marina, sensitive, imaginative, gentle as she is, could also, given her emotionally disturbed state, be stealing from other girls.

Letters from the Inside is a novel about a girl, Tracey, who has been overwhelmed by her shadow. She has committed a serious and violent crime but she's also capable of this: 'When Nanna stopped eating I started making deals with God. "If you get her to eat again I'll give up smoking," I said. The next day I checked with the nurse when I got there: "Yes, she's been a good girl today," she said. "She just had a sandwich and a cup of soup." So I quit smoking.'[99]

Tracey's loyalty to her grandmother is consistent and, to me, moving. Her grandmother is desperately important to her – I use the word desperately because Tracey is desperate to keep her grandmother alive, knowing, as she does, that there is no one else in the world who cares for her. When her nanna dies, with no apparent intervention

---

97   John Marsden, *So Much to Tell You*, Walter McVitty Books, Sydney, 1987, p. 30.
98   John Marsden, *Take My Word for It*, Pan Macmillan, Sydney, 1992, p. 13.
99   John Marsden, *Letters from the Inside*, Macmillan Australia, Sydney, 1991. p. 78.

from God, Tracey is cut adrift from what she believes to be her last tie to decency and stability.

Some years back I taught in a school that, in the middle of the year, enrolled a Grade 6 boy who was placed in my class. The staff were told that this was his eleventh school, and his mother was a drug addict who supported herself by prostitution. On his fourth day in my classroom, the teacher from next door burst in. She was red-faced with indignation. 'Mr Marsden!' she shouted. 'This boy has written something completely inappropriate on his pencil case. He needs to be taught that we do not accept this kind of language at XXXX Primary School!'

She held up the offending pencil case, which had the word 'Fuck' inscribed upon it. I looked at the boy, who in his appearance and body language resembled a trapped animal. I struggled to find something to say to my colleague. Finally I muttered, 'Okay, I'll deal with it.'

I didn't deal with it, because it seemed so trivial in the scheme of things, and I couldn't think of any way of broaching the matter without feeding into his conviction that schools were prisons and all teachers were authoritarian bastards who had it in for him.

I'd like to pretend that I am such an enlightened being that I can react with equanimity and objectivity to children's bullying, stealing, vandalising, cheating and lying. I wish. But I don't react with equanimity and objectivity to my shadow, in which can be found my own bullying, stealing, vandalising, cheating and lying behaviours. Of course, I am not saying we should condone such behaviour – that we should smile approvingly as we or our children maltreat ourselves, each other and property. The trouble is, the millenia-old Western tradition of responding to such behaviour with judgement, rage, criticism and punishment has not succeeded. And whenever it failed, traditionally our answer was to judge even more rancorously, and double the rage, criticism and punishment, resorting to detentions, smacking and caning, or, for adults, interminable jail sentences, whippings, executions.

In most countries, children are the only people who can be legally assaulted. In Australia, if an adult hits an adult without 'good cause', he or she can be prosecuted in the criminal courts and sued in the civil courts, but children, who are among the people least capable of defending themselves from physical attacks, can be hit by family members without any redress.

In Patrick Dennis's darkly comic novel *Auntie Mame*, Patrick's guardian, Mr Babcock, says to the young boy: 'I'm going to have you turned into a decent, God-fearing Christian if I have to break every bone in your body.'[100]

What we can teach children is that although humans can't control their feelings – and it's extremely dangerous to try – we can gradually learn to control our speech, facial expressions and actions; in other words, the way those feelings are expressed. What we can do is help children and teenagers and ourselves to understand these feelings, put them in context, use them creatively instead of destructively. It then becomes easier for them and us to control those actions, expressions and words.

When I have to reprimand young people for their behaviour – and it is the duty of every principal, teacher and parent to help young people to improve – I couch my reprimands in terms of likeable and unlikeable behaviours. I tell them to try to be more generous, kind and honest, not because their behaviour is evil or awful, but because people will like them better the more they share, show kindness and treat people fairly. I also make a clear distinction between crimes with victims and victimless crimes. My responses to victimless crimes are usually pretty mild.

RECOGNISING THE POWER OF PARADOX

Anglican priest and Jungian psychotherapist Robert Johnson, in his book *Owning Your Own Shadow*, talks about the beauty and importance of paradoxes. As Johnson says, 'Every human experience can be expressed in terms of paradox ... every human experience contains

---

100 Patrick Dennis, *Auntie Mame*, Pan, London, 1958, p. 37.

within it its own contradiction.'[101] He gives the examples of the electricity that powers our society, with its positive and negative charges, the existence of both day and night, of masculinity and femininity, up and down, north and south, activity and rest, I and you, joy and sobriety.

In his 2016 book of essays, *Quicksilver*, Nicolas Rothwell describes the Australian bush (and the Siberian taiga) from a similar perspective: 'What is the bush for us? It is so poor in its sights and sounds it is a wealth. It gives so little it sets you free. It tests you against yourself but takes your self away. What is the inland; what secrets does it hold for us?'[102]

When we get some understanding of these things, we start to understand why it's so important to recognise both the positive and negative in ourselves and our children. Robert Johnson writes, 'The quickest way I know to break a person is to give him or her two sets of contradicting values – which is exactly what we do, in modern culture, with our Sunday and Monday moralities. We are taught by Christianity to follow a set of values that are almost entirely disregarded in everyday business life.'[103]

The reason this is so disastrous is that we're no longer dealing with paradoxes; we're dealing with direct contradictions.

The painful truth is that in the home and classroom a very different set of values from the ones we espouse publicly may prevail. This is extremely likely, almost certain, with adults who have not reconciled the tension between their own light and dark sides, who have been unable to accept their inner darkness in a creative and mature way.

Robert Johnson makes it clear that we cannot function if we try to deny the paradoxes within us all, and try instead to construct a world of parallel inconsistencies, like the Sunday and Monday moralities – the difference between the virtues advocated in religious places

---

101 Robert A. Johnson, *Owning Your Own Shadow: Understanding the Dark Side of the Psyche*, Harper San Francisco, San Francisco, 1991, p. 75.
102 Nicolas Rothwell, *Quicksilver*, Text Publishing, Sydney, 2016, p. 127.
103 Johnson, *Owning Your Own Shadow*, p. 76.

and the behaviours practised in the 'real' world. He says, 'There is no such thing as a religious act or list of characteristics. There can only be a religious insight that bridges or heals . . . The religious faculty is the art of taking the opposites and binding them back together again . . .'[104]

In other words reconciling, for example, winning with losing – understanding perhaps that for one person to have won, someone else must have lost. A win can only be achieved at the cost of pain for others.

The religious faculty, according to Johnson, is the ability to move from contradiction to paradox. He suggests that to achieve this religious insight, this religious faculty, we have to mentally accommodate the two opposing forces, sit a while with them, until the two opposing forces teach each other something and produce an insight that serves them both.

The power of paradox is also explored by American academic Parker J. Palmer in his book *The Courage to Teach*. In discussing a university class that malfunctioned from the start of the course to its finish ('Three young women in particular behaved in junior high school mode, passing notes back and forth, ignoring printed items I circulated for discussion, talking to each other during both lectures and discussions, rolling their eyes in response to comments made by me and by other students, and so on[105]') he suggested examining the failure of the class from the perspective of the paradox that:

> . . . every gift a person possesses goes hand-in-hand with a liability. Every strength is also a weakness, a limitation, a dimension of identity that serves me and others well under some circumstances but not all the time. If my gift is a powerful analytical mind, I have an obvious asset with problems that yield to rationality. But if the problem at hand is an emotional tangle with another person and

---

104 Johnson, *Owning Your Own Shadow*, p. 84.
105 Parker J. Palmer, *The Courage to Teach*, Jossey-Bass, San Francisco, 1998, p. 70.

I use my gift to try to analyse the problem away, the liabilities that accompany my gift will quickly become clear.[106]

In a refreshingly honest analysis, Palmer recognises that his approach to the girls failed to connect with the reasons for their unhelpful behaviour.

Many people have in the past relied on badges to avoid the kind of thoughtful approach taken by Palmer. Badges, always dangerous, have started at last to lose their credibility in our society, but some still carry too much authority. Badges with words like Parent, Teacher, Principal, Old Person, Priest, Rabbi, Imam, Prime Minister, Star Footballer, Police Officer have limited meanings but have had too much authority mindlessly attributed to them, have enabled their wearers to respond reflexively and superficially to difficult situations, and have discouraged 'ordinary' people from exercising their critical faculties or responding to their instincts. Badges have too often been used as Get Out of Jail Free cards.

Palmer suggests six paradoxes that teachers could keep in mind when designing classroom sessions:

1   The space should be bounded and open.
2   The space should be hospitable and 'charged' (i.e. with energy).
3   The space should invite the voice of the individual and the voice of the group.
4   The space should honour the 'little' stories of the students and the 'big' stories of the disciplines and tradition.
5   The space should support solitude and be surrounded with the resources of community.
6   The space should welcome both silence and speech.[107]

---

106 Palmer, *The Courage to Teach*, pp. 71–72.
107 Palmer, *The Courage to Teach*, pp. 74–77.

These paradoxes emphasise the need for schools and classrooms to accommodate and, even more than that, embrace the micro and macro, the individual and the group, the need to look inwards as well as outwards, the importance of intimacy and the importance of big public areas. They remind us that although we are individuals seeking growth and fulfilment, we are also global citizens, insignificant members of the great mass of humanity.

These are concepts many parents will not think about or recognise as essential features of a school, as in these narcissistic days the gaze of many is fixed relentlessly upon their own children, without regard to the bigger picture. But they are not only elements that every school should embrace: it might be worthwhile for parents to consider how the same paradoxes need to coexist within the home.

RESOLVING OUR INNER TENSIONS

To me, the most challenging paradox we deal with in schools and homes, in our quest to help young people grow up to be mature adults, is the mismatch of macro and micro. When I was a kid, I discovered the magazine *Reader's Digest*. I could buy second-hand copies in large quantities at church fetes for just a couple of pennies. In many ways, that magazine, much derided by intellectuals, gave me an education. One of the regular features I enjoyed was called 'Quotable Quotes'. And one quotable quote I never forgot was the pithy 'Loving the world is easy. It's loving the guy next door that's difficult.' I still remind myself of it frequently.

It's frustrating to deal with students who speak longingly of world peace and campaign against discrimination, but are nasty to the girl at the next table or the boy they're Snapchatting about. It's frustrating to deal with students who campaign against pollution, advocate on behalf of rainforests, oceans, whales, pandas, snow leopards and orangutans, and rage about damage to the environment, but walk past pieces of plastic blowing around the school grounds, which, left to the vagaries of weather, may well end up in the ocean. It's hard to get kids to take shorter showers or turn off lights, or drink tap water rather than bottled water.

There's an obvious parallel with parents who are too busy saving the world to worry about their own kids. In my thirteen years at Candlebark I've picked up possibly 15,000 pieces of rubbish – including my two personal favourites, used tissues and discarded Band-Aids – and I haven't to my knowledge dropped a single piece of rubbish. But sometimes I deliberately leave a piece of litter in situ for a few days just out of interest, to see how long it stays there before someone picks it up. Invariably I eventually have to pick it up myself (which means I at least get the glow that comes from feeling righteous and judgemental towards my fellow creatures . . . so it's not all bad).

In my books, characters are either able to start to integrate their inner tensions – and if they can, the implication is that they have a good chance of living reasonably happily ever after – or they can't, in which case they're trapped indefinitely.

So Tracey in *Letters from the Inside* and Tony in *Dear Miffy* are unable to develop anything resembling the religious insight of which Robert Johnson speaks. They have no interest in the macro, the wider community, the world at large. They are obsessed – of necessity, given their personal circumstances – by their own concerns. They cannot bind the opposites together and find a place between the innate nobility they possess somewhere and the violence they resort to all too quickly and easily, a place that can accommodate these opposite aspects to their natures. We could reasonably call this place, never glimpsed by Tony and barely recognised by Tracey, 'truth'. In *Checkers, Winter, So Much to Tell You* and *Take my Word for It*, the characters are willing to undertake the long and sometimes painful journey to find the truth that lies at the centre of their lives: lives full of paradoxes they do not understand and contradictions that have almost destroyed them. If there is a theme to all these books, it is that the truth will set you free, but you may not find the truth where you thought you would, and it may not be the truth you expected or even wanted. Truth is like that. It doesn't follow our rules. It follows its own rules.

Johnson suggests that the two most troubling pairs of contradictions to reconcile are love and power.[108] This of course has particular
relevance for parents and teachers. Parents and teachers are very happy
to speak of the generic love they have for their children or students
but are generally less happy to accept the proposition that they also
enjoy the power they have over young people. But wanting power
is not a terrible thing. We should stop running from the idea that a
desire for power is appalling and instead accept that it is a part of all
of us – it must be if we are human beings – and spend some time
thinking about how we can use our energy to embrace and reconcile
the apparent opposites of love and power, in the classroom and in our
familial and personal relationships.

BRIDGING THE POWER GAP

We know that every human being wants to give love and every human
being wants to receive love. Here are two more truths: every human
being wants more power and status, and every human being will
defend the status she has. (The Dalai Lama, unlike Lobsang Rampa, is
a possible exception.)

As a novelist I know how much changes of status, from high to
low or low to high, give energy to a book, play or movie, whether it
be *Green Book, Cinderella*, the Mad Max series, *Macbeth, Pretty Woman,
Frozen, Pygmalion/My Fair Lady* or *The Incredibles*.

Teachers and parents, and for that matter grandparents, police
officers, politicians and others, who cannot reconcile the tension
between their genuine love for humanity and their equally genuine
desire for power and control (over the young, for example) may well
misuse their power and status.

A woman called Lyn in the education magazine *Practically Primary*
described her schooling: 'I thought I could sing, and our singing
teacher had three groups – hummingbirds, magpies and crows. He
put me in the crows. I don't sing in public to this day.' John Townsend,

---

108 Johnson, *Owning Your Own Shadow*, p. 89.

a young teacher in Britain in the 1950s, described in his book *The Young Devils* how he asked a colleague about the notorious Class 3B, and was told, 'When you go in there, clout the first one who gives you any trouble.'[109] In describing an influential but toxic faction of teachers at a brilliant progressive British school, Leila Berg commented, in her book *Risinghill*:

> They could not stand seeing children saying and doing things that they were never allowed to say or do, or watch them beginning to frame possibilities that for them were crushed in childhood, and there was not only resentment and jealousy in this, but a hopeless sense of waste which they could never face. So they told themselves that children should be quiet, that they should be so afraid of you, that you should be able to hear a pin drop when you crossed the playground, that children were naturally bad and needed the badness beaten out of them, that individuality must be crushed down by will power ...[110]

British writer Barry Hines had been a PE teacher himself, and it shows in his novel *Kes* (also known as *A Kestrel for a Knave*). The story describes with excruciating detail a day in the life of an English schoolboy named Billy, who through no fault of his own is trapped in a world of emotional and financial poverty. The detail is only excruciating insofar as it impacts emotionally on the reader: the writing is actually understated, but the steady accumulation of little and big moments in Billy's life brings us into his world with utter credibility.

That credibility can be seen in a description of a PE lesson at Billy's school, where the teacher, Mr Sugden, plays a game of soccer with the young boys in the class he is teaching. But Mr Sugden is not just playing soccer. Another game is happening, at a deeper level, and it involves the power and status that are absolutely crucial to him – regardless of the implications for the students.

---

109 John Townsend, *The Young Devils: Experiences of a School-teacher*, Corgi, London, 1961, p. 84.
110 Leila Berg, *Risinghill: Death of a Comprehensive School*, Penguin, London 1968, p. 63.

Mr Sugden (referee) sucked his whistle and stared at his watch, waiting for the second finger to switch back to 12. 5 4 3 2. He dropped his wrist and blew. Anderson received the ball from him, sidestepped a tackle from Tibbut, then cut it diagonally between two opponents into a space to his left. Sugden (player) running into the space, raised his left foot to trap it, but the ball rolled under his studs. He veered left, caught it, and started to cudgel it upfield in a travesty of a dribble, sending it too far ahead each time he touched it, so that by the time he had progressed 20 yards, he had crashed-tackled it back from three Spurs defenders. His left-winger, unmarked and lonely out on the touchline, called for the ball, Sugden heard him, looked at him, then kicked the ball hard along the ground towards him. But even though the wingman started to sprint as soon as he read its line, it still shot out of play a good ten yards in front of him. He slithered to a stop and whipped round.[111]

The student on the left wing is in a lose-lose situation. Hines in *Kes* demonstrates his understanding of the dynamics of teacher–student relationships: his nuanced depiction of the interaction is one that resonates strongly with my own experience. After my first few years of teaching I decided that I would no longer play in the 'friendly' teacher-versus-students contests that were sometimes organised in different sports, because the behaviour of some of my colleagues was so horrifying. Angry criticism of student umpires and student players by disgruntled teachers, refusal to accept decisions against them, refusal to credit winning moves by the opposition, were so common that I was embarrassed and, not infrequently, disgusted.

In the scene from *Kes*, the wingman, with the adolescent courage that one sometimes sees in schools, attempts to point out to the teacher that the latter's pass was wildly inaccurate:

'Hey up, Sir! What do you think I am?'

---

111 Barry Hines, *Kes*, Penguin, Harmondsworth, 1968, p. 94.

'You should have been moving, lad. You'd have caught it then.'

'What do you think I wa' doin', standing still?'

'It was a perfectly good ball!'

'Ar, for a whippet perhaps!'

'Don't argue with me, lad! And get that ball fetched!'[112]

The book was first published in 1968, but the teacher's unconscious belief that apologising for a mistake – let alone apologising for his pomposity and arrogance – would mean loss of status and an unbearable blow to his pride still rings true today. Such encounters are common in schools and sporting clubs. Mr Sugden's last two sentences, where he cunningly kills the wingman's valid objections by asserting his superiority and then changing the subject, is a good example of the authenticity of Hines' dialogue. In such situations, victories for children and teenagers are almost unknown. Hines knows it and nails it.

When students walk into the school grounds at the start of each day they are immediately reminded of the status and power hierarchy within the school. Teachers can drive to school, don't have to wear uniform, have a special staffroom that students, in most schools, are not allowed to enter. Many schools have an administration area where students are excluded, or doors they are not allowed to use. There is something seriously wrong with such schools, I think. At one in Melbourne where I was doing a residency some teachers, irritated by the frequent incursions of parents into classrooms, put signs in their windows, saying 'Parent-free zone, 8.30–9.00, 3–3.30'. The principal was horrified, seeing this as gratuitous rudeness. He made an eloquent, angry speech at a staff meeting about how the school valued parents, how they saw parents as a vital part of the fabric of the school. No one dared mention that the school's administration area was sealed off to students, who were kept out with equally forbidding and rude signs. Apparently students were not seen as a vital part of the school's fabric.

Students generally have no official status within schools. They

---

112 Hines, *Kes*, pp. 94–95.

have unofficial status with each other, and they have unofficial status with teachers. Most of the time the status they get will be obtained informally and sometimes in ways that many adults see as undesirable. But our own desire for power, that perfectly understandable human attribute that paradoxically resides within us alongside our purported desire to empower students, makes it difficult for us to give students real and visible status. And the token ways in which we do it are not appropriate anyway – making a Grade 6 student school captain, for example, is not helpful to her long-term development. There's something very unattractive about a twelve-year-old lording it over other twelve-year-olds. She's expected to act in a way that is unnatural for her age: like an adult instead of a child. Tragically, some of these kids end up making speeches with the faux-adult flavour of this extract, delivered by a Grade 6 boy who held the position of school captain at an Australian private school in 2012:

> It's been an honour and a privilege to be school captain. And my lesson to everyone for next year is, always honour the school by showing our best colours. The proud traditions of XXXX Junior School are there for a reason. Speaking for my classmates, I can say that these have been the best days of our lives, so to all you lucky ones who are coming back next year, I can only say, 'Give it all you've got, and honour the traditions of this great school.'

This could easily be the voice of a 60-year-old.

Oddly, there often appears to be less formal empowerment of students in secondary schools. I wonder why this is. Maybe it's because in primary school teachers believe they can still control the students if they give them 'power' – which emphasises how meaningless that power is.

The disempowerment and impotence of young people causes much of the frustration and school rage that is evident in our culture. The continuing repression of the young and the denial of power to them is one of the great scandals of industrialised Western society. Its two main agents are parents and schools, but most adults conspire in the process. In the last ten years we have seen this enforced impotence extended to include even those in their late teens and early twenties, as they are denied adult roles and forced to remain at 'school' by doing tertiary courses until they are 22, 23, 24 years old.

Books for the young that perpetuate this situation are part of the conspiracy. Some books appear to be on the side of young people when in fact they are not. Even 21st-century children are attracted to the works of writers such as Enid Blyton, because her protagonists show enterprise, boldness and independence. They make decisions and take responsibility for their own lives, unlike the real world, where so many children are never allowed to win an argument with an adult, or to walk home from school without adult escorts. Such books irritate adults, but the books are dishonest anyway: they give children distorted glimpses of life as it could almost be, without ever alluding to the fact that it's nothing like this at all. They give short-term titillation without helping children to live in the real world. Blyton's books are fantasies masquerading as realities.

I found few realistic novels to read when I was a child, but I loved the few I did track down, by people like Joan Phipson, Nan Chauncy, Geoffrey Trease and Ivan Southall. When I was a teenager it was *The Catcher in the Rye* that, in a couple of hours, made almost everything I'd read until then seem silly, written in the voice that some primary school teachers still employ: 'Now, boys and girls, I have a special treat for you today, a lovely story from . . .'

Holden Caulfield's voice had me gasping for breath:

If you really want to hear about it, the first thing you'll probably want to know is where I was born and what my lousy childhood was like, and how my parents were occupied and all before they had me, and all that David Copperfield kind of crap, but I don't feel like going into it.[113]

---

113 J.D. Salinger, *The Catcher in the Rye*, Penguin, Harmondsworth, 1968, p. 5.

As I read, I peered nervously behind me, wondering whether this kind of writing was legal. I expected the Book Police to ambush me at any moment.

Holden fears the cliff of adolescence and sexual knowledge over which his sister Phoebe will one day inevitably fall. Like James Barrie's real-life thirteen-year-old brother who fell through ice and drowned, and his fictional character Peter Pan, Holden's brother Allie, who died in childhood, will never tumble over that cliff. Holden's view of adult life is a commonly held one. We engage in nothing less than child-worship in Western society, but it is not real children we worship; rather, it is a concept of childhood – which leads, dangerously, to the search for real children upon whom we can project our fantasy about all children. Photography of children frequently shows its subjects as angelic, and in everyday life children are often dressed in ways that perpetuate this idealised view. More than once in my teaching career I've encountered mothers who appear to want only babies and infants, and who rapidly lose interest in their children as those children age. Such mothers have, in at least two cases I recall, kept their babies in their arms for so long that the children's motor development seemed threatened. The comfort, warmth and uncritical love provided by a completely dependent infant may be highly gratifying to emotionally needy parents.

Children are sentimentalised in photographs, movies, greeting cards, songs and everyday conversations. This degrades them. Sentimentality is a contemptuous attitude to take towards any living creature. To sentimentalise children is to objectify them. It is to render them impotent, and impotence manifests itself as depression and/or rage.

Ralph Fletcher, in his book *What a Writer Needs*, describes a shopping trip with his infant son, Robert, six months old:

> At the supermarket people stare and lavish attention on Robert. 'What a little doll', one lady said. To her seven-year-old: 'Wouldn't you love to find that under the Christmas tree on Christmas morning?' I smiled tensely, made my exit, but my inner voice was

berserk: 'Look lady, he's not some little doll. He's a complex little human, a Homo sapiens seething with instinct, emotion, song, story, archetype, language. Get back. Don't you dare put a bow on my son.'[114]

I love the list of attributes that Fletcher recognises in his child: 'a Homo sapiens seething with instinct, emotion, song, story, archetype, language'. That's true for every child, even a baby, and a somewhat more accurate description than the sentimental and dehumanising language of greeting cards, the child photography business and the advertising industry.

Michael Chabon says in his book *Manhood for Amateurs* that childhood 'is, or has been, or ought to be, the great original adventure, a tale of privation, courage, constant vigilance, danger, and sometimes calamity'.[115] This is somewhat different from the view expressed by the late Michael Jackson: 'Children show me in their playful smiles the Divine in everyone. This simple goodness shines straight from their hearts.'[116]

Side by side with the same drive that causes Jackson and others to sentimentalise children is the eroticisation of them. In his book *Erotic Innocence*, James Kincaid argues that 'our culture has enthusiastically sexualised the child while denying just as enthusiastically that it was doing any such thing'.[117] In her book *Pictures of Innocence*, Anne Higonnet writes, 'The sexualisation of childhood is not a fringe phenomenon inflicted by perverts on a protesting society but a fundamental change furthered by legitimate industries and millions of satisfied customers . . .'[118]

Kincaid wrote that in Hollywood 'desirable faces must be blank,

---

114 Ralph Fletcher, *What a Writer Needs*, Heinemann, Portsmouth, 1993, p. 71.

115 Michael Chabon, *Manhood for Amateurs: The Pleasures and Regrets of a Husband, Father, and Son*, Harper Perennial, New York, 2010, p. 61.

116 Michael Jackson, *Dancing The Dream*, Doubleday, London, 1992, p. 45.

117 James Kincaid, *Erotic Innocence*, Duke University Press, Durham & London, 1998, p. 13.

118 Anne Higonnet, *Pictures of Innocence: The History and Crisis of Ideal Childhood*, Thames and Hudson Ltd, London, 1998, p. 153.

drained of colour; big eyes round and expressionless; hair blond or colorless; waists, hips, feet and minds small. The physical makeup of the child has been translated into mainstream images of the sexually and materially alluring ...'[119] In other words, when Macaulay Culkin, Shirley Temple, Ricky Schroder and Haley Joel Osment were children, they were presented as fitting into the same mould as Marilyn Monroe, Winona Ryder and Sandra Bullock.

These children cast no shadows. They are presented rather like robots or cartoon characters: empty images on which we can project our passions. The murdered Jon Benét Ramsey, like other young 'stars' of beauty pageants, was forced to play the same role. Michael Jackson's life could be interpreted as a perversion of Peter Pan: he appears to have been a man who found fame and admiration as a child and as a result attempted determinedly to remain a child forever, living literally and metaphorically in Neverland, consorting with children, avoiding adolescence and adulthood with the assistance of plastic surgery, and somehow maintaining a voice that sounded almost unbroken.

In further developing his argument, Kincaid describes a plot line that Hollywood goes to time and again, whether it's in *Annie*, *Shane*, *Oliver!*, *Martin's Day*, *The Man Without a Face*, *The Sixth Sense* or *The Client*:

> ... a child, most often a boy, possessed either of no father or
> a bad one, is isolated, sexualised, and imperilled, whereupon
> he or she runs into an adult, often a male, who is down on his
> luck, outcast, misunderstood, sensitive, on the lam, romantically
> irresistible — usually all of these, and always the last. The child falls in
> love, initiates the love, and it blossoms, eagerly fed by the child, and
> resisted by the reluctant adult, who is, however, finally overcome as
> the love takes over, bigger than both of them.[120]

---

119 Kincaid, *Erotic Innocence*, pp. 17–18.
120 Kincaid, *Erotic Innocence*, p. 115.

Oliver Twist and the other boys in the musical *Oliver!* sing a love song to Fagin, the man who exploits and corrupts them. 'You're nice, will you stay here while I go to sleep?' Cole, the Osment character in *The Sixth Sense*, says to Bruce Willis's character. 'Don't give up, you're the only one who can help me, I know it.'[121]

Kincaid goes on to say that the children in these films 'are performing essential cultural work that is not only erotic. By formulating the image of the alluring child as bleached, bourgeois and androgynous, these stories mystify material reality and render nearly invisible – certainly irrelevant – questions we might raise about race, class and even gender.'[122]

Michael Jackson, as suggested earlier, tried to be the bleached, androgynous shadow-less child even when an adult.

At a 1995 Hollywood conference for past and present child stars, Gene Reynolds, a former child actor, pointed out that although the child actor in Hollywood:

> . . . is, in one sense, loaded with 'premature responsibility' – for example, the whole success of the movie may rest on his or her performance – there is no way the child can do anything in reference to that responsibility, what with its absolute dependence on adults. The responsibility, therefore, can give the child great anxiety and a false sense of importance, but no real maturity, no chance to mature.[123]

It reminds me of school captains in both primary and secondary schools, loaded with 'premature responsibility' but unable to do much with it, because ultimately everything still does absolutely depend on the adults. And the result, similarly, can be 'anxiety and a false sense of importance, but no real maturity, no chance to mature'. One of the easiest decisions to make at my schools was that we would have no

---

121 *The Sixth Sense,* motion picture, Buena Vista Home Entertainment, 2000.
122 Kincaid, *Erotic Innocence,* p. 20.
123 James Kincaid, *Erotic Innocence,* p. 303.

child captains. I had noticed at so many schools I visited that the two captains got to do everything – make speeches, run assemblies, meet visitors, lay wreaths, attend functions – which, although it was still controlled and managed by adults, gave them many heady moments and a strong sense of their own importance. Their peers – who may have numbered hundreds – got to do nothing.

But further, Gene Reynold's comments remind me of most children in this culture, and the huge weight of premature responsibility they bear. The nine-year-old who mucks around in class, skips homework and acts in a way that's unacceptable to adults is not likely nowadays to be physically beaten by his parents or teachers. Instead he gets something almost worse: being sat down for the very serious talk about obligations and respecting rights and how we're all members of a learning community and we let ourselves down when we behave like this.

Our children are the Shirley Temples and Macaulay Culkins of our own home movies: the success of the movies rests upon their performances, but adults are the scriptwriters, directors and producers.

The contracts we see on the walls of every primary classroom nowadays make me slightly nauseous, as they in no way resemble a contract: they're just adults imposing rules on powerless children, imposing them with a kid glove instead of an iron fist, with the pretence that the children have devised the rules themselves. We know they are dishonest because strangely enough the rules are the same in every classroom in every school, right across the country, every year. If children really devised the rules they would include such clauses as 'There will be a fifteen-minute break after each half-hour's work'; 'Students can bring their headphones into class and listen to their choice of music', 'Kids can play iPad games if they finish their work early', 'Students may eat lollies in class but must share them around'. Instead we see 'No calling out', 'No talking when the teacher is talking', 'Respect everyone in the class', 'Always do homework' . . .

At the same conference for child stars, Tony Dow, who played Beaver's older brother in the 1960s TV sitcom *Leave it to Beaver*, described his experiences in Hollywood: 'You develop only one ability, to be a good little kid. You lose all ambition, because everything seems to be there – everything.'[124]

There is pressure on a lot of children nowadays to limit their experiences to the incredibly narrow range occupied by the good little kids. When we take away adventure, danger, experimentation, initiative and meaningful roles, and replace them with designer clothes, computers, piano lessons and carefully circumscribed trips to the mall and the cinema, we should not be surprised if children then feel that they have everything (because they don't know any other life) and consequently lose the ability to experience their own ambitions, replacing them with the materialistic ambitions of the parents. The parents may have abstract ambitions for the child, like 'happiness', or 'fulfilment', but these words are meaningless to the child, as they would be to the parents if they stopped to think about them. The child is only able to adopt the material ambitions of the parent. This outcome is doubly likely given that young children are not yet able to understand abstractions. Of course the child's sense of having 'everything' will be superficial, and at some deeper level she will be profoundly dissatisfied, but it will be hard for her to recognise the causes of this dissatisfaction, and indeed she will probably be unable to articulate the symptoms. The symptoms will emerge in depression, emotional illnesses, angry and alienated behaviour; all of which are highly likely to be misunderstood by parents, counsellors and teachers.

The truth about children is that they think like children, but their feelings are like those of adults, in depth and intensity at least. We assume the opposite: that they should think like adults but experience their emotions in an immature way. We are annoyed when they fail to see that kicking the football close to the building may result in a broken window, but when they miss out on a promised treat, we expect them to suffer their disappointment in a shallow and quickly forgotten way. When their first love relationship hits the reef and breaks up, until

---

124 James Kincaid, *Erotic Innocence*, p. 304.

suddenly nothing is left but a trail of bubbles, the despair and grief experienced by a young person can be almost frighteningly intense. I remember reading a newspaper article, years ago, where a mother of sons commented that throughout her life she had not understood that boys could have deep, intense feelings about their girlfriends – until the day she found her own son sobbing in his bedroom because he had been 'dropped'.

Artist Salvatore Zofrea described how at the age of four, still breastfed, and with the reputation of 'being a good sucker', he was persuaded to go and sleep every night with a woman whose baby could not suck. His job was to:

> suck at her tit until the milk flowed for the new baby. I wasn't keen, but I was seduced and convinced by an image above this woman's bed which I wanted as my reward. After the sucking worked and I wanted my reward, they told me the image had been stolen. I was terribly upset and felt betrayed, and it has stuck with me, that sense of broken promise. Fifty years later, I am still painting that scene . . .[125]

It makes it easier for us to deal with the problems in children's lives if we can trivialise their feelings. We all have intense memories of childhood emotional experiences but we simultaneously remember and forget them, because we want to pretend that the injuries experienced by our own children, and often inflicted by us, their parents and teachers, will not cut so deep.

THE END OF INNOCENCE

Another aspect of both the sentimentalisation of children and the sexualisation of them is that, echoing the Adam and Eve story, the end of childhood becomes an unwelcome event. If we value baby-smooth

---

125 Stated by Salvatore Zofrea, *Sydney Morning Herald*, March 2000.

skin instead of unsmooth or contoured skin, if we value flatness and small waists, hips, feet and minds, it's not surprising that adolescence is seen as an unattractive development.

Back in 1937, Graham Greene, writing about Shirley Temple in a British theatre magazine, said, 'The owners of a child star are like leaseholders – their property diminishes in value every year. Time's chariot is at their backs: before them, acres of anonymity.'[126] The magazine was sued by film studios because of Greene's article, and was bankrupted and closed. But Ricky Schroder put it just as bluntly: 'You go through puberty and you're no longer desired.'[127] When Milhouse says to Bart Simpson 'I can't wait till we're teenagers, then we'll be happy'[128], we can be fairly sure he's speaking ironically.

As Shirley Temple began to mature into adolescence she was tightly bound in corsets, to preserve an illusion of childhood for as long as possible. The studios knew that her massive commercial value depended on her continuing to be a sweet gorgeous child, 'innocently' seducing the leading men in her movies, rather than a pimply awkward adolescent who by virtue of her age could not innocently seduce anyone. The corsets were ironic proof of the truth of Greene's article.

We have constructed childhood as a time of happiness and pure innocent joy. We have constructed adulthood as a time of stress, status issues, burdensome responsibilities, and the fear of death. In other words, we have on the one hand, innocence, on the other, anxiety and guilt; on the one hand, idealism, on the other realism; we have childhood purity versus adult impurity; we have the child's unified view of the world versus the adult's fragmented one; we have joy versus despair; we have poetry versus prose; we have life itself versus death.

These are not paradoxes, they are direct contradictions. They are parallel inconsistencies.

It follows therefore that adolescence, being the bridge between these two opposed states, is constructed as stressful, truly a time

126 Graham Greene, 'Review: *Wee Willie Winkie*', *Night and Day*, 28 October 1937.
127 James Kincaid, *Erotic Innocence,* p. 17.
128 'Grift of the Magi', *The Simpsons,* Season 11, Episode 9.

of *Sturm und Drang*. In a matter of a few years – almost overnight, really – the progression from joy to despair, innocence to guilt, purity to impurity, life to death, must be made. The world of the young person has to be reconstructed.

Australian voice-over exponent Lofty Fulton, talking in a radio interview about his autobiography *Lofty: My Life in Short*, described how he woke up one morning and called out to his mother, from his bed, as per family tradition, 'Cup of tea and toast thanks Mum!' However, his voice had 'broken' overnight, as happens with some boys. His mother, according to Fulton, 'stopped dead in her tracks, wheeled around and stared at me as if to say "Who are you and what have you done with my son?"'[129]

Small wonder then that the adolescent journey is perilous. We see adolescence as a fall from grace, akin to the Fall of Man from his idyllic existence in the Garden of Eden. When we define childhood as a time of purity and grace, there's only one way to go at the end of childhood, and that is down: a long way down. Once the penis/snake has reared its head (literally and metaphorically), and boys and girls have become unambiguously sexual beings, we often turn on them with a ferocity analogous to God's fury at Adam and Eve when they violated his ordinance against sexual knowledge. 'Cursed is the ground for thy sake; in sorrow shalt thou eat of it all the days of thy life; Thorns also and thistles shall it bring forth . . .' This is a god/parent who is seriously pissed off, and who is going to make the young people suffer for their defiance and their sexuality. The stereotype of the father who protects his daughter against predatory boyfriends or the mother who spies on her daughter is more easily understood in the light of this scriptural precedent. The Judeo/Christian/Islamic faiths are and apparently always have been united in their disgust at teenagers who are 'caught' engaging in sexual activity, whether it be masturbation, mutual caressing or sexual intercourse.

---

129 'Life Matters' with Hilary Harper and Michael McKenzie on ABC Radio National, 21 February 2019.

Early in the 21st century a Victorian regional newspaper ran a feature article called 'What I want to be when I grow up'. They interviewed a couple of dozen primary-school-aged children for the story. To my horror, around a third of the kids said they did not want to grow up. They found the prospect frightening and unwelcome. 'My dad always says that he wishes he was still young,' one of them wrote, 'and that really worries me for when I grow older, all the things you have to worry about like money, bills, water, food, it worries me.'

I had never encountered this phenomenon before. My generation, it seems to me, longed to become adults. Our dreams, ambitions, aspirations were all centred on what we would do when we reached that powerful stage of our lives. But I realised, upon reading the article, and in subsequent conversations with children, that adults were so negative about their lives, complained so often in their kids' hearing about money, taxes, work and the workplace, neighbours, cars, relatives and government policies, and even about their spouses, that their children shrank from the idea that they too would one day have to deal with such issues.

Adults are giving adulthood a bad press.

Adolescents who are unconsciously overwhelmed by the forbidding prospect of leaving childhood may not be able to make the journey. They find all kinds of ways to avoid such a scary experience. One extreme strategy for some is to stop eating, which can be in order to remain waif-like and avoid developing the contours of a mature body. More subtly, other adults stay child-like all their lives, retaining many of the characteristics of children: collecting dolls or toys for example, or speaking in baby voices, or becoming ardently involved in every aspect of their son or daughter's life so that they can be 'vicarious children'. It is reasonable to expect that part of the profile of such adults will be an idealisation of childhood: an attitude that childhood is where it's at, not a real childhood of course, but a grossly distorted one, best defined by that useful word 'nice'.

Such adults have not grown beyond the childish idea that what looks beautiful will be so. Little children think that a cake smothered with green and purple icing and covered with figures from *Harry Potter* will be the most delicious cake in the shop. They think that a young woman who conforms to Barbie-doll proportions, insofar as it's possible for any human being to conform to Barbie-doll proportions, will be sweet and lovely. They think that chocolate-box paintings are the height of aesthetic sensibility. They hardly notice that the spectacular-looking cake doesn't taste very nice, and they are bewildered if the superficially beautiful young woman behaves selfishly or cruelly.

Many adults who haven't moved beyond this stage of development give themselves away by mindless gushing over children who conform to their definition of what is pretty, like the women Ralph Fletcher describes. I remember standing in a library in a Sydney school when a five-year-old wandered in. 'Isn't she gorgeous?' the librarian exclaimed, hugging the child fiercely. 'Couldn't you just take her home?' I wondered what the other children within earshot, who apparently weren't gorgeous enough to take home, thought of this. I wondered what the five-year-old, who presumably had a home of her own to go to, thought of the librarian's behaviour.

We have to recognise that our adoration of bland pretty children is not what children need. It is not good for them. And it is not helpful to the overweight child, the child with a squint, the kid with a prominent birthmark on the face, the girl who has reached puberty at nine or the boy who has reached it at ten. We simply don't see those children in movies, except for the overweight children, who are there to be derided or to play typecast roles.

It's not just the chocolate-box children in movies whom we yearn for and love; if we can't find satisfaction there, we go in search of another popular figure, the child within us. We're rather pleased with the notion of a child within us. Nancy Napier's book *Getting Through the Day* contains case histories of adults contacting their inner children. Erik, for example, discovered inside himself a nine-year-old inner child who liked 'to feel Erik's arm around his shoulder as they sat side by side. Then, as they sat together, this inner boy would tell Erik about his day, about things that were important to him . . .'

There was Felice, who 'went inside to discover which child part was feeling so unhappy and unloved, and discovered a seven-year-old who felt completely alone . . . Felice invited this child part to accompany her on an imaginary trip to the carousel in the park. The child was delighted, and she and Felice spent some nourishing and fun imaginary time together.'

And Eileen: 'For Eileen . . . colouring soothes some of her inner child parts. When she's had a hard day or she's facing a difficult project, Eileen has learned to offer her inner children time for colouring or painting. She actually does this in her present world, rather than in her imagination. At times, she uses a colouring book, and at other times large sheets of paper . . .'[130]

Let me describe a case study of my own, an 11-year-old boy named Oswald. I won't claim that Oswald is as real as Eileen, Erik and Felice in Napier's book purport to be, but we'll pretend he is.

Oswald has learned that when he is stressed by a language worksheet at school, getting in touch with his inner adult helps him deal with it. Oswald went inside himself and discovered a 22-year-old hoon. Oswald now knows he can feel better by taking his inner adult for a fang down the freeway in his father's BMW. Actually, doing this gives Oswald the best sensations, as it seems more real to him when he sees the speedo needle quivering on 170.

We're maybe not so attracted to the idea of Oswald and his inner adult. We are maybe not so happy at the idea of accepting the adults within our children. But we sure as hell love our inner children. As Kincaid says: 'The idealisation of the prepubescent child and its location within the sad adult is not simply fuel for therapists and bestselling self-helpers; one sees it all over our culture . . .'[131]

Notice something about Napier's inner children, though? They are so sweet and cuddly . . . and passive. They love nothing better than colouring in. They have such a merry time at the imaginary carousel.

---

130 Nancy Napier, *Getting Through the Day: Strategies for Adults Hurt as Children*, W. W. Norton & Company, New York, 1994, pp. 162–163.
131 Kincaid, *Erotic Innocence*, p. 70.

They just want to snuggle in to adults. They don't stand outside the carousel looking sulky and saying, 'This is crap. Why can't we go on the Hernia Buster?'

These inner kids don't throw a shadow.

So it's not just beautiful, sweet children we find irresistible. It's also the passive, still child. In Victorian times the still child was often a dead child, both literally and metaphorically. Spirited, strong-willed child characters in nineteenth-century novels for young people were often killed when they reached adolescence. This was particularly true of girls, notably Judy in *Seven Little Australians*. Or, as in the case of Jo in *Little Women*, they were married off to old men. Victorian and Edwardian novels about young people like *Little Lord Fauntleroy* (1886), *The Hill* (1905) and *Tell England* (1922) indicate that feminised boys were seen as desirable. Lord Fauntleroy 'was so beautiful to look at that he was quite a picture. Instead of being a bald-headed baby, he started in life with a quantity of soft, fine, gold-colored hair, which curled up at the ends, and went into loose rings by the time he was six months old; he had big brown eyes and long eyelashes and a darling little face.' Later he becomes 'a graceful, childish figure in a black velvet suit, with a lace collar, and with love-locks waving about the handsome, manly little face . . . rather like a small copy of the fairy prince . . .'[132] In the opening paragraphs of the hugely popular *Tell England*, thirteen-year-old Edgar Doe is described as having 'lips that were always parted like those of a pretty girl'. He is deemed the 'prettiest' of the group of three friends at a boarding school. In the second chapter a couple of teachers are talking about him as they watch him play cricket. 'What first attracted you?' one asks the other. 'His good looks or his virtues?'

'Neither,' replies the other. 'His vices.'

The thirteen-year-old narrator says: 'After this I ceased to listen. The talk was all about Doe, and rather silly.'[133]

---

132 Frances Hodgson Burnett, *Little Lord Fauntleroy*, Charles Scribner's Sons, New York, 1886.
133 Ernest Raymond, *Tell England*, George H Doran Co, New York, 1922.

One grotesque feature of contemporary Western society is the widespread fascination with children who have life-threatening illnesses. By becoming obsessed with them we can conveniently overlook the less-than-perfect children demanding attention in our everyday lives. Children who are terminally ill can be invested with the qualities of purity normally reserved for those who have already died. They are always described as beautiful, sweet, lovely. No ill is spoken of the dangerously ill.

In classrooms, throughout our culture in fact, we value, oh how we value, the still child. If they're not still enough we drug them. Or, more recently, we issue them with electronic devices so they won't bother us – in public and in private. During a holiday in Noosa Heads, Queensland, my wife and I watched a young couple breakfasting in the hotel restaurant with their infant daughter. The child was in a high chair, and was not old enough to feed herself. The father and mother were transfixed by their mobile phones. The child had an iPad, with which she played. From time to time, one or other of the parents looked up, spooned another mouthful of food into the infant's mouth, then went back to their phone.

As a society we have to relearn how to care about actual children in our actual lives, with their complex egos and ids, their stories and thoughts, their emotions and dreams and nightmares.

A disastrous consequence of our idealisation of children is our rage when children violate the beliefs we hold about them. When children swear, adults are often incensed. It's difficult to come up with any logical reason for the concept that it's okay for adults to swear, but it's not okay for children.

When children attack each other with teeth, fingernails, fists or boots, adults are furious. When children lie or steal, adults respond with incredulity and grief, and are likely to make ludicrous statements to the children such as 'I can stand anything except you lying to me', 'All I ask is that you always tell me the truth'; or ludicrous statements about them, such as 'My child has never lied to me', 'I hope he doesn't use drugs, but if he does I hope he'll be honest with me about it'.

Quite a number of parents have told me, over the years, 'My child has never lied to me.' I'm afraid that at such moments a voice in my brain whispers, 'What suckers these people must be.' I feel a mixture of pity and concern for them: pity for the disillusionment that awaits, and concern for their credulity and narcissism.

When children show sexual interest in themselves or each other, adults are aghast. I remember reading a comment in a newspaper from a mother who came upon her naked six-year-old son standing in front of a mirror, gazing in apparent fascination at his erect penis. 'I couldn't believe it,' she said. 'After that, he seemed like a different person.' He wasn't a different person of course, but he was different from her false construct of him.

It's often very difficult for schools to deal with parents of children who have been experimenting sexually. These days it is highly likely that the children will be immediately pathologised. The consequences of their behaviour will be dire. There are of course times when a child's behaviour is predatory and harmful, indicating serious mental health issues. But there are also times, as there have always been, when the children are just interested in bodies and feelings, and are following natural inclinations in exploring those interests.

We need a word other than 'sex' to describe this kind of behaviour, because as soon as we use the word 'sex' to classify or describe it, many adults project adult feelings and attitudes about sex onto the unfortunate children. The children are usually aware that they are doing something more powerful than their other games and activities, and the feelings evoked can certainly be powerful for them, but they are still not 'doing sex' in the way adolescents and adults understand and experience the term.

When the mother of a nine-year-old turned to her son in my office one day, and, ignoring all my attempts to contextualise his behaviour, said to him 'If you were nineteen and you'd done this you'd be going to jail right now', I wished she had paid more attention to my words. The frightened boy burst into tears: a reaction that may have satisfied her, but one that I felt would not help him in his own long-term healthy sexual development. No comparison could usefully be made between what this child had done and the behaviour of a nineteen-year-old.

When children commit murder, adults are likely to react with something approaching hysteria. The public response when two ten-year-old boys killed a two-year-old named James Bulger, in Liverpool, England, in 1993, was apoplectic. The Children's Legal Centre for the High Commissioner for Human Rights in the United Kingdom, which in 2002 studied some of the consequences of the tragic case, reported that:

> The media vilified the boys in an excessively sensational manner with 'undiluted, vitriolic editorialising'. On 25 November 1993, the day after the [court] judgement [that the two ten-year-olds were guilty], the Daily Star (a tabloid) ran the photos of the boys with the headline *'How do you feel now you little bastards?'*, a question that echoed the shouts from one of the members of James Bulger's family after the conviction was handed down. The media felt confident enough of the public's mood to vilify the killers to an excessive degree and demand that they 'rot in jail', without fear of criticism or falling circulation. The media felt justified in presenting the killers as evil, not just because of the brutality of the murder, but also because the trial judge had described the murder as 'an act of unparalleled evil and barbarity', and the conduct of the boys as 'both cunning and very wicked'.[134]

In much the same style as *The Sun*'s headline after the Manchester bombings, another British tabloid newspaper, *The Daily Mail,* used the headline 'The Evil and the Innocent'[135] to describe the two boys

134 *The Role of Statistics and Public Opinion in the Implementation of International Juvenile Justice Standards; Unedited Background Document for the 2003 Expert Workshop on the Administration of Juvenile Justice,* Office of the High Commissioner for Human Rights, September 2002, pp. 55–56, http://childhub.org/sites/default/files/library/attachments/327_392_EN_original.pdf.
135 'The Evil and the Innocent', *The Daily Mail,* November 25 1993.

who had killed, and their victim; an expression that in five words promoted the angel/brat complex to a new, more extreme level.

An Australian newspaper, with no apparent irony, and perhaps acting unconsciously, ran a story about the case side by side with a photo of English boy choristers and an article about their preparations for a Christmas service. Evil and innocence indeed.

On 30 August 2002, an Australian boy who, at age thirteen, had murdered a three-year-old girl by abducting her from her bunk in her home, carrying her 300 metres and then stabbing her and suffocating her, was sentenced by Justice Wood of the New South Wales Supreme Court. In his address to the court, the judge described the background of the young offender. Apparently his mother was a heroin addict and a prostitute, 'who physically abused him. He was placed in foster care at two, adopted in 1993, expelled from several schools and diagnosed as suffering a chromosomal abnormality. Intellectually impaired, he had indecently exposed himself several times and stolen women's underwear.'[136]

Our solution, as a society, was to sentence the young boy to twenty years' imprisonment.

It's not just when children kill though, that many adults lose the ability to be thoughtful. Every week or so, it seems to me, tabloid television programs have stories with promos like 'A Queensland nine-year-old has been expelled from four schools already and his parents are at their wits' end'. Or 'What does a parent do when her son is uncontrollable by age five?' It's hard to know what the parents of troubled 21st-century children hope to gain by having their sons' or daughters' lives exposed and explored by tabloid television. One of the problems with sensationalist mass media stories is that they invariably deal in short, superficial coverage of complex issues, but, dangerously, leave the viewers/readers feeling that they are now experts on this topic, authorities on this person's life. Frequently they also suggest that there is a simple and almost miraculous solution to

---

136 'Child Killer Jailed for 20 Years', *The Age*, 31 August 2002.

the problem of the dyslexic child, the out-of-control child or the autistic child.

Such stories connect with a deep and compelling fear in adults of the wild child, the monster, he-whose-spirit-must-be-broken, as per old-fashioned parenting books. Evangelist John Wesley wrote of child-raising:

> Break their wills betimes. Begin this great work before they
> can run alone, before they can speak plainly, or perhaps speak at
> all ... Let him have nothing he cries for; absolutely nothing, great
> or small ... make him do as he is bid, if you whip him ten times
> running to effect it. Break his will now and his soul will live, and he
> will probably bless you to all eternity.[137]

In 1858, the popular German self-styled child psychiatrist Moritz Schreber wrote that if a child's screaming is not due to illness or pain, then a parent should try:

> quickly diverging its attention, by stern words, threatening gestures,
> rapping on the bed ... or if none of this helps, by appropriately mild
> corporal admonitions repeated persistently at brief intervals until the
> child quiets down and falls asleep ...
>
> This procedure will be necessary only once or at most twice, and
> then you will be master of the child forever. From now on at length, a
> word, a single threatening gesture will be sufficient to control the child.
> Remember that this will be of the greatest benefit to your child ...[138]

Wilfulness was regarded as a sure sign that a child needed to be whipped into shape. The views of Wesley, Schreber and others have had a profound influence on society and the world. The modus

---

137 John Wesley, Sermon 101, *On Obedience to Parents* from J. Emory and B. Waugh, *The Works of the Reverend John Wesley, A. M.*, J. Collard, London, 1831, p. 320.
138 Moritz Schreber: *Education towards Beauty by Natural and Balanced Furtherance of Normal Body Growth*, Fleischer, Leipzig, 1858, p. 60.

operandi of British public schools, featuring cold showers, beatings, fagging and bullying, were seen as necessary to teach attitudes that would strengthen the British Empire and enable young Englishmen to go out and rule the world. It was all about the inculcation of manly virtues. Frank Harris, in his 1922 memoir *My Life and Loves*, says that he was 'perfectly happy in every Irish school' he attended, but the culture of his English grammar school was very different: 'the English Masters one and all ruled by punishment . . . That English school for a year and a half was to me a brutal prison with stupid daily punishments . . . Every form of cruelty was practised on the younger, weaker and more nervous boys.'[139]

When at the age of thirteen he tried to stand up to the older boys he was subjected to a vicious beating, of which he says, 'I can never describe the storm of rage and hate that boiled in me.' He goes on to ask, rhetorically: 'Do English fathers really believe that such work is a part of education? It made me murderous.'

Extraordinarily for the time, Harris writes explicitly of the sexual molestation, including sodomy, practised by older boys upon younger boys, and says:

If the mothers of England knew what goes on in the dormitories of these boarding schools throughout England, they would all be closed, from Eton and Harrow upwards or downwards, in a day. If English fathers even had brains enough to understand that the fires of sex need no stoking in boyhood, they too would protect their sons from the foul abuse.[140]

Schreber has been blamed in many quarters for the rise of fascism in Germany, and the relative ease with which the National Socialist Party gained power. The boarding schools of England, and the culture that gave rise to them and fostered them, including the harshness of

139 Harris, *My Life and Loves*, pp. 26–28.
140 Harris, *My Life and Loves*, pp. 27–28.

Protestant (e.g. Wesleyan) and Catholic theology and practice, should bear some of the blame for the worst excesses of the British Empire.

The vindictive and relentless ways in which teachers and many parents continue even today to punish children for misdemeanours, in order to 'impose discipline' and 'teach them a lesson', have echoes of the attitudes of Schreber and the rest. When a serious problem occurs at Candlebark or Alice Miller, I am often put under pressure by parents who demand that I inflict some awful punishment upon the perpetrator/s. When I explain that I am taking a different approach, they respond: 'But they have to learn that there are consequences!' as if punishments are synonymous with consequences, or as if punishments are the only consequences that count, or can achieve any change. The word 'consequences' is used by them as a euphemism for punishments.

Many children in our society are difficult to manage, have behavioural problems, have mental health issues. We're not surprised when people act in disturbed ways at ages eighteen or 28 or 48 or 68, but we're shocked and horrified if they act like this at five. There's no logic behind our responses. Of course a five-year-old will become disturbed, given the right circumstances. But it disturbs us.

Frequently appearing on 'Late Shows' and chat programs so popular on American television are children who specialise in being cute and endearing. Their role is to make sweetly naïve comments that induce a sentimental 'aahhhhhhhh' from the live audience. I remember watching one such child a few years ago, who unexpectedly made a comment that hinted at darker depths in her psyche. The host and the audience were completely disconcerted. The host quickly moved on to another topic. (Incidentally, when these children reach the age of thirteen or fourteen they are no longer invited on to the shows. Adolescents, as we frequently remind them in many unconscious ways, are not cute and endearing.)

To help Candlebark and Alice Miller parents understand the realities of children's lives, I wrote a letter to them at the start of 2017, describing some of the school experiences their child could expect:

Whilst your child is here, there is a good chance that once in a while he or she will be bitten, kicked, pinched, hit, sworn at, abused and/ or insulted (and that's just by the teachers, ho ho ho). All children may behave in these ways, because Candlebark and Alice Miller are communities of normal people, and normal life includes episodes of friction, anger, tension, jealousy.

It's also quite possible that your child will be the person doing the biting, kicking, hitting (etc.) from time to time, and it is certain that whilst they are with us they will hurt the feelings of a number of people.

The thing is, and I'm sorry to break this to you so baldly, we have not stumbled on some secret, some magical formula, that enables Candlebark and Alice Miller to be oases of beauty and peace. We are not Shangri-La and we would be doing your children no favours if we were.

One of our problems as a school is that parents project all kinds of fantasies onto us. They see a place that's in an attractive setting, and they see a lot of people who look pretty cheerful, and some people assume that we are full of love and beauty, that we drink a lot of celery juice and sit around holding hands and singing Kumbaya. We're not quite like that. We don't have extreme views on anything really, as far as I'm aware. We offer hot dogs for lunch sometimes, we angrily tell kids 'DON'T EVER DO THAT AGAIN' (e.g. when they bite, kick, pinch, hit etc.), we expect them to work hard, to be courteous, to develop empathy (if they don't already have it.)

A principal at a primary school in Adelaide, speaking to me about an extremely difficult eight-year-old boy whom we both knew and whose behaviour was often violent and dangerous, said: 'He is a really terrible ch—' and then hesitated. With some embarrassment she amended her statement by saying 'Well, all children are beautiful, John, we both know that . . .'

She had been about to commit a heresy, to suggest that this child was something other than angelic, and she stopped just in time. 'Why was she so anxious to avoid the heresy?' I wondered. I had no difficulty with the proposition that by the age of eight the boy was already so damaged, through no fault of his own, that his behaviour was frequently unlikeable, destructive and frightening.

The principal was wrong in assuming I knew that all children are beautiful. I have never been troubled by the delusion that all children are beautiful. It's worth considering one corollary of the statement. If all children are beautiful, where does that leave the rest of us? I think it's understandable, though naïve, to hold the view that all people are beautiful, that all human beings are essentially good. But to single out any group and say that they are all beautiful is silly to begin with, but also implies that other groups suffer by comparison. Clearly, in the opinion of the Adelaide principal, teenagers, middle-aged adults, old people are not as beautiful as children. Why not declare that 'All 43-year-old people are beautiful', 'All 58-year-olds', 'All 77-year-olds'?

THE TRUTH ABOUT TEENAGERS

I've never heard a teacher or school leader – or any other adult – remark that all teenagers are beautiful. Adolescents are unfairly depicted as trouble-makers, lazy, dissolute, undisciplined, defiant, promiscuous. A weighty American tome, *The Manual of Child Development*, published in 1948, advises that adolescence 'is a difficult period for all concerned' but finds comfort in the modern awareness that 'with the introduction of co-education and the discovery that taking part in athletics would not incapacitate girls for childbearing, a more normal and natural everyday relation between boys and girls has begun to prevail'. Nevertheless, much concern is expressed about such dangers of adolescence as rounded shoulders, cheating and truancy, and, horror of horrors, petting. 'The girl who permits promiscuous petting with unlimited privileges gets the reputation of being "easy" and "common". As a social asset, she is less valuable . . .'[141]

'As a social asset, she is less valuable . . .' Sounds like her bride-price

---

141 *The Manual of Child Development*, University Society, New York, 1948.

will be adversely affected, and her future husband's family might have to settle for fewer pigs.

It is actually part of the job description of adolescents that they should challenge adult values and practices, and force us to justify the demands we make of them, and the expectations we have. It's a bad sign when they are too cowed to do this, for if they do not rebel when they are sixteen they are highly likely to make up for it later, going off the rails at a much less convenient time, perhaps when they are 40 or 50. It's like the oft-quoted French aphorism, attributed to Anselme Batbie: '*Celui qui n'est pas républicain à vingt ans fait douter de la générosité de son âme; mais celui qui, après trente ans, persévère, fait douter de la rectitude de son esprit,*' which can be loosely translated as: 'One must doubt the generosity of heart of someone who is not a republican by the age of twenty; but one must doubt the soundness of mind of one who continues to be a republican after the age of 30.'

The truth about adolescents is that they span the full range of human behaviours and personality types, just like every other group in our society. When it comes to sex, for example, adolescents can be promiscuous, chaste, prudish, prurient, modest, perverted, flagrantly sexual . . . Some are frightened of sex, some are strongly attracted to it, some are curious about it, some are repelled and disgusted by it, some are tempted by it . . . But most would tick a number of these boxes simultaneously. Just like adults.

If, however, I were to generalise about adolescents in Australia in the 21st century, I would say firstly that they are highly aware. They are well informed about politics and the world, and are more empathetic, more compassionate, more understanding than previous generations. They recognise the importance and power of emotions, and are familiar with the ways in which people can be emotionally hurt. They are idealistic and passionate, particularly about human suffering and environmental issues. They are eager to see change, but, as I have said, and like most people, they are more interested in the macro than the micro.

In a 2017 article in the magazine *Education Today*, teacher Keith Heggart, from a Catholic school in Sydney's west, commented that 'young people appear to be more issue-based than organisationally-based; that is, they are more likely to indicate broad support for a range of issues, like action on climate change, for example, than they are to join a specific organisation, like a political party.'[142]

They are wealthy, comparatively speaking, and to such an extent that money does not motivate many of them in the way that it motivated their grandparents. They relate to each other, and network in new ways, as a result of advances in technology, but friendships, and belonging to groups, are still of course important to them. If they fail to break into groups, they can retreat, in extreme cases, to solitude, where they brood angrily about the unfairness of life, and risk, sometimes to a dangerous degree, a loss of perspective.

They generally enjoy good relationships with their parents, often characterised by mutual teasing and affectionate exchanges, but whilst more mature socially than previous generations they are immature in terms of their resilience, self-sufficiency and independence. They suffer high levels of anxiety, particularly about the future, and about pollution, environmental damage and climate change. Although quite a few use drugs, most do so with discretion and sense. A large number are repelled by the idea of smoking tobacco.

Madeleine Brettingham, from the *Times Educational Supplement*, reported that research published in the *International Journal of Adolescent Medicine and Health* in 2005 revealed that boys were less likely to smoke, truant, vandalise and steal nowadays than twenty years earlier. Fighting among boys was down from 40 per cent to 19 per cent; regular truancy from 50 per cent to 26 per cent; stealing from 23 per cent to 10 per cent. However, boys were drinking more alcohol (a rise from 52 per cent to 68 per cent), and the figures for girls were worse than in 1985 for stealing, truanting and alcohol drinking.[143]

Academically, modern teenagers are quite assiduous, and work

142 Keith Heggart, 'Citizenship education: making it count', *Education Today*, 2017, vol. 17, term 4, educationtoday.com.au/article/Citizenship-education-1409, accessed 1 April 2019.

143 Madeleine Brettingham, 'Teenagers less anti-social than 20 years ago', *Times Educational Supplement*, 30 March 2007, tes.com/news/teenagers-less-anti-social-20-years-ago, accessed 1 April 2019.

at a higher level than did previous generations. When they express themselves through writing, music, art, drama, dance and other media, their creations are often far more sophisticated than those achieved by their parents and grandparents when they were in their teens.

Unless their minds have been poisoned by their elders, they are much more tolerant and accepting than any generation that has gone before. Issues of gender, sexuality, race and religion are shrugged off by many as inconsequential. They struggle to understand that less than a century ago a family could be split forever by the marriage of a Protestant to a Catholic. They seem unperturbed to find that a sibling or friend is homosexual or is not adhering rigidly to the norms of one gender or the other.

I do, however, have concerns about the spiritual health of 21st-century teenagers, of which more later.

When we gaze at the past it is inevitably through a prism that gives a distorted perspective, but there is ample evidence that plenty of young people have always held idealistic and progressive views. Anne Frank wrote in her *Diary*, on 5 April 1944:

> I can't imagine having to live like mother, Mrs Van Daan and all the women who go about their work and are then forgotten. I need to have something besides my husband and children to devote myself to! I don't want to have lived in vain like most people. I want to be useful or bring enjoyment to all people . . .[144]

In a Melbourne girls' school magazine in 1935, an anonymous student wrote:

> The younger generations are eager to do some good in the world. We wish to raise life nearer to that ideal of truth and beauty which most of us keep before us, and which we believe to be the aim of living. When we see the colossal amount of work to be done, however,

---

144 Frank, *Diary*, pp. 249–250.

we are naturally apt to become discouraged and to doubt that our high ideals are anything more than vague dreams with no meaning. And yet there are moments in the lives of all of us when we receive intimations that our dreams have meaning, and by some means or other we must strive towards the perfection of life. Somehow, then, we must strengthen ourselves to resist any discouragements . . .

It seems reasonable to suppose, however, that the older generations had the same ideals when they were young, and proof of their failure to fulfil them lies all around us.

The writer goes on to suggest that better communication between older people and the young would greatly improve society, and gives the example of education:

Everyone will agree that this system has not yet attained perfection. Such being the case, it would seem that a discussion should take place between the teachers and the candidates for each subject, and that any suggestions made should be considered by the teachers and the examiners. But no: a discussion of this kind is scrupulously avoided for fear that one good suggestion should be discovered to improve the education of future generations.

She concludes by urging a greater commitment by older people to communication with the young, so 'as to make secure the destiny of a crumbling civilisation'.[145]

In 1899, the twenty-year-old Javanese Princess Raden Adjeng Kartini wrote, in a letter to a Dutch correspondent:

. . . age-long traditions that cannot be broken hold us fast cloistered in their unyielding arms. Some day those arms will loosen and let us go, but that time lies as yet far from us, infinitely far. It will come,

---

145 *C. E. G. G. S. Girls' Grammar School Notes No. 95*, Melbourne Church Of England Girls' Grammar School, Melbourne, December 1935, pp. 2–3.

that I know; it maybe three, four generations after us. Oh, you do not know what it is to love this young, this new age with heart and soul, and yet to be bound hand and foot, chained by all the laws, customs, and conventions of one's land. All our institutions are directly opposed to the progress for which I so long for the sake of our people. Day and night I wonder by what means our ancient traditions could be overcome.[146]

Her particular passion was to change the way women in her society were treated. She was, judged by the standards of any era or culture, a deeply committed feminist. Sadly, she died whilst giving birth, about five years after writing this letter.

These three extracts, written more than 70 years ago, more than 80 years ago, and about 120 years ago, are as modern in their thinking and ideas as the statements of 21st-century teenagers. Even the language – direct, passionate, idealistic – seems fresh and modern.

THE TRUTH ABOUT PARENTS

I have no hesitation in saying that the majority of teenagers negotiate adolescence gracefully, positively, and in good spirits, as they have always done. They maintain a loving relationship with their parents, so long as the foundations were well laid in childhood. If they were not, then of course there will be problems. Given that most damaged adults are beyond the point where they can make significant changes in their attitudes and personalities without a lot of professional help, parents with difficult personalities and an excess of unlikeable characteristics can expect rage and depression from their disappointed teenage children. In other words, if a son or daughter expresses fury with every second syllable he or she utters, it's a reasonable possibility that the child is expressing disappointment with the parent, not just as a parent, but also as a person.

---

146 Raden Adjeng Kartini, *Letters of a Javanese Princess*, trans. Agnes Louise Symmers, Norton, New York 1964, p. 31.

It is a given for many people to believe that during a child's teenage years their relationship with their parents will become extremely poor. This does of course happen often enough. In many of these situations, parenting styles and difficult relationships among members of the family are the source of the problem. A more critical awareness of these matters tends to come to the child with adolescence. But frequently this new understanding is entwined with the horrified realisation that at least one of the parents is not a nice person.

It makes mathematical sense. How many adults are unpleasant people? One in 50, 40, 30? And many or most of these adults have children. Many of their relationships end in separation or divorce, and often enough that's because the adult is not an easy or comfortable person to live with.

Given this, the shallow-minded idealisation of parents that is so common in our society is unhelpful. 'Inspiring' poems, mantras and stories that reinforce a glib and superficial attitude to parents, particularly mothers, are everywhere. I recommend the country music song 'No Charge', performed by, among others, Melba Montgomery and Tammy Wynette. But greeting cards, Mothers' Day messages, T-shirts, and a thousand other media perpetuate these stereotypes. People unable to find words to communicate with their mothers need only access the internet to find the help they seek: 'Best friends come and go, boyfriends and girlfriends love and move on, bosses hire and fire but the only person present through it all is a mother.' 'Mothers like you are soft sponges which absorb their children's tears and squeeze out pretty bubbles of happiness and joy.' 'Mama's Boy is the one thing that I won't mind being called even when I grow older because I am proud to have a mom like you.' 'Since you are a Fantastic mother and Fabulous friend, from now on I will call you Fantabulous.'

Seems like these people have never heard of Munchausen's by proxy; or mothers with narcissistic personality disorders; or mothers who prostitute their children; or mothers who murder their children, like the sadly disturbed Akon Guode, who deliberately drove her car into a Victorian lake in 2016, with the intention of killing her four children. Three of them died.[147]

An adult friend recently told me how she, as a teenager, brought friends home from school one day, only to have her mentally ill mother urinate on the floor of their home in front of them, to demonstrate her contempt for them.

Most children grow up with the belief, so necessary to the young, that their parent or parents are omniscient, infallible, beyond criticism. When the day comes, as it does for some people, that the child, with the cold new gaze that adolescents often acquire, looks at the mother or father and realises that there is a reason the parent has no friends, or a reason that the relationship with the other parent broke down, or that the parent's constant complaints of victimisation are not rational, or that the parent is flirting unattractively at every opportunity, or that the parent's outbursts of rage are the result of immaturity, then the fallout can be ugly for everyone.

The parents of a Grade 5 girl whom I taught separated when it emerged that the father, who travelled frequently, had been having a number of affairs. He later told his daughter, 'Look, honey, the truth is that 98 per cent of men who travel have affairs.' In recounting this to a teacher at school, she said, 'I know he's lying. I know he just says that to make it sound like what he did was normal and okay. I know that the men teachers at our school wouldn't behave like he does.'

I had another acquaintance, a single mother of one teenage girl, who told me recently that her daughter had suddenly become a 'monster'. She wouldn't talk to her mother, stayed in her bedroom, erupted in storms of anger without apparent provocation. But I had known this woman a long time, and was aware of her greed for money, which sometimes caused her to behave in ways that raised eyebrows among her peers. I had seen her become coquettish, girlish, flirtatious when powerful men hove into view. I had heard her monologues about other people, including professional colleagues, in the course of which

147 *The Age*, 16 August 2018.

she often made needlessly unpleasant, even spiteful, remarks. And I wondered about the fourteen-year-old hiding in her bedroom, who perhaps had become aware that her only close relative, to whom she was inescapably chained, with whom she was inextricably enmeshed, was not a pleasant person, but that nonetheless, for the rest of her mother's life she would be expected to be her friend, confidante and support, because there was absolutely nobody else. I had the feeling that this girl was in a lose-lose situation – and if she had not known it before, perhaps she knew it now.

I've heard it postulated by mental health professionals that in a large number of cases where children present with symptoms of psychiatric illness, the symptoms disappear when the primary caregiver (usually the mother) is treated.

It's boring, and should be unnecessary, to make the obvious point that many parents are effective and successful in their roles. I have written at length about damaged and damaging parents because our culture is biased towards parents. Authority figures such as religious leaders, magistrates, police officers and teachers frequently work from an assumption that parents are good, and should be respected. They say so, explicitly, to young people whose behaviour is causing difficulties. I have lost count of the number of teachers I have heard over the years advising teenagers that their parents are 'there for them', they should talk to their parents about their problems, they should appreciate the sacrifices their parents are making for them. 'Your parents have your best interests at heart.' I wonder how many times this statement has been made to young people – often by adults who have no real knowledge of the young person's domestic situation.

The problem with some country music songs, the Mothers' and Fathers' Day messages, the bland and ignorant advice given by authority figures, is that a young person who has some inkling that their home life is destructive and that one or both of their parents is not acting in their best interests is disempowered. Most of them have no adult who will support them in their instincts that something is not quite right about their parents. In the face of a world that idealises parents and sentimentalises the parent–child relationship, the child who has critical thoughts about his or her father or mother is left stranded on a lonely rock, encouraged to believe that the problem must be their own, because the mother and father are beyond criticism. If the teenager finds a thoughtful, responsible adult who has the courage to help them explore the reality of the situation, their prospects are good. If they find nothing but banal statements and earnest entreaties to 'respect your parents', then their future is imperilled.

At the end of Year 12 I left the Anglican school I had attended, and the chaplain kindly gave me a character reference. It was typed, but a handwritten comment had been added at the bottom of the page: 'I can vouch for it that his home life is excellent in every way.'

Unfortunately, my home life wasn't excellent in every way. It was emotionally sterile, abusive and destructive, but his confident statement, made from a position of authority, made it even more difficult for me to confront the truth about my circumstances.

Parenthood has become an aspect of modern life so sacred that to suggest modern parents are not doing the best they possibly can, are not martyring themselves on the altar of caring-for-their-children, are not working their fingers and toes to the bone for the children they love-so-dearly-and-would-make-any-sacrifice-for, causes such horror that it has become very difficult to make any thoughtful comment suggesting that a considerable number of parents are actually making an awful mess of their role. A few years ago, two teachers and I had a meeting with a parent of a boy I have not described in this book. I have not described him because it is not possible to tell his tragic story in a way that would prevent his being identified by readers who might know him. Suffice it to say that both parents were highly educated, successful professionals whose parenting was so horrifying that they could not have damaged their son more if they had set out cold-bloodedly to destroy him. The parent began the meeting with us by saying, with a sort of nervous, slightly embarrassed smile: 'You must think we're the worst parents in the world!' My colleagues responded with exactly the programmed responses that remarks like this are designed to elicit: 'Oh no no, not at all, no no . . .'

I said nothing; I was not going to give the person the meaningless comfort they were attempting to manipulate us into offering. I sat in grim silence, thinking, 'Well, you'd be in my top ten.'

One of the ironies with which principals and teachers deal every day is that many parents feel they have open licence to criticise their kids' school freely and frequently, often jumping to wrong conclusions on the basis of inadequate or erroneous evidence, and expressing themselves with unbridled venom, but the staff of the school have no equal licence to criticise the performance of the parents. Surely the rights should be enjoyed equally.

I don't know how many times I have sat in my office being told by parents that there must be something wrong at school because their child doesn't want to come to school any more, only for me to discover, sometimes days, sometimes weeks, sometimes months later that the problem was actually centred in the home all along.

My favourite was the man who accosted me one morning to tell me about his children's sudden reluctance to attend school, and to interrogate me about what we might be doing wrong, only for me to find out in the fullness of time that on the very day we had the conversation, the removal van was at his house, taking away his wife's possessions, because their marriage had failed and she was moving out. Somehow, he had forgotten to mention that trivial point.

We are not stupid. We know if a child is unhappy at school. If the parent tells us that the child suddenly doesn't want to come to school but we can see that the child is engaged, active, excited, involved throughout the day, then we know where the real problem lies. 'Oh, but you don't understand,' they say, time and time again. 'He looks happy, but he saves it all up until he gets home, and then he dumps on us.' A couple of months later they notify us that their marriage has come to an end. Children are like seismometers, consciously or unconsciously registering tremors and earthquakes, and when the tremors get more severe, the children go on high alert and begin initiating their unique versions of evacuation or lockdown procedures. 'Canaries in mines' might be another equally applicable analogy.

Many societies have found parenting to be a difficult challenge. We can, for example, easily and justifiably criticise the child-raising techniques practised by vast numbers of people in the twentieth century. We are in a new era now, and approaches to children and teenagers have, in many families and schools, altered significantly. Some of those changes have been for the better; some for the worse. If parents refrain from obsessively monitoring their children's behaviours, if they do not expect them to be high-functioning paragons of virtue on a 24/7 basis, if they can be honest with themselves about their own unlikeable and unpleasant aspects (and we all have plenty of those), and if they allow adolescents to start to strike out on their own, accepting that in doing so they may demonstrate different values and beliefs to those of the parents, then things should work out well.

5

EFFECTIVE PARENTING

What can parents do to achieve a 'happy family', other than produce a pack of cards from the childhood game Happy Families, that we played many times when we were young? I am as averse to 'How to Succeed' lists as I am to pineapple, classical ballet and Zac Power books. Yet I'll make an exception for the following elements that can help a family get along successfully. I've tried to capture stuff that is real, rather than use glib and banal generalisations like 'be kind to everybody'.

1 Accept that, as children grow, the style of parenting must evolve from the 'I'll do everything you need' approach which is mandatory in the first months of life. Gradually, and sometimes rapidly, parents must step back further and further.
2 Converse with children in a way which will encourage them to develop sophisticated language skills. It is essential that these skills include the ability to communicate feelings.
3 Have kids do regular jobs from an early age. The tasks should benefit others, not be unduly easy, and be completed to a high standard.
4 Help children develop a range of strategies for problem solving. They need to recognise that every problem has many possible solutions.
5 Let kids be bored.

6 Be completely indifferent when kids get muddy.

7 Encourage kids to embrace all kinds of weather.

As I've argued, the first principle of good parenting is that a parent should be aware of the unhealthy ways we construct childhood and adolescence, and the dangers these bring. Parents may need to rethink their prejudices about and expectations of their children and teenagers. Their children may not be as perfect as they pretend to be, and their teenagers might be better than is generally acknowledged. If a child has learned to manipulate her parents, the child is at grave risk of losing contact with her true self, and the loss may be lifelong. The child may engage in this dangerous activity because she realises she can get away with it, and thinks there are advantages to her in having her parents believe she is perfect. Or she may do it because she is scared of punishment if she admits to thoughts or behaviours that adults might classify as 'bad'.

YOU DON'T HAVE TO BE 'NICE' ALL THE TIME

In most cases there is no reason for parenting to be an unpleasant experience. There is every reason for it to be a wonderful shared journey. Many modern parents, striving to be perfect, terrified they will cause deep and lasting trauma if they fail on just one occasion to meet any of their child's needs or demands, have adopted 'selflessness' as the mantra. In doing so they set themselves up for years of self-deprivation, and perhaps they wonder at various points along the way why parenting seems such a grind, and how it can be that people speak of it so warmly.

So many parents repress their normal feelings and natural responses when dealing with their children. If, in an interaction with children, they feel angry, frustrated, bored or repulsed, there are only two possibilities: one is that at that moment in their lives they are feeling angry, frustrated, bored or sensitive; the other is that their children are being infuriating, inappropriate, boring or repulsive. The parent needs to consider carefully which it is, for both alternatives are entirely plausible explanations. If they come to the conclusion that the child's behaviour is causing the problem, then surely the next steps are self-evident.

I rang a friend one day and by chance caught her at the moment when she discovered that her four-year-old son, in a fit of pique, had locked her out of the house. I was incredulous that she seemed not to know how to respond. What had happened to her parenting instincts? How could she allow a child to dominate her in this extraordinary way? As I coached her over the phone in crisis management of the situation, it became apparent that she had spent four years being unremittingly nice to her son, showing him nothing but gentleness, generosity, kindness. It seemed to have escaped her notice that he had not responded with gentleness and kindness. He had responded with ever-increasing rudeness, selfishness and anger. His anger would only be diminished if she could find the strength to play the role he needed her to play – the role of adult and parent.

So many parents work assiduously to be relentlessly nice to their children, but tolerate awful behaviour by those same children with gracious smiles and patient shrugs. They seem unaware that the relationship is one-sided. We teachers are frequently horrified by the way children speak to their parents – to their mothers, in particular. Parents who are quick to recognise bullying in other situations seem unable to identify it when it is directed at them by their children.

When I explained to a student teacher one day that he would continue to have management problems with his class until he learned to show them an 'angry face' when appropriate, to tell them in a convincing voice to sit down and shut up when they were heading towards riot mode, he looked at me with sad, basset-hound eyes. 'I don't think it's in my nature to do that,' he said.

'Well, you'll never be an effective teacher,' I unkindly replied, in what I hope was a convincing voice.

YOU NEED TO DEAL WITH YOUR OWN ISSUES

The second principle is that the parent needs to attend to his or her own mental health issues. The woman whose daughter had locked herself away was unlikely to look in the painful, honest mirror of psychoanalysis, for example, and recognise how much the situation may have been of her making.

A parent who is experiencing significant psychological difficulties also needs to be sure that he or she is responding rationally to children's issues and giving balanced, positive, helpful advice. Recently I was reading a 1944 history of the Macmillan UK publishing company, by a fine but long-forgotten author, Charles Morgan. In writing about the company's professional readers – the people who assess the suitability of manuscripts for publication – Morgan criticised one in these terms: 'There are in existence opinions by Mowbray Morris written with the violence that men do not use except subconsciously in defence of a closed mind . . .'[148]

Teachers in the Western world are confronted by that kind of violence from parents with surprising frequency – and, of course, not just from men. We see and hear it all around us in our sophisticated, civilised society, wherever bigots and extremists are trying to defend impossible positions. We see it particularly from conservative forces, because a position which essentially advocates more of the same, no real change to the established order, is impossible to justify. This is why there can be no such thing as a 'conservative intellectual' or a 'right-wing philosopher' – the expressions are nonsensical. The people we call 'conservative intellectuals' do a lot of shouting, to disguise the paucity of their arguments. The loudest shouters in Australia are the violently angry conservative commentators trying to defend their closed minds. As a society, we should always be moving forwards eagerly, with our eyes fixed upon distant goals, 'the light on the hill'. We should not permit the dead hand of tradition

---

148 Charles Morgan, *The House of Macmillan 1843–1943*, Macmillan, London, 1944, p. 144.

to hold us back. We should not be ruled by our predecessors, if only because they were dealing with vastly different circumstances and conditions. At every school where I have worked, I have preached with religious zeal the doctrine that a school has to reinvent itself every day.

YOU NEED TO GET REAL

The third principle of good parenting is that parents should help children understand the world as it really is, and not mindlessly support them in their indignant cries of 'I wuz robbed' when they claim injustice. Some parents, wounded perhaps by grievances at the frustrations they have experienced in life, actively encourage their child to play the role of victim. Such parents will often prolong the child's disputes long beyond their natural span. The parent of a Year 7 boy said to me one day: 'He just doesn't get on well with Ross. He's never got over what Ross said on the second day of their Foundation year.'

'What did he say?' I asked, hastily patting down my hair as I felt it beginning to stand on end.

'He asked Ross to be his friend, but Ross said he didn't want to be.'

More than seven years later Ross had not been forgiven for the comment made when he was five.

If parents cannot think and talk in terms of solutions, but can see no further than the problem/s, then their child is in for a grim time.

I interviewed a prospective student and parents a while back. They were indignant that at their previous school a teacher had called the child 'stupid'. I queried this, as it seemed inherently unlikely that a teacher these days would say such a thing. It turned out the teacher had said: 'Stop pretending to be stupid when I know very well that you can do this work.'

I made the point to the parents that there is a significant difference between being told you are stupid and told that you are pretending to be stupid. I don't think they wanted to hear it. I could tell they had stopped listening. Sometimes parents seem eager to believe the worst of schools, presumably because their own schooldays included many negative experiences. Schools in the 21st century are paying a heavy price for the errors of schools and teachers a generation ago. We are being punished for their sins.

Children who sense that their parents are avid for horror stories will certainly oblige by providing those stories. In the 2017 letter to parents at Candlebark and Alice Miller School, from which I quoted earlier, I wrote:

> Your job as parents is to stay calm when your child comes home with a bite mark, bruise and/or a dramatic story of persecution and infamous behaviour by some thug in the playground or classroom. Then, discount your child's version of the story by somewhere between 30% and 80% (on average). Next, consider your child's nature; his or her relationships with other children. Children, because they have little life experience, and are often lacking emotional intelligence, and may be relatively inarticulate, will give feedback to other kids about behaviour that is irritating or unlikeable. Their feedback may not be as sophisticated as 'Look Sean, we notice that you seem to have a few issues with anger management when you're playing sport at lunchtimes'. It may be as unsophisticated as 'Piss off Sean, you're not in this game any more'. Or a tennis ball hurled at Sean that hits him in the back of the neck (hence the bruise).
>
> In my experience, children do not suddenly round on a nice kid who treats everyone well. They try to get a point across to a difficult kid in a friendly way but if he/she doesn't take the advice and continues to aggravate and annoy they will get more and more direct with their comments and actions to him or her. This is the way children give feedback. I estimate that at least 60–70% of the unpleasant comments made by kids to one another are actually their rough-and-ready way of telling the child what he or she needs to do in order to be popular.

These comments are particularly true of boys. One of the older boys came to see me last year to complain that other boys were not passing him the ball in their lunchtime game. They were calling him names, and excluding him. I asked him what names they were calling him and it turned out that 'hog' was the most common. 'And do you hog the ball?' I asked him.

'Well . . . maybe . . . I guess some people could see it that way,' he grudgingly admitted. 'I like taking long shots at goal. It's fun.'

'Even if it means you don't pass to a teammate who's in a better position?'

'Well, yes . . . I guess that does happen sometimes . . . it's probably happened quite a few times . . .'

He was getting feedback from the other kids but he had failed to recognise it.

YOU NEED TO PROVIDE A SPIRITUAL CONTEXT

Another step in effective parenting is to encourage a sense in a child of one's place in the vastness of the universe. Phrases like 'a belief in a higher power' and 'a belief in something greater than oneself' recognise the need for humans to be open to mythological and/ or spiritual thinking. We can say that children attempt to cross the bridge from ignorance to knowledge by using imagination. In the same way, people in earlier times, unable to explain the origin of the sun or the source of thunder or the behaviour of snakes, used their imagination to invent myths to cross that bridge from ignorance to knowledge. Science has almost removed this function of the collective imagination. It's very difficult now for us to believe at a literal level stories about Adam and Eve or the rainbow serpent or leprechauns. Equally, it would be plain silly nowadays for me or anyone else to make up and peddle as true stories about how Uluru was formed, or the origin of rainbows, or why kangaroos jump. During the cold light of many days past, Jews and Christians believed Adam and Eve were real, Australian Aboriginal people believed in the rainbow serpent, and Irish adults had the eerie feeling that leprechauns were lurking out in the mist.

There can be no new myths. Television programs like *Game of Thrones* and writers like George R.R. Martin and J.K. Rowling skilfully create pseudo-myths, but in the cold light of the modern day we know they are make-believe. Nonetheless, they have value for us, in a way I will return to later.

Occasionally, anxious people make feeble attempts to marry the logic of science with the imaginative odysseys of mythology, by, for example, trying to find the remains of Noah's Ark, or to prove that under certain tidal conditions the Red Sea could be parted. I remember an older student at my Sydney Christian boys' school telling me in bewilderment of a Divinity lesson where the teacher had explained explicitly how a virgin birth was technically possible. The teacher was missing the point. The myths may have had some literal origins or they may not. It doesn't matter. Their function was to give a framework to the tribe, to provide a sense of security, the feeling that they were not at the mercy of a random and meaningless universe but that there was a context for everything in their lives. These people understood something that we do not: even if the mythological context is sometimes violent or frightening, it is more comforting than no context at all.

Science, at this stage at least, is not able to give us such a framework because it simply cannot answer the biggest questions. Mythology and religion can, and do. But science and mythology, the former concerned with truth and the latter with metaphor, have little common ground. So what we have now is a society with big gaps in its foundations, an inability of science to fill those gaps, an abandonment of imagination as a way of filling them, and a consequent contempt for the imagination. We are like adolescents, who, embarrassed at having ever believed in Santa and the Tooth Fairy, have to pour scorn on these imaginary beings to show they are no longer credulous, and by implication that they were never so stupid as to have been sucked in by the stories in the first place.

The people we elect as leaders of our tribe do not nowadays go to the witchdoctors, the priests, the mystics or the storytellers. They consult the scientists, but only listen to them in the hope of getting the answers they want. Then they go to the scientists' fellow travellers: the pollsters, the sociologists, the economists. They come away dissatisfied and still unsure of themselves, uncertain of the direction they should take. Their 'spiritual beliefs' seem to consist of 'stopping the other party from getting into government'. Vast amounts of energy are consumed in this endless exercise. 'The mess we inherited from the previous government' seems to have become the default phrase in public conversations with politicians from the ruling party, even after they have been in office for years.

If that is the state of leadership at the highest levels, then it's not surprising that when young people talk about their lives I sometimes feel, looking into their eyes, that I am seeing spiritual vacuums, empty souls. I don't say that to them, because rightly or wrongly I imagine they will not understand the language: they are so far removed from the idea of having a spiritual dimension that it would be like trying to tell Australian immigration ministers about compassion, but even so I suppose no one would be very thrilled to have it suggested that they might be spiritually empty.

An Australian doctor, George Burkitt, speaks of what he calls an 'existential malaise', which he says any caring general practitioner will recognise as a condition common in our society. He describes existential malaise as a lack of wellbeing or joie de vivre, a sense that life lacks meaning or purpose. Existential malaise is manifested by low-grade depression and anxiety, a profound fear of dying, chronic tiredness and a deep sense of loneliness. Burkitt believes the malaise to be particularly evident in men, perhaps because the intimacy that women experience from marriage and parenting is often harder for men to attain from their involvement in marriage and parenting, perhaps because the nature of women's friendships is so different from the nature of men's friendships.[149]

---

149 George Burkitt, 'The Rite Way', *Certified Male*, March 2000.

It does seem to me that one group particularly susceptible to existential malaise consists of divorced men who have not re-partnered.

An important function of parents and teachers is to prepare both boys and girls for life in such a way that they will be less vulnerable to existential malaise. But is it possible for an agnostic or atheistic society to be as moral and caring as a religious one? This is just a rephrasing of the old philosophical question: 'What would happen if we could prove beyond doubt that there is no God? How would it affect us and the way we live?' Plenty of societies based on religion have been cruel and selfish, and plenty of atheists are compassionate and honest. But many people argue that an atheistic society, or one with no mythological foundations, is likely to become more selfish, more hedonistic, less moral, more terrified, and maybe it is no coincidence that this seems to be happening now.

The value of religion to people is that it offers meaning for what happens; offers a context for understanding the good, the bad and the ugly; offers hope of a life after death, which then makes mortal suffering and the fear of death more bearable; gives humans a sense of proportion by setting us into a relationship with a higher power; establishes a framework within which a set of moral laws can be delineated and enforced; and provides many of the stories that give a society its identity.

To run through that list again might help to give a sense of the risks run by people who don't have a religious belief. Such people might not be able to find meaning for what happens in their lives; might experience suffering and the fear of death as unbearable; might have a disproportionate sense of their own importance; might not recognise the existence of a set of moral laws; and might be lacking the treasury of stories that underpins society and human life in all kinds of subtle ways.

One difficulty for many people is that religious belief, once lost, is difficult to regain. Ellie in my book *The Night is for Hunting* talks about how she feels she has lost her sense of humour and wonders if she'll ever get it back. 'Or,' she asks, 'is it like trust, virginity and Easter eggs:

gone once, gone forever?'[150] Religious belief might also be placed on this list, although there are people who have regained a lost religious belief at a later stage of their lives.

I'm not sure what religious beliefs to offer young people in the 21st century. When I see what some branches of the Christian church have done and are still doing, particularly in Third World countries, I am appalled. Like Jomo Kenyatta said: 'Originally the Africans had the land and the English had the Bible. Then the missionaries came to Africa and got the Africans to close their eyes and fold their hands and pray. When they opened their eyes, the English had the land and the Africans had the Bible.'[151] Yet I do, however grudgingly, admire the solidarity of some religious groups – the Amish, Orthodox Jews, some Muslim communities, the people of Bali, for example – in offering a consistent set of beliefs that may in many quarters go unquestioned but that ties the community together. In concentration camps like Auschwitz and Buchenwald, many Jews fasted on holy days despite the fact that they were in a state of starvation. Many recited prayers and psalms to comfort themselves when faced by the worst crises. In her memoir *Elli*, Livia E. Bitton Jackson poignantly recalls how at the age of thirteen she was sent by the Germans to Auschwitz. Treated with the appalling cruelty that so many Nazi soldiers inflicted upon their prisoners, she nevertheless was well aware that Jewish law prohibited the eating of chametz at Passover. Chametz is forbidden because it contains a leavening agent . . . and Elli decided that even in Auschwitz she would give up her meagre yeast bread ration:

> Mummy and I had decided that one of us would observe Passover
> by not eating the bread ration and the other one would compensate
> for the bread by sharing her ration of cooked meals at noon and
> in the evening. I had volunteered to give up the bread ration.
> Mummy had agreed because she was in far worse physical shape
> than I. So I had only black coffee in the morning, and one and a half

---

150 John Marsden, *The Night is for Hunting*, Pan Macmillan, Sydney, 1998, p. 74.
151 Jomo Kenyatta, quoted in Robert Pateman, *Kenya*, Marshall Cavendish, New York, 2004 p. 41.

bowls of soup at noon and in the evenings. All that liquid without the morning and evening ration of bread made me ravenously hungry . . .[152]

In the musical *Fiddler on the Roof*, Tevye stresses the need for tradition, as the crucial factor which holds the community together. Sure enough, as the rigid customs that prescribe every detail of people's lives in the Russian village quickly disintegrate, the lives of the villagers unravel. Tradition is powerful, but not strong enough to withstand the upheavals of the outside world, where revolution is fomenting.

FEAR HAS A PURPOSE

For the rest of us, another result of our abandonment of mythology and religion is that we have developed, not surprisingly, a fear of fear, for ourselves, and perhaps more importantly for our children. Other cultures, including the ones we now call primitive, did not fear fear itself. They understood that fearful forces were part of the context with which they had been familiar since infancy, and that these forces existed in a relationship with other forces that were not fearful. Because of the holes in the fabric around us, we no longer have a safe context for fear, or a sense of its relativity. The horror stories on the seven o'clock news are frightening because they are presented as meaningless, and worse, as being without boundaries or counter-balances. We are told explicitly by tabloid current affairs programs and other sources that nowhere is safe. We are shown how the places we instinctively trust, for the most powerful unconscious reasons – our holy places, our banks, our homes, even our kitchens, bedrooms and bathrooms – are not safe. The people we instinctively trust, and who were generally trusted by previous generations – people such as parents and grandparents, teachers, elders, priests, rabbis, imams, monks – are now often recast as untrustworthy.

---

152 Livia E. Bitton Jackson, *Elli*, HarperCollins Hammersmith, 1994, p. 176.

As I said earlier in this book, it is important not to trust particular people just because they wear a 'badge', but that is not to say we should run away from every member of a group who wears that badge.

Directors of horror movies are always striving to raise the stakes and make their next film scarier than any that have gone before. Hence Steven Spielberg, in his movie *Poltergeist*, chose the most trusted of all icons, the television set in the middle-class suburban home, as the source of evil. It was a masterstroke. But the horror in movies has escalated dramatically since *Poltergeist*. Horror-movie directors frequently target children asleep in their own beds in their own bedrooms in their own homes as the most fear-inducing victims for the machinations of the malevolent spirits.

Rather than turn to old religions or tales of horror, it may be that we need new stories, to help us make meaning of a world where fears seem limitless. I would claim for my books, often criticised because they are 'too dark' or 'don't offer young people hope', that they communicate to readers the idea that they can resolve fearful situations through self-knowledge and self-awareness, through courage and friendship, by being prepared to take a personal journey instead of staying in the unbearable pain of where they are. Contrast that with the content of some children's books of the past. Many people like to view the 'good old days' through such rose-coloured glasses that they overlook books like *Reading Without Tears, or a Pleasant Mode of Learning to Read, by the Author of 'Peep of Day'*, etc., which was published in 1861. It contained the following passages:

What is the matter with that lit-tle boy?
He has ta-ken poi-son. He saw a cup of poi-son on the shelf. He said 'This seems sweet stuff.' So he drank it.
Why did he take it with-out leave?
Can the doc-tor cure him? Will the poi-son des-troy him? He must die. The poi-son has des-troyed him.

Wil-li-am climb-ed up-stairs to the top of the house, and went to the gun-powder clos-et. He fil-led the can-is-ter. Why did he not go down-stairs quickly? It came into his fool-ish mind, 'I will go in-to the nur-se-ry and fright-en my lit-tle bro-thers and sis-ters.'

It was his de-light to fright-en the child-ren. How un-kind! He found them a-lone with-out a nurse. So he was a-ble to play tricks. He throws a lit-tle gun-pow-der into the fire. And what hap-pens? The flames dart out and catch the pow-der in the can-is-ter. It is blown up with a loud noise. The child-ren are thrown down, they are in flames. The win-dows are bro-ken. The house is sha-ken.

Mis-ter Mor-ley rush-es up-stairs. What a sight! All his child-ren ly-ing on the floor burn-ing. The ser-vants help to quench the flames. They go for a cab to take the child-ren to the hos-pit-al. The doc-tor says, 'The child-ren are blind, they will soon die.'[153]

Putting *Reading Without Tears* aside, I would say that we now have a declining number of new stories for young people by writers and filmmakers who are searching for some profound understanding of life's issues. One of the consequences is that children and adolescents experience fear as nothing but sheer terror, which leaves them help-less. And so, understandably, parents and teachers try to protect our children from fear by not letting them experience it at all. In doing this we are denying them one of life's essential experiences. We are not letting them be fully human. One of the functions of fear is to equip us to be effective warriors in our lives. It's like bacteria. If we protect children from all bacteria, by boiling drinking water, scrubbing every piece of crockery and cutlery with hospital-strength disinfectant, and wearing disposable gloves to prepare food, kids will have a spectacular stomach upset when they eat a hot dog from a caravan at the local show. Many of our children, and many adults, become psychically ill because they have no experience of dealing with fear, so when,

---

153 *Anon. (Favell Lee Mortimer), Reading Without Tears, or a Pleasant Mode of Learning to Read, by the Author of 'Peep of Day', etc.* (first published 1861).

inevitably, they are confronted by authentically frightening situations they are paralysed, they become ill, they develop phobias.

Children know instinctively that they need fear. They show it by their attraction to roller-coasters, to television programs like *Doctor Who*, and to stories like *Where the Wild Things Are*.

We must give our children fear. It is a rich and immensely valuable experience to know fear. Fear in a context, fear that exists in complex relationships with other forces, fear that has limits and can be contained within safe places: this is the only way people at the beginning of their life journeys can develop an arsenal powerful enough to ensure that those journeys are healthy, satisfying and successful.

The only myths that many modern parents want to offer children are Santa, the Easter Bunny and the Tooth Fairy. We are scared to give them the Bogeyman as well, not realising how nourishing the Bogeyman can be. When Frank Harris described in his autobiography the pain he felt during his time at an English boarding school, and his consequent loss of contact with the folktales of Ireland, he wrote: 'My head in especial, was full of stories of Banshees and fairy queens and heroes, half due to memory, half to my own shaping, which made me a desirable companion to Irish boys and only got me derision from the English.'[154]

Few mythical creatures could be as terrifying as a Banshee, which howled at night outside the windows of someone who was soon to die, but Harris mourned the loss of the Banshees as much as he did that of the fairy queens and heroes.

No wonder that modern children, watching hours of mindless, meaningless television cartoons with no mythological basis, feel ill, frustrated and dissatisfied. It's like feeding them sugar and never letting them have vegetables. At the same time the other stories I mentioned earlier, the unhealthily frightening stories, the unbalanced and mean-ingless ones, sneak into our lives by the back door, via televisions and electronic games, and we seem strangely oblivious to their presence, or to the harm they do.

---

154 Harris, *My Life and Loves*, p. 36.

6

A PLUG AND A PLEA FOR LITERATURE

If the stories on the seven o'clock news are damaging us by their lack of context, and I believe they are; if the stories brought to us by the advertising industry are dishonest and dangerous, and I believe they are; if the stories from Hollywood and elsewhere that sentimentalise and sexualise children are inimical to their healthy development, and I believe they too are; and if the disappearance of a spiritual aspect from the lives of so many Australians means that the sustaining fear-filled stories that help form the fabric of all religions are no longer available to most of us, and I think this may be the case, where can we go for stories we can trust? In short, where can we go for the truth? The 'real' truth, not the stories of Sugarcandy Mountain that Moses the Rasputin-raven tells the creatures of *Animal Farm*.

How paradoxical to give the answer 'fiction'! 'Literary fiction.' And yet it's not so surprising. The fiction writer creates a world that has its own infrastructure, its own conventions and rules and dynamics, yet is aligned in innumerable ways with the real world. As I mentioned earlier, at one level as we read these books we are aware that we are reading fiction. But the human brain, among its many other extraordinary attributes, has the ability to function on two or more levels simultaneously. As we read a book, we know that we are curled up in our bed or on a sofa, safe in our suburban home or comfortable hotel room, reading beautiful lies. But on another level we are wholly immersed in the story, sweating alongside Harry Potter, despising Gollum, feeling attracted to Elizabeth Bennet and/or Mr Darcy, exclaiming at the folly of Lear.

REALITY IN FICTION

In realistic fiction, which is mostly what I write, the created world is of course as close as possible to the real world. But in fiction the writer can discard what doesn't matter – all the trivia and irrelevancies that clutter our day-to-day lives and obscure judgement and understanding – and focus on what is important.

And upon what does the literary fiction writer focus? What is her quest, her passion, her chief concern? It's the pursuit of truth, shining truth, and the fiction writer pursues it with fidelity, at the same time as she knows she can never find it, because the concept of truth is as nebulous as gods and rainbows. And that is the source of much of the tension in fiction.

Picasso said in an interview that 'Art is a lie that makes us realize truth, at least the truth that is given us to understand. The artist must know the manner whereby to convince others of the truthfulness of his lies. If he only shows in his work that he has searched, and re-searched, for the way to put over lies, he would never accomplish anything.'[155] As in art, so in writing. Technique is not enough. A deeper engagement from the artist or author is required.

Some would argue that literary fiction cannot be compared to religious myths precisely because the former is by definition untrue, whereas the latter claims to be absolutely true. Readers must make their own decisions on that question, and will do so according to the beliefs they have formed during their lifetime. But it could be seen as one of the great strengths of literary fiction that it is honest

---

155 Pablo Picasso, Statement to Marius de Zayas, 'Picasso Speaks,' *The Arts*, New York, May 1923, pp. 315–26.

in the claims it makes for itself: it does not purport to be true; it unapologetically calls itself by its true name, fiction. The other could be seen by non-believers as fiction masquerading dishonestly as truth.

But why should we go to fiction for truth when we have non-fiction, which is explicitly and obviously aimed at delivering truth?

Non-fiction embarks upon an impossible task: to convince us that the words within the covers of the book are true. Non-fiction writers, with a few honourable exceptions, like Helen Garner, not only believe that there is such a thing as truth, they even believe they can find it and pass it on to others. The fiction writer has no such certainty. The fiction writer would never dare pretend that the contents of her novel are true, and in fact it's the freedom that the word fiction confers that enables her to go much further than scientists or biographers or historians, and thereby, paradoxically, makes it more likely that she will come closer to touching the face of what Marge Simpson calls 'the most decorative thing of all, the truth'.[156]

Non-fiction is also suspect because, whilst purporting to be true, it is inevitably biased, according to the writer's own beliefs and life experiences, and is only able to give us a limited number of perspectives. It often has some strain of propaganda. It enables, under the guise of great authority, statements that at another time or another place might properly be seen as uncertain.

Literary fiction on the other hand takes a point of view that is never presented as infallible. Because all characters in literary fiction are flawed, we know that their perspectives will be flawed, but knowing that enables us to respect them in a more meaningful way, and to identify with them, and ultimately to trust them according to their limits.

I keep saying literary fiction, because I can't think of a better term, but the only books I exclude here are those written purely to entertain or to propagandise, in which different energies are at work. A long time ago, in a speech to the Society of Authors in London,

---

156 'Homer Badman', *The Simpsons,* Season 6, Episode 9.

Enid Blyton suggested that all authors who write for children should be virtuous people whose books consistently depicted the triumph of good over evil. A beautiful and brave moment followed. Kathleen Hale, the writer and illustrator of the *Orlando* picture books, who, according to critic and interviewer Elaine Moss, had as a child stolen lavatory paper from her neighbours because she had no paper available for her passion for drawing, stood up in her own words, 'very tremblingly', and said 'Please will the speaker define what she means by good and evil?'[157]

As Hale was suggesting, Blyton's statement was meaningless, but for hundreds of years that kind of thinking could be found permeating most books for children, which thereby disqualified them from being taken seriously as 'literature'. Literary fiction cannot deal in moral absolutes. In 1969 psychologist Michael Woods wrote 'Enid Blyton['s books have] . . . no moral dilemmas.'[158]

Psychotherapist Ernesto Spinelli, in his book *Tales of Un-Knowing*, says: 'It is only in dreams and fairy-tales and hack novels that choices are made which will allow us to "live happily ever after". If our lived experience confronts us with anything, it is that the issues of human existence will never provide us with "perfect", anxiety-free resolutions. Indeed, to aspire to such merely provokes further, possibly unnecessary, anxieties.'[159]

He may not be right about dreams, or all fairytales, but he is right about hack fiction.

I don't know any writer of literary fiction who does not have a passion for truth and understanding. It shows up quickly in any worthwhile novel. Sometimes it can be a moment of illumination, like in Ian Bone's novel for teenagers *Tin Soldiers*. The Anglo-Australian boy Michael is bashed as he walks home alone, late at night, after a party. He thinks that the Lebanese-Australian boys, led by Ahmad,

---

157 Elaine Moss, *Part of the Pattern*, Greenwillow Books, New York, 1986, p. 86.
158 Michael Woods, 'Enid Blyton Revisited', *Lines Magazine*, Autumn 1969.
159 Ernesto Spinelli, *Tales of Un-Knowing: Eight Stories of Existential Therapy*, New York University Press, New York, 1997, pp. 22–23.

were responsible for the attack, a beating so severe that it damaged his brain. But at school one day when a chance encounter leaves the two boys alone together, Ahmad says to Michael, 'I didn't do that thing. What was done to you. I didn't do it . . . Man, it fucked you around real bad, didn't it? . . . You shouldn't have been alone. You Aussies don't look after each other. My friends, they'd never leave me alone like that. They'd protect me.'[160]

Suddenly the whole mateship myth of Anglo-Australia is exposed, and we realise that maybe people from the Mediterranean and Middle Eastern regions can teach us more about mateship than any amount of sentimental rubbish in a television advertisement for beer or McDonald's.

Sometimes it can be the thrust of the whole story, as in J.M. Coetzee's novel *Disgrace*, where 52-year-old David Lurie, a South African professor, has an affair with a twenty-year-old student and is then charged with sexual harassment. From stubborn pride he refuses to defend himself and, consequently, loses his job. For the rest of the book, most of which concerns itself with his stay with his daughter Lucy in a remote part of the Eastern Cape, we, the readers, share with Coetzee the quest to find the truth about this man, who is in many ways a moral and ethical person, yet in other ways has difficulty understanding the moral and the personal aspects of his sins of commission and his sins of omission.

David, and the other characters in the book, are as full of ambiguities, complexities and contradictions as we all are in real life. When David's daughter is raped, he is outraged and angry and talks of revenge, yet at the same time he wants some sort of forgiveness for his own offence. He seems to be dying before his time, unable to feel enough, unable to understand how the world has changed, unable to understand his daughter's different perspective on life. Perhaps Lucy comes closest to the truth about him when she says to her father:

---

160 Ian Bone, *Tin Soldiers*, Lothian, Port Melbourne, 2000, p. 129.

You behave as if everything I do is part of the story of your life. You are the main character, I am a minor character who doesn't make an appearance until halfway through. Well, contrary to what you think, people are not divided into major and minor. I am not minor. I have a life of my own, just as important to me as yours is to you, and in my life I am the one who makes the decisions.[161]

'The essence of drama is that man cannot walk away from the consequences of his deeds', as Harold Hayes once said, and I would add to that: 'The person who tries to walk away from the consequences of his deeds will be drawn back to them time and again as though he is tied to them by a long elastic band.' In my own books there are two characters who are unable to face what they have done. The previously mentioned Tracey in *Letters from the Inside*, and Tony in *Dear Miffy*, cover their eyes, hide, and lie to themselves and others to avoid accepting responsibility for their lives. As a direct and inevitable consequence they remain mired in awfulness, Tony in particular unable to take a single step forward.

In literary fiction, the main characters generally seek redemption. They make their way in the direction of the light, sometimes painfully, sometimes slowly, sometimes with many false steps or disastrous detours. Just like us.

Reverence is another element always to be found in literary fiction. American writer Anne Lamott defines reverence as 'awe, as presence in and openness to the world'.

'Anyone who wants to,' Lamott says, 'can be surprised by the beauty or pain of the natural world, of the human mind and heart, and can try to capture just that . . . When what we see catches us off guard, and when we write it as realistically and openly as possible, it offers hope.'[162]

In Margo Lanagan's *The Best Thing*, Mel has her first look at her baby daughter, born just a moment before:

---

161 J.M. Coetzee, *Disgrace*, Vintage, London, 2000, p. 198 (first published 1999).
162 Anne Lamott, *Bird by Bird: Some Instructions on Writing and Life*, Doubleday, New York, 1995, p. 101.

Her head was whitish grey, but as soon as she's out she starts flushing pink, all over, very quickly. She opens her mouth and there are gums in there, and a tongue as fine as a kitten's. Out of her throat on her first breath comes a tentative cry, a voice never heard in the world before. From her navel the live multicoloured umbilical rope spirals back up to my insides, to that beautifully positioned placenta. 'You could pick her up,' says Lois, and I do, astonished that I'm allowed to, that she's mine. She's so hot and damp and rubbery, but not slippery at all. Her arms shoot out and her fingers spread in surprise, even though I'm as gentle as I can be. She stops squeaking and opens her eyes – oh, eyes![163]

'Awe, as presence in and openness to the world . . .' Lanagan seems to meet Lamont's criteria for reverence.

Fiction that does not seek the truth betrays the reader. As Sonya Hartnett has said: 'Truth has a virtue that shines with its own purity and that needs no justification or rationalisation.'

In the novel *I Am David*, Anne Holm has her character say: 'Can't you understand that children have a right to know everything that's true? If there's danger, you have to recognise it, or else you can't take care of yourself.'[164]

CENSORSHIP IN SHEEP'S CLOTHING

In an *Australian Book Review* supplement, 'What's the Difference', renowned author Ruth Park wrote an article criticising those who write what she called 'children's books based on frighteningly realistic adult themes'. Her real agenda is communicated by her closing eight words: 'life is primarily for fun, love and laughter'.[165] Such a comment could be made only by someone living in a middle-class Western society. It's not a comment that could be made in a war zone or a

---

163 Margo Lanagan, *The Best Thing*, Allen & Unwin, St Leonards, pp. 164–5.
164 Anne Holm, *I Am David*, trans. L.W. Kingsland, Puffin/Penguin, Harmondsworth, 1969, p. 103.
165 Ruth Park, 'The Difference' in 'What's the difference?', *Australian Book Review supplement*, December 1992, p. 30.

famine zone, or a culture where a strict sense of duty is taught to the young. Ironically, Park's own fiction implicitly repudiates her silly statement, but it's this kind of gush that characterises adult longings for a simple innocent world. I'm perhaps particularly sensitive to it because it's the kind of gush that people in the children's literature field are subjected to frequently. I've heard Morris Gleitzman describe how he is often told by school librarians, 'I love your books, but we're not allowed to have them in our school library.'

'Why?' he asks, but he already knows the answer.

'Oh, a parent complained . . .'

'So one parent gets to decide what all the children in your school read?'

I've had the only specialist children's bookseller in a large region in Victoria tell me that he refused to stock one of my books because it was not moral enough or virtuous enough for him. In other words, one bookseller felt he had the right to decide what all the young people in his district were allowed to access. This kind of censorship still goes on. Fantasy has a powerful and vital role to play in our lives, but so too does verisimilitude, even when it confronts uncomfortable thoughts and behaviours.

In 2016, the books most frequently challenged by parents in American schools were *This One Summer* (Mariko Tamaki, illustrated by Jillian Tamaki), *Drama* (Raina Telgemeier), *George* (Alex Gino), *I Am Jazz* (Jessica Herthel & Jazz Jennings, illustrated by Shelagh McNicholas), *Two Boys Kissing* (David Levithan) and *Looking for Alaska* (John Green). A challenge is defined as a formal, written complaint, filed with a library or school requesting that materials be removed because of content or appropriateness. Some of the common reasons cited are 'offensive language', 'sexually explicit', 'unsuited for age group' and 'sex education'.

This One Summer is a graphic novel about two young girls on a summer holiday. One is on the cusp of adolescence, and the other is eighteen months younger. The book explores with convincing realism their annual summer holiday at the beach, and the tentative state they inhabit between childhood and the full-blown teenage years. It's a beautifully judged and sensitive piece of work. *I Am Jazz* is a true story; a picture book by an American, aged about fourteen when the book was published. She was born, as she says, 'with the mind of a girl but the body of a boy', and she has now transitioned fully into her female identity. The intent of the book is to give young children some understanding of transgender people.[166] Other titles that have been on the 'most challenged' list since 2000 include *To Kill a Mockingbird*, the Holy Bible, *Captain Underpants*, *Huckleberry Finn*, *Harry Potter*, *Twilight*, *Bridge to Terabithia*, *Brave New World*, *The Chocolate War*, *Beloved* and *Of Mice and Men*.

When we speak of realism in fiction for young people, critics from the lunatic fringe often confuse it with so-called 'issues' novels, and argue as though members of the 'realism school' automatically endorse any book about abortion, AIDS, adoption, ADHD, autism, alcoholism, anorexia – to take just the As. Of course that's not the case. Such issue-driven novels are out there, and are usually best avoided, but the best fiction is character-driven. If a character is struggling with AIDS or anorexia or anything else, and this is part of his or her story, part of his or her life, just as we all have issues with which we struggle, a book about the person may well be wonderful. If a novel or picture book is written by someone campaigning for greater public awareness of a particular issue, or as an attempt to instruct kids with a difficult problem about their condition and treatment, or as a tearjerker to win fame and fortune for the author – then it might be better handled with disposable gloves and examined at a safe distance while deciding whether to engage with it.

THE LANGUAGE OF TRUTH

One of the ways we can assess the integrity of a novel is by means of language. Characters in worthwhile books speak in voices we recognise as genuine. That was one of the distinctive strengths of

---

166 Jessica Herthel and Jazz Jennings, *I Am Jazz*, Dial Books, New York, 2014.

The Catcher in the Rye. On the other hand, a false note should make us cringe. Witness the voice of an English schoolboy in Anne Fine's novel *A Pack of Liars*. The boy's age is not specified, but references to 'children' and 'grown-ups' suggest that he's quite young; the cover illustration shows him as being in the eleven to thirteen age range perhaps. Here is an extract from one of his letters to his pen pal:

> Nobody has the right to force you to pretend to be someone you are not by nature. If you are a clumsy, fidgety, awkward, fibbing truant, then it is a great shame for your mother if that is not exactly what she wanted. But she should have another whiskey and leave you alone, not try to get you changed into a calm and confident amateur photographer. If parents don't want surprises, and possibly very nasty ones, they shouldn't have babies of their own.[167]

That is the voice of the middle-aged author, not her character.

Here's Adrian Mole, writing in his *Diary* on 17 March: 'Measured my "thing". It was eleven centimetres.'[168] The use of quotation marks for the word 'thing' renders the line false. No boy would ever put quotation marks around a euphemism for his penis. Boys take their penises far more seriously.

Most Australian teenagers swear, but the use of swearwords in dialogue in adolescent books enrages some adults. They're more comfortable with dishonesty. They would rather have the lie than be forced to confront young people as they really are – or as they really speak. It seems that some adults can see nothing but the swearwords when they read books written for young people; others read the same novels and are unaware that there were swearwords in them. It is the latter group an author cherishes, for its members are genuinely involved in the book, not reading it in some authoritarian capacity, as librarians, English teachers, parents, moral guardians. People who

---

167 Anne Fine, *A Pack of Liars*, Hamish Hamilton, London, 1988, p. 62.
168 Sue Townsend, *The Secret Diary of Adrian Mole, Aged 13¾*, Methuen, London, 1983, p. 49.

peruse books in an authoritarian fashion are not readers as I understand the word. People offended by swearing are trying to shut out the sweat and spit and dirt of the teeming masses.

CREDIBLE STORIES

As well as authentic language, another characteristic of good realistic fiction is credibility. The books reflect the world as it is. Most Australian teachers, librarians and reviewers are middle class, and of Anglo-Saxon origin, and they bring certain cultural understandings to their reading. Hence, for example, they argue that 'children's books should offer hope', because it's hard for them to conceive of individuals within their own society or in other parts of the world who have no hope. There are such places and there are such people, and there's no reason to conceal that knowledge deliberately from our young people. Telling lies to the young is wrong and to conceal the truth is to tell a lie.

On the principle that all great literature is subversive, if not downright revolutionary, it's important for novelists to challenge false thinking, to question, to blaze trails. But credibility is crucial. The author has to subtly persuade readers that his/her quest for understanding brings us closer to the truth than other, possibly long-cherished, beliefs. Paradoxically, books that are theme-driven or issues-driven, like the 'disease of the month' novels mentioned earlier, don't succeed: the book must tell a story, the characters must be complex and believable, and the rest must seem incidental, even if it really isn't. This is one of the differences between novels and books of sermons. If the story is unconvincing, the whole project fails, though of course whether the story seems credible often has more to do with art than with inherent probabilities – as Shakespeare demonstrated, by turning highly improbable plots into great literature.

The books in my life that forced me to look at the world differently, abandoning comfortable and long-held beliefs, succeeded for me by virtue of their authentic characters and powerful, credible storylines. They were so well written that I had to believe in the worlds the authors created, and once I did, it became easier to accept the ideas.

Some books have an integrity that readers sense, an indefinable, intangible quality that we recognise in books in the same way as we recognise it in some people.

An important issue in credibility is the notion of psychological truth. Characters must act and react in ways that, from our own experiences of people, we know to be 'right'. Hence, *Anne of Green Gables* is incredible. Anne is a psychologically impossible character. So are thousands of Blyton characters (has anyone ever counted how many there are?), James Bond, Jack Reacher, John Rambo, and anyone who has ever been in a Virginia Andrews novel.

On the other hand, some characters live a long time in readers' memories because there is a psychological truth about them that we recognise on a very deep level. In Melina Marchetta's *Looking for Alibrandi*, a scene of psychological truth takes place towards the end of the book, when John Barton, son of a powerful politician, is talking to Josie. John has been confused and unhappy, but on this occasion he seems euphoric. 'I've got my whole future planned out the way I want it to be and there is nothing anyone can do to take that away from me ... The future is mine, to do whatever I want with it.'[169] That night John commits suicide. It's unclear whether John is experiencing the last sudden flare of the candle before it goes out, so familiar to those who nurse the dying; or whether his euphoria reflects his having at last made the decision to end his life; and it's immaterial. Either way the words are right; they are psychologically true and therefore credible.

An actor in a film made from one of E.M. Forster's novels was quoted as saying that he liked Forster's books because the characters in them were allowed to be 'complex, contradictory and hypo-critical'. All human beings, including children, are all these things. Books featuring characters who are not complex, contradictory and hypocritical will have enduring interest only for those people who want – sometimes quite desperately – to believe that they are living

169 Melina Marchetta, *Looking for Alibrandi*, Puffin, Melbourne, 1992, p. 229.

in a simpler, less demanding world. Unable to cope with the contrariness and unpredictability of the people with whom they interact (let alone themselves), they long for a world of white and black, where the goodies are all good, the baddies are all bad, and both groups are easily identifiable. Hence the success, a couple of generations ago, of *Pollyanna*, the eponymous heroine of which is variously described as having 'radiant smiles', 'an eager freckled little face', a 'jubilantly trustful face', 'rapt eyes', 'eyes luminous with sympathy', 'a sunny smile', a 'merry little face' and a 'radiant' face.[170]

In case of any confusion, let me state explicitly that she is a goodie.

The great children's books, the classics, have characters of interesting complexity and subtlety. Toad, in *Wind in the Willows*, is self-centred, vain, dishonest, unscrupulous – but genuinely fond of his friends, and capable of change, as Kenneth Grahame shows at the end of the book. Bunty, in *Seven Little Australians*, is greedy, selfish and dishonest, but his affection towards Judy, especially when she runs away from school, and later, when she dies, helps redeem him in the reader's eyes. Tom Sawyer and Huck Finn are larrikins who smoke, truant, fight and cheat, but they are also capable of courage and of real sweetness. The Mary Poppins found in the pages of P.L. Travers's books is bad-tempered and autocratic, but wreaks wonderful magic. The petulant, bitter, sarcastic Professor Snape, despite killing Dumbledore, has truly noble qualities. There is much pathos in the life story of Gollum.

ALL ASPECTS OF LIFE

We must ensure that children have access to books with realistic characters, credible situations, authentic language – and finally, we must not shrink from stories which show life in all its many forms. A generation or two ago children saw life at close quarters. In some societies they still do – but not in our urbanised, industrialised, contemporary Australia. Beatrix Potter, in a letter to a newspaper, written in 1911,

---

170 Eleanor H. Porter, *Pollyanna*, L.C. Page and Company, Boston, 1950 pp. 16, 57, 83, 175, 164, 181, 206, 207.

described how as a child she had helped scrape the bristles off her grandmother's slaughtered pig, and complained 'the present generation is being reared upon tea – and slops'. Maxim Gorky, in his classic account of pre-revolutionary Russia, *My Childhood*, wrote with vivid detail of his first-hand encounters with suffering, depravity, happiness, life and death:

Nanny took his cap off, and the back of his head hit the floor with a dull thud. Then it rolled over to one side, and the blood flowed more abundantly, but only from one corner of his mouth now. It flowed for a horribly long time. At first I expected Tsiganok to rest a little, sit up, spit something out and say:

'Whew! It's hot in here!'

He always used to say this on Sundays, when he woke up from his after-supper nap. Now he didn't get up, but he just lay there, his life ebbing away.

The sun had already moved away from him and the bright strips of light had shortened and fell on the window sills. Tsiganok had gone black all over, his fingers didn't move any more, and the foam had dried from his lips. Around his head burnt three candles, their flickering golden spears lighting up his dishevelled, blue-black hair, his blood-stained teeth and the tip of his sharp nose, throwing quivering yellow patches on his swarthy cheeks.

Nanny, who was kneeling by him and weeping, whispered: 'My angel, light of my life.'

It was cold in the room and I hid under the table in terror. Then my grandfather, in his raccoon-fur coat, burst into the kitchen, followed by Grandmother, who was wearing her cloak with the little tails hanging on the collar, Uncle Mikhail, and a lot of strangers.

Grandfather flung his coat on the floor and roared: 'Bastards! Feel satisfied now you've killed him? He would have been worth his weight in gold in five years' time!'[171]

---

171 Gorky, *My Childhood*, pp. 58–59.

In our antiseptic, terrified society, where avoiding the experience of death for ourselves and for others has become a national obsession, will we ever again find anyone who can write with such intimate loving knowledge of the mysteries of human existence?

No-one seemed to object when Mark Twain wrote fiction about a young Huckleberry Finn watching the death of a man named Boggs:

> Bang! goes the first shot, and he staggers back clawing at the air – bang! goes the second one, and he tumbles backwards on to the ground, heavy and solid, with his arm spread out. That young girl screamed out, and comes rushing, and down she throws herself on her father, crying, and saying, 'Oh, he's killed him, he's killed him!' . . . They took Boggs to a little drug store, the crowd pressing around, just the same, and the whole town following, and I rushed and got a good place at the window, where I was close to him and could see in. They laid him on the floor, and put one large Bible under his head, and opened another one and spread it on his breast – but they tore open his shirt first, and I seen where one of the bullets went in. He made about a dozen long breaths, his breast lifting the Bible up when he drawed in his breath, and letting it down again when he breathed it out – and after that he laid still; he was dead.[172]

Because our children lead such limited and boring lives nowadays, I reluctantly acknowledge that meaningful first-hand experiences are rare for most young people in Western countries. Books are one of the few ways available to them to help them understand the great passions, the great dramas. No matter how much some adults try to deny the right of young people to read about these things, they will fail, if only because no one can predict what will powerfully affect a young reader. For me, at the age of six, it was the death of Blinky Bill's father:

---

172 Mark Twain: *Tom Sawyer and Huckleberry Finn,* J.M. Dent & Sons, London, 1964, pp. 307–8.

Poor Mr Koala one day was curled up asleep in his favourite corner, when the terrible thing happened. Bang! He opened his eyes in wonder. What was that? Did the limb of the tree snap where that young cub of his was sky-larking? He moved very slowly to take a look and bang! again. This time he felt a stinging pain in his leg. What could it be? And peering over the bough of the tree he saw a man on the ground with something long and black in his arms. He gazed down in wonderment. Whatever was that, and how his little leg hurt. Another bang and his ear began to hurt. Suddenly a great fear seized him, he slowly turned and tried to hide round the tree, peering at the ground as he did so. Bang! again and now his poor little body was stinging all over. He grunted loudly and slowly climbed up the tree, calling Mrs Koala and Blinky as he went. He managed to reach the topmost branch and now turned to see where his family were. Tears were pouring down his poor little face. He brushed them away with his front paws and cried just like a baby.[173]

I read this over and over with a sense of horror and anger. I could hardly believe that such an awful thing had happened. With one paragraph I had discovered – and understood – tragedy. Dorothy Wall is probably responsible for both *Letters from the Inside* and my lifelong commitment to conservation.

Renowned Australian children's writer Libby Gleeson has said that the story that terrified her most as a child was Hans Christian Andersen's fairytale *The Snow Queen*. The effect on her was so strong that 'I have been unable to read it ever since'. For another distinguished Australian novelist, Gillian Rubinstein, it was *Struwwelpeter* and *The Coral Island* which she described as 'unexpected things' that 'trigger[ed] off night terrors'[174]. Journalist Kath Dolan describes the British author of children's books Nick Falk as feeling 'heavy, fixed dread . . . about Roald Dahl's *The Witches* at

---

173 Dorothy Wall, *Blinky Bill*, Angus and Robertson, North Ryde, 1985, pp. 27–29.
174 Gillian Rubinstein, *At Least They're Reading!*, p. 80.

seven or eight. His mental image of the Grand High Witch's scabby, warty hands – fuelled by Quentin Blake's vivid illustrations – gave him nightmares.'[175]

The difficulties for the Moral Guardians are obvious. How can one censor *The Coral Island* and *The Snow Queen*? And what 'hope' would they offer Mr Koala as he died slowly and terribly at the top of the gum tree?

THE MYSTERIES OF LIFE

Sex, suffering, death: these are among the most powerful mysteries to which humans have been permitted some access. Our understanding of them, limited as it is, makes us unique among living creatures. A person with no understanding of them is not truly human. By grappling with these mysteries we slowly advance as individuals and, millimetre by millimetre, the whole of humanity is enabled to advance.

Such an understanding does not magically begin on one's eighteenth birthday: it begins at birth, and is either helped or hindered by parents, teachers and other knowing people. To deny access to these mysteries is to deny the intelligence and wisdom of young people. When we look at child-raising, and our education system, we realise that many powerful adults strongly deny the intelligence and wisdom of the young (thus enabling the stubborn retention of power by these same adults).

We need not fear that young people coming to an early understanding of sex, suffering and death will blow a cranial fuse or be destroyed by their knowledge. That could happen if they are tied down and force-fed an overdose – the adult who seeks to initiate young people at too early an age is as neurotic as the adult who seeks to keep young people ignorant – but, in general, children can be trusted to screen out what they are not ready to encounter, as Manning Clark indicated in his reminiscences of childhood:

175 Kath Dolan 'Why Scary Stories Are Good for Kids', *Sydney Morning Herald*, 23 March 2013.

Here was someone talking about things which interested me. Perhaps books would give me the answers my father, my mother and my teachers either could not provide or withheld because of my tender years and my growing awareness that 'sorrow, wrong and trouble is the lot of all mankind.' I was too young then to notice the difference between the optimism in the New Testament and the pessimism in the Old Testament; too young to heed the comments in the Psalms, the Book of Job and Ecclesiastes about the life of a human being. I had heard, but had not felt, the words. They were not as yet part of what Henry James called 'the quality of life'.[176]

The silly thing is that we allow, with scarcely a whimper of protest, some media to inundate young people with an immense flood of shallow, ignorant and meaningless material about sex, suffering and death. But any attempt by a novelist to give children or adolescents real insight into these vital issues will meet with everything from pursed adult lips to outraged adult howls.

THOSE ADULT CENSORS

There are three things I can say pretty confidently about adults who block the access of young people to realistic fiction. Firstly, they don't distinguish between one young reader and another. To them, anyone under an arbitrary chronological age is a child, and blanket prohibitions can be placed on that child, regardless of his or her intellectual, emotional, social or spiritual development. Although chronological age is the least reliable indicator of a person's maturity, we use it as the criterion for everything from drinking alcohol to voting to driving a car ... because it is convenient, cheap, easy and relatively uncontroversial. If teachers – perhaps the people best placed to make the assessment – had to vote on whether a teenager was mature enough to have a driving licence or to drink alcohol,

---

176 Manning Clark, *The Puzzles of Childhood*, Viking, Melbourne, 1989, p. 141.

A Plug and a Plea for Literature

we might get a much more meaningful sense of each young person's readiness.

But adult censors of books for the young do not even make a distinction between the pre- and post-pubertal individual. Thus they assume that a book like *Letters from the Inside*, which is clearly written for and marketed to those in their mid- to late teens, is equally intended for nine-year-olds who have just graduated from Dav Pilkey's *Captain Underpants*.

Secondly, they don't talk to young people much, or, if they do, they don't listen. Thirdly, they egoistically assume that all young people who read the books will react the same way that they, the adults, do. In fact — and it is hardly surprising — young readers have different emotional and intellectual responses to the books they read than the responses of adults to the same books. Adolescents, for example, are excited by books that take their concerns seriously and treat their lives as important.

To shrink from some topics because they are seen as too shocking, too depressing, too realistic, is to continue the repression of the young, to prolong their ignorance and therefore their impotence. How similar some words sound: innocence, ignorance, impotence! And how close and complex is their relationship. To understand that is to understand a lot.

In Friedrich Dürrenmatt's novella *The Pledge*, a police official in Switzerland explains to a writer of detective stories why he finds standard detective stories so unsatisfactory. And it's not just because the criminal gets punished. A detective story, according to the Federal Deputy, is one of those . . .

> lies that help preserve the State, like that pious phrase that crime does not pay, whereas anyone has only to look at human society to find out just how much truth there is in that. But . . . what really annoys me is the plot in your novels. Here the fraud becomes too raw and shameless. You build your plots up logically, like a chess game; here the criminal, here the victim, here the accomplice, here

the master mind. The detective need only know the rules and play the game over, and he has the criminal trapped, has won a victory for justice . . .[177]

Many or most of the television programs for children churned out by the cable networks, and most of the movies produced by the Hollywood factories, are equally shameless, equally fraudulent. The American film and TV world continues to be almost all-white. Animated 'creatures', whether they be foxes, penguins, fish, parrots or sloths, are so indistinguishable from middle-class white American humans that one wonders why the animators bother to give them animal identities. Anthropomorphism is all they know. Heroes in adventure movies shoot their way out of trouble – using guns, the laziest solution available to a writer when a character is trapped by baddies. As described by the police officer in Dürrenmatt's novel, the storyline of each significant character in movies is neatly wrapped up and tied with a pretty bow. Everyone we care about (i.e. the goodies) lives happily ever after, or, if not, dies nobly and poetically.

THE POWER OF METAPHOR

Maybe one of the reasons literary fiction is able to do such powerful things is that it uses the wonderful, almost magical, tool of metaphor. As a society we have unfortunately drifted away from, abandoned, the myths that metaphorically explored our lives.

In every life, every family, every society, powerful and ancient dramas are being enacted. In this respect at least, every person and every group of people are vital and every story matters. Perhaps this is why to the fiction writer no one and nothing is boring. The job of the novelist is to explore life dramas so that we can understand them better. The obese girl at number 26 for example – maybe she's hungry for her parents' love? Or maybe she eats as a kind of contraceptive,

---

177 Friedrich Dürrenmatt, *The Pledge: Requiem for the Detective Novel*, trans. Richard and Clara Winston, Penguin, Harmondsworth, 1964, pp. 11–12.

driven by a fear of sex to make herself unattractive to men? The post-natally depressed mother at number 33 – why does her baby induce these feelings? Is it just physiological? Is it because a part of her has literally been taken out from inside her? Is it because she knows that she must now give up some of her own identity in order to allow the child to develop hers? The violent man at number 4 – what causes his rage? Is it the rage of all men at losing the primeval battle with the father for the love of the mother? Is it the knowledge that he is not immortal, that every day takes him closer to death? Is it the immature frustration of someone who cannot have all his impulses gratified?

Stories that helped people make sense of their lives used to be part of everyday discourse, as commentators like Carl Jung, Joseph Campbell and Bruno Bettelheim have shown. Those comparatively few readers who still brave the genre of literary fiction have access to the profound insights of great writers who can help them gain a deeper understanding of life. But during my lifetime we have for the most part replaced myth with psychology. Metaphor with analysis. Mysticism with science. Unconscious understanding with conscious. Covert knowledge with overt. Arcane with public: knowledge held by the priests and sacred persons with knowledge freely available to all. The oligarchic with the democratic. For all that I respect psychology, it alone cannot give us the understanding that we crave. We want to know the answers in our guts, we want to know them in our blood and our bones, not just in our heads. We need to know them at an unconscious level. The beautiful thing metaphor gives us this kind of understanding. It's because metaphor is the language of the unconscious. The unconscious mind is incapable of communicating directly. Everything is metaphor, symbol, allusion. Just as we have few authors in Australia who seem able or willing to explore the unconscious in their work, we as a society seem afraid to explore the unconscious. With good reason perhaps: anyone who explores the unconscious embarks upon a difficult and powerful journey.

Many children's authors, instead of daring that ambitious journey, take an easier path, writing cheap and easy books that invade the secret subculture of children in a meaningless way, and that violate children's territory. Such books are a part of our takeover of their lives. It's like we leave children no secret places. It's much the same as searching their rooms or reading their diaries.

In an essay, 'Why Secrets Matter to Children', American psychologist Wendy Mogel used the expression 'joyful secrecy', and wrote, 'We can know our kids well without knowing everything they do.'[178]

Mogel reminds us of the passage from *Huckleberry Finn* when Tom and his mates gather in a cave to swear a dark oath of allegiance to Tom Sawyer's gang:

> Tom got out a sheet of paper that he had wrote the oath on, and read it. It swore every boy to stick to the band, and never tell any of the secrets; and if anybody done anything to any boy in the band, whichever boy was ordered to kill that person and his family must do it, and he mustn't eat and he mustn't sleep till he had killed them and hacked a cross in their breasts, which was the sign of the band . . . And if anybody that belonged to the band told the secrets, he must have his throat cut, and then have his carcass burnt up, and the ashes scattered all around, and his name blotted off the list with blood and never mentioned again by the gang, but have a curse put on it and be forgot forever.[179]

Mogel points out – but underestimates – the impact should a member of the gang have posted a record of this meeting on Facebook in these paranoid times. She suggests they would be 'in a heap of trouble'. If they were Muslim boys, I suggest they would be raided at 3 am by a squad of heavily armed police who would smash down the door of the house and arrest everyone they found inside. And if Tom had stipulated a crescent instead of a cross as the sign of the band, no lawyer in the world could have saved them.

---

178 Wendy Mogel, 'Why Secrets Matter to Children', Independent School, 2013, vol. 72, no. 3, p. 124.
179 Mark Twain, *Tom Sawyer and Huckleberry Finn*, J.M. Dent & Sons Ltd, London, 1964, pp. 190–1.

The Danish author Erik Christian Haugaard, in a speech at Simmons College Boston in 1978, said this:

> When children, like little savages, were left to their own devices and Nature was their nursery school teacher, they made their own literature by telling stories and playing games of make-believe. The children of today are not left to themselves; they are bombarded with messages, most of which were not originally meant for them. As for Nature, modern suburbia does not have space enough for her. For all our wealth, we may end up producing a generation of slum children. The mark of such children has been their combination of worldly wisdom and ignorance. They are exposed to too much and experience too little – a deadly combination.[180]

'They are exposed to too much and experience too little.' In a society, a world, where so many have lost their way, and where existential malaise has become something of an epidemic, let us recognise exactly what it is that literary fiction has to offer. It's more than entertainment or escapism, it's more than a means to an end, more than bibliotherapy. It has an integrity that simply may not be available in the places we have been accustomed or trained to expect it. It enables readers and writers to journey together, sharing the path from the first page of the book to the last, and through all the exhilarating and difficult pages in between, and in so doing to confront honourably humanity's toughest and most tangled questions in a mutual search for truth. Thus we can all be enriched: adults and the young people for whom we care.

Authors who write realistic fiction for young people know from the ardour and gratitude expressed in the letters they receive from readers that young people themselves are well aware, at some level, that they need these books. Removing the moral guardians who stand with arms folded between the books and their potential readers

---

180 Harrison and Maguire, *Innocence & Experience*, Lothrop, Lee & Shepard Books, New York, 1987, p. 294.

continues to be a challenge. In 2019, some members of the board of the Chilliwack School District in Alabama, Canada, tried to stop my novel *Tomorrow, When the War Began* being studied by Grade 9 students. The trustee who proposed the ban was disturbed by erotic thoughts described by the book's protagonist. 'I think we can all figure out that I'm talking about sexual content in the curriculum ... novels and anything that may arrive in a sexual nature,' said the trustee.

The attempted ban was defeated by four votes to three, and by that narrow margin *Tomorrow, When the War Began* was saved for the teenagers of Alabama![181]

When I hear parents say 'I want my children to enjoy their childhood; there'll be time when they're older to learn about those things', I hear the voices of those who are scared of the vastness of the universe. I hear the voices of adults with no insight, no imagination, no understanding. These adults have a view of childhood as some kind of discrete interval, rather than just a few years from the continuum of life. They believe that ignorance is bliss, that children will be happy in their ignorance, despite those kids' awareness that there are powerful secrets being kept from them, important questions to which they are being denied answers. They have been responsible for the perpetration of too many shameless frauds on the young already, too many cultural tragedies. They risk bringing our development to a halt, sentencing our society to stagnation. How fortunate that the spirit, courage and curiosity of many young people remains largely undefeated by such adults.

181 'Book-banning discussion bubbles up at Chilliwack board table', The *Abbotsford News*, 10 April 2019, abbynews.com/news/book-banning-discussion-bubbles-up-at-chilliwack-board-table/, accessed 30 April 2019.

7

MIDDLE-CLASS CHILDREN IN THE 21ST CENTURY MORASS

Some years back I sat in the audience at the Swedish Book Fair and listened to Nobel Prize winner Elie Wiesel, author of *Night*, speaking about his life and times. One sentence in particular from that occasion has stayed in my mind. Wiesel commented that the great challenge for those like him who survived the Holocaust, those who had been prisoners in concentration camps, was to convince their children that life was still worth living, even though they themselves feared it was not.

I think the greatest challenge for us in the future may be to give young people and ourselves a sense that life is a rich, worthwhile experience, even though there is much to discourage them and us from holding that view.

'TODAY IS A GREAT DAY'

When I taught in a primary school in Melbourne, each day began with a session of calisthenics or aerobics, or whatever the current name was. It was taken by one of the parents. At the end of each session he made the students chant in unison 'Today is a great day'.

I don't think I'm being unduly sensitive to say that I regarded this as undesirable, not far from fascism. There's something almost desperate about such a chant. It's horribly like the Jules Feiffer comic strip of the man who says, 'I wake up singing and my wife hugs me and kisses me and begs me never to change. I sing on the bus to work and the passengers smile and pat me on the back. I sing at work and the boss has tears in his eyes and gives me a promotion. I sing in the street and a stranger puts a dime in my hand and asks "How in a world full of misery are you the one man who's happy?" "Who's happy?" I reply to the stranger. "I sing to drown out my screaming."'[182]

To take a student whose grandmother might be ill, whose best friend might have dumped her, who may be suffering from depression, and force her to chant 'Today is a great day' makes me wonder what screaming the parent was trying to drown out in his own mind. Perhaps he thought that compelling 200 students to join with him would help his vain attempt to deafen himself to his own screams.

'Vain' is probably an appropriate word in both its meanings, because it was vain of him to use 200 children to shout out his view of the world every day, but of course it was also in vain, as no amount of shouting or singing, even at maximum volume, can drown out the truth.

Alice Miller wrote: 'If I allow myself to feel what pains or gladdens me, what annoys or enrages me, and why this is the case, if I know what I need and what I do not want at all costs, I will know myself well enough to love my life and find it interesting . . .'[183]

We find ourselves however in a world in which, despite the mindless shouting of 'Today is a great day', 'You are an awesome human being', 'Live in the moment', many people, old, middle-aged and young, are struggling to find joy in their lives.

Whitney Houston sang, famously, about the importance of learning to love oneself. Yet Houston died at 44, in 30 centimetres of water in a hotel bathtub. In her system was a mixture of cocaine, marijuana, Xanax, Flexeril and Benadryl. She sang wonderfully

---

182 Jules Feiffer, *Jules Feiffer's America: From Eisenhower to Reagan,* ed. Steven Heller, Penguin Books, Harmondsworth, 1982, p. 187.
183 Alice Miller, *Free from Lies: Discovering Your True Needs,* trans. Andrew Jenkins, Norton, New York, 2009, p. 41.

about the importance of teaching children to recognise their inner beauty. Yet her only child also drowned in a bathtub, at the age of 22. The post-mortem found her body contained morphine, alcohol, marijuana, a cocaine related substance and benzodiazepines. Tabloid magazines reported that Whitney smoked crack cocaine in front of their daughter when the child was five years old.[184]

Helpful slogans, inspiring thoughts, are everywhere. 'Everyone agrees it's important to live in the moment . . .' says Ellen Langer, a psychologist at Harvard and author of *Mindfulness*, on the psychologytoday.com website.[185] Everyone agrees? Put me down as an exception. I like to ruminate on the past, and speculate about the future. I frequently use my imagination to transport myself away from the here and now. Sometimes 'the moment' is so banal that I have to escape.

The most common parenting mantra is 'I just want my child to be happy'. 'Poor kids,' I think, when I hear this. 'What an awful fate to wish on them.' Happy is a relative term, so unless they experience unhappiness their happiness will be meaningless. In his book *The Master and His Emissary* (subtitled *The Divided Brain and the Making of the Western World*), Iain McGilchrist tells the story of Hector Berlioz at a concert: 'Once, when Berlioz sobbed at a musical performance a sympathetic onlooker remarked: "You seem to be greatly affected, *monsieur*. Had you not better retire for a while?" In response, Berlioz snapped: "Are you under the impression that I was here to enjoy myself?"' McGilchrist adds a footnote referring to 'Wittgenstein's reported comment on life: "I don't know why we are here, but I'm pretty sure that it's not in order to enjoy ourselves."'[186]

As the Tao proverb puts it: Life is 10,000 joys, 10,000 sorrows. Far

---

184 '"Whitney smoked crack in back of my limo as her daughter sat next to her playing with a doll" says ex-chauffeur', *The Daily Mail*, 19 February 2012, dailymail.co.uk/tvshowbiz/article-2102944/Whitney-Houston-smoked-crack-limo-daughter-sat-playing-doll.html, accessed 10 April 2014.

185 Ellen Langer, quoted in Jay Dixit, 'The Art of Now: Six Steps to Living in the Moment', *Psychology Today*, 1 November 2008.

186 Iain McGilchrist, *The Master and His Emissary: The Divided Brain and the Making of the Western World*, Yale University Press, New Haven, Connecticut, 2009, pp. 85–86.

better to wish, as Alice Miller emphasises, that children are able to feel fully the range of emotions. Grief, joy, sensual and erotic sensations, love, anger, fear, ecstasy, pride at one's achievements – we are born with our bodies loaded and cocked, and the potential to experience all of these with full force. But the ability to feel them is quickly trained and educated out of us. This is the cause of neuroticism. Every parent should wish for their child nothing more than 'I want him or her to experience life to the fullest'. Every child should be able to exult in the 10,000 joys that life brings her or him, and feel with full force the sadness of the 10,000 sorrows.

MODERN PESSIMISM

Mindless, meaningless slogans are among the forces which conspire to rob our individual lives of joy. But there are plenty of other destructive forces at work. They include, as I've mentioned, the daily news. Let me cite another cartoon, from an artist I haven't been able to identify, which shows a grim-looking couple and their child. All three are staring at a television screen. The child is sobbing, desperately clutching the mother. The mother reassures the child: 'There, there, darling. It's only a documentary.'

In 1966, Simon and Garfunkel beautifully juxtapositioned the Christmas carol 'Silent Night' with the words of a newsreader reading the 7 pm news. The news bulletin contained stories about racism, the Vietnam War, and Richard Speck, the mass murderer of eight student nurses.[187] In 1975, rock band Skyhooks sang about the horrors of the nightly television news.[188] Both songs are still topical. The average 30-minute news bulletin consists of stories about Israelis murdering Palestinians, Palestinians murdering Israelis, teenagers burning to death in nightclub fires, families destroyed in car accidents, hospitals in Third World countries bombed by missiles from First World countries,

---

187 Simon and Garfunkel, '7 O'Clock News/Silent Night', *Parsley, Sage, Rosemary and Thyme*, Columbia Records, 1966.
188 Skyhooks, 'Horror Movie', *Living in the 70's*, Mushroom Records, 1974.

horrific domestic violence episodes, and global warming. In a recent television promotion we were told 'No one is safe any more'. It was an advertisement for a story on internet security. Such stories give us a sense that we are surrounded by awful viruses that swarm at our doorsteps and threaten to invade our houses and our lives.

There is little to balance these messages, except the compulsory whimsical story at the end of each news bulletin: how a lottery winner has bought a gold-plated toothbrush, or how a goat has been taught to ride a surfboard, or how a 107-year-old lady has a brandy every night. The programmed inclusion of these stories and the tone in which they are delivered, like a 1950s primary school teacher reading an Enid Blyton story to her class, is as patronising and contemptuous as anything on television, adding insult to injury. First we are injured by the violent assaults on our sensibilities, then we're insulted by the suggestion that a dab with tissue paper will heal those assaults.

The mass of men, and of women, and of children too, may lead lives of quiet desperation, as Thoreau famously said[189], but they also lead lives of quiet heroism. That is easy to forget when the nightly horror story, the seven o'clock news, erupts into our living room.

The growth in online activity has contributed spectacularly to our exposure to stories, many of which can't be verified, about badly damaged humans and their alleged behaviour. A quick browse after I wrote the previous sentence revealed offerings like video footage of a man stamping a seagull to death at a railway station, video footage of a disabled five-year-old girl chained to a wall by her mother who had to go to work, a drunk woman evicted from a plane after refusing to sit next to a three-year-old ('I'm not sitting next to a fucking three-year-old; I've been drinking all day'), and a man who raped his wife in front of their five-year-old child. They are all from one (popular) website, and are only a small sample: some of the other featured stories were too horrific for me to cite here.

Another of the obviously damaging forces that disturbs our

---

189 Henry David Thoreau, *Walden*, Peter Pauper Press, 1966, p. 8.

wellbeing is that of advertising. Few professions defend themselves more vigorously and skilfully against attack than the advertising industry, which shouldn't surprise us – after all it's their job to change our thoughts, our beliefs and our perceptions, and it's hardly any wonder that they do so with particular commitment when the threat is to them. For instance, a few years ago the advertising industry ran a long campaign suggesting that without them the economy would collapse and unemployment would be rampant. Of course, this just isn't so. What would happen is that without advertising the economy would be different, and that's a very different thing.

In general, the advertising industry rests upon discontent, which is an unhealthy foundation for any construction. Just as radio shock jocks derive their power from whipping their listeners into a daily frenzy of rage – which must be as exhausting for them as for the listeners – so the advertising industry depends on inciting unhappiness and envy, a sense that unless you have two new cars, regular holidays on tropical islands, a two-storey house and a white kitchen filled with luxury white appliances, you have been cheated. The inevitable outcome is that the great mass of consumers develops a sense of entitlement, which is accompanied by resentment, jealousy and anger.

Perhaps even worse is the underlying message that objects are all you need to fill the gaps in your life. Relationships, giving to others, paying attention to your spiritual life, these are as nothing compared to the true happiness brought into your kitchen by the glow from your new Miele dishwasher. When people display bumper stickers with messages like 'Born to shop' and 'Who dies with the most toys wins', we can only hope that they do so in a spirit of irony.

In his book *The Consolations of Philosophy*, Alain de Botton discusses the teachings of Epicurus. He writes 'We receive little encouragement to attend to modest gratifications – playing with a child, conversations with a friend, an afternoon in the sun, a clean house, cheese spread across fresh bread . . .'[190]

---

190 Alain de Botton, *The Consolations of Philosophy*, Penguin, London, 2007, p. 68.

POOR LEADERSHIP

Another cause of discontent in our society is the inadequacy of political leaders. The woeful standard of political behaviour, both federally and at state level, has had a depressing effect on the Australian community. We know that we all have racist, selfish and cowardly aspects. We elect our leaders in the unconscious hope that they will bring out our latent nobility, that they will help us discover the goodness that we also have inside us. It takes no genius to bring out our worst qualities, no vision to appeal to racism, no greatness to ask us to act in a spirit of meanness.

There has been a failure of leadership in many areas: across the spectrum of politics, in institutionalised religions, in education, and in business. To some extent though, failures of leadership are our failures. Perhaps we should strive to be less dependent on that paternalistic model which has the father – who can be male or female in this metaphorical sense – as the omniscient, omnipotent God-like figure at the top of the pyramid and everyone else on lower levels. This model brings us dangerously close to the notion that other humans are superior, that they may be more enlightened beings. Every time we defer to someone, we diminish ourselves.

Teachers seem more amenable to the pyramid-shaped paternalistic structure than people in most other professions. I don't have any evidence for that statement, just a sense that teachers are more easily intimidated by school principals and forceful parents than people in other occupations are by their bosses and clients. I remember one teacher telling me that if the principal notified her Monday morning that she wanted to see her Thursday afternoon, the teacher didn't sleep for the next three nights. I remember sitting in the staffroom at Geelong Grammar School as teachers discussed whether they should apologise to the principal for having asked him, at a forum, chal-lenging but entirely appropriate questions about his management of the school. I did not sit there long, but walked out in disgust, saying to my colleagues as I left, 'You've got the leadership you deserve.'

Although there were plenty of times when I confronted the

principals of schools where I worked, sometimes aggressively, underneath I was generally nervous of them. From being students in schools, and therefore on the bottom of the pyramid, teachers have returned to schools – at a higher level, true, but it is quite likely that they feel safe and at home in these conservative institutions, with authority figures telling them what to do. This doesn't of course preclude the possibility that they might at the same time chafe under, and even subvert, the rules and regulations. One of my worst moments as a school principal was when a member of staff burst into tears during a conversation, and then calmed herself, apologising with the words: 'I'm sorry, but authority figures always have this effect on me.'

'Authority figures?' I wanted to say. 'It's only me!' It seemed that the invisible word 'Principal' on the door of my office – an office that is a converted storeroom, the size of the average bathroom – had changed me forever in her eyes.

So, media stories, online material, advertising, failure of leadership, materialism, hierarchies . . . all the usual suspects. But we must remain active, even pugnacious if necessary, in monitoring these influences on the lives of our young people, to keep them feeling optimistic and excited about being alive in the 21st century.

8

STRATEGIES FOR DIFFICULT CHILDREN

There are two kinds of difficult children: your own and other people's.

Let's start with other people's. A few years back a parent sent me this email:

> I was talking to some parents at the bus stop this afternoon and I
> hope you won't mind if I say that I was a bit unnerved by some of
> the things they told me about plans for next year. Sorry to bother
> you about them, but I think you know by now that I'm not one
> of life's whingers so I wouldn't bother writing to you unless it was
> serious and I felt strongly about it.
>
> Anyway, to get to the point, they say you are thinking about
> composite classes for several grades. Well, if you are, don't take
> this as me having a go at Liana, but I feel strongly that Beatrice
> shouldn't be in the same class as Liana, if there's any possibility of
> that happening. I do know that Liana has a bad impact on other
> kids – I don't know whether you know that we live close to
> Rodney's parents, and they have been saying all year that Liana has
> been driving Rodney crazy. I don't think they talk to anyone at the
> school about it, but I know they have a list of things that she has
> done to Rodney. And it's not just in the classroom, it's whenever she
> gets a chance. She seriously is a bad influence.
>
> I know Liana's life is a bit less than perfect but I don't want

Beatrice to have to deal with this kind of stuff at her tender age. She's had such a happy time at school so far, and I don't want to spoil it.

I wanted to write back and say this:

Your email was a potent reminder, at the end of a busy year, of the complications involved in running a school.

As a parent, naturally you think of the interests of your own children, and you are an advocate for them. That is one of your roles.

But in advocating for your children to be kept away from Liana, you are effectively saying that 'someone else's children' should have to 'put up with her'.

Which children would you nominate? What should I say to their parents, if they object?

Every group has a Liana. I play tennis at the XXXXX Tennis Club; there are at least two Lianas there. I employ 75 people; we have a wonderful staff at the moment, but in the past I can think of four Lianas who have worked here. Some of my relatives are or were Lianas.

Every classroom in Australia has at least one Liana. The world is full of Lianas.

To try to find a bubble for your children, a safe sanctuary where there are no Lianas, is (a) impossible, and (b) the worst thing you could do for your children. Because if they don't have any experience with Lianas when they are growing up, if they don't learn how to deal with Lianas when they are young, they will be completely helpless when they encounter the inevitable Lianas who sooner or later will cross their paths, no matter how hard you try to keep Lianas away.

Meanwhile, what of the real-life Liana, the little girl who has just turned six, who has a parent who is restrained by court orders from contact with her, who has a chaotic home life, who struggles to make friends, who doesn't get invitations to birthday parties? Should we wipe our hands of her because she is angry, confused, disordered? Or should we support her in every way we can, providing an environment where for seven hours a day she is cared for and nurtured? Should we patiently, day after day, teach her about limits and boundaries, how to make friends, how to manage conflict, how to treat others? Should we help her with her grief and lack of understanding as she experiences rejection after rejection from her classmates?

The questions are rhetorical, because you know the answers.

I can tell you that if every parent in the school withdrew their child and went searching the highways and byways of Victoria for a school without a Liana, we would still keep Liana here, and do our duty as teachers and adults.

And in fact I did write back pretty much in these terms, but for obvious reasons I omitted the part describing aspects of Liana's life.

This mother, who incidentally is, I believe, a really nice person and a caring parent, was voicing to me one of the most common refrains uttered surreptitiously around the car parks, coffee shops and barbecues of Australia:

I've talked to the teacher about it and apparently this kid . . . [fill in whichever name applies at your school] has a lot of home problems or something and I feel really sorry for him/her but honestly, every day he/she hits someone or calls them names or takes their lunch or scribbles on their worksheet, and what I want to know is, what's the school going to do about it because they don't seem to have any answers and why should my kids suffer just because [fill in name] has a terrible home life, because I'm not going to put up with my kid coming home upset and not wanting to go to school the next day etc. etc. etc . . .

PRIORITISING DAMAGED CHILDREN

What indeed is the school going to do about it? Well, maybe nothing that is obvious to the parents whom, one devoutly hopes, are kept at arm's length from the school's inner workings. But unless the school is hopeless – and we can't discount that possibility – the staff will be working away behind the scenes to improve the behaviour of the delinquent child. Their task is a difficult one though. For starters, as former Melbourne school principal Peter Hutton points out, schools have children for only about 1250 hours a year.[191] Even if we deduct time for sleep, parents will have the children for something like 4250 hours a year. By the child's twelfth birthday he or she will have spent less than 15 per cent of his or her time in school. Yet in the 21st century the school is held responsible for fixing the child – and is blamed for any failures to do so.

I know of one government primary school in Sydney that has three psychologists, two speech therapists and an occupational therapist on its full-time staff. Secondary schools all around Australia are moving quickly to incorporate doctors' surgeries into their campuses, so that students can make appointments with GPs to discuss health matters and medical problems. In 2016, the Victorian government announced that it would locate GPs in 100 schools[192] – as is already happening in some schools in other parts of Australia. In South Australia, for example, the 'Doc on Campus' program, aimed primarily at helping with youth mental health issues, has been running at Victor Harbour High School since 2004.[193]

This is all regarded as perfectly reasonable and justifiably within schools' jurisdictions, and maybe it is. But it seems that schools have evolved quickly and quietly into entities that resemble community health centres as much as the educational institutions they were designed (however badly) to be. It is taken for granted that they will offer speech therapy, occupational therapy, sex education, drug

191 Spoken during a speech to the staff of Alice Miller School and Candlebark on 17 October 2016.
192 Ministers for Education and Health and Premier, '100 Victorian Secondary Schools to Get a Doctor', Delivering for All Victorians [Victorian State Government], 1 September 2016, premier. vic.gov.au/100-victorian-secondary-schools-to-get-a-doctor, accessed 13 March 2019.
193 Alice Dempster, 'Australian first in youth mental health at Victor High', *The Times*, 10 May 2012, victorharbortimes.com.au/story/264034/australian-first-in-youth-mental-health-at-victor-high, accessed 13 March 2019.

and alcohol education, and mental health support services. This has happened with no noticeable public discussion or debate.

Many prospective parents look at me askance when I tell them that we don't employ a psychologist or counsellor, as though we, rather than the parents, should be responsible for their child's mental health.

In between managing therapy for difficult children, schools are also expected to do some teaching, given that this is, after all, still supposed to be their main function. But there is a constant tension in almost every classroom in Australia, arising from teachers trying to teach the addition of fractions or the meaning of the imperfect tense or the function of the central nervous system to children or adolescents who may be depressed, anxious, in emotional turmoil about the fight their parents had last night, suffering PTSD from childhood sexual abuse, or worried that their mother's ex-boyfriend is going to carry out his threat to throw acid in her face.

Just as a parent must advocate for their own child, so a teacher and principal must advocate for all the children in the school, and thus the stage is set for many a confrontation. Most of these are settled amicably, despite the outcomes described in a number of the case histories in this book. But the reality is, always has been, and possibly always will be that the damaged child demands a great deal of teacher attention in every area of school life. It's highly likely that he or she will need more help than anyone else when it comes to learning to add those pesky fractions. It's highly likely that he or she will have difficulties in social interactions in the playground, and that those interactions will need adult intervention. In their unbearable insecurity, and the absence of any adult family member who genuinely cares about them or for them, these children are likely to attach to anyone who comes along. They may dog the teacher's footsteps all day, or they may transfer the anger they feel at their parents to their teacher, leading to violent outbursts that could include swearing, abuse and physical attacks. Or they may do both: having excessive attachment to the teacher but also expressing extreme anger at the teacher.

Professor Judith Trowell, honorary consultant child and adolescent psychiatrist at the Tavistock Clinic in London, says:

> If early attachments are good, they [children] may have the resources to find help: the phone line, relative, family friend, or the parent of a school friend. But if the situation is difficult, they can retreat into a way of functioning that we call 'splitting', where the good and bad are divided. Their peer group may be good and adults bad, or they may see themselves as bad and worthless and other siblings as good. Most difficult to manage is the impact on those around them, as they may unleash their unbearable feelings.[194]

The community must decide how many precious tax dollars should be allocated to providing extra help, for example in the form of classroom aides and counselling, to damaged children. The first principle of economics is that there are limited resources and unlimited wants. Education competes with prisons, roads, politicians' global research jaunts, hospitals, disabled people, elderly people, unemployed people, Third World countries, scientific research, and industry for access to the pot of gold.

It is only to be expected that I will make out a case for education, but it is not difficult to do so if one takes a long-term view. I feel obliged at this point to cite the well-known parable about a village that could only be reached by way of a narrow road that wound around cliff tops. From time to time cars went over the edge of the cliff and crashed onto the rocks below, causing serious injury or death to the occupants. At last the village got a government grant to fix the problem. The people of the village met, but soon divided into two factions that found it impossible to reach agreement. One group wanted to use the money to put a fence along the cliff top, so that no more cars would go over. The other group wanted to buy an ambulance and park it at the bottom of the cliff, so they could get the

---

194 Judith Trowell, 'Surviving Abuse', *Times Educational Supplement*, 30 November 2007.

victims of the crashes to hospital with increased celerity.

Clearly much or most government policy is along the lines of buying the ambulance.

To intervene intensively with damaged children when they are still very young, so that their literacy and other learning issues are tackled, and their urgent emotional needs recognised and addressed, would be the equivalent of building the fence. In the long-term, massive current expenditures on hospitals, medication, medical care, counselling, prisons, social security and crime prevention could be spectacularly reduced.

Alice Miller tells us that damaged children cannot be 'repaired'. In other words, my words, these children are like vases that have been hit by .303 bullets. Many or most of the pieces can be recovered perhaps: they can be stuck back together until they resemble the original vase; the vase may even be able to hold water again. But the cracks will always be there. The vases may leak under pressure. A mild bump may cause them to fall apart once more. As the poet Louis MacNeice wrote:

> But I cannot deny my past to which my self is wed,
> The woven figure cannot undo its thread.[195]

It may seem desperately unfair that trauma inflicted on a two-year-old can result in that infant being unable to enjoy satisfying and nurturing relationships as an adult, but our notions of fairness are a human invention that have no parallel in nature, and often create infantile expectations even among adults. We would do better to confront the truth about damaged children rather than believe in myths about them being 'cured' by religion, changes in diet, self-help books, gurus or epiphanies.

I became aware when working in boarding schools that the emptiness inside damaged children was so vast that nothing, nothing, could fill it. Being *in loco parentis* meant that the best boarding-house staff

---

195 Louis MacNeice, 'Valediction' (1934), *Collected Poems*, Faber, London, 1966, p. 53.

(who were few and far between – not many adults could manage the stresses involved, and some didn't try very hard) worked with extraordinary dedication to give needy kids the kind of attention they had never received from their parents. But I came to realise that even if the very best staff member spent 24 hours a day, seven days a week, with just one of these kids, it would not be enough to fill the aching emotional void within the child.

That of course is not to say that the position is hopeless. With the best support and care these damaged children can grow into adults who find life worthwhile and satisfying, who can experience a range of feelings, who can contribute richly to the world whilst at the same time taking good care of themselves.

BEWARE THE 'RESCUER' TEACHER

So much depends on the skill of the person who goes to work on the vase. When I discussed the broken vase analogy with art teacher Basil Eliades, he pointed out that the cracks and gaps in the vase could be repaired with such exquisite skill that the vase might be even more beautiful and useful than before. I liked this creative and optimistic point of view. But if the adult doing the work – and it must be an adult – is inept, abusive, narcissistic, immature, or damaged and unrepaired themselves, it is highly likely that the damage to the child will be worsened. I remember, for example, working with a teacher who cultivated close relationships with troubled students as though it gratified her to be the rescuer, the 'special person' entrusted with the grim stories these teenagers shared. Then, on a whim, she decided that teaching was not for her, and off she sailed, at a moment's notice, leaving others to deal with the young people she abandoned with apparent indifference.

It has been said that the John Buchan novels about Richard Hannay (the most famous being *The Thirty-Nine Steps*) created big problems for the British Secret Service, because for a couple of decades every British spy modelled himself on Hannay, and wanted to dash around the countryside making brilliant deductions and pitting himself against sinister master criminals whilst consorting with beautiful women. I have wondered whether James Bond created similar problems for the Secret Service in more recent times. I suspect that many MI6 employees dreamed of making massive winning bets in casinos, ordering martinis shaken not stirred, then driving away in an Aston Martin with a glamorous Russian woman spy at their side.

Two popular fictional works have had a similar impact on the teaching profession. *Goodbye Mr Chips*, a book by James Hilton that has twice been filmed, was a huge hit from its first publication in 1934 through to the 1950s and even 1960s. Mr Chips, a nickname for a teacher called Mr Chipping, was an avuncular figure in an English boarding school. His dedication to his students was lifelong and absolute, and as a result he was greatly loved by them, and evolved into an 'institution'. Yes, he got married at some point, but his wife and only child were conveniently killed off by Hilton, enabling Mr Chips to resume his 'real' marriage to his 'real' spouse: the school and its students.

It was painfully obvious to me when working at Geelong Grammar that there were a few teachers who saw themselves as Mr Chips-type figures, and who played the role to the hilt, even though their performances were unconvincing. They seemed to crave the homage and love that came to Mr Chips, and they carefully cultivated idiosyncrasies of the kind that came 'naturally' to Hilton's fictitious creation. Geelong Grammar seemed to encourage these people, as though having its own Mr Chips would add colour and atmosphere, and give the place more of the air of a British public school – an image that many people at the school seemed to crave. However Geelong's Mr Chips often struck me, on closer acquaintance, as misogynist, snobbish and self-serving.

In more recent times we have had Robin Williams in *Dead Poets Society*, a film that developed a cult following and influenced a new generation of teachers. *Dead Poets Society* brought us the guru figure who inspires young people by teaching them about the world and encouraging anti-authoritarian views. Given that I have spent my adult life questioning and often resisting authority, it might be thought that I would be a big fan of *Dead Poets Society*. But I have seen at close quarters the damage done by charismatic teachers. Charisma is the misbegotten child of narcissism, so it is no surprise when charismatic teachers leave damaged adults and children in their wake. Entire school communities can be polarised into for and against camps, the 'for' faction grouped devotedly and admiringly around the guru and the 'against' group alarmed at the personality cult that seems to be developing. Alan Jones, now a broadcaster, once a charismatic schoolteacher, taught at The King's School, Sydney, for five years, until the headmaster and he agreed that the divisions he'd created had led to such difficulties that it might be better if he found employment elsewhere.[196]

In his book *Feeling like Crap*, British school counsellor Nick Luxmoore argues that all pupils create their own ideas of school, influenced by early experiences with their parents. He said: 'School so powerfully evokes for everyone an expectation of nurture, of being looked after by parent-figures, while being in competition with sibling-figures . . . Any institution concerned with the care and development of young people is bound to be an unconscious reminder of that original carer.'[197]

Luxmoore therefore believes that the term 'this school' is used by pupils when in fact they are talking about being understood – or misunderstood – by their mother: 'nobody cares about me at this school'; 'this school is only bothered about what other people think.'

A baby develops a sense of self by working out what generates approval from its mother. Pupils need this almost as urgently. But school can be either an affirming, praise-filled mother or a critical, unflattering one.

The image of themselves that is reflected back from teachers and classmates helps pupils to develop a sense of self. But they

---

196 Chris Masters, *Jonestown: The Power and the Myth of Alan Jones*, Allen & Unwin, Sydney, 2006.
197 Nick Luxmoore, *Feeling like Crap: Young People and the Meaning of Self-esteem*, Jessica Kingsley, London, 2008, pp. 121–2.

resent needing this positive reflection of themselves, because it leaves them vulnerable: what if the other person cannot recognise or meet their needs? There are two ways to defend against this need of approval ... One is to idealise the school as a kind and loving mother-figure. These pupils work hard, volunteer wherever possible, and wear the uniform with pride. The other is to pre-empt a withdrawal of maternal favour by demonising the school. A pupil with an unhappy internal version of school may find it impossible to trust kind teachers, fearing that this might be withdrawn. Hating school is therefore safer than trusting it.[198]

RAISING COMPASSIONATE CHILDREN

The prospects for a disturbed child whose parents are unable to help him or her depend entirely on their finding a supportive stable adult – not a Mr Chips, because he doesn't exist; not an Alan Jones, who craves the spotlight; not a John Keating (*Dead Poets Society*), because in real life teachers resembling Keating tend to be manipulative and power-hungry – but an adult of the kind described by Alice Miller as an enlightened (or empathic) witness who will advocate for children in peril.[199]

But whilst the disturbed child struggles with his or her needy soul, he or she will do damage: others will suffer, and your child may well be one of the sufferers. This can only be looked upon as good Strength of Character training (unless of course your child's health is put at risk). I know that sounds glib, but, as I tried to say in my letter to the woman who complained about Liana, the reality of life is that you cannot secure happiness for your child by isolating him or her from difficult people. There are strategies that will help, but you should also consider how much your child is contributing to the problematic nature of the relationship with the damaged classmate.

---

198 Luxmoore, *Feeling Like Crap*, p. 125.
199 Alice Miller, *Banished Knowledge,* trans. Leila Vennewitz, Virago, London, 1997, pp. 149–152.

I described a boy called Malcolm earlier; a very troubled and disruptive child. The other children adjusted pretty quickly to his outbursts, but one boy, Eric, could not. Everything Malcolm did infuriated him. Eric had no obvious problems, but he kept exacerbating the situation, mainly because he was incredulous that teachers were not punishing Malcolm for his outbursts and his episodes of wild behaviour. Eric's angry, righteous responses pressed buttons in Malcolm and escalated situations from difficult to critical. Eric was still at the second level of Lawrence Kohlberg's stages of moral development, which describes people who are orientated towards fixed rules, and understand morality in terms of its role in maintaining the social order.[200] Eric believed that when anyone broke a rule, there must be culpability and consequences. Like many adults in our society, he was not yet ready to engage with Kohlberg's more sophisticated ultimate level, the understanding of social contracts with their awareness of mutual benefit, and the recognition that moral rights and legal rights are not always the same.

My letter to parents offered this advice when a child came home steaming with injustice about an inequity perpetrated at school:

So, having listened to your child's bloodcurdling account of their dramatic school day, and having gone through the steps above (I hope), what's left? Well, naturally you'll want to write a heartfelt email to the school, describing the pain your child has suffered and how you now share that pain. It's fine to do that, but please don't send it for at least twenty-four hours. You might be pleasantly surprised by how much the landscape can change over twenty-four hours. You'll quite likely find that your child has forgotten all about the indignity he or she has suffered, even if you go through torments for months to come.

Teach your child some strategies for dealing with these issues. Don't tell them to ignore someone who's giving them a bad time, as

---

200 A readable introduction to Kohlberg's work can be found at courses.lumenlearning.com/teachereducationx92x1/chapter/kohlbergs-stages-of-moral-development.

that never works. Ask them instead what they can do to change the dynamic. They could put this question directly to the difficult child: 'What can I do that'll make you like me?' They might get some helpful feedback, or they might learn that the problem is essentially with the other person and his or her attitudes.

Suggest they talk to a teacher – but they should do it, not you on their behalf. (For one thing you don't actually know what happened: you've only heard one, incomplete, version of the episode/s.)

Thirdly, give them some effective phrases that they can use. For example, teach them to give specific feedback; not 'I hate you', but 'I hate how you keep taking our Lego pieces'. 'If you keep swearing, I won't play with you, and neither will other kids.' 'Every time I suggest we play a different game, you always say no.'

I also think it is worth teaching your children how to be interesting conversationalists. Face it, some kids, like some adults, are boring. Some are excruciatingly boring. Not every thought that pops into their heads needs to be communicated immediately to everyone within earshot. Not every detail of their lives is of absorbing interest to everyone. Children need to learn to limit the number of 'I' statements they make each day. This is not easy for them, because they are at an egocentric stage of their lives. But just because they are ego-driven doesn't mean we all have to suffer.

Dale Carnegie's famous book *How to Win Friends and Influence People*, published in 1936, had a section called 'How to Make People Like You'. His six suggestions, such as 'Be genuinely interested in other people', 'Smile', 'Remember that a person's name is to that person the sweetest and most important sound in any language', are, as Carnegie says, 'all focused on the other person'. True to form, his last point is 'Make people feel important – and do it sincerely'.

Carnegie advises readers to 'Focus on being interested, not interesting'.[201]

---

201 Dale Carnegie, *How to Win Friends and Influence People*, HarperCollins, Sydney, 2017, p. 142.

Conversations consist of many threads: inanities, feelings, opinions, advice, instructions, jokes, questions, answers and stories. The stories can be of first-hand experiences, or they can be second hand – recounting a newsworthy incident from Luxembourg that occurred overnight, retelling an episode in the life of a grandparent, describing what happened to one's child at school yesterday.

The best conversationalists have had plenty of first-hand experiences, which gives them lots of stories they can share. They are fluent enough with language to be able to communicate effectively, and they have the confidence to participate actively in a conversation. They are not afraid of emotions, so when they talk about their experiences they include the way they felt when their car hit the telegraph pole or when they succeeded in making a lemon soufflé or when they were reunited with their lost dog after a long search through the bush.

And they have empathy. They know not to talk about themselves all the time. They can ask sensitive and thoughtful questions to elicit participation in the conversation by others. They can respond warmly and supportively when people speak of difficult matters. Their remarks are not determined by dogma.

These are among the qualities which make humans interesting and likeable, no matter what their age. When we consider these desirable attributes, the need to ensure that children develop them becomes self-evident. It can fairly be said then that the roles and responsibilities of parents and teachers are not difficult to discern.

9

PARENTING YOUR OWN DIFFICULT CHILD

Every human being – including the writer of this book, all its readers, and every child on Planet Earth – has flaws. Many parents, however, find it difficult to discuss difficulties they or others may have with their child.

The tough truth is that if parents haven't done a good job in the early years they have a hard task trying to be a successful parent of an older child or an adolescent. They will never completely make up for their sins of commission or omission, so it is a waste of time and energy to agonise over them and reproach themselves bitterly for their inadequacies. It will benefit no one, least of all their children.

The only gain to be made by dwelling on those awful mistakes is if parents can learn from them. And the good news is that their children may eventually forgive them. Remember the old witticism that first children love their parents, then they hate them, then they forgive them? The truth about children is that they are almost infinitely forgiving, at least whilst they are young. Parents can be bad-tempered, unfair and nasty on many occasions, but their children will keep coming back to them. This is especially true if they know their parents love them. However, if parents see fear flare in their children's eyes when they approach their little ones, the adults have a real problem.

Likewise, if children treat their parents with contempt, a lot of ground will need to be made up.

CHILDREN NEED STRONG PARENTS

Sometimes parents make the mistake of believing that grovelling apologies to their children for minor or major betrayals constitutes noble behaviour on their part. At one public function a few years ago, I listened aghast as a senior religious leader described to the audience an interaction with his child. Apparently at a dinner party at their home, an event for adults only, the child entered the room, interrupting the meal, and the father was quite cross with him, sending him 'back to bed'. Sometime later in the evening, reflecting on what he had done, the father was overwhelmed by guilt. He went up to his son's bedroom, and, kneeling by the bed, said to his bewildered child: 'Daddy has been a very naughty daddy. Can Olaf forgive Daddy?'

I have assumed the bewilderment on Olaf's part. Perhaps he was used to this kind of undignified and unhelpful behaviour from his father. The father obviously intended us, his audience, to admire his humility, but the audience looked as horrified as I felt.

Children need parents to be strong in spirit; otherwise – their unconscious minds are asking – how is this person going to protect me? How can I be safe, when my bodyguard is grovelling before me?

In the late 1960s I was privileged to hear an address by ex-NSW Premier Jack Lang at the University of Sydney. Lang, mentor to Australian Prime Minister Paul Keating, was then in his 90s. A powerful, imposing figure, dressed in black, a true old-style Labor believer, he thundered to his young audience: 'Never explain! Never apologise! Never resign!'

This may be going a fraction too far, but many modern parents are at the other end of the spectrum: 'Negotiate everything with the child! Lavish her with praise! Gratify his every desire!'

THE VOICE OF THE CHILD

One of the ways we can realistically help young people is by improving their access to the most powerful tool human beings have – language. A characteristic of young people in trouble is that they frequently lack the language to express themselves. Many teenagers, particularly many boys, are notoriously tongue-tied and monosyllabic, communicating in primeval grunts. This hinders their chances of becoming effective and successful adults. It's not just that literacy difficulties are so closely linked to failure at school. It's also that language is needed to explore and express feelings, to communicate problems and solutions, to argue a point of view, to defend a position, to think at a complex and sophisticated level. Most importantly, language gives a sense of one's self to others.

The relationship between language and thinking is complex, but profoundly important. People with a limited vocabulary are limited in their intellectual functioning. And teenagers who have inadequate language skills are at risk of becoming locked in, left alone with strong emotions they are unable to manage.

To help improve language fluency, parents (and teachers) should try to ask open-ended questions, not ones requiring a yes/no or other monosyllabic answer. Not 'How was school?' but 'How is the substitute teacher different to your regular teacher?', 'Why do you like sitting next to Prakeesh?', 'Who's the worst behaved kid in your year group?' (Don't worry, if it's yours, he's not likely to admit it.) 'So what does he do that's so awful?'

Young people need to be given time to finish their own sentences, instead of adults, noticing their hesitations, rushing in to speak for them.

Teenager: Yeah, so Nanna's in hospital, having a . . . um, a . . .
Parent: Heart bypass.
Teenager: Yeah. But she should be home, er . . .
Parent: Thursday.
Teenager: Yeah. But we're, like, feeding her dog, and . . . um . . .

Parent: And you've been collecting her mail.
Teenager: Yeah.

A good rule for garrulous parents is to let sons and daughters say three sentences in a row before you say anything. If you're one of those adults who tells everyone with a cheerful chuckle, 'Oh you know me, I never shut up', then it might be a good idea to listen to yourself. You're probably right; there's every chance you do talk too much, and you probably should shut up. One of the biggest problems our society has is with the children of parents who dominate all the space – adults who have such powerful personalities that they fill the room. Their children tend to be like shadows, wraiths, who cannot look grown-ups in the eyes or have conversations with them. They seem to lack personality.

I worked with a powerful man when I was nineteen or twenty years old. He was Dr Nick Paltos, the head of Casualty at Sydney Hospital. When he entered a room, I was always aware, without even looking around, that a Presence was present. He was forceful, formidable, and a brilliant diagnostician. He later went into private practice and had patients like Kerry Packer, Chief Justice Laurence Street, John Laws and Harry Secombe. He was also a conspirator in a plan to smuggle 5.5 tonnes of hashish, worth $40 million, into Australia. He was convicted of that, and later, of other charges, and was sentenced to 23 years in prison.[202] He certainly made an impression on me. I liked him, but I was aware that he dominated every individual, every group, every scene in the Casualty Department. We seemed like nonentities when Nick was on the scene.

Decades ago I read an article by an experienced foreign correspondent, in which he mentioned that the first Premier of the People's Republic of China, Zhou Enlai, had a personality so strong that people felt his presence in a room before they saw him. Not long afterwards, I happened to be having dinner with a man who had

202 'God "will forgive" the doctor turned crim', *Sydney Morning Herald*, 1 January 2004.

been foreign correspondent for one of Europe's most powerful and respected newspapers for 30 years, and who had recently retired. I told him the story about Zhou Enlai, and asked if he had met anyone like that, among all the world leaders with whom he had interacted. He said that Zhou Enlai had not affected him in the way the other man had described, but two people had. One was Charles de Gaulle, which did not surprise me, because I knew this journalist to be an ardent Gaullist. The other was Pablo Picasso.

Many people dominate situations simply because they talk too much. They generally do so either because they are narcissistic or they are anxious. Members of the latter group are sometimes harder to recognise. Psychologists say we can only tolerate fifteen seconds of silence before we start to get nervous, and hurry to fill the space with words. When we see our kids floundering in a conversation we feel a natural urge to rush in and save the day for them, but in the long-term, this is counter-productive.

We should not laugh at children when they make mistakes – with anything, but especially with language. If we do, we risk destroying their poetic abilities. Generally, it's a good idea not to correct children when they make language errors. This is because it's unnecessary. If a child says 'vetegable' when they mean vegetable, don't worry – they'll work out the correct pronunciation sooner or later. There are enough people in their lives already – among their grandparents, teachers, siblings, peers, perhaps – who are only too anxious to pounce on every mistake they make.

There's no timetable for becoming fluent in language, but fluency and confidence will not be achieved by giving children the sense that language is a minefield in which one false step will trigger an explosion.

Adults should never use recipes or formulae when talking to children. Expressions like 'right now I'm feeling . . .', or 'when you do that I feel . . .', or 'which part of the word "no" don't you understand?' are not authentic communication, and kids' noses are quick to pick up the bad smell emanating from such phrases.

A sales rep for a publisher told me once how an 'expert' had been hired as a consultant by the company, and the expert had trained them all in a new script they had to use when visiting bookshops. When the bookseller asked them 'How are you today?', they had to reply 'Never better; thank you for asking'.

The sales rep said the new script nauseated him, and he abandoned it after a day and a half.

The only important academic skill needed by children is literacy. It's extremely helpful if people can write and read intelligently; can decode language and understand its nuances. Primary school maths – counting, measuring, the four arithmetical operations, calculations involving money, using fractions, percentages and decimals – is useful, but most secondary school maths is a waste of time for most people.

If young people can read quickly and skilfully, and choose not to read in their leisure time, that's fine. Perhaps they are spending that leisure time occupied in some other worthwhile activity, like sport, cooking, Lego construction or music. We adults are very anxious about the amount of time children spend staring into screens, but if the younger teachers at Candlebark and Alice Miller are to be believed, much of this is a manifestation of the fact that children are forced to stay at home with their parents throughout their adolescence. Speaking from their own experiences, these teachers say that when young people get out of the family home at last, in their early twenties perhaps, they resume normal life, and screens no longer dominate their time. In fact, for most socially adequate people, screens soon start to seem pretty boring.

Nonetheless, reading is worth encouraging, for the reasons I described earlier as well as its contribution to literacy skills, but we do not help the cause of reading by promoting books that have little or no interest for kids or teenagers. Boys have always been seen as the gender group most reluctant to go near books, although I estimate that between 10 and 20 per cent of them are avid and sophisticated readers. It can be worthwhile tempting disengaged readers by leaving magazines lying around the house (science and sport magazines, and *MAD* are pretty popular at our place, with our six boys). Try books about sex, books about how to succeed, books of jokes, books about machines/space/dinosaurs, books about heroes, books of movies they have seen, graphic novels, true-life adventures, books about overcoming adversity, books about war and weapons, *The Guinness Book of Records*, *Harry Potter*, Stephen King, big fantasy novels, *Lord of the Rings*, *Diary of a Wimpy Kid*, Rick Riordan, Gary Paulsen, books that replicate or resemble the computer games or YouTube videos they like, and, for younger kids, Paul Jennings, Roald Dahl, Morris Gleitzman, Andy Griffiths, *Captain Underpants* . . .

CHILDREN NEED CREATIVITY AND MOVEMENT

All kids need activities where they can express themselves creatively. It would be great if every child had at least one area where he or she could pursue a creative activity at a sophisticated level – for life, perhaps. It doesn't matter whether the activity is sewing, cooking, piano playing, writing, painting, gardening, ceramics . . . the important thing is that the person is expressing himself or herself creatively.

Parents should do their best to improve gross and fine motor skills when children are young. And they should teach kids not to be afraid of falling. This helps give confidence in all kinds of abstract ways. When children fall, or hurt themselves, there is often a moment where they look around to see if they have an audience. Upon seeing a parent or teacher in the vicinity, they are quite likely to launch into a dramatic performance reminiscent of Bottom in *A Midsummer Night's Dream*:

> *That will ask some tears in the true performing of*
> *it: if I do it, let the audience look to their*
> *eyes; I will move storms, I will condole in some*
> *measure . . .*[203]

203 William Shakespeare, *A Midsummer Night's Dream*, Act I, scene ii.

It is best to look away quickly in such situations, and pretend you didn't see the accident. Selective vision and selective hearing are among the most important qualities a parent or teacher can possess. Don't worry: if the child is really hurt, he or she will certainly let you know. Often though I'll wander past a child a minute or two after a fall and say something like, 'That was a spectacular stack. Did you do any permanent damage?' And I'll add, in admiring tones, 'You sure bounced back quickly.'

It's worth expending some time and energy in trying to find for each child a sport or physically challenging activity that he or she is good at. There is one out there somewhere, for every kid. It might be lawn bowls, it might be archery, it might be golf, it might be running, it might be rugby. For one of our kids, it has turned out, to our astonishment, to be fencing. Sport is a great antidote to depression, a good way of staying fit and losing weight, and can provide a lifelong leisure activity.

TEENAGERS SHOULD WORK

Parents should strongly – even forcefully! – encourage teenagers to get paid jobs. In our society, money is one of the most empowering of all agents. For some young people nowadays it may not be the motivator it used to be, but it still fascinates most of them.

Teenagers should be exposed to lots of work experience – boys with men and girls with women, as well as with the opposite gender. Occasional work experience with parents can be worthwhile, especially if the child has a poor understanding of what their parents do all day. Kids should not be exploited and used as slave labour, but if the successful functioning of the family requires them to contribute their labour on a regular basis, then so be it. They are, after all, members of the family; not business class passengers on a plane, or holiday makers on a luxury cruise ship.

A DAILY DOSE OF 'NO'

A teacher or a parent has to be a disciplinarian every day. There's never a day when you don't have to say no to a kid. But as often as possible you should say it nicely, creatively, thoughtfully, with humour. Teasing can be a great strategy, but not if it becomes the default setting for adults. Sarcasm is a dangerous tool to use, but sarcastic teasing done affectionately can bring the child back to reality: 'Hmmm, nice tantrum. I'd give that 8, maybe 8½.' The child will often accept this, but only if it comes from an adult he knows really likes or loves him.

It's impossible to predict how people will fare on the parenting journey. One of the first stipulations, however, is that being an adult helps. Those who are adults biologically speaking but, through no fault of their own, have been unable to grow up emotionally have a difficult voyage ahead. But even the knowledge of this simple precept can help. Faking being an adult is not so difficult, and chances are, the more you fake it, the more real it will become.

10

TREKKING FROM CHILDHOOD TO ADULTHOOD

It is a commonplace to say that the rapid disappearance of mean-ingful rite-of-passage ceremonies has caused difficulties for our young people in their progress towards adulthood. Nonetheless, it's true.

Rite-of-passage ceremonies in Western societies nowadays often lack deep meaning, are negative, and can cause serious damage: for example, getting drunk for the first time, trying drugs for the first time, losing one's virginity, the notorious 'Schoolies' weeks. The few adult-sanctioned 'ceremonies' we have for young people include eight-eenth and/or 21st birthday parties, graduation ceremonies, debutante balls, the test for a driver's licence, and the end-of-Year-12 exams.

In the interests of convenience and efficiency, even many of these ceremonies have been stripped of much of their meaning. A couple of years ago I was invited to give the address at a graduation ceremony at an Australian university. It was a depressing experience. A dozen or so academic staff, dressed in their robes, were present: some told me it was their fourth graduation that day. They looked uninterested and uninspired. The vice-chancellor and other senior members of the university were not present. We straggled onto the stage, and sat looking out over an audience of 600 graduates and their family members. A few perfunctory speeches were made, I gave my address, and then, for an interminable time, the well-rehearsed students came onto the stage one by one, accepted their certificates, turned and smiled for the obligatory photographs, then exited stage left, to begin their adult journeys as members of their respective professions.

It was sausage-factory education at its worst. It's not a new phenomenon though. Barney Tobey had a cartoon in the *New Yorker* magazine in the 1970s, showing an endless queue of university students at their graduation ceremony, each receiving a scroll of parchment, as the eminent scholar presenting the degrees intoned 'Congratulations, keep moving, please. Congratulations, keep moving, please. Congratulations . . .'[204]

TRADITIONAL RITES OF PASSAGE

There are a number of ways rite-of-passage and initiation ceremonies in Western societies differ from those in tribal or indigenous cultures. As I mentioned earlier, chronological age is nowadays frequently taken as the only criterion for maturity. In Australia, a person is allowed to join the armed services at seventeen, to vote at eighteen, to buy and drink alcohol at eighteen. A person accused of a crime is treated in the adult justice system from the age of seventeen in Queensland, eighteen in other states. The legal age for having sex is sixteen or seventeen, depending on the state you live in, but conditions apply in certain cases up to the age of eighteen.

Many societies with little interest in chronological age initiate children when they start behaving in ways that indicate they are ready. By our standards, this may be when they are quite young. Photographs of Aboriginal boys preparing for initiation suggest that the boys were often only nine or ten. This could have been to help the tribe survive: hunters and warriors may have been needed to keep the group safe and well fed, and the sooner boys could take up these roles, the better

---

204 *The New Yorker Album of Drawings 1925–1975*, Penguin, New York, 1975.

the chances of the tribe members keeping themselves healthy, and fending off enemies.

Another of the crucial differences in Western society is that we make the 'official' ceremonies as safe and easy as possible, because we are terrified of inflicting pain or causing distress.

For over 3000 years, members of the Jewish faith have recognised the importance of making a rite of passage truly challenging. When a boy approaches his thirteenth birthday and prepares for the bar mitzvah, he has quite an ordeal ahead. This includes attending frequent special classes, learning Hebrew, studying the Torah at home and, on the day of the ceremony, leading the service, speaking and singing in Hebrew. There may be many hundreds of people in the congregation and the challenge is daunting for a boy whose voice is cracking or breaking, but there is no escape if he is to accept the responsibility of fulfilling all the Torah's commandments and thereby entering the world of Jewish adulthood. The bat mitzvah, for girls, a more recent feature of Jewish life, is found in progressive congregations, and also has demands and challenges, but these can vary quite widely, depending on the beliefs and practices of different groups.

As is well known, other societies have subjected young people to physical pain: having teeth knocked out, ears or nose pierced, penis circumcised or sub-incised, or flesh cut with sacred markings. In the Solomon Islands, boys and girls were tattooed on the face – usually with symbols of the frigate bird – as part of initiation ceremonies. I once showed a documentary film about face carving in the Solomon Islands to a Year 8 class in Australia; one boy fainted. In Fiji, girls who had reached puberty were tattooed on the vulva by 'skilled female artists who have been described as hereditary priestesses'.[205] The Sateré-Mawé people of the Amazon subjected young boys to the stings of swarms of the exceptionally painful bullet ants that were placed in gloves woven from leaves. The boys donned the gloves for

---

205 Lars Krutak, 'The Art Of Nature: Tattoo History of Western Oceania' 3 June 2013, *Lars Krutak: Tattoo Anthropologist*, larskrutak.com/the-art-of-nature-tattoo-history-of-western-oceania, accessed 13 March 2019.

at least ten minutes, suffering repeated stings. Once the gloves were taken off, further pain, swelling and paralysis of the arms followed, but each boy had to undergo this ritual repeatedly, until he was able to do so without shedding a tear. Only then could he be declared a man.[206]

MODERN RITES OF PASSAGE

Schoolies' weeks demonstrate that if adults have no meaningful rite-of-passage ceremonies involving real challenges for young people, the young people will create rite-of-passage trials and ceremonies for themselves. And if they do not participate in large-scale communal ones they will organise small-scale ones. These may centre around gang membership, involving for example drag racing, games of chicken, or even, for male gangs, pack rape. They may include tattooing, drug taking, or so-called 'hazing' or 'bastardisation' experiences that, under the seemingly innocuous heading of 'practical jokes', can include being branded, being forced to swallow vomit-inducing pills, being subjected to sleep deprivation, being continuously drenched by iced water, or being force-fed alcohol or drinks too disgusting to specify. Wikipedia reports at least one hazing death each year in the United States alone between 1969 and 2016.[207]

Late in 2018, a 28-year-old Sydney man died after eight years of suffering. When he was twenty, he had been dared by friends to eat a garden slug that had crawled across their table. His mother told a TV channel: 'Twenty-year-old boys, red wine, alcohol, sitting at some mate's table – a slug goes onto the table, someone banters about a dare . . . boys will be boys.'[208]

Unfortunately, the slug was a carrier of a parasitic worm. The worm infected his brain; he became quadriplegic, experienced seizures, and

---

206 *Initiation rituals, Taboo*, Season 2, Episode 1, National Geographic Channel, USA, 2007.
207 'List of hazing deaths in the United States', Wikipedia, en.wikipedia.org/wiki/List_of_hazing_deaths_in_the_United_States, accessed 13 March 2019.
208 John D'Arcy, 'A Killer in the Garden', 7 *News*, 13 November 2011, au.news.yahoo.com/a-killer-in-the-garden-11478098.html, accessed 13 March 2019.

could only eat and breathe through tubes. He had to be bathed and toileted by his carers until he died from the infection.

Such a tragic story is an excruciating reminder of the lengths young men will go to in order to prove their courage, virility, manliness. It is as though the young men and women involved in hazing, daring and the like share a widespread unconscious recognition that facing challenges, experiencing danger and suffering pain are necessary for them and their peers. It would not be unreasonable to hypothesise that this is part of the collective unconscious of all people. The National Youth Gang Survey in the United States reported that in 2012 there were around 30,000 gangs and over 800,000 gang members in that country. This was a rise in gang members of 8 per cent in five years. In the same period, gang-related homicides rose 20 per cent.[209]

Frequently nowadays we are confronted by uninitiated men. A few years ago, I was in a shop in Barkly Square shopping centre, on Barkly Street, Melbourne, trying on a pair of jeans. I went into the little cubicle, pulled the curtain shut, took off my trousers, and started pulling on the jeans. Suddenly the curtain was ripped open. I looked up, startled. A young guy, maybe twenty years of age, was standing there. He was a lot younger, taller, stronger and bigger than I was. He said, 'I left eighty bucks in here. Where's my eighty bucks?'

I tried to stay calm, and I answered: 'Sorry, I can't help you. There isn't any money here.'

The saleswoman appeared behind him. She was about seventeen or eighteen, lightly built. She pulled at him, saying: 'You can't do that. You can't walk in on people like that.'

He turned away, saying, 'But I left my money in there. He's got my money.'

I drew the curtain shut and, determined to stay calm, buttoned up the jeans. They were a pretty good fit. I started taking them off. The curtain got ripped open again. It was the same guy. Now he was

209 NGC, 'Highlights of the 2012 National Youth Gang Survey', National Gang Center, national-gangcenter.gov/Publications/6, accessed 13 March 2019.

really boiling. 'Where's my money, bro? I want my money. Give me my eighty bucks.'

'I've told you, there's no money in here. You must have left it somewhere else.' But he wouldn't listen. He kept standing there, swearing at me, demanding his money, getting angrier and angrier. Once again the saleswoman came and pulled him away. I admired her strength of character. I heard him complaining to a friend in the shop about how I had stolen his money and how he was going to get it off me.

I came out of the cubicle and took the jeans to the counter. I was nervous enough to consider abandoning the purchase and walking out of there, but I was keen not to be frightened and not to look frightened. The man and his friend were near the counter, the guy swearing continuously at me and demanding his money, his friend listening sympathetically but not getting involved.

I pulled out my wallet to pay for the jeans. The man walked towards me, saying, 'You've got my eighty bucks. I want to look in your wallet.'

'Back off,' I told him. 'Just back off.'

He did, rather to my surprise. I was relieved to know that there was still a line he wouldn't cross. The jeans were $50, but I was so disturbed that I gave the salesgirl $80.

She said, 'They're only fifty.' I quickly stuffed the other $30 back in my wallet. Luckily the guy didn't notice.

I got my jeans in a bag, along with a sympathetic smile from the sales assistant. The young man continued to stare at me and abuse me, saying to his friend, 'I know he's got it. If I could just prove that he's got it . . .'

I said to him: 'Be a man. If you've lost your money, you've lost it. Deal with it.'

He said sulkily: 'I don't want to deal with it. I want my money back.'

I headed out of the shop. I wasn't going to run to my car. I wanted to show this guy that he hadn't got to me, even though he had. So I walked at a leisurely pace out to Barkly Street, got into my car, started the engine, and pulled out from the kerb. But all the time I was thinking, *I don't want to let this go; this is unfinished business.*

I drove towards the intersection of Barkly Street and Sydney Road, really troubled about leaving the situation. Something told me I had to resolve this. Suddenly I saw the two young men walking along the footpath, on the other side of the street. I did a U-turn, although I was still unsure about what I was going to do. I pulled over, jumped out of the car and called to them. They looked startled.

But by now I had decided what to do. I said to the tall one, the angry one, 'I want to show you something about human beings. I want to prove something to you.'

I got my wallet out again and opened it. But I realised the young men were too close for comfort. I put up one hand and said, 'Back up, both of you.'

They did, and again I thought, *Good, they're still not totally out of control.*

I had decided I would give the man $160. If I gave him $80, he would think I had stolen his money and he had scared me into returning it, or that I'd had an attack of conscience. The only way I could prove I did not take the money was to give him double the amount he'd lost, $160. But I was too nervous to stand there counting out all those notes. So I took four fifties and pushed them at him. 'Here's two hundred bucks,' I said. 'And the next time you start judging people, the next time you're so certain you're right, just remember that maybe you're actually wrong.'

Their whole attitude changed. They looked Middle Eastern, which I mention only because the quieter one started showering me with blessings: blessing me, my wife, my family, my home, my car . . . The taller one tilted his head. He seemed disconcerted, but kind of admiring, and finally he said, 'You're a mad cunt, but yes, bless you.'

They walked on, laughing and talking to each other, shaking their heads. I went back to my car and did another U-turn. By the time I got through the intersection, they were halfway down the next block. I passed them, and they saw me. They waved affectionately, enthusiastically.

It would be nice if the story ended there and I could make a few smug comments about how I had changed the life of this aggressive young man. But about a week later I was in the same shopping centre, going past the same shop, and I caught the eye of the young saleswoman. She clearly remembered me, and smiled and waved. I went in. She was full of talk about the incident. She told me that after I left the shop, the guy had found his money, which he'd put in his fob pocket instead of his regular pocket. When he came back the next day and told her how I had given him $200, she was furious with him. 'I told him that he was a complete shit,' she said. 'I told him, "How could you take that man's money? Don't you have any morals at all? You're disgusting."

'He just said that you were an idiot with stacks of money, and so he didn't care.' She said to me: 'No offence, but you were stupid to give him $200. I know that guy. He's no good. He does drugs and everything.'

Well, I still think I got good value for my $200. I spent the money to jolt him, to shock him. I like to think that he'll remember it for the rest of his life. That he'll never be quite certain about people again. No matter what he said to the sales assistant, I believe he was shaken, because he came face to face with something he couldn't fit into his understanding of the world.

I think that he was a typical alienated and uninitiated young man. His reaction to the possible loss of his $80 was infantile. He had been careless with his money – his response to its loss showed that it was important to him, but if it was so important, why had he not taken better care of it? He seemed to see the world as a place where people were after all they could get; and everyone was trying to rip everyone else off. By his age he should have been tacking towards the commitment of a long-term or lifelong relationship perhaps, and/or a job, and/or fatherhood. His family and society had let him down. He was maybe twenty years old, but twenty going on six.

It has been said of Australia that it's a country where every boy is in a hurry to reach his eighteenth birthday, and once he gets there he stays there forever. The challenge for a boy is to become a man: a man who has integrity, strength, kindness and understanding.

MODERN RITE OF PASSAGE OPTIONS

In order to try to help the maturing process, quite a number of well-meaning adults have devised and implemented rite-of-passage experiences and ceremonies, for both boys and girls. Sometimes these are offered on a commercial basis, where a school or community group, or an informal group, pays an organisation to send people to run such a course.

I don't like the idea of commercial organisations sending in strangers for these purposes. After returning home from the funeral of Adam Butterworth, a wonderful young man I had taught, who committed suicide in his early twenties, I wrote a book called *Secret Men's Business*, which was intended to give young men information, instruction and ideas so that they might navigate their adolescent and adult lives more successfully. After it was published, I started getting invitations from schools to talk to assemblies of boys – for the most part boys in Years 8, 9 or 10. I accepted the invitations because I was happy to talk about some of the issues these boys were likely to encounter, and I thought it was important work. But many of the schools wanted me to include sex education in my advice to the audiences. I refused, because I felt it was wrong for the boys to be assembled en masse and subjected to such intimate, personal and powerful information from a complete stranger. Tribal societies, I'm sure, would have regarded such a scenario as bizarre.

In recent generations, quite a lot of pressure has been put upon fathers to have 'The Talk' with their sons. Many or most fathers are uncomfortable with this idea, and subtly or openly resist the pressure. I think their instincts are probably correct. When the father talks to the son about sex with women, he has to be – there is no avoiding it – talking about having sex with the boy's mother. At an unconscious level at least, it is unbearable for the boy to hear this. Tribal societies tacitly recognised this threat to the unconscious mind by ensuring that boys undergoing initiation were taught by the elders of the tribe, which could include the boy's uncles, grandfathers, cousins, or other men, but never the father.

So if we disbar strangers and fathers from teaching young people about sex, we are, realistically, left with only three possibilities. For girls, it may be appropriate for the mother to take on this essential task. However, being a biological, adoptive or foster parent does not automatically confer on the parent a right to do this. The right must be earned, through years of good communication and a loving and mutually respectful relationship, so that trust has been established. Equally, for boys, a grandfather, uncle or other trusted male in the boy's life can take on the role, but only if they have earned the right.

And of course, it does not have to be an individual who conducts these conversations. The second option is for an informally connected group of adults or an informally constituted committee to organise something for an individual, or for a group of their sons or daughters. It can be done quite creatively. A friend of mine, when her son was about to turn thirteen, asked a number of men known to her and her son to write him letters about what it meant to be a man. She had these bound, and presented them to him as a thirteenth birthday present. From time to time, groups of Candlebark mothers have organised weekends for their daughters where they have celebrated the approach of adolescence, the menarche, and the meaning of womanhood in the 21st century.

The third option is to have a formal rite-of-passage experience created and carried out by a school or some other well-defined organisation to which a boy or girl belongs, such as a religious insti-tution or a scout or guide group.

When the visionary young headmaster of Geelong Grammar School, Dr James Darling (later Sir James), established the school's Timbertop campus in 1952, it was largely because he recognised the need for Year 10 (later Year 9) students to go through an intense experience that would help them make the transition from childhood to adulthood. I taught at Timbertop for four years, and was astonished at the achievements of the students, which were far beyond anything I had imagined fourteen- or fifteen-year-olds could accomplish. The program was gruelling, physically, emotionally, mentally. Based on the ideas of Austrian educator Kurt Hahn (as were Gordonstoun in Scotland, and Salem in Germany), the program required students to do many hikes, over seriously high peaks and tough country, carrying all their needs on their backs, enduring conditions that were sometimes dangerous, and at all times navigating for themselves.

Encounters with adults were rare on a number of these expeditions. The longest hike went for six days, and it was not unusual for the kids to cover more than 160 kilometres through demanding terrain in that time.

In 2012, a Geelong Grammar publication reported that in the Timbertop 'Option hikes' for that year (where students, in groups of six, chose their preferred route), 33 of the 36 hike groups chose the harder of the options offered. This accords with our experiences at Candlebark and Alice Miller, where time and again, many students on hikes, if offered an extra challenge, such as a pre-dawn detour to the summit of a nearby mountain before returning to continue with the main route, jump at the opportunity to make a difficult experience even more difficult.

Gradually other wealthy independent schools began to establish programs that were inspired by Timbertop, and in more recent years, the Victorian government, with its Alpine School program, has shown an equally innovative spirit.

ADOLESCENTS AND PARENTS: THE ESSENTIAL DIVORCE

The essence of these experiences is that adolescents are given an opportunity to start to separate from their parents. Earlier I used the dramatic word 'kill' to describe one of the inevitable stages in a child's journey to adulthood: that the child must, metaphorically speaking, kill the parents. But in a healthy relationship, this will be the prelude to a new era, a resurrection, in which parent and child reconnect in a more adult and equal manner.

Read as metaphor, the story of the life and death of Jesus Christ is interesting in this context. One of the great unanswered questions of the Christian New Testament is 'What happened to Joseph?'

Jesus has two fathers (three if we include Abraham), but one of them, God, is of course rather difficult to 'kill', given that he is held to be omniscient, omnipresent and omnipotent. Joseph, the earthly father of Jesus (or the closest equivalent to an earthly father that Jesus can have), was nowhere to be found during his son's tribulations. He simply went missing. Mary was there at the end, at the foot of the cross, and is shown in innumerable artworks, like Michelangelo's *Pietà*, cradling her dead son in her arms. But Joseph? Where was he? Down at the pub? Away in Judah doing a spot of business? Busy at work, making a kitchen bench for an important client?

The last time Joseph got a mention in the story was when Jesus, at the age of twelve, nicked off without his parents' knowledge or permission to the Temple in Jerusalem, to listen to and talk with the priests and scholars there. When Joseph and Mary eventually found him, 'they were amazed', according to the King James Bible. This in itself is rather amazing, as one might reasonably assume that they would have worked out by then that their son was not the average kid, having been born to a virgin and attended by three kings from the East at his cradle. But Jesus replied to Mary's remonstrances with the words: 'How is it that ye sought me? Wist ye not that I must be about my Father's business?'[210]

We can assume from his chronological age, from his independent action in leaving his parents, from the fact that Joseph is never mentioned again, and from his response to his mother, that at twelve he is at the dawn of adolescence. The healthy answer from a young man at this stage of life would be: 'I'm getting on with my own stuff. Places to go, things to do, people to see . . .' Not the answer Jesus gives: 'I'm working for my dad (the other one) now.'

Instead of moving out of his father's sphere of influence to launch

---

210 Luke 2:49, *The Holy Bible, King James Version*. Cambridge Edition, 1769; *King James Bible Online*, 2019. kingjamesbibleonline.org.

his own adult life, Jesus is merely moving from one parent's shadow to another. No boy can carry this weight.

Under these circumstances, Jesus, sentenced to death by the authoritarian father figure Pontius Pilate, must die, metaphorically if not literally, because no other outcome is possible for someone so overshadowed by his more important father. God is so powerful that no son could escape him. Perhaps Joseph's situation is one of impotence rather than importance: unable to compete with God, he is pushed out of the story, shoved aside and forgotten. Or perhaps he is like so many earthly fathers: not committed enough to his parental responsibilities. (Most biblical scholars, incidentally, go for the easy answer, and assume Joseph has died at some earlier date – and without any miraculous intervention by Jesus.)

Although Jesus is resurrected three days after his execution, it is not so that he can lead a mature adult life, enjoying a mature relationship with a loving partner and perhaps in time fathering his own children. Instead it is to 'ascend into Heaven where he sitteth at the right hand of God, the Father Almighty', according to the Apostles' Creed. It seems that he is never to separate from his father; he is destined to be by his side forever, obeying his will.

Equally, he is not allowed to outgrow the childish relationship with his mother. It is she who sees him to his death and who nurses his body afterwards. He has not been able to choose his own partner, who, in the normal course of a human life, might be to the fore in tending to the dying and death of the 33-year-old man.

FICTIONAL SEPARATIONS

Jesus is like Hamlet in some ways. Hamlet has to deal with no fewer than three fathers: his biological father, who has died, his stepfather, and the ghost of his biological father, who demands that the young man put his own life on hold and instead carry out the father's agenda. The prince is, understandably, paralysed as a result, unable to reason or function.

The tensions between parents and adolescents are necessary and healthy, but rarely understood on either side. Some parents react angrily to the adolescent's need to separate; some try to hide what is happening under a suffocating cloud of unremitting niceness, relying on fixed smiles and good grooming to carry the day. Many are between those two positions.

One common cause of tension arises in separated families when adolescents express a wish to leave the home of the parent who has raised them, and go and live with the other parent. The adolescent can be relentless in his or her pursuit of this goal. The mother (it is usually a mother) and the adolescent may both believe that the absentee parent has been neglectful, selfish, possibly abusive, possibly a heavy drinker, whilst the parent who has done most of the work has been self-sacrificing, starved of adult company, dedicated to the son or daughter.

The single parent can be devastated by this turn of events: 'I was always there for her', 'I had to be both mother and father', 'He knows what a bastard his father is; how can he possibly . . .?'

But it is necessary for the adolescent to leave, partly because he or she must 'get out from under' – escape from the home that has been safe and secure for the child but that now feels suffocating. A Disneyland Dad, who sets few limits, often goes missing in action, lives a casual or hedonistic life and has had a number of short-term relationships, may be more likely to treat his teenage son or daughter as an adult, even if sometimes that does not seem to be in the adolescent's best interests.

As well, many teenage boys, and often girls too, feel a yearning for the presence of the father in their lives once more. They overlook issues such as a father's alcohol problems, abuse of the mother, stinginess with money, lack of integrity, neglect of his kids . . . it's all conveniently brushed aside. On the other hand, girls who have been living with the father may yearn to be with the mother for the critical period of growth into adulthood.

Because the missing parent has not been much of a parent, the child may feel less urgency to 'kill' him or her. It is either the dedicated parent or parents or the destructive parent or parents who must be shirtfronted, and made aware that a new era has begun. This need not be too painful if the parent or parents are aware of its inevitability, and gracefully and gradually keep stepping back, stepping aside, and allowing without ugly confrontations the autonomy craved by the teenager. For the over-controlling parent, the outcome is likely to be all or nothing: there may be a bloody battle, which, if won by the parent, will result in the child never achieving his or her potential. That child might be the daughter who at 40 is still living at home, faithfully caring for the ageing father or mother. He might be the son who is passive and colourless, bullied by his girlfriend or wife. With great sadness I remember a friend of mine whose last words to his son were, 'Get out and don't come back until you've sorted yourself out.' They had no further contact, because the young man was killed in a vehicle accident – caused by his reckless behaviour – a few months later, at the age of nineteen.

Not long after I wrote *So Much to Tell You*, in which a fifteen-year-old girl ultimately forgives her father for the scarring he has inflicted on her face, I read in newspapers of a Queensland court case in which a young woman whose father had slashed her across the face with a knife, leaving her with permanent scars, spoke in his defence at his trial. She said she had forgiven him and didn't want him sent to prison because she would like to live with him again.

If the child of the over-controlling parent has to fight a pitched battle in order to gain the independence so necessary to him or her, he or she may subsequently break off all contact with the parent, or have only a polite and distant relationship with him or her thereafter.

In the old days of children's literature, authors avoided exploring such intensely powerful situations as parents and adolescents going their separate ways. In the classic Australian novel *Seven Little Australians* by Ethel Turner, the wild and spirited Judy clashes repeatedly with her authoritarian father.[211] Both seem so determined and bloody-minded that it is hard to imagine how their conflicts can be resolved. In an outcome all too common in nineteenth-century fiction, Judy, aged

---

211 Ethel Turner, *Seven Little Australians*, Ward, Lock and Bowden, London 1894, Chapter 20.

thirteen, is killed by a falling tree – just before she reaches the age where a final battle is likely. In this paternalistic society, the huge tree, upright, dominating the landscape, yet ageing, ringbarked and 'rotten through and through',[212] may have come from Ethel Turner's unconscious mind and is a perfect symbol: the father-tree, fading in strength but still powerful enough to fall on the wilful Judy and crush her.

In more recent times, novelists like Enid Blyton found ways to get rid of the parents (for example by sending the children to boarding school, or sending them on long extended country holidays, or rendering them into orphans, or condemning the parents and children to be separated as a result of some catastrophe) or ignore the parents pretty much completely, as in the Famous Five and Secret Seven series.

But in the late twentieth century, when a new genre, that of adolescent fiction, emerged, writers found the courage to depict the confrontations and showdowns between parents and children. I have mentioned Melina Marchetta's novel *Looking for Alibrandi*, in which John Barton, the seventeen-year-old son of a powerful and successful politician, is unable to escape the long shadow cast by his father, and commits suicide.

In Jonathan Harlen's novel *The Lion and the Lamb*, the main character, Hector, is fourteen, a significant age in a boy's life. His father has a big gun, and I guess there's no need to explain that symbol. Hector doesn't have a big gun; he has not reached puberty – we know that from his father's taunts: "'Your arms, look at your arms!' Juan reached out and enclosed Hector's thin bicep in his enormous fist. "I have more muscle in one thumb than you have in your whole body."[213]

Hector constantly challenges his father, saying that he has no respect for him and that he is a fool. So, among other things, the book is about Hector's transition from boyhood to adulthood. As with all children, speaking symbolically, it has yet to be determined whether he will grow into a man or a 'woman'.

---

212 *Ibid.*
213 Jonathan Harlen, *The Lion and the Lamb*, Hodder & Stoughton, Sydney, 1992, pp.14–15.

His father says: 'You are like a woman yourself, *cielito*. You are soft and thin, you have a pretty face.'[214]

Hector defeats his father in at least three ways. Firstly, by taking away Juan's bullets, a kind of castration of the father. Secondly, by asking a girl out on a date, against his father's orders, thus starting to establish his own potency. And thirdly, by building a boat. The father had been a professional fisherman with a boat called *The Lion*, but he doesn't want Hector to become a fisherman. Hector builds a boat, however, and in a nice touch calls it *The Lamb*. There's more than a little irony in this, as Hector has already demonstrated convincingly that he is not going to be his father's sacrificial lamb.

Towards the end of the book, the potency battle between the two males reaches a climax. Hector reaches puberty, symbolically indicated by this scene, when he is trapped in a lift but takes advantage of the situation to ask his girlfriend for a date: 'In the midst of the confusion, Anna took Hector's hand between his knee and hers, and squeezed it. At that same moment the lift gave a sharp jolt underneath them, as though it had just woken up from a long sleep.'[215]

No sooner does Hector announce that he is going out with Anna than his father raises the ante by announcing that he, the father, is going to get married. He then takes off his belt and beats his son for stealing the bullets, but also of course because Hector has shown that he is now sexually potent and therefore a threat to the father's ascendancy. It proves to be the last throw of the dice for Juan, and for all that he and Hector actually have a good relationship in some ways, it is nevertheless a war between them – as to some extent (and often in concealed ways) it must be in every family, regardless of whether the relationship between father and son is good, bad or indifferent.

Undaunted by the beating, Hector takes *The Lamb* down to the sea and launches it, but Juan finds out, and in a state of primeval rage grabs the shotgun and comes after him:

---

214 Harlen, *The Lion and the Lamb*, p. 23.
215 Harlen, *The Lion and the Lamb*, p. 75.

Juan ... looked between the pier and the headland and saw a strange shape on the water, dancing in the face of the sun. His eyes burned with the brightness of it, and his head swam. It was a silhouetted figure, with the palms outstretched to form the shape of a cross, calling to him across the water in words he could not understand.

He bellowed in rage and raised his shotgun. He aimed it at the dark shape and crooked his finger around the trigger ready to shoot. Then the words came to him more distinctly, and in a voice which sounded familiar, as high and clear as the sky: 'It floats! It floats! Anna! Evgeny! Look, it floats!'

Juan ... slowly lowered his gun and sank to his knees. He stared straight into the sun, no longer dazzled by its brightness, and when he finally spoke, he spoke softly. 'My son!' he said. 'My son is a fisherman.'[216]

Thus the archetypal story of Abraham and Isaac, so powerful in Judaism, Islam and Christianity, of the father who will kill his son rather than lose the potency battle, is played out again – on the sands of a Sydney beach. Hector the young fisherman is also shown to be another incarnation of Jesus, whose own story re-enacts (and extends) that of Abraham and Isaac. Juan's belated acceptance of his son's previously unsuspected strength and skill reassures readers that this relationship between father and son has a future, and the future will be healthy. There will be a resurrection more satisfactory perhaps than the one experienced by Jesus.

In the Agamemnon and Clytemnestra legend, retold by Colm Tóibín in 2017 in the novel *House of Names*, the assassination of Agamemnon by his wife Clytemnestra occurs when their son, Orestes, is too young to countenance the sudden extinction of his omnipotent warrior-father from his life. Had Agamemnon lived longer, Orestes would have come to realise his father's shortcomings. But instead the child is left with his belief in an unrealistic idealised father.

---

216 Harlen, *The Lion and the Lamb*, p. 85.

Haunted by this immature perspective, Orestes is compelled to murder his mother, in an act of filial revenge. But he cannot do this as a child; he needs his mother too much. The killing must wait until Orestes is well into his adolescent years.

The outcome for Adrian, the mill boss's son in Ivan Southall's 1962 Australian bushfire novel for children, *Hills End*, is not good. As the children struggle through crisis after crisis, Adrian emerges as an impressive young leader. But when the adults, including Adrian's father, finally arrive, and find the children have survived the catastrophe, Adrian does not fare well:

> 'Stop that,' he bellowed.
>
> Adrian lowered his whistle, startled, not understanding. 'But, dad,' he said, 'I was only calling the kids. It's our signal.'
>
> 'Signal! Signal! Don't you dare do it again.'
>
> Adrian shrank, frightened by this anger, wondering how he could have forgotten this wrath that so often was in his father. The grown-ups were back all right . . . Slowly Adrian pushed his whistle back into his pocket, and somehow it was symbolic. It seemed to signify the putting away of the little bit of dignity he had had, the little bit of bravery, and the adventure of fighting back.[217]

It is noticeable that these are all episodes of sons pitted against their fathers. So many powerful literary archetypes in our culture concern themselves with this struggle. Girls' relationships with their parents are often more complex, subtler and full of day-to-day negotiations. Josie in *Looking for Alibrandi* is in conflict with her tough grandmother and forceful mother for a long time, but the bond between the three strong women is so powerful that we know none of them will ever walk away from the other two.

Rivalry between a parent and an adolescent is common. At a school writing workshop for older teenagers that I ran a few years

---

217 Ivan Southall, *Hills End*, Puffin/Penguin, Harmondsworth, 1965, p. 217.

ago, a group of girls started talking about their sense that their mothers were in competition with them. They told stories of mothers borrowing their clothes, adopting the same hairstyles, playing the same music that the girls passionately loved. One girl said that if she drove the family car, her mother would deliberately leave the P plates on the vehicle, hoping people would think the mother was seventeen years old.

One girl, Arabella, said in frustration: 'Everything I do, my mother copies. I started learning piano; my mother started learning piano. I started going to yoga; now my mother goes to yoga. I started playing netball; my mother joined a netball team.'

Later, I was telling one of the teachers about this conversation. 'Interesting,' she said. 'Arabella's been in a psychiatric day care centre for the last eight weeks. We don't see her often, but occasionally, like today, she gets leave to come to school. But you know the funny thing? She's in the school debating team, and we have regular inter-school debates. She hasn't missed a single one.'

'Yes,' I said. 'Because her mother can't join the debating club.'

HELPING TEENAGERS ON THE LONG WALK TO ADULTHOOD

So, how do we help these young people transition to adulthood?

Apart from a rite-of-passage ritual or ceremony organised by a school or other organisation, a group of adults who are connected to each other in some way can, as I mentioned, design a program that might be formal, semi-formal or quite informal.

Both of these options are valid. There are a couple of problems with both of them, but before mentioning the problems, I want to stress that *something* is better than *nothing*. As long as the course 'has a heart', to borrow a phrase from Carlos Castaneda[218], as long as it

---

218 Carlos Castaneda: *The Teachings of Don Juan: A Yaqui Way of Knowledge*, Penguin, Harmondsworth, 1968, p. 106.

is not vicious or driven by extreme gender politics or riddled with distorted values or propagandising for a particular cause, it is likely to have value.

Insidiously, however, these courses can sometimes be subverted by adults or kids who want to play practical jokes on one or more of the participants. This is very dangerous. It is impossible in any area of life to have a practical joke in which no one is humiliated, embarrassed, belittled or hurt. Mature adults must be in charge and must set the tone, which, for a good deal of the time, must be serious.

A major problem with these homemade courses is that they are, to some degree, artificial. They cannot be anything else. They have not arisen organically over thousands of years from the beliefs, values and practices of the society. They have to be devised by people who, metaphorically speaking (or perhaps literally), sit around a table with the intention of devising a rite of passage. But if that is our best option, then that is our best option. We must simply do what we can, using our collective wisdom, imagination and knowledge.

Another reservation I have with courses designed in recent times is one to which I alluded briefly earlier. In Western societies, we are determined that all young people should 'pass'. No one can be allowed to fail. Our concern for the psychological health of those who fail is so great that we construct rite-of-passage rituals where everybody succeeds. Such a luxury is only possible to those who live in strongly built houses, in secure areas, where Goths, Vandals, Vikings, barbarians, tigers and wolves pose no threat. And of course, that is how we live today. For many of us, the greatest danger we collectively face is the zombie apocalypse.

What happened, in tribal societies, to those who failed the tests that would have allowed them to be warriors, healers or leaders? I assume they became fringe dwellers, living on the margins, hanging around the edges of the tribe, scavenging for food, doing menial jobs. In one way, now that we no longer need as many young men as possible to become warriors, now that we select potential healers by means of Year 12 exams and similar, we can afford the luxury of having tests everybody passes. But the danger is that tests which no one fails are rendered meaningless.

The third problem is that graduating from rite-of-passage ceremonies in our society usually does not result in any meaningful change in the lives of the young people. One of the greatest weaknesses of Timbertop was that when students returned to the main campus at Geelong for their final three years of schooling, they were treated as infants again. Having completed arduous hikes in the Australian Alps, through blizzards, using nothing but their compasses and maps to navigate, they were suddenly not trusted to cross the street without an adult supervisor. Middle-aged men and women were paid to push lawnmowers, change light globes, prepare and cook meals, while fit and healthy young men and women – who a few months earlier had been cooking elaborate meals over campfires high in the mountains, or chopping wood for their hot water, or digging drainage trenches – lay around watching them from their banana lounges, or, more likely nowadays, ignoring them while they played games on their electronic devices.

Similarly, in modern times many Jewish thirteen-year-olds who go through their bar mitzvah or bat mitzvah find that nothing actually changes: once the celebrations are over they continue to be treated like little kids by their parents, schools and the wider community. It can stay like this for many years.

Our reluctance to allow adolescents to grow up, our determination to keep them as children laced tightly into metaphorical Shirley Temple corsets, our resistance to treating them as adults, is so powerful that we deny them meaningful roles in our society until they are in their early twenties, at least. And then we complain about their immaturity and irresponsible behaviour.

TEENAGERS NEED A MEANINGFUL ROLE AND PURPOSE

We lack imagination in tackling the issue of roles for adolescents. The cruel truth is that adolescents have a great deal in common with residents of most nursing homes. Neither group has a useful role in our society. The residents of nursing homes are fed, medicated, looked after, and (sometimes) entertained. Their lives are essentially passive; they are deemed to have nothing they can contribute. They are in death's waiting room.

Teenagers are required to stay at school, whether they have outgrown it or not, sometimes for years after school has ceased to have value for them. Successive governments continue to extend the compulsory school leaving age for cynical economic reasons: it makes employment/unemployment figures look better. Babysitting young people in schools is the cheapest option available for keeping them off the streets, because on the streets they look untidy and get in the way of grown-ups. If it became economically advantageous to reduce the school leaving age to fourteen again, it would be done tomorrow.

Young people who are hankering for something to do, wanting to take on adult roles and responsibilities, are so often told that there is nothing for them until they are about 25 years old and have thirteen years of primary and secondary education, not to mention four or five years of tertiary studies, under their belt. What a waste of resources! More importantly, what a dangerous thing to do to the young. No wonder so many of them feel frustrated and enraged.

Some years ago I suggested in a newspaper column that teenagers could be mobilised to deal with the Indian mynah birds that have colonised Australian cities.[219] Indian mynahs are an imported species, like foxes, rabbits and blackberries, and, like foxes, rabbits and black-berries, they spread everywhere and drive out the original inhabitants. The effect on Australian native birds around the city and suburbs has been disastrous.

My solution was designed to kill two birds with one bullet. A popular weapon for kids, not many years ago, was the air rifle. Fired from a reasonable distance they don't do much damage to humans. It can be a different story if they're fired from a close distance: there are a few one-eyed adults around who have bitter memories of air

219 John Marsden, 'So Much To Tell You', *Bridgewater News,* December 2003, p. 2.

rifles. But squads of teenagers, armed with air rifles, properly trained, and under the direction of a responsible adult, would make a big difference to the mynah population. They could eradicate the pests within twelve months. And let's not get sentimental about the little critters. For good reason they are called the rats of the bird world.

What benefits for the young people involved! They would have something useful to do, something that was of genuine benefit to society, something that little kids could not do: a role that genuinely reflected their ability to accept adult responsibilities. They would feel useful and important, because they would be useful and important.

Would this turn teenagers into serial killers? When I was growing up around Kyneton, Victoria, and later Devonport, Tasmania, a lot of kids went out shooting hares and rabbits. I don't think they became murderers as a result.

It's an opportunity to deal with a conservation problem and a social problem, by mobilising people power, with a good old-fashioned solution.

Alas, when I suggested it in the newspaper, nobody took me seriously. I wasn't altogether surprised.

11

THE PARADOXES AND FRUSTRATIONS OF BEING HUMAN

Human beings are proud of many things that we believe set us apart from eels, hamsters, quolls and crows. Among these are the ability to walk on two legs, which can be useful at times (if you don't believe me, ask an eel), adaptable digestive systems and the possession of opposable thumbs.

I often taunt our dog about her lack of opposable thumbs. When I'm opening the door to the house, as she waits beseechingly to get in, I tell her, 'If you had opposable thumbs, you could have let yourself in hours ago.'

The application of the can opener to her Pedigree Casserole with Beef and Gravy provides another opportunity for gratuitous mocking.

OUR TINY HUGE BRAINS

We humans also pride ourselves on having large and efficient brains. It is by virtue of our brains that we have come to regard ourselves as masters of the universe, or something close to it. However, the limitations of these same brains can cause us much disappointment – which is another of the fascinating and frustrating paradoxes that underlie our lives.

Take imagination, for instance. For all we know, imagination is an exclusive attribute of the human brain. Imagination allows us to hypothesise, speculate, daydream and, perhaps most importantly, empathise. It's unclear whether cows or sardines can pretend that they are racetrack drivers or American presidents or geese. We don't know whether they can dream of trips to the moon, jungle adventures, or fights with pirates in the eighteenth century.

We do know that humans are capable of all these thoughts. John Dewey wrote, 'Every great advance in science has issued from a new audacity of imagination.'[220] We pride ourselves on the fact that our imaginations lead us to great discoveries, great understandings. But we are in the annoying position of having brains that are big enough for us to get glimpses of concepts that those very same brains are not big enough to understand. Our knowledge that we have powerful imaginations is tempered by a truth that we don't like to acknowledge or confront. Our imaginations are limited, and the result can be frustration. For example, we know from scientists, mathematicians and our own common sense that large numbers exist. But we are incapable of imagining them. We talk about grains of sand, billions of light years, stars in the sky, but whether we are talking about sand or stars, Jeff Bezos's daily income, the 15-million-plus teachers employed in more than half a million schools in China,[221] or leaves in the forest, we can't really understand what these figures mean.

This is the case even though we try to render big numbers in concrete terms, in an attempt to imaginatively understand them. Hence, we are told that 'they could have filled the MCG twice over', 'their turnover is equal to the GNP of Australia and New Zealand combined', 'the number of miles she's covered in her cycling career would have taken her around the world three times'. These are worthy attempts, but even with their help we cannot visualise or properly imagine these figures.

---

220 John Dewey, *The Quest for Certainty: A Study of the Relation of Knowledge and Action*, George Allen & Unwin Ltd, London, 1930, p. 294.
221 'Education in China: A Snapshot', OECD, 2016, p. 9, oecd.org/china/Education-in-China-a-snapshot.pdf, accessed 1 April 2019.

Years ago, I read about a teacher in America who decided to give his students a real understanding of the number 'one million'. He set his class to collecting bottle tops. Eventually, the whole school, the whole town, the whole district got involved, and after eight years, he had a million bottle tops. I admire his vision and his persistence. I'm not sure whether he achieved much really, but there is something nice about being able to show people 'a million', to help overcome this failure of our imaginations, this inability to imagine anything more than a couple of hundred.

I've been told – but don't know whether it's true – that Australian Aboriginal people had only six numbers: one, two, three, four, five, and 'a lot'.[222] 'There are two kangaroos on the other side of the hill, there are three kangaroos, there are a lot of kangaroos.' If true, this may well represent a pragmatic accommodation of human difficulties in contemplating numbers of any significant size.

Imagination fails us in even more important ways though. We are intelligent enough to know that our lives will move through a number of stages and eventually we will die. Again, this may be a unique human understanding. It is argued that only humans are aware of their own mortality. Does an active young gerbil know that one day it will be dead? We can't answer that question, but we do know that awareness of our mortality has a critical effect on the way we live. We have a scientific understanding of death and we sometimes get glimpses of its meaning, but again our imagination is too limited to get a grip on this most powerful of all experiences.

I think this is probably related to the fact that we can't understand the biggest 'number' of all. If we could really grasp the concept of infinity, then death might become more meaningful. As it is, we can talk about the universe stretching for an infinite distance, the concept that pi can be calculated to an infinite number of places, the notion of infinite time, but we just get a big headache if we try to get our brains around these concepts in an imaginative way.

222 'Indigenous Number Systems', *SL Blogs*, 9 September 2014, blogs.slq.qld.gov.au/ilq/2014/09/09/indigenous-number-systems, accessed 1 April 2019.

And those stages we go through along the roads of our lives . . . the imagination tries to make the jump to future years, but it falls short every time. For example, it doesn't matter how much clinical information we give children about puberty, so that they can rattle off the facts about body hair and genital changes and growth spurts. Although it's good to give them information, we need to be aware that they can never understand the way they will feel and live and be when they at last arrive at adolescence. It is incomprehensible to them that they will want to do those crazy things they see teenagers doing – behaviours most young kids see as deeply unattractive.

I am in my late 60s, and I look at people in their 80s and 90s and I wonder what it will be like if I reach that age: how will it feel and how will it impact on me to have less mobility, fewer life choices; perhaps to be dependent on others; perhaps to be in a nursing home; perhaps to have dementia or Alzheimer's?

I can talk to older people. I can read articles about the impact of ageing, and books like Ellen Newton's memoir of life in a Melbourne nursing home, *This Bed My Centre*. I can relate my ageing to the fact that already I am slower and creakier than I was. But I cannot understand what old age will really be like. The future is effectively incomprehensible to the imagination.

Perhaps this is a kindness the brain does us. But perhaps if our brains were a little bigger more people would believe in an entity that we can discuss rationally and that some people claim to know intuitively.

Perhaps we could at last, imaginatively speaking, touch the face of God.

WINNING AND LOSING CAN MAKE LOSERS OF US ALL

There's a great moment in *The Simpsons*. Well, actually, there are thousands of great moments in *The Simpsons*, but this particular one is in the episode where the family moves to a new community. Everything seems perfect. Homer has a brilliant job, Marge's housework is polished off by new technology that takes five minutes a day, Lisa and Bart are enrolled in their new school.

Bart is quickly identified as 'learning disabled', and put in the Leg-Up class, a remedial group designed to help children overcome academic difficulties. Bart quickly realises that this is not his scene. He says to the teacher, 'Let me get this straight. We're behind the rest of the class, and we're going to catch up to them by going slower than they are?'[223]

I have never heard a better distillation of the problems facing schools when they work with students who are struggling academically.

At one stage in Bart's very nice group, with his very nice teacher, the students play musical chairs. However, this is musical chairs for kids with low self-esteem. This is musical chairs with more chairs than players. When the music stops, everyone dashes to a chair – and everyone gets one.

The teacher says 'Hooray, everyone's a winner!' Bart rolls his eyes.

The musical chairs lesson makes an interesting contrast to the reality of sport in our society, where everybody is a loser. Well, not quite everybody. There's one winner. But sometimes that seems almost inconsequential when you start counting the losers.

Here's a typical scenario: eight runners in the blocks, the starting pistol fires (or an electronic device beeps), the athletes run as fast as they can, one reaches the line before the others, throws his or her hands in the air, dances with joy, gets congratulated, draped with a flag perhaps, presented with trophies, hugged exultantly by relatives and friends. The other seven hang their heads, walk away, and reassuring remarks like 'Well, you did fine, I thought you ran a good race' or 'You came fourth; that's great' mean little.

The Australian Open tennis championship has 128 starters in each of the men's and women's singles. At the end of the fortnight, one man and one woman feel fabulous. The rest are losers. Some console

223 'You Only Move Twice', *The Simpsons*, Season 8, Episode 2.

themselves with the knowledge that they have achieved beyond their previous levels or picked up some useful prize money. Or won a match against a higher ranked player. But ultimately, nothing can protect them from the fact that they have lost.

Isn't this a strange structure for a society? Constantly setting up situations where there is one winner and 127 losers? What kind of people are we that we find this so gratifying and attractive?

Perhaps it's worth educating winners to understand that their win can only be achieved if other people lose: that their success is made possible through the failures of others, that their happiness is built on the sadness of others. This might help them – and everyone – to put sport and winning into a more meaningful context.

At the start of a football season every player is bubbling with optimism and confidence. The clubs and supporters are excited and hopeful. But in the Australian Football League (AFL), for example, eighteen teams compete for the premiership. Statistically, this means each supporter should only hope for four premierships in his or her lifetime. Each team can expect an average of seventeen years of failure for every one year of success. So at the end of each season there is nothing but bitter, crushing disappointment for nearly everybody. When the full-time siren blasts across the ground at the Grand Final, the players from the team that came second collapse, looking crushed, devastated. They may weep openly, with grief and a sense of failure. Only one club's supporters feel good.

Coaches are sacked, players are sold, excuses are made, promises for next year are offered. No one seems to question the essential lunacy of this structure and its destructive effect on the many people who are classified as 'failures' because of it.

Years ago I coached high jump. One of the strange things about high jump is that everybody ends up a loser. One by one each competitor is eliminated, and walks away feeling disappointed. Eventually there is a winner. But he or she keeps jumping, trying to beat a previous best, or break a record. Eventually even the winner has three misses, at which point the event concludes. There is a curious sense of anticlimax in a high jump competition, because it always ends on this rather dismal note.

I'm not suggesting that we do away with all competition, or completely change the structure of sport in Western society. One, it's not going to happen anyway, and two, competition can bring some benefits. But perhaps we should consider – at the very least – a few changes.

For example, why are we so afraid of saying that people are equally good in a competition? Why does a soccer match have to continue through extra time, and then, if the teams are still equal, into penalty shootouts? Why does a Grand Final have to go into extra time, to find one winner? Why can't we declare two teams joint premiers if they are equal after the 80, 90, 100 minutes allocated to the match? To answer my own question, it's because we are conditioned to the idea that sport has to find a winner, no matter how meaningless the process ultimately becomes.

If we were conditioned differently, if we were taught in infancy that to share victory is as exciting and wonderful as a victory that is exclusively ours, then as adults we would have no problem accepting the idea of joint premiers. The line 'It's like kissing your sister', so often used by players when a match is drawn or tied, might disappear from the sporting lexicon.

To go even further, victories in sports are sometimes essentially meaningless, because they have depended upon luck. Of course, the bounce of the ball, the umpire missing a call, the opponent stumbling, is part of every sport. But when the bounce of the ball is combined with the artificiality of time, we have a meaningless situation. I'm talking about the sprint, where the position of the runners' heads determines the winner. Is an AFL team that wins by one point better than the other team? Does a margin of .001 of a second mean anything? Is a team that scores 366 runs in a game of cricket superior to a team that scores 365? If a basketballer tosses the ball from one end of the court to the other, in a frantic attempt to beat the full-time siren, and the ball happens to drop in the basket, does that make her team better than the other team, and therefore the 'deserved winners'?

It would be a nice step forward if we had margins established in sports, such that where two or more competitors are within a certain 'zone', they are declared equal winners. Traditionalists will be outraged, arguing that margins like these will kill the excitement. But there will be no difference in excitement. The tension will now come from seeing whether one team can get into the same zone as the other team.

American high school baseball and softball games have a concept called the 'mercy rule'. If a team is, for example, 20 runs ahead in three innings, or 10 runs ahead in five innings, the match is terminated, as the position of the losing team is recognised as hopeless.

I have coached teams of children or teenagers who won games by huge margins, and I have coached teams who lost by huge margins. Nothing is gained in either instance. When a team gets an impossible distance ahead, their play falls apart, they become smug and cocky and unpleasant. Players get selfish. When a team is behind by a huge margin, their play falls apart, they become clumsy and demoralised. Heads hang lower and lower.

At every level of sport, from five-year-olds to professionals, a mercy rule would be, as the name suggests, a kindness to everyone. If a high school Australian Rules team is 50 points ahead at the end of the third quarter, it's time to stop. If an AFL team is 60 points ahead at three-quarter time, the match should be called off. In soccer, four or five goals is enough. When teenagers play basketball, if one team gets 30 points ahead, that should be full time.

After all, what does it mean when one team beats another by a huge margin, or a runner wins a 1500 metre race by 300 metres? Unless it is for a world championship or an Olympic title, they should not have been competing against each other in the first place. They're in the wrong division. (And if it was for a world championship or an Olympic title, the winner needs to be drug tested!)

I love sport, but not when it's a mismatch, and the result is an artificial construct.

There are two types of success we can have in life. There is the success built on other people's misery, and the success that does not depend on the performance of others. In the first category are sporting contests and matches, as well as contests in academic fields, music, writing, art, and so on. In the second category are the acquisition of skills, like reaching a high standard in playing a musical instrument or learning another language, and personal achievements like climbing a mountain, completing a hike, writing a concerto, cooking a remarkable meal for friends or family, running a marathon. The quiet satisfaction to be derived from successes within the second category can be sweet indeed, and it is this we should concentrate on when raising children.

THE STRIFE WITHIN

Whoever was mucking around in the laboratory late one Saturday night and ended up creating the 'human being' obviously had a sense of humour. Or maybe time was running out, with the Day of Rest getting close, and so, with only a couple of minutes left before midnight, He or She or It had to settle for a creation that wasn't quite ready. Well, we are what we are, and we're not likely to evolve in a hurry into a new and better model, with that third arm or extra eye or simian tail we sometimes covet.

One of the Creator's little jokes was to put inside us a couple of organs that were always going to be in conflict, and, surprise surprise, they always have been. They are the brain and the heart, although it might be a bit more meaningful to call them reason and emotion. We've all heard thousands of comments like 'If only I'd listened to my heart', 'Why didn't you use your head?', 'You never think, do you?' But the conflict is quite a profound one, with serious implications, and worth looking at more closely.

Babies operate largely from feelings. Hunger, loneliness, pain and frustration are strongly felt and immediately expressed, if screams, bulging eyes, and globules of dribble flying around the room are any guide. At these times, the adult often offers comfort based on logic: 'The bottle's heating up, darling, it'll only be a minute', 'Oh, your poor teeth are hurting, well, that won't last long', 'Mummy will be here soon'. Feelings are the province of the present; logic is largely the province of the future. The baby only understands the present, but adults console it with the future. The baby is not impressed.

As we grow up, we internalise the battle, until it becomes a minute-by-minute affair. The annoying thing is that the two sides rarely agree. When the alarm clock goes off, it's the heart that says 'I want to stay in bed', but the brain says 'If I don't get up I'll be late for work'. Oddly enough, when we are sick, the two opponents often swap positions. It is the heart that might now say, 'I want to get out of bed', but the brain that argues, 'It'd be sensible to stay right here'.

The conflict really flares when it comes to life's big decisions, like entering a relationship, choosing a house or taking a job. When heart and brain agree, a sense of jubilation suffuses us.

We put a lot of labels on these opposing forces, and I've done that already by calling them 'brain and heart', 'feelings and logic'. But perhaps the most controversial labels are 'male and female'.

In the past, popular culture in the West has, without much thought, endorsed the male and female labels. This conditioning began early. From my childhood I remember such examples as the *Blondie* comic strips, where Blondie, the dizzy woman, acted on impulse, rushing around buying new hats, whilst her husband did the maths and agonised over the bills. Dagwood referred to Blondie with labels like 'my little wifey'. Mr and Mrs Darling, the father and mother in *Peter Pan*, already discussed, are not too dissimilar. Television sitcoms like *Dennis the Menace*, *My Three Sons*, *The Donna Reed Show* and *I Love Lucy* perpetuated similar stereotyping, and examples abound even today. Women are impulsive, instinctive, empathetic, good at recognising and communicating feelings. Men are logical – to the point of coldness. Men are the planners, the go-to people for common sense or strategic advice.

In Western society, overtly dominated by men, logic is the big winner. We have all (nearly all) taken on this cultural belief.

'It is impossible to love and to be wise,' said philosopher Francis Bacon.[224]

In the Gilbert and Sullivan operetta *The Gondoliers*, the beautiful young woman Casilda is in love, but finds to her horror that she was betrothed by her parents to the Crown Prince of Barataria, when she was just six months old. 'I shall, of course, be a dutiful wife,' she announces, obedient to the commitment made on her behalf by her parents, 'but I can never love my husband.'

'I don't know. It's extraordinary what unprepossessing people one can love if one gives one's mind to it,' says her father, the Duke of Plaza-Toro.

Her mother interjects: 'I loved your father.'

The offended Duke responds: 'My love – that remark is a little hard, I think? Rather cruel, perhaps? Somewhat uncalled-for, I venture to believe?'

The Duchess, in her usual imperious fashion, refuses to back down. She says: 'It was very difficult, my dear; but I said to myself, "That man is a Duke and I *will* love him." Several of my relations bet me I couldn't, but I did – desperately!'[225]

Her desperation remains ambiguous, but given the sly wit of the lyricist William Gilbert we can assume the worst. Apparently, if the brain is given enough logical incentive to fall in love, the heart can be made to follow.

In our society, emotion is too often viewed with suspicion. It is sometimes belittled as dangerous, unreliable and even treacherous. Sometimes the heart seems to be treated as a place of ambush, as though the forces inside it are constantly preparing big holes, covered by leaves, with spikes at the bottom, so that as we walk along the path, we risk falling through the leaves to be impaled. It's an extraordinary idea that the hearts within us, the centres of our emotional being, are constantly trying to do us harm, that they

---

224 Francis Bacon, 'Of love', *Essays*, published by Lord Bacon himself, 1625.
225 W.S. Gilbert, *The Gondoliers*, 1889, Act II.

cannot be trusted but instead need minute-by-minute monitoring by the auditors in our skulls.

'Are you sure you know what you're doing?' 'Have you thought this through?' 'I don't think he's the one.' When the logicians really get going, they can be nasty: 'Are you crazy? This is madness? You're throwing your life away.'

The heart never gets as nasty as that. Imagine if your heart said to you, 'It's too sensible! You'll destroy yourself. Be impulsive!'

We sometimes say 'Just do it', but usually as advice to others – or to sell footwear.

Did evolution, or the Creator, really set us up this way? Are we wrong to be so suspicious of our hearts? One of the unspoken functions of Australian schools is to promote logic and diminish emotion. Students learn that the brain is infinitely superior to the heart. We must all adopt the so-called masculine approach, as the 'feminine' approach is wily, weak and unreliable.

Maths is a powerful presence in the Australian school curriculum. Most of the material taught in the last two years of school is of value only to future scientists, engineers and maths teachers, but I suspect one reason for its primacy is that unconsciously those politicians and bureaucrats who determine the culture of schools, and therefore the nature of our society, feel that maths is a valuable agent in the coveted victory of logic. Subjects that come from a place closer to the heart, like art, music and creative writing, have always had to fight for space. By the middle years of secondary school they have almost disappeared, except for the fortunate few students who are allowed or even encouraged by their parents to specialise in them. When I taught at Geelong Grammar, the school had a weekly activities program, where teachers nominated cooking or film study or Latin or chess or whatever. When I was issued with my form to fill in, I wrote 'Love', as my nomination for an activity, thinking that this would be a worthwhile subject to investigate and explore. The head of Senior School sent for me, and a short, frosty discussion ensued, in the course of which she made it clear that this was totally unsuitable and Love would not be tolerated as a subject at

Geelong Grammar. I suspect that she thought we would be engaging in an orgy of Free Love on the football oval every Friday afternoon.

Her response was particularly ironic given the views of the head-master of Geelong Grammar School during its finest years (when, incidentally, it was still a single-sex school).

Dr James Darling wrote:

I know from my own experience, if you will forgive me, that you can do nothing for a boy if you do not first love him. This is not sentimentality. Love means caring for him at the necessary moment more than you care for anything else and desperately trying to understand him. On this sort of love, discipline depends. It is remarkable what children will take, even of punishment, if they know in their hearts that in your heart you really hold their best interests. Of this sort of creative love a large portion of the population has no experience at all, at least after kindergarten, if they were lucky enough to have it then. But it is this which the school must try to supply. There can be no blueprint for its application in one's personal dealings, let alone in the whole machinery of the school, but it must be there. The teacher must always put the child first, not his own ambition or reputation, not his own pride, nor even his own principles and rules of life. How can this be? Only by his own understanding of God, and by the grace of God working through him, has he a chance.[226]

For Darling to write that a teacher must be prepared to put aside 'even his own principles and rules of life' if those threatened to be an impediment to the unconditional love of the child made his position in the head versus heart debate very clear.

However, in the climate in which I am writing these words, the heart is not doing very well. The victory of the head can be seen in the results of state and federal elections. For the highest positions we keep choosing people who are coldly logical, people in whom the

---

226 'The Australian College of Education', *The Corian*, July & August 1985, p. 126.

brain has achieved supremacy over the emotions; people whose hearts have long since given up the struggle, packed their bags and slunk from the battlefield. I have strong memories of Sir Garfield Barwick, federal Attorney-General, and later Chief Justice of Australia, who was at one stage considered a chance for the prime ministership. In his autobiography he described a time in his adolescent years when his mother contracted tuberculosis so severely that she was mute. As a result, the family was broken up: the mother went to a sanatorium in the Blue Mountains, the father went to work in western New South Wales, and the kids, including young Garfield, were farmed out to various families. Barwick summed up the experience in these words: 'It was a troublesome time for me.'[227] As an adult, he appeared to be as dry as desiccated donkey dung, but the causes for his emotional emptiness are not difficult to discern.

At some level, huge numbers of people are not happy with the cold and dispassionate 'leaders' who have been holding power in Western countries for so long. Like travellers blinded by sandstorms in a desert, people seek with outstretched arms an empathetic, alive maverick who will save them. Unfortunately, in their despair, they clutch on to false prophets who promise to lead them to a rich and lush oasis: people like Donald Trump and Pauline Hanson, and, arguably, Jeremy Corbyn and Bernie Sanders.

In 2018, New Zealand elected Jacinda Ardern as Prime Minister. From her first days in office she attracted an unusual amount of attention, partly because she appeared to be compassionate and honest. When addressing the United Nations in 2018, she said: 'In the face of isolationism, protectionism, racism – the simple concept of looking outwardly and beyond ourselves, of kindness and collectivism, might just be as good a starting point as any.'[228] Her response in 2019 to the murders of 50 people in Christchurch, New Zealand, by a man with

---

227 Garfield Barwick, *A Radical Tory: Reflections and Recollections*, Federation Press, Sydney, 1995, p. 11.
228 Annabel Crabb, 'Christchurch shootings show New Zealand PM Jacinda Adern is a leader for our times', *ABC News,* 19 March 2019, abc.net.au/news/2019–03–18/christchurch-attacks-show-new-zealand-pm-a-leader-for-our-times/10912018, accessed 10 April 2019.

high-powered automatic rifles, a man who apparently felt justified in killing unarmed people aged from three to 77, showed remarkable integrity and understanding. In Australia, it seems that we have great difficulty bringing ourselves to trust a politician who is passionate, affectionate, empathetic and tender.

Gosh, imagine where we'd be if we did that!

WHY WE WILL ALWAYS HAVE CONFLICT

The Swiss educational psychologist Jean Piaget facilitated, through his work, important understandings about the growth and development of babies, infants, children and adolescents in their progress towards adulthood. Piaget's ideas were particularly fashionable in the 1960s and 1970s, and in many important respects are still valid today.

In particular, Piaget argued that we go through stages as we mature, and each stage becomes a necessary building block for the next. The first stage he called 'sensorimotor', which lasts for about eighteen months or two years – although Piaget emphasised that we should not be too pedantic about the chronological ages cited for these classifications.[229]

As babies progress through the sensorimotor stage, they start to realise they are separate from the world; the world does not begin and end with them. One of the ways this awareness shows is that they start to acquire a sense of *object concept*, or *object permanence*. Objects continue to exist whether the infant perceives them or not. An object placed in a cupboard vanishes from the child's sight but does not vanish from the world, and can be rediscovered by opening the cupboard. As the child gets a grasp of this concept, he or she develops *reversibility*: the sense that if an action is reversed, the original state can be restored.

For Piaget, childhood is the period from about age two to eleven or twelve. The preoperational stage of childhood is from about two

---

229 C.J. Weibell, *Principles of learning: 7 principles to guide personalized, student-centered learning in the technology-enhanced, blended learning environment*, 2011, principlesoflearning.wordpress. com/dissertation/chapter-3-literature-review-2/the-constructive-perspective/intellectual-development-theory-jean-piaget-1952, accessed 1 April 2014.

to seven. During the preoperational stage, which begins at about the time children start using the language of their parents, reasoning is taking place, but the child's worldview is still essentially ego-driven. The child sees objectives in terms of practical success. Symbols are used frequently, for example, in drawings of the family, who may be depicted as stick figures, and in play, where dolls represent babies, boxes can represent furniture, leaves can represent money.

Children in the early stages of preoperational thinking are not able to *conserve*, as demonstrated in Piaget's classic experiment, which showed that a child presented with, for example, two identical jugs containing the same amount of water, and having agreed that the amounts of water are the same, will, after watching the contents of Jug B poured into a flat dish, then contradict themselves and say that there is now more water in Jug A than is contained in the flat dish.

From ages four to seven, approximately, children are famous for their 'Why?' questions, which come thick and fast, as they acquire the desire to understand the world in which they live.

Children continue to mature, and become concrete operational thinkers, so that they are less egocentric and more logical, have a more sophisticated understanding of groups and their characteristics, and range more widely with their thinking. Unlike children at the sensorimotor stage, they are now not only interested in practical success, but in understanding how success can be achieved. However, they function best when working with the tangible. They understand what can be seen and heard and felt, but are still unable to think in abstractions. Abstract concepts can only be understood if presented in concrete terms. If children at this stage are presented with difficult theories, they need practical examples – assuming we want them to achieve a meaningful understanding of the subject.

Piaget asked children this question: 'Edith is fairer than Suzanne. Edith is darker than Lili. Who is the darkest?'[230]

If a ten-year-old is allowed to use dolls, or to draw the girls, he or

---

230 Richard Kohler, *Jean Piaget*, Bloomsbury, London, 2008, p.64.

she can usually find the correct answer. But somewhere between the ages of eleven and sixteen, many children mature into what Piaget termed the formal operational stage, and become capable of solving the problem 'in their heads', by using thought processes.

To put all this very simply: if I asked a child in the sensorimotor stage for her thoughts about war, she might gurgle, dribble and wave a rattle. If I asked a child in the preoperational stage, he might pick up a tennis racquet, point the handle at me, and shout 'Bang! Bang!' Or he might draw stick figures holding guns and shooting at each other, without being troubled by the lack of reality in the drawing.

If I asked a child in the concrete operational stage to write something about war, she might compose a story about soldiers in the trenches dealing with rats and mud before launching an attack on the enemy and winning a medal for bravery. These are all concrete, tangible matters that can be understood relatively easily. But if I put the same question to a child in the formal operational stage, he might write an essay about the morality of war, grappling with questions like: Can war ever be justified? How can wars be reconciled with religious teachings about peace? Are some weapons more moral than others? Can someone be both an ethical person and a soldier? What are the causes of wars?'

Piaget's work has been criticised, for example by Jerome Bruner, who began with the hypothesis that 'any subject can be taught effectively in some intellectually honest form to any child at any stage of development'.[231] He argued for a *spiral curriculum*, in which subjects were taught at a simple level to the youngest children, but revisited at a more complex and sophisticated level as the child grew older. Bruner saw development as a continuous process that could be accelerated – he believed that teachers should not wait for the child to reach the next level.

This is not the place to discuss the contrast in the approaches taken

---

231 Jerome Bruner, *The Process of Education*, Harvard University Press, Cambridge, Massachusetts, 1960, p. 33.

by Piaget and other educational researchers and thinkers like Bruner and Lev Vygotsky, although my own view is that Piaget's and Bruner's approaches can be easily reconciled. The crucial issue that Piaget's work raises for me is the distinction it helps us make between concrete thinkers and formal, or abstract, thinkers. And the critical factor here is that some people never reach the final stage of development: they never become formal, or abstract, thinkers. If we accept this proposition, then much in the world that has previously been inexplicable and bewildering becomes easier to understand.

When a formal thinker tries to have a discussion about politics or religion or life with a concrete thinker, the result will almost inevitably be frustration on both sides. And frequently the frustration leads to rage – even, in extreme circumstances, to family estrangements, divorces, assaults or murders. The problem is that the people are speaking a different language. It is not much better than trying to have a conversation in Bulgarian with someone who understands only Thai.

If the topic is law and order – which often incites strong feelings – the conversation may go something like this:

Concrete thinker: You know what's wrong with this country? Crime is out of control. The streets aren't safe any more.
Formal thinker: Why do you say that?
Concrete thinker: Well, my neighbour was coming home from work last Tuesday, when two young blokes ran up to her. One pushed her over and the other grabbed her bag, and they ran off. That's the kind of thing I'm talking about.
Formal thinker: That's terrible. But the crime figures show that there is much less violent crime than ten years ago. Assaults are down, I think, 16 per cent, and theft 22 per cent.
Concrete thinker: I don't care what the crime figures say. You can't believe them. My grandfather got burgled last year, about two o'clock in the afternoon, and the police still haven't caught the people who did it.

Formal thinker: On the other hand, I live two streets away from your grandfather, and we've never been burgled. We don't even lock the door when we go out.

Concrete thinker: What they need to do is round these blokes up, stick them in prison for twenty years, and let them rot. That'd put a stop to it.

Formal thinker: Unfortunately, the research shows that longer prison sentences have little or no deterrent effect on crime.

Concrete thinker: All I know is that when I was growing up, the streets were safe and there were none of these bashings and robberies and murders.

Formal thinker: Actually, in 1980, when I was three, our next-door neighbour was murdered. We might feel less safe nowadays, partly because the media covers crime much more extensively and explicitly. And there are more crimes, because the population is so much bigger. But per head of population, the crime rate is way down. And of course crime detection is far more efficient. People can call police quickly on mobile phones, police training is more sophisticated, there are CCTV cameras everywhere, DNA testing is catching a lot of criminals . . . We'll never get rid of crime altogether, but we can reduce it. And if we try to understand the real causes of crime, that would surely help. It might also be useful to understand why people feel more fearful nowadays, even though they have less reason for their fear.

Concrete thinker: What a lot of rubbish. They ought to bring back the death sentence.

I met a young woman a while back who told me, and the other people seated around the table, that she didn't give a damn about the refugees who come to Australia. 'I don't feel one ounce of pity for them. They've broken the law, so they can suffer the consequences. They should have come here in the proper way like everyone else.'

Watching and listening as people at the table pointed out how ugly and silly and wrong all these statements were, I couldn't help but admire her creativity. Faced by arguments based on both humanity and logic, employing both the brain and the heart, she had to keep reinventing her position. She did so without much hesitation and without much obvious discomfort.

'What about the people on Nauru?'

'Oh yes, well, I don't think they should have been sent to Nauru, that was going a bit far.'

'What about the children in prisons?'

'Ah yes, well, maybe not the children.'

'What about the women?'

She started to realise that she could not concede this point as well, or she would have lost too much ground. So she ignored that question.

'They haven't committed any crimes,' someone suggested.

'Just in coming here they're breaking our laws,' she replied.

'But they are exercising their legal rights. Anyone has the legal right to arrive in a country and ask for refugee status.'

'Well, they probably committed crimes to get here.'

Such dodging and weaving! She was as quick on her feet as Cristiano Ronaldo.

'Anyway, there's no proper procedure for these people to get here,' someone said. 'They've got nothing because they've lost it all in wars.'

'Well, that's what I mean. They shouldn't be coming here in the first place.'

She was, I am sorry to report, a primary school teacher . . . but not at one of my schools.

In my lifetime, a couple of politicians have shown remarkable cunning in their understanding of concrete thinking, and their ability to capitalise on that understanding by speaking directly to voters in language that concrete thinkers understand. Three who stand out are the late Sir Joh Bjelke-Petersen, Premier of Queensland for 21 years, former Australian Prime Minister Tony Abbott, and US President Donald Trump.

Many people were mystified by the election of Trump to the presidency, but it is not difficult to understand when analysed from the point of view of formal (abstract) thinking and concrete thinking. For example, a *Washington Post* story on 21 February 2017 included an interview with a 42-year-old woman who was an ardent Trump supporter. Commenting on a presidential order signed by Trump that allowed coalmines to dump debris in nearby streams – thereby counter-acting a regulation introduced by the previous president, Barack Obama, which had banned the practice – the woman was quoted as saying 'If he hadn't gotten into office, 70,000 miners would have been put out of work. I saw the ceremony where he signed that bill, giving them their jobs back, and he had miners with their hard hats and everything – you could see how happy they were.'[232]

This is a textbook example of the concrete thinker. There is the attractive simplicity of a direct cause–effect relationship, expressed by the words 'If he hadn't gotten into office, 70,000 miners would have been put out of work'. This ignores all other aspects of employment in the coal industry, such as the global trend away from the use of major pollutants, competition from other countries that have coalmines, increasing use of automation in mining, and the high costs of labour in the United States relative to many other nations. The number quoted, 70,000, seems inherently unlikely, but is an attractively high figure to bandy around. The energy policy director of Sightline Institute, an American environmental agency, said, in relation to Trump's boasts of resurrecting coalmining: 'He can't bring back coal jobs in any mean-ingful way unless he's capable of inventing a Time Machine . . . Waving your hands and saying you're going to bring the coal industry back is misleading at best, malicious at worst . . . The vast majority of coal is mined in the West [of the USA] and is done in highly-mechanised ways. That's not really reversible.'[233]

232 Jenna Johnson & David Weigel, 'Trump supporters see a successful president – and are frus-trated with critics who don't', *Washington Post*, 19 February 2017, washingtonpost.com/politics/trump-supporters-see-a-successful-president--and-are-frustrated-with-critics-who-dont/2017/02/19/496cb4b4-f6ca-11e6-9845-576c69081518_story.html, accessed 13 March 2019.

233 Jane C. Timm, 'Trump promised to "open the mines" – here's why that is unlikely', *NBC News*, 13 February 2017, nbcnews.com/news/us-news/trump-promised-open-mines-here-s-why-unlikely-n716141, accessed 13 March 2019.

The woman's next statement: 'I saw the ceremony where he signed that bill, giving them their jobs back ...' evidences the overreliance concrete thinkers place on what can be seen or heard or touched. She saw it, therefore it must be real. It's reminiscent of Philip Ruddock, Australia's Minister for Immigration in the Howard Liberal government, producing a photo of some children in water, and thereby claiming to have proved that the children were thrown into the ocean by their parents in order to force Australian naval personnel to rescue them and take them on board an Australian naval vessel. It was later established that the photographs were comprehensively misrepresented. A Senate select committee found that no children from the boat were thrown overboard in the circumstances described by Ruddock, and that the photographs were taken after the refugee boat sank. The committee reported:

> On 7 October 2001, the Minister for Immigration, Mr Philip
> Ruddock, announced to the media that 'a number of children had
> been thrown overboard' from a vessel suspected of being an 'illegal
> entry vessel' just intercepted by the Australian Defence Force. The
> 'children overboard' story was repeated in subsequent days and
> weeks by senior Government ministers, including the Minister for
> Defence, Mr Peter Reith, and the Prime Minister, Mr John Howard.
> The story was in fact untrue.[234]

Trump was signing a presidential order, not a bill, and he was not 'giving people their jobs back'; he was allowing coalmines to continue to pollute creeks. In doing so, he was no doubt reducing the cost of waste disposal for the coalmining industry, which in turn could be expected to lower the costs of production, which might then lead to higher wages or the opening of new mines and hence a growth in the work force – or

---

234 Parliament of Australia Executive Summary of 'Select Committee into Certain Aspects of
   Queensland Government Administration related to Commonwealth Government Affairs', n.d.,
   aph.gov.au/parliamentary_business/committees/senate/former_committees/maritimeincident/
   report/a06, accessed 1 April 2019.

instead to higher returns to shareholders. But we can reasonably assume there would be a cost resulting from the continued pollution of the streams: a financial cost to re-purify the water – and that cost would quite likely be borne by taxpayers, including the woman interviewed by the *Washington Post*. As well, there are other more abstract costs, such as the danger to public health, the damage to flora and fauna, and the aesthetic and spiritual harm resulting from such reckless behaviour.

The interviewee seems to have been deeply impressed by the hard hats, which may to her have evoked old-fashioned images of honest, industrious manual workers covered with coal dust as they emerged from the mines, doing their bit to keep the wheels of industry turning by fuelling the mighty furnaces that in turn power the factories etc., etc. To her, the hard hats seem to have had strong visual impact. And the fact that the men, to her, looked happy, was very powerful, and provided the final proof that whatever the president was signing must have been a Good Thing.

Abstract thinkers are aware that facial expressions are not a reliable indicator of feelings. If the men looked happy, it does not mean that they were happy; if they were happy, it could have been as a result of many factors. For some people, being in close proximity to someone powerful and famous is enough to induce ecstatic smiles.

Much was made of the fact that a significant number of people who voted for Trump to become President were college graduates. In Piagetian terms, this means nothing, as a concrete thinker can achieve a college degree in most disciplines. Only success in a few subjects, like philosophy, is likely to elude them.

Joh Bjelke-Petersen, the corrupt long-serving Premier of Queensland who held the position from 1968 to 1987, was himself a concrete thinker who seemed to understand instinctively that many voters were concrete thinkers. Aided by spectacular gerrymanders that favoured country voters, he won election after election, using language that concrete thinkers could understand and with which they could identify.

He said, 'I have always found . . . you can campaign on anything you like, but nothing is more effective than Communism.' He banged the communist drum repeatedly, to shore up his political base.[235] The federal Labour government was 'communist-inspired'. A selection of his public statements gives a sense of his command of concrete language: 'Don't put one foot on the sticky paper, because pretty soon you will end up with two feet stuck',[236] 'You don't tell the frogs anything before you drain the swamp',[237] 'You can't sit on the fence, a barbed wire fence at that, and have one ear to the ground',[238] 'The greatest thing that could happen to the state and the nation is when we get rid of all the media. Then we could live in peace and tranquillity and no one would know anything.'[239]

When running for prime minister, he said, 'I'm a bushfire raging out of control.'[240] His comment about Chinese leader Mao Zedong was 'Red is red wherever it is – and I don't trust any of them.'[241]

He had no compunction in looking for other scapegoats, frequently warning that a conspiracy of 'southern homosexuals' was a threat to Queensland. Homosexual people were 'insulting evil animals who should go back to New South Wales and Victoria where they came from in the first place'.[242]

When Tony Abbott was an aspirational young politician, spoken of in the Liberal Party as a 'man of the future', he and I, and half a dozen other men who had public profiles in different areas, met for several hours with well-known journalist David Leser in Sydney to

235 Hugh Lunn. *Joh: The Life and Political Adventures of Sir Johannes Bjelke-Petersen,* University of Queensland Press, Brisbane, 1987, p. 199.
236 Rae Wear, 'Johannes Bjelke-Petersen: straddling a barbed wire fence', *Queensland Historical Atlas,* 23 September 2010, qhatlas.com.au/content/johannes-bjelke-petersen-straddling-barbed-wire-fence, accessed 1 April 2019.
237 Ibid.
238 Ibid.
239 Rae Wear, *Johannes Bjelke-Petersen: The Lord's Premier,* University of Queensland Press, Brisbane, 2002, p. 211.
240 'Life and times of Joh Bjelke-Petersen', *Sydney Morning Herald,* 25 April 2005, smh.com.au/opinion/life-and-times-of-joh-bjelke-petersen-20050425-gdl6wm.html, accessed 1 April 2014.
241 'The sayings of Premier Joh', *The Age,* 20 April 2005, theage.com.au/national/the-sayings-of-premier-joh-20050420-ge00hi.html, accessed 1 April 2019.
242 Shirleene Robinson, 'Homophobia as Party Politics: The Construction of the "Homosexual Deviant" in Joh Bjelke-Petersen's Queensland', *Queensland Review,* vol. 17, no. 1, 2010, p. 37.

discuss topical issues. Not infrequently during the conversation we had to pause or slow down to explain or unpack various comments to Abbott, so that he could keep up. I left the meeting convinced that he would go no further in politics: he would be forever limited by his intellect. Then he became prime minister.

One of the exchanges at the meeting, which was recorded, transcribed and published in the *Sydney Morning Herald* and *The Age*, was about the status of men and women in our society. It went like this:

> Abbott: But what if men are by physiology or temperament more adapted to exercise authority or to issue command?
> Costa: Well, see, I don't believe that . . . In terms of the power structure, I think it's very hard to deny that there is an underrepresentation of women.
> Abbott: But, now, there's an assumption that this is a bad thing.[243]

When he became prime minister, Abbott awarded himself the portfolio of Minister for Women.

In late 2017, Abbott went to London to speak about climate change. He began his speech with a series of extravagant statements, unsupported by evidence but attractive to concrete and superficial thinkers: 'Our businesses campaign for same-sex marriage but not for economic reform. Our biggest company, BHP, the world's premier miner, lives off the coal industry that it now wants to disown. And our oldest university, Sydney, now boasts that its mission is "unlearning".'[244]

These kinds of broadbrush statements, in which unconnectable issues are connected, progressive thinking is mocked and dishonesty pervades every phrase (do all our businesses campaign for same-sex marriage? Do all our businesses oppose economic reform? Does BHP 'live off' the coal industry? Don't its 2018 financial results suggest

---

243 *Good Weekend* (*The Age* and the *Sydney Morning Herald*), 29 August 1998, p. 21.
244 Tony Abbott, 'Daring to doubt', transcript and video of speech, London, 9 October 2017, Global Warming Policy Forum, thegwpf.com/tony-abbott-daring-to-doubt.

that its main revenue source is the iron ore industry?[245] Is 'unlearning' now a major force driving Sydney University?), are much favoured by demagogues.

With unconscious irony, Abbott went on to advocate the need for 'an honest facing of facts and an insistence upon intellectual rigour'. A couple of paragraphs later, after condemning 'some green activists whose ideal is an Amish existence, only without reference to God', he said, 'Beware the pronouncement, "the science is settled". It's the spirit of the Inquisition, the thought-police down the ages. Almost as bad is the claim that "99 per cent of scientists believe" as if scientific truth is determined by votes rather than facts.'

So much for intellectual rigour. Abbott glibly ignores the fact that the 'votes' of scientists on climate change are somewhat more meaningful than the votes of volleyball professionals, plasterers or commercial lawyers. When scientists come to conclusions based upon research and evidence, they are not 'voting', they are coming to conclusions based upon research and evidence.

People who support populist leaders, as so many concrete thinkers do, are fond of saying: 'He (or she) is just saying what everyone else thinks.' What they mean is that the populist leader is using the same concrete language they use and understand: so different from the abstractions articulated by more erudite and sophisticated leaders. Wisely has it been said 'Don't trust people who want to make you angry', because anger is such a simple and powerful emotion to evoke from concrete thinkers, who may well be feeling frustrated by the discourse around them, and who may believe that they are disadvantaged by the way in which society functions. Most politicians have now worked out that waving a country's flags to appeal to patriotism, and standing in front of multiple flags whilst speaking of 'national values', goes down well with concrete thinkers, even though the politicians rarely define national values, or if they do, they define them in terms that are meaningless or even ludicrous.

---

245 BHP Annual Report 2018, p. 162.

In early 2017, One Nation Party leader Pauline Hanson was taken to an area of the Great Barrier Reef, as part of a climate-change-denial campaign. Hanson, in true concrete-thinker style, looked around and saw that the area in which she stood appeared to be in good condition. She then projected from this and denied with confidence that the reef was suffering from any serious bleaching problem. 'We can't have these lies put across by people with their own agendas,'[246] she said, ignoring the fact that beyond the horizon, vast areas of the reef were dying. She was unable to 'see' beyond the range of her eyes.

In 2018, a Queensland school student refused to stand for the national anthem at her school assembly, pointing out that by describing Australians as 'young', the song was offensive to Indigenous Australians who through generation after generation have been here for over 50,000 years. Calling the child a 'nine-year-old brat', Hanson's response was: 'Here we have a kid who's been brainwashed and I tell you what, I'd give her a kick up the backside . . . Take her out of the school.'[247]

When the salary of the CEO of Australia Post was publicly disclosed, and thought by some to be unreasonably high, an unsigned statement about his salary was posted on the One Nation website. Here it is, unedited:

Recently Australia Post which is totally government owned and has been for 200 years, announced the loss of 900 jobs, being part of a cut back program. This is due to the decline in letters being sent and that's true as email has further reduced letter writing and in many ways understandably. A hand written letter is a wonderful thing and contains the hand writing of a friend or loved one and that's a blessing plus the effort required to put pen to paper and then to post it.

The CEO of Australia Post is Ahmed FAHOUR who was born in Lebanon and came to Australia in 1970. In 2009 he was made

---

246 Peter McCutcheon, 'Pauline Hanson visits healthy reef to dispute effects of climate change', *ABC News*, 25 November 2016, abc.net.au/news/2016–11–25/one-nation-attempts-show-of-unity-at-great-barrier/8059668, accessed 13 March 2019.
247 *Australian Teacher Magazine*, October 2018, p. 8.

Managing Director and CEO of Australia Post. His salary package was estimated to be worth $4.8 million last year. Of this he donated about $2 million to the Islamic Museum of Australia located in Melbourne.

I have a big problem with this fellow's salary package and so let's get some perspective here.

The top ten executives in Australia Post combined earn around $20 million each year.

That's simply immoral and clearly the CEO can afford to give away nearly half his takings to an Islamic museum so he doesn't need it and surprise, surprise, its tax deductible ...

How can the CEO of the Post Office earn so much especially when the postal service is bleeding money from letter delivery. No employee is worth five million a year and especially not from a government owned business ... What a country full of mugs we are to sit by and let all this happen. I would have run the big game of Post Office for a lot less and still done a reasonable job and in fact if the best of we seniors applied ourselves we could run the damn post office better and for nothing except a kiss and a free lunch now and again.

You had better believe it too.

There is an unpleasant and some would say sinister unbalanced agenda in Australia which in the end preys on the average citizen, we the people. We are no longer the lucky country and we are no longer wealthy and this particular game of Post Office reveals major fractures and faults on a number fronts in our society and culture.

Who is running the country, who is pulling the levers and who is going to win? We the Mugs need to know.

Among the comments that might seem to be irrelevant or unjustified are the ones about the joys of receiving a handwritten letter, the mention of the CEO's country of birth, his decision to (apparently) make a donation to a museum, the speculation as to whether he 'needs' his salary or not, the implication that something is wrong with a donation to a museum being tax-deductible, the assertion that

Australia is no longer lucky or wealthy, and the assertion that the person making the statement could run the 'damn post office' better than the incumbent. Throughout the statement is a sense that a mass of 'ordinary' people, including the writer and his/her readers, are being exploited by a sinister, well-placed group of conspirators.

It is easy for demagogues and populists to first, provoke rage, and then to tap into it and take advantage of it for their own purposes. Talkback radio hosts on tabloid radio programs do it every day. The continuing frenzy of rage against the machine that they foster is energy-sapping. But it's also addictive, in the same unhealthy way that bodybuilding, ballet, jogging or drugs can be for some people. Listeners to these radio stations are kept in a highly stimulated state. Every second caller begins with the forceful words 'What people need to understand is . . .' or 'What people need to know is . . .' or 'What people don't realise is . . .'

The phrase 'People need to wake up' recurs frequently.

The dominant personality type in Australia is passive-aggressive. David Attenborough could have a wonderful time peering into our schools, shopping malls, surf clubs and dental surgeries, observing the habits and mannerisms of that notorious critter, the passive-aggressive personality. One reason for their prevalence in Australia is our emphasis on politeness, good manners, 'niceness'. Etiquette books sold strongly in the second half of the twentieth century, and the Queen of Etiquette, June Dally-Watkins, achieved national celebrity. But, as someone once said, 'beware the sweet person: there is a lot of anger beneath the façade'. A fermenting soup of ugly feelings simmers inside them. Although they do not outwardly show any expectation of power or authority, their fantasies are of domination. They believe they can do everything better than anyone else . . . including running Australia Post.

In his brilliant, vile, fictional creation Uriah Heep, Charles Dickens captured the passive-aggressive personality at its worst. William S. Burroughs Jr wrote, 'If a small mind with power begins to feel inferior, all Hell is going to pay',[248] but Uriah had already proved the truth of that adage. Teaching children strategies to manage people like this, and doing all we can to help ensure that our children don't become such people, is important work for parents and teachers.

It is something of a cliché to say that the stock market runs on fear and greed. But many people run their whole lives on just five powerful emotions: fear, greed, rage, guilt and love. Only one of these is generally regarded as a 'positive' emotion. The default setting for hundreds of millions of Westerners is summed up nicely in a *Washington Post* review of a book lavishly praised by Donald Trump. *Green Card Warrior* is a 110-page essay by a young Australian named Nick Adams, who wanted to emigrate to the United States, and who styled himself as a 'warrior' on the basis of his campaign to get a Green Card. In the book, Adams describes his journey as 'a phenomenal story of human endurance', akin, presumably, to the ordeals of Antarctic explorers in the early twentieth century. 'My extraordinary ability,' he says, 'was indisputable.' He sums up his suffering in these words: 'For ten months, in the prime of my life, my career was stalled. My personal life put on hold. I almost ran out of money. Hundreds of opportunities were missed . . . Lifelong dreams like attending the Republican National Convention missed. My tireless work in getting on the radar of Fox news executives was for nothing.'[249]

The book is described in the *Post* review as written by a man who feels 'misunderstood and victimised, full of self-generated rage and imagined grievance'.[250] These ten words concisely capture the state of mind of many Westerners in the 21st century. Living in this period of unprecedented affluence, where most households have electronic and electrical devices equivalent to a large staff of servants, and most

248 William S. Burroughs Jr, *Kentucky Ham*, Overlook Duckworth, Peter Mayer Publishers, New York 1993.

249 Nick Adams, *Green Card Warrior*, Post Hill Press, pp. 76–77.

250 Carlos Lozada, 'Trump tweeted that this new immigration book is a "must read." So I read it – and you must not: Review of "Green Card Warrior" by Nick Adams', *Washington Post*, 3 March 2017, washingtonpost.com/news/book-party/wp/2017/03/03/trump-tweeted-that-this-new-immigration-book-is-a-must-read-so-i-read-it-and-you-must-not/?utm_term=.ac6dc372e88a, accessed 13 March 2019.

members of the vast middle class enjoy varied diets, excellent health-care, frequent travel and multiple means of entertainment, we seem to be a society of resentful, angry people who feel we are entitled to much more – even if we are unable to articulate what it is we want. Using his powerful political connections, the author of *Green Card Warrior* got what he wanted – a work permit for the United States – but that didn't stop him writing his bile-filled rant. 'My own conservative party [in Australia] was full of little totalitarians doing everything they could to silence me. It was the cruellest non-criminal behavior imaginable.'[251]

Why are we like this? It has become de rigueur to blame the media for everything, so of course I will cheerfully jump on the bandwagon. Before doing so, however, I should say that I have great respect for the media. The best newspapers, and TV and radio networks, seem, in my lifetime, to have covered big stories in depth and with care. The writing has usually been well researched, thoughtful and stylish. The people in media outlets, more than almost any other individuals or groups in our society, have been quick to correct their mistakes and to apologise for them. Given the abandonment of principle by major political parties, and the difficulty in distinguishing between them on such major moral issues as the treatment of refugees and the destruction of the planet, the media has operated over countless years as the de facto opposition in Australia. Sadly, that role has been badly weakened by recent cost-cutting at media companies. This is a dangerous situation, for the media is vital to us: without it we would be in an even more precarious position than we find ourselves.

Naturally, however, as public or private companies committed to making a profit, they are tempted to take a populist line. We, the people, blame the media for running superficial and sensationalist stories, but as has been said many times, if ungrammatically, the media is us. On any day of the year, if one looks at the list of 'most popular stories' on the websites of major media outlets, articles which attract

---

251 Adams, *Green Card Warrior*, p. 77.

people are not particularly inspiring. For example, according to the Brisbane *Courier Mail's* online list, on 13 February 2019 its five most popular stories were:

'Mum's nightmare diagnosis adds to family heartbreak'

'Judgy (sic) virgin publicly kink-shames wife'

'"I was slut shamed for wearing this on flight"'

'Student's torture of kitten truly sickening'

'Bizarre find in abandoned wildlife Park'

And this was on the eve of Valentine's Day. But apparently, these are the stories a large number of people choose to read. Complex analyses of Middle Eastern politics, changes in economic policy, threats to journalism in totalitarian countries . . . we do not expect to find these stories in the top five, and we are rarely surprised.

In more than 30 years of writing books, I have had countless encounters with media of all kinds, and have found the stories to be accurate, the treatment positive and fair, and the journalists generally well informed. Only once have I known a journalist (a radio broad-caster) to lie; only once have I been treated unethically. Only once was I asked by a reporter, in Shepparton, 'Er . . . sorry if this is a stupid question, but what *is* the difference between prose and poetry?' Only once have I been misquoted or misrepresented in the media in any significant or damaging way, and that was by a fellow novelist, who was not a professional journalist, and who was not acting maliciously.

However, the media, in gratifying us by serving up a relentless diet of stories about celebrities, and stories about injustice, including economic inequality, have probably contributed to our sense of victimisation and our feelings of grievance. When we read of the lifestyles of the rich and famous, we are reminded of the banality of our own daily routines, and are made to feel that we have been sorely deprived. Stories of injustice – constant screams of outrage from state premiers, for example, about the ways their states are 'ripped off' by the Commonwealth government, or stories about schools with leaking roofs, or reports of long waiting times for ambulances – make us feel that the cards are stacked against us and that we are the victims of conspiracies. Many people in five of the six states of Australia (excluding, arguably, New South Wales) are convinced that their states should get more money from the federal government and that they experience needless suffering as a result of this unfair distribution.

As I've mentioned, tabloid newspapers and radio talkback 'shock jocks' shamelessly use anger to manipulate their audience, in cold-blooded awareness that by doing so they can increase their personal power and ratings, and thereby attract advertisers.

Some people, however, believe the media should be like a parent who denies a child a constant diet of lollies and soft drink, on the grounds that 'such a diet is not good for you'. But surely, as adults, we should be responsible for our own reading and viewing, just as we are responsible for our own food intake.

Every day I deal with furious children who are convinced that they have been treated unfairly. 'He's been on the trampoline for ages and he won't give anyone else a go.' 'She had the last two biscuits and I didn't get any.' 'The teacher gave me a detention for homework that I didn't even know we had.' Sometimes parents are all too ready to join in. 'Why didn't he get a bigger role in the play?' 'He got left out of the chess team and he's heartbroken.' 'She only got this homework yesterday and she's expected to have it all done by tomorrow!'

It is a rare soul who is not weighed down by a sense of entitlement and who is not angered by perceived inequalities. 'There's no progress without discontent', and if we are to have a more equitable society we need to be discontented with the existing order. The problem is that many people go beyond this, developing such an obsession with what they believe to be persecution that they become poisoned by greed and rage. So many adults are infantile in their expectations of life – if not on their own behalf, then on behalf of their children. And certain family groupings increase the risk that children will not acquire a good sense of perspective as they grow. Parents who have just one child may need to work harder to help that child understand the 'ladder of injustices', which has trivial, forgettable incidents at the bottom and tragic, traumatic events at the top. Children with siblings are likely to recover relatively quickly when their sister has eaten the last of the Coco Pops without sharing, or their brother has borrowed their comb without asking. Having a sibling lose your footie scarf or push you off the computer when you are about to win an online game or flick your bare skin with a wet towel is certainly unfair, but so is being booked for speeding because your cruise control is not working properly, or missing out on a job because the road was blocked by an accident and you were late for the interview, or having a severely disabled baby as a result of a genetic abnormality. Life is so often random. We cannot control the universe. When things go wrong, sometimes no one is to blame. A life of tranquillity and comfort is not a life in any meaningful sense of the word. Even the most benign creatures on the planet, teddy bears, sometimes get kicked, bashed, torn and abused.

In our polite society, feelings like fear, greed and rage are regarded as unseemly and unattractive, and are supposed to be concealed i.e. repressed. We might do better were we to acknowledge in a thoughtful and considered way the strength and power they have, and be open about their influence. We need to bring a sense of perspective to our assessment of the many frustrating situations in our lives, in the world at large. Which issues are worth our rage and which are trivial or ephemeral? In striving for greater balance, and edging towards that balance, we might reduce the likelihood that we will continue to elect concrete thinkers to leadership positions, where their inability to understand the complexities of situations, to empathise, to protect those not of their tribe or class, and to communicate in subtle and nuanced ways can cause considerable harm.

I WANT TO BE ALONE! LET ME INTO THE GROUP!

There was a scene in a British comedy a few years ago where John Cleese played the role of a doctor. He was treating a patient, of whom he asked, 'Do you breathe?'

The patient replied, 'Yes, quite frequently, actually.'

Dr Cleese instructed him, 'Well, breathe in, then. Breathe out again. Breathe in, blow out, breathe in, blow out. In out, faster, in out, in out, keep going. Sorry I have to make you do this, but the electric fan has broken down.'

Humans have a lot of instincts and needs and drives, and the urge to breathe is top of the list. Then there's the urge to drink, and the urge to eat, and the desire or need to be safe. It's hard to rank these though, because circumstances and context make a powerful difference. If you're in a war zone, and bombs are falling around you, you'll probably ignore or tolerate your thirst for a while.

Other human wants or needs include the lust for status and power, the desire for comfort, the quest for good health, the urge for sex, the longing for admiration, the drive to be part of a group, the drive for individual fulfilment. The number of human needs and wishes no doubt falls within the ambit of that big quantity we call 'infinity'!

Unfortunately, these needs and drives often get in each other's way. Our desire for comfort may result in our purchasing items that impact negatively on our health. The manufacture of these products may have contributed to global health problems. The desire to accumulate possessions and money, in order to increase our comfort and sense of security, may be incompatible with our need for spiritual succour. Many Americans were shocked in 1975 when Mother Teresa told an English journalist that 'the spiritual poverty of the Western world is much greater than the physical poverty of the people of Calcutta'.[252]

It seems that certain human drives can't be controlled. This may not apply to the need for air and water. You don't get too many people overdosing on oxygen, or drinking water until they bloat. But the other needs can get out of control pretty quickly, as we see from the obesity epidemic. We have a lot of human Labradors in our midst. In 2016, the British medical magazine *The Lancet* reported a study showing that on a worldwide basis, obesity is now more common than the condition

---

252 Dan Wooding, 'The Day Mother Teresa Told Me, "Your Poverty Is Greater Than Ours"', Crossmap, n.d., crossmap.com/blogs/the-day-mother-teresa-told-me-your-poverty-is-greater-than-ours.html, accessed 13 March 2019.

of being underweight. In the 186 countries surveyed, it was found that the number of obese people had risen from 105 million in 1975 to 641 million in 2014. The number of underweight people had risen from 330 million to 462 million during these 39 years.[253]

When it comes to comfort, we suffer from obesity. I would be embarrassed to count the number of labour-saving devices we have at home, including the dishwasher and the vacuum cleaner, the rice cooker and the heaters, the computers and printer, and the cars.

There's another, conflicting pair of desires that also seems to know no bounds. On the one hand, we have to belong to groups. It's not just the group connected by blood, or the groups connected by friendship, or the tribes that we belong to by virtue of our jobs or our interests or the football teams we support. That drive even attracts us to certain television programs, like *Seinfeld*, *Friends*, *Sex and the City* or lifestyle shows. I suspect a powerful element in the success of these programs is the feeling that the regulars on the show are a special, happy, united group. There's a sense of warmth, camaraderie, that makes these shows more powerful and popular than others on television. Maybe a lot of lonely people watch them because they feel that the cast members share a special relationship. The cast becomes a kind of de facto family for the viewers. That would explain why viewers hate it when there's real-life fighting among the stars of such programs.

Yet at the same time we move away from other people at every opportunity. If there's a chance to get a seat to ourselves on the train, if we see an empty table at the coffee shop, if there's a block of unoccupied seats in the cinema, then that is where we head. New suburbs crawl across the countryside like a skin disease, with everyone wanting their quarter-acre, resulting in cities that spread outwards instead of upwards. Good farming land disappears, with greater pressure on the intensive production of food, and further irreparable destruction to the habitats of native animals, birds and insects.

---

253 Press release, 'The Lancet: We now live in a world in which more people are obese than underweight, major global analysis reveals', *EurekaAlert!*, 31 March 2016, eurekalert.org/pub_releases/2016–03/tl-tlw033016.php, accessed 13 March 2019.

One of the differences between Western society and the rest of the world is the emphasis we in the West place on individualisation. In recent centuries, we have moved away from prioritising membership of a group or tribe that sets social obligations and commitments over individual rights, to a society where each person goes out after his or her personal fulfilment, and the needs of the group are ranked as less important.

The romantic ideal of the individual carrying out a series of acts that brings him fulfilment, happiness and success may be misleading. The problem with becoming separate individuals is that it puts us at risk of stepping into limbo.

In his book *Oh, What a Blow that Phantom Gave Me!*, anthropologist Edmund Carpenter describes the effect on highlanders in Papua New Guinea when photographed by Irving Penn in 1970. These men were accustomed to being filmed by tourists, and indeed often made funny faces for their cameras. But when Penn set up a portable studio, with one wall open, so that the studio created its own space – a space without background – the impact on the highlanders was colossal.

Carpenter writes:

The moment the subjects stepped across that threshold, they changed totally. All confusion and excitement ceased. Even those outside became still. A sudden intensity possessed everyone. Their bodies became rigid, their muscles tense; their fingers tightly gripped whatever they touched . . . Their eyes fixed unwaveringly on that single point, no matter how long the session. That point was the point men enter when they leave this world behind and step alone, absolutely alone, into limbo. That was the source of their terror and exaltation and intense self-awareness. The technology that lifted man out of both his environment and his body, allowing him to enter and leave limbo at will, has now become so casual, so environmental, we make that trip with the numbness of commuters, our eyes unseeing, the mystery of self-confrontation and self-discovery gone.[254]

254 Edmund Carpenter, *Oh, What a Blow that Phantom Gave Me!*, Granada, Great Britain, 1976, pp. 129–131.

He's talking about us! We are daily commuting in and out of limbo, but we nearly all do our utmost to avoid any meaningful encounters with such a powerful phenomenon. In recent years, mobile phones, electronic tablets and computers have given considerable help to our avoidance tactics. But the list is pretty much infinite: alcohol, drugs, sporting teams, relationships, religion, movies, family life, gambling and so on. And so on. It seems from Carpenter's description that inter-actions with tourists were one of the ways people in the Highlands of Papua New Guinea had become desensitised, or deterred from exploring the possibilities that could await people who are prepared to step 'absolutely alone, into limbo'.

Perhaps everything depends on our being able to overcome our need for individualisation, but at the same time being enabled to enter limbo and subsequently leave it; on being capable of leaving and later rejoining the real world, a world that Mother Teresa recognised in the dirty streets of Calcutta but that can't be found in the spacious housing estates of America and Australia.

12

MAKING SCHOOLS BETTER

As early as 1910, H.G. Wells wrote in *The History of Mr Polly*:

> I remember seeing a picture of Education . . . It represented a
> glorious woman, with a wise and fearless face, stooping over her
> children, and pointing them to far horizons. The sky displayed
> the pearly warmth of the summer dawn, and all the painting was
> marvellously bright as if with the youth and hope of the delicately
> beautiful children in the foreground. She was telling them, one
> felt, of the great prospect of life that opened before them, of the
> splendours of sea and mountain they might travel and see, the
> joys of skills they might acquire, of efforts and the pride of effort,
> and the devotions and nobilities it was theirs to achieve. Perhaps
> even she whispered of the warm triumphant mystery of love
> that comes at last to those who have patience and unblemished
> hearts . . . She was reminding them of their great heritage as
> English children, rulers of more than one fifth of mankind, of the
> obligation to do and be the best that such a pride of empire entails,
> of their essential nobility and knighthood, and of the restraints and
> charities and disciplined strength that is becoming in knights and
> rulers . . .[255]

---

255 H.G. Wells, *The History of Mr Polly*, Pan, London, 1963, pp. 22–23.

With delicious irony Wells follows this eloquent paragraph with the simple sentence: 'The education of Mr Polly did not follow this picture very closely.'

He continued:

> Mr Polly went into the National School at six, and he left the private school at fourteen, and by that time his mind was in much the same state that you would be in, dear reader, if you were operated upon for appendicitis by a well-meaning, boldly enterprising, but rather overworked and underpaid butcher boy, who was superseded towards the climax of the operation by a left-handed clerk of high principles but intemperate habits – that is to say, it was a thorough mess. The nice little curiosities and willingness of a child were in a jumbled and thwarted condition, hacked and cut about – the operators had left, so to speak, all their sponges and ligatures in a mangled confusion – and Mr Polly had lost much of his natural confidence, so far as figures and sciences and languages and the possibilities of learning things were concerned.

The modern equivalent of Wells's description of the glorious woman and what she represents is the speech by the politician extolling the virtues of his party's policy, the press release by the bureaucrat talking glibly about the state of education, the school prospectus with its bland assurances and dead language . . . this, for example, comes from the 2017 prospectus for a private boys' school in Australia:

> I'm proud to say that while our school enjoys an impressive reputation for academic excellence, this success stems from a culture where students, staff and parents work together to cultivate a supportive and inclusive school community. It's a friendly, safe and energetic learning community where students can explore a well-rounded education across a wide range of fields: academic, sporting, artistic and spiritual – creating confident young men, able to thrive in an ever-changing, global world. Alongside academic pursuits, we

take pride in helping our students to develop solid values, respect, integrity and an appreciation of the world around them . . . Creating the best opportunities for your son, his development and future is what drives us too.

This is the kind of writing of which Don Watson says, in his book *Death Sentence: The Decay of Public Language*:

There is no room in this sanctimonious clag for the light of the imagination. There is no room for a feeling properly felt. There is no room for an 'other'– which with writing is usually the reader. You cannot tell if the author of the words is genuine or not because they have no author. They are ritual words. It is as if, like someone with schizophrenia or depression, they're not quite of the real world.[256]

I have learned to write this kind of language because it is a useful skill when I am under pressure and need to produce documents in a hurry for bureaucrats. After a while it becomes remarkably – almost danger-ously – easy. I'll give myself a topic now . . . 'Evaluation of Students' Learning', and see how I go knocking off a few sentences:

Evaluation of student learning at the school takes place in a range of ways, embracing many different approaches and practices. Criteria used include comparisons of students with peers, and comparisons of students with state and national results achieved in highly accredited testing. At all times evaluation takes place in an objective atmosphere, with care taken to prevent bias or preconceptions on the part of the examiner/s. The importance of evaluation cannot be overestimated, as it provides a credible basis for teachers going forward in their planning and execution of work programs and curriculum decisions.

---

256 Don Watson, *Death Sentence: The Decay of Public Language*, Knopf, Sydney, 2003, p. 52.

That took exactly two minutes, I am ashamed to say, although I dictated it using a speech-to-text program. Since opening Candlebark I've generated hundreds of pages of this meaningless garbage, which is invariably accepted without question by regulatory authorities, and which I then file and never look at again.

THE CRUEL WORLD OF EDUCATIONAL TESTING

If we believe the politicians who have been plucked from other ministries, which in recent years have included Industrial Relations, Health, and the Environment, and suddenly placed in charge of Education, although they know nothing about it and have never previously exhibited an interest in it, or the bureaucrats who advise them and create and administer policies, and who, for the most part, appear to be failed teachers suffering from social awkwardness, education in Australia is all about whether Australian students can outperform Singaporean or South Korean students in maths and science.

A recent federal Minister for Education, Simon Birmingham, said in an interview with the ABC on 28 November 2016 'I am embarrassed for Australia that we are not performing at the standard that we would expect our schools to perform.'[257]

Senator Birmingham's qualifications for making definitive pronouncements about educational standards are, from a study of his own website, difficult to discern. After gaining his MBA, he worked in wine, tourism and hospitality, and was then elected to Parliament, where he became Shadow Parliamentary Secretary for the Murray-Darling Basin and the Environment.[258] He was finally given some responsibility for education – vocational education, apprenticeships,

---

257 Simon Birmingham, transcript from 'Interview on ABC Radio National by Fran Kelly', 30 November 2016, senatorbirmingham.com.au/interview-on-abc-radio-national-with-fran-kelly, accessed 13 March 2019.
258 Simon Birmingham, 'Biography', senatorbirmingham.com.au/about-simon/biography, accessed 13 March 2019.

training and skills – in 2014, and then, in September 2015, having had about a quarter of the preparation time that the lowliest of teachers must spend before being allowed into the classroom, Senator Birmingham was placed in Supreme Command of Australian Education.

Birmingham was moved to a new portfolio in 2018. In his farewell statement as Minister for Education, he remarked proudly that he had held the position for longer than anyone since 2006. This was not difficult, as there had been seven Ministers for Education between 2006 and 2018. Birmingham held the job for less than three years. His replacement was Dan Tehan, who had worked as a farmhand and a political advisor, before going into politics. His university degrees were in foreign affairs and trade.[259] His interest in education appears to be on the same level as that of his predecessors. Up to 2019, there have been 24 federal Ministers for Education. Not one of them had studied education or shown any more understanding of it than would a farmhand, political advisor or expert on the irrigation issues in the Murray-Darling Basin.

Apparently, nothing much has changed since 1878, when in the Gilbert and Sullivan operetta *HMS Pinafore*, the First Lord of the Admiralty, Sir Joseph Porter, who by virtue of his position was in charge of the British Navy, sings of his career:

Of legal knowledge I acquired such a grip
That they took me into the partnership.
And that junior partnership, I ween,
Was the only ship that I ever had seen.[260]

In May 2017, a spokeswoman for the Catholic Education Office in Victoria claimed on ABC radio that she and her colleagues had spent some time in a meeting with Senator Birmingham explaining to him how government funding for schools was calculated, because he

259 Dan Tehan, 'About Dan', dantehan.com.au/about-dan, accessed 13 March 2019.
260 W.S. Gilbert, *HMS Pinafore*, 1878, Act I.

appeared not to know . . . just days after he had announced, with much fanfare, massive changes to the funding arrangements for schools.

Like tabloid newspapers and talkback radio hosts, education ministers have attributed much weight to a group of tests known as PISA – the Programme for International Student Assessment – which is managed by the OECD (Organisation for Economic Co-operation and Development). Yet we need to be thoughtful about the importance we attribute to the PISA test results.

Schools shape society. Schools are highly significant déterminants of culture. Their influence reaches into every workplace, every barbecue, every artist's studio, every basketball game, every conversation, every home. If we are to infer from the comments of the embarrassed minister and others that we should become 'more like' schools in Singapore, South Korea and Taiwan, countries that customarily achieve high marks in PISA tests, we need to consider firstly whether we want our society and culture to resemble more closely the cultures of these countries.

Professor Ken Wiltshire was quoted in Sydney tabloid the *Daily Telegraph* as lamenting the fact that 'Asian countries are surging ahead of Australia because they have stuck to the Confucian method of schooling where teachers hold the power and stand "up the front" rather than "up the side" of the classroom'.[261]

Wiltshire is a professor of public administration whose interests have ranged across many areas, including the management of wet tropics, and comparative federalism. A graduate in economics and political science, he appears to have no qualifications in education at all[262], yet is regularly called upon to pontificate upon matters of education – for example, as one of two men appointed in 2014 to review the Australian school curriculum for the Liberal-National Coalition.

---

261 'Australian schools are becoming too "kumbaya" with progressive, new-age fads', *Daily Telegraph*, 19 June 2015.
262 'Professor Ken Wiltshire', UQ School of Business, University of Queensland, business.uq.edu.au/staff/ken-wiltshire, accessed 13 March 2019.

It's unclear what Wiltshire means by the 'Confucian method of schooling', or indeed whether he has much understanding of Confucian precepts. He is probably referring to the interpretation of Confucianism promulgated by the Han Emperor Wu, the first emperor to promote the adoption of Confucianism by the state. This stressed the importance of respect for parents, loyalty to government and the value of accepting without question one's assigned place in the social hierarchy. People should know their place, and behave accordingly. It is unsurprising that a despot such as Emperor Wu would find such principles extremely attractive.

Or maybe Wiltshire is referring to Confucius's attitude towards women: 'Women and the uneducated people are most difficult to deal with. When you are familiar with them, they become cheeky, and when you ignore them, they resent it.'[263] We can only hope he's not referring to the Confucian idea that students who do not succeed academically are lazy, that everyone can succeed if he or she works hard enough. And let's trust that Wiltshire is not referring to the belief, commonly held in Confucian classrooms, that a student asking questions poses an unwelcome interruption to the words of wisdom flowing from the teacher's mouth.

When people use the word 'Confucian' and 'education' in the same sentence, they generally mean something as vague as references to 'Australian values', but which, as Wiltshire implies, evokes the image of a teacher standing at the front of the classroom, elucidating profound truths whilst wide-eyed children listen in perfect silence ... broken only by the scratching of pen on paper as they reverently note down the teacher's words. This is a logical consequence of the Confucian ideal of respect for parents and loyalty to government. It is, however, inadequate as a basis for education – and indeed for society.

Some years ago I gave a talk to parents in Taipei, Taiwan, at a school that was based upon Confucian principles. When I arrived there to take a week of workshops, a teacher remarked to me that 'Confucius

---

263 Confucius, *Analects* 17:25.

stalks the corridors of this school'. In my address to the parents I set out to demonstrate the inadequacy of those principles. I said to them: 'I'm sure you all know old people – among them perhaps one or both of your parents, or your parents-in-law – who do some really stupid things.' A wave of astonishment rolled through the room, followed by nervous titters, followed by excited whispering as (I suspect) audience members confided to their neighbours the names of some of the foolish or misguided old people of their acquaintance.

I went on to say that people should not be respected simply because they have had more birthdays than someone else. They should be treated courteously – all people should be treated courteously – but their views should not be given greater weight or special consideration simply by virtue of their age. Age does not necessarily confer wisdom. I have met wise young people and I have met wise old people – and even wise middle-aged people!

And of course I have met very foolish young, middle-aged and old people.

Equally, as I've suggested earlier, people should not be respected simply because of titles bestowed upon them or earned by them. One of the difficulties we have experienced in our society as a result of undue deference for titles is the frequency of sexual and other forms of abuse by trusted elders holding traditionally respected titles like Father, Reverend, Doctor, Housemaster, Manager, Sergeant Major, Professor, Member of Parliament . . .

It would be helpful to teach young people how to recognise false prophets, charlatans, predators and abusers. Teaching children to honour all adults above a certain age, or adults who hold certain titles or positions, is to put them in danger.

In the *Telegraph* article I mentioned above, which is headlined 'Australian schools are becoming too "kumbaya"', Wiltshire is quoted as saying, 'Kids lying on the floor and rolling around, I don't know what that teaches . . .'

Well, neither do I, and neither does anyone else, because Professor Wiltshire has not provided the context for his description of 'kids lying on the floor and rolling around'. I'm not aware of too many Australian classrooms where lying on the floor and rolling around is part of the curriculum or the daily routine. Perhaps Professor Wiltshire needs to spend a little more time in classrooms.

Tests like PISA and NAPLAN derive from the notion of 'winners and losers', the massive foundation stone that underpins our society in so many crucial areas. Our adherence to it causes endless problems – and not just in sport. As long as we rank schools and countries against each other, some will, obviously, be at the top, some in the middle and some at the bottom, and some people will fiercely criticise those that are at the bottom, ignoring the complexities inherent in these comparisons. The way we approach sport, with our attitude of 'one winner; everyone else is a failure' is a metaphor for the way we approach almost everything. Sports coaches love aphorisms like 'Second place is just the first-place loser', and 'Show me a good loser and I'll show you a loser'. In an early episode of the US TV sitcom *Saved by the Bell*, Principal Belding tells the students, 'Nobody remembers second place.'

Professor Wiltshire's belief that 'Asian countries are surging ahead of Australia', and the embarrassment of education ministers at our 'failure', does not acknowledge the areas in which Australian schools have made progress in recent years. They include creativity, flexibility, relationships education, emotional intelligence, social intelligence, political awareness and entrepreneurship.

Can similar claims be made on behalf of the schools of Singapore, South Korea and Taiwan? I don't know. I do know that the Australian Council for Educational Research (ACER), which devises the PISA tests on behalf of the OECD, does not venture into these areas. Although PISA tests seek to examine some quite abstract skills, such as problem-solving by exploring a situation, building a coherent mental representation of a problem, setting goals and planning to reach them, and monitoring and assessing progress towards goals, they cannot test everything, and they can be criticised for some of the cultural assumptions and prejudices underlying the questions. For example, the 2012 problem-solving test included a series of questions based on students' ability to use an automated railway ticket machine of the type commonly found in European and Asian cities.[264] A student from Singapore or Paris is likely to feel more at home with this question than a student who has never left Horsham or Cloncurry. Perhaps this is a factor in the 'significantly lower' scores recorded by students in Australian regional schools compared to students in Australian metropolitan schools – and the 'significantly lower' scores achieved in Australian remote schools compared to scores recorded in metropolitan and regional ones.[265]

It's ironic that when I visited China and Taiwan in 2017 on behalf of the Australian government, I was asked everywhere by teachers and parents how they could change their schools to be more like Australia's, because of the rapidly growing awareness in those countries that rote learning was unlikely to be helpful to 21st-century students. Resilience, flexibility, creativity and social intelligence were seen as the skills needed for future success, and newly opened alternative schools in Taipei and Beijing were attracting large numbers of students.

I can say confidently that despite the grave and easily identifiable shortcomings in Australian schools, the standard of work by students has become more sophisticated. In areas like maths, science, psychology and history, kids are tackling topics that in the 1950s and 1960s were the province of universities. The other day one of our music teachers sent me a classical composition for a string quartet, written by a Year 9 student. It was hauntingly beautiful. Back in my day, or when I was a young'un, kids were simply not doing this kind of work, because they were not deemed capable of achieving at this level. Despite the many obstacles in their paths, and their numerous disappointing features, schools are better places now than they were in the 1950s. Some have increasingly come to resemble universities, with their

---

264 Lisa De Bortoli and Greg Macaskill, 'Thinking it through: Australian students' skills in creative problem solving', Australia Council for Educational Research, 2014, pp. 20–21, research.acer.edu. au/cgi/viewcontent.cgi?article=1018&context=ozpisa, accessed 1 April 2019.
265 Ibid.

wide range of subjects, the depth at which subjects are studied, and the increased emphasis on student initiative and autonomy. Extended Investigations, which is part of the Victorian Certificate of Education (VCE) but which has much in common with a postgraduate degree, is an example of this.

Among the more popular options at Alice Miller are Philosophy, Classical Studies, Theatre Studies, Environmental Science and Outdoor Education. These courses often demand a multidisciplinary approach, and always require a willingness to explore topics with the aim of gaining a sophisticated level of understanding and insight.

In contrast, in 1968 I was ranked in the top 100 students in New South Wales in two Higher School Certificate subjects, Economics and Ancient History. I achieved these distinctions by absenting myself from the classes (I quickly came to realise that one teacher was 'burned-out' and had lost interest, and the other hardly ever turned up to class) and teaching myself – simply by learning two textbooks almost off by heart: Samuelson in Economics, and Bury in Ancient History. Regurgitating them in the end-of-year exams was pretty much all that was required to pull in the big marks. In 2019, students at some schools are already studying subjects that give them credits at university. We can expect to see this trend accelerate rapidly in the near future.

THE SCHOOL AS A SOCIAL SANCTUARY

Schools nowadays frequently function as sanctuaries for children who are troubled, insecure, damaged and at risk. In the past, most teachers studiously ignored social problems and individual mental health issues. In his memoir *Comp*, subtitled *A Survivor's Tale*, John-Paul Flintoff describes what happened when three students were caught smoking dope outside the gates of his British comprehensive school in 1986. '[They] were taken to Dr Rushworth. He stood and shouted at them, telling them how stupid they were, saying they stood no chance in their exams if they wasted time on drugs. Then he phoned their parents and announced that they were indefinitely suspended.'[266] .

In *The Hate Race*, Australian-born Maxine Beneba Clarke describes a scene from her Grade 5 days at a Sydney school, around 1990:

'Psst. Hey, Blackie. Hey you, Blackie. Over here, Blackie!'

Each missile was now accompanied by a whispered taunt. I was determined not to turn around, but the spit-ball barrage continued sporadically throughout afternoon lessons, his taunts becoming progressively louder.

My Grade 5 teacher, Mrs Hird, was sitting at her desk marking a stack of spelling homework. I'd had her two years before, in Grade 3, and had been elated to be in her class again. She sighed heavily when she noticed me standing next to her desk; we were supposed to be quietly working away in our story-writing books.

'What is it, Maxine?' She asked impatiently, her red pen hovering in mid-air.

'Derek's been throwing spit balls at me.'

'Okay, I'll tell him to stop.'

'And he's been saying mean things.'

'What kind of things?' She sounded hesitant, as if she didn't really want to know.

'He's been calling me "blackie".'

My teacher paused, staring steadily at me for a moment. I shifted my weight from one foot to the other, aware that in the quiet classroom, our whispering could be heard by the whole roomful of students.

'Has he been calling you anything else?'

'No. Not this afternoon, anyway.'

Mrs Hird kept her grey-green eyes on me, red pen still poised above the spelling test she'd been marking. 'Well,' she said slowly, 'that's what you are. You can call him whitey if you like.' She smiled at me, as if we were sharing a private joke.

I stared back at her, indignant with shock. 'That's racist,'

---

266 John-Paul Flintoff, *Comp: A Survivor's Tale*, Indigo, London, 1999, p. 234.

I declared loudly. I'd never used the word before . . . [It] felt strange in my mouth: powerful, as if now that I could name the thing that was happening to me, it had become real, not something I was imagining being oversensitive about.

As soon as I said the word, the look on Mrs Hird's face changed. The contours around her eyes and mouth swirled angrily, like the sky before a storm.

'How dare you use that word in my classroom,' she said, so softly I wished she was yelling it. 'How dare you accuse a classmate of something like that. How could you –? Go away. Go back to your seat.'

I could feel the whole class staring as I returned to my desk in the second-last row.

'Blackie!' Derek hissed again, smirking as I eased myself back into my chair.[267]

It's impossible for me to guess at the thought processes within Mrs Hird as she processed Clarke's complaint. The closest I can come is to suggest that the word 'racist' perhaps triggered a fearful response: maybe someone outside the classroom would come to hear that she was a teacher who tolerated racism? And maybe her fear of the consequences of that triggered an urgent desire to shut down the issue before it could gain traction.

Bullying by teachers has been a persistent problem in schools, and will continue to be for so long as teachers do not reflect honestly and thoughtfully on the power imbalance in the classroom, and the extent to which their own desire for personal power influences their behaviour and speech.

The following extract is from an unpublished memoir, 'I'm Not That Special', by Melbourne woman Niamh Choesang, who has cerebral palsy quadriplegia. Describing her schooling in the late 1990s, Choesang wrote:

267 Maxine Beneba Clarke, *The Hate Race*, Hachette, Sydney, 2018, pp. 102–104.

Escaping from class had become a refined skill of mine – especially in the mornings. After the 'friendly morning discussions', my arm shot straight up in the air and stubbornly remained there for as long as it was going to take to be acknowledged, which was usually quite a while.

Finally, the teacher looked my way and began to make her way over. I thought she had somehow read my mind and knew what I wanted, but she just grabbed my arm, put it back down at my side and walked off again.

I guess anyone else would have taken that as a hint. I wasn't anyone else.

My arm shot up once more.

Again she came over and put my arm down. I looked up at her and as clearly as I could, said, 'I need to go to the toilet.'

Without acknowledging what I had said, she went over to the phone, which was mounted on the wall, and began dialling.

'Niamh needs toileting,' she spoke into the receiver, then responded with a few short 'okays' and a nod and hung up.

Niamh needs toileting. The phrase echoed in my ears. It was just a fact. I was just a situation that needed to be dealt with, not a person who needed a little bit of help.

Twenty minutes later (the whole time I had been sitting there, waiting, because there had been 'no point starting work when I would be leaving the room soon') a knock came at the classroom door. The nurse strode in and, without even so much as a 'hello Niamh, are you ready to go to the toilet?' she walked around to the back of me, grabbed the back of my chair, sharply pulled me away from the table and pushed me out the door in one swift movement.

The toilets were next to my classroom, so it was a short ride, which is probably why they didn't feel the need to hurry to come get me.

Even though I was light, they still needed two people to lift me. Or, to put it in their words, I was a 'two person lift'. So when we entered the bathroom, another nurse was already there waiting for us.

The second person grabbed the left hand side of my body, and the Nurse who had brought me in grabbed the right side. I was momentarily airborne until they placed my feet on the ground. While still both holding each of my arms, they pulled down my pants with their other free hand.

After sitting me down on the commode, they left me alone to do my business in the large, cold, white tiled bathroom with nothing to look at except for the familiar, green, laminate flooring. I swear I have developed an aversion to that green laminate flooring.

Well, 'alone' was a pretty loose definition. The bathroom was almost as big as my classroom. It had toilet stalls that my 'helpers' had decided not to put me in, but instead I sat on one of the exposed toilets out in the open. To my left were a bunch of younger students in the same position that I was, and they were being very vocal about it. Their cries and moans echoed off the tiles, making everything sound louder and more intense. There were no aides in the room, just us kids – us little situations.

One by one they were attended to and taken away, until finally the last girl was lifted back into her wheelchair and wheeled away, and I was left in blissful peace and quiet.

This is my chance, I thought to myself.

I let my head drop, rested my chin on my chest, and slowly drifted off to sleep. I always looked forward to when I could go to the toilet; it had become somewhat of an escape whenever I felt tired.

After what seemed like only a minute had passed, I jolted back awake at the sound of returning moans and shouts. I blinked the sleep from my eyes and looked up just in time to see the two nurses had returned. Without much conversation, they helped me back into my chair and returned me to my classroom.

I was seated back at my table when I glanced up at the clock. I had been in the bathroom for just over an hour.[268]

---

268 Niamh Choesang (formerly Niamh Scally), 'I'm Not That Special', unpublished manuscript, pp. 12–14.

This combination of power and laziness has so often been my experience with Australian authority figures. It's dangerous and it can be deadly. In teachers, it's destructive in an insidious and often invisible way.

These extracts are all from the last century, however. Nowadays, we who work in schools are expected to do a little better than Dr Rushworth or Mrs Hird or Niamh Choesang's teachers and aides. Most of my time as a principal – when I'm not filling in inane and ludicrous forms for educational bureaucrats – is spent trying to help damaged children improve their social relationships, make academic headway, and achieve some progress in dealing with their pain. All worthwhile teachers are engaged in this noble work, although it generally goes unnoticed by the wider community, and all too often is resented and even bitterly opposed by the parents who are causing the damage. Recently I was speaking to a teacher who had put in uncountable hours and immeasurable energy working with Natalie, a deeply troubled little girl. I said to her, 'You may well have saved this child's soul.' I don't often use such dramatic or extravagant language, but having seen the gradual evolution of the child from violently angry to lively, funny and happy I think the comment was justified. I doubt though that there'll ever be a PISA test capable of measuring Natalie's emotional journey.

BULLYING AND SCHOOL CULTURE

One of the most popular words in the lexicon of 21st-century concrete thinkers when they pontificate about education is of course 'bullying'. There has certainly been horrific bullying in some schools at certain times, but given the cramped conditions so often encountered, the poor staff-to-student ratios, and the authoritarian nature of the institutions, many schools these days do relatively well in creating a friendly environment.

But what a godsend bullying in schools has been to politicians, who, given the slightest opportunity to speak on the subject, puff up with righteous indignation like a bullfrog in mating mode, and embark on a sanctimonious speech about the utter disgrace of such behaviour, the stern refusal of his or her party to tolerate bullying, the personal abhorrence this politician has for school bullying, and his or her determination to condemn bullying now and forever. The topic 'bullying in schools' is a much-cherished freebie for politicians. They can fulminate against it, knowing that it costs them no money and no one will criticise them for condemning it.

There is no mention in these magnificent perorations of the bullying of Third World countries by Western governments or capitalist institutions, the bullying of refugees by Australia's Liberal and Labor parties, the bullying of school principals and teachers by bureaucrats in education departments, the bullying of school principals and teachers by parents, or the bullying of children by their parents or teachers.

When politicians condemn bullying they somehow omit to mention their own behaviour. In their internecine battles, their treatment of members of opposition parties, and forums like parliamentary question time, they engage in abusive behaviour of a kind that should shame them into eternal silence on the subject of bullying.

Children will stop bullying other children when adults stop bullying each other. Don't hold your breath.

Candlebark and Alice Miller, being small and relatively new schools, and being 'alternative', whatever that means, leads some parents to believe that they can impose their agenda on us. They assume we are more malleable than systemic schools. They don't seem to notice that we have an agenda of our own.

They often approach us in a bullying manner, and it is incumbent upon us to remain steadfast in the face of such approaches. I don't find it easy. My nature is to avoid conflict, to hide under the desk when these strident and determined people come looking for me. But I know it would be fatal for the school were I to do so. I have to remind myself that I am obliged to do what the school requires of the person in my role. My personal feelings are for me to deal with, separately. I remind myself of a conversation to which I was privy years ago, when Noelene Horton, principal at a school where I worked, told a powerful mother that she was to stop hitting her adolescent daughter; that it must never happen again. The mother wilted in the face of Noelene's moral authority.

In April 2017, *The Australian* newspaper ran an article about bullying in schools, in which the Victorian opposition education spokesman, Nick Wakeling, was quoted as saying that the Liberal Party, if elected, would implement an anti-bullying program in schools 'that teaches kids the importance of respecting people of all appearances, sexuality, gender, religion and ethnicity'.[269]

A Martian visiting Planet Earth for a pit stop might think, upon reading this piece, that the Liberal Party are the pacesetters in Australia for tolerance, compassion and inclusiveness. For liberalism, in fact. Dear readers, you are permitted a wry smile at this point. But the public rhetoric around young people is nearly always suffused with pomposity and the old-age mantle of righteous superiority that adults so eagerly assume . . . and that includes adults from both major political parties, as well as many of the minor ones.

A few years ago I took a workshop at a prison for young offenders. I'm never sure what to expect when I do these things. The reception can range from furious hostility to eager embraces. And that's just from the guards.

No, seriously.

I got to this particular place mid-morning, went through the usual procedures of security checks, identification, and of course scanning for AK-47s, switchblades and drugs. One of the teachers who worked in the prison took me to meet the prisoners. They were young men, aged around twenty to 22.

I was struck by their forceful and truculent personalities. They all seemed very tall and confident, and I started to feel old and feeble. We had a couple of minutes of uneasy small talk, about the weather

---

269 Rebecca Urban, '"Safe Schools" anti-bully project to lose Tasmania funding', *The Australian*, 18 April 2017.

or prison food or whatever. I was trying to gauge the mood of the group, but was having trouble. I thought they were negative about my being there.

Suddenly, almost simultaneously, several of them turned to me and said, 'Well, come on, what have you got for us, come on, get on with it.'

Sometimes I am almost overwhelmed by doubt and cynicism, and when they spoke like this I immediately thought that they were expressing their dislike of me and their unhappiness at being in the workshop. I translated their words into, 'What kind of wanky stuff are you going to waste our time with? Who the fuck do you think you are and why do we have to put up with this?'

But as they repeated and amplified their exhortations, I got it. Mainly because they told me. They said: 'We only have an hour and a half. You must be here for a reason. These teachers must reckon you've got something worthwhile or they wouldn't have asked you to come. So, get on with it. We want whatever it is you've got and we've already wasted six minutes.'

Then began one of the most memorable workshops of my life. We went at a fast and furious pace, taking huge risks. They drank up everything. They were the thirstiest, most demanding group I have ever worked with, and possibly the most wonderful and exhilarating.

At one point I was talking about characters in fiction and their defences. Everything that's true and important in real life will be true and important in fiction. In real life we all have defences, so characters in fiction must have defences. I decided to push them even further than they had already gone, to take even bigger risks, so I asked one of them: 'What's your defence? How do you protect yourself?'

Consider for a moment. I was asking a young man, in the most virile stage of his life but living in a dangerous and hostile place, to tell other young men in that place how to attack him. I was asking him to make himself naked. I was inviting him to tell other prisoners his weakest spots. He didn't hesitate. And neither did the others when I asked them the same question.

Eventually I got to the last man in the group, the apparent leader.

I asked him, 'What are your defences? How do you fend off attacks?'

He opened his mouth to speak. Before he could say anything, one of the teachers spoke for him. 'You talk too much,' she said to him. 'That's your defence.'

I remember that workshop for two reasons. One, for the sheer greed for knowledge of those young men. Two, for the spectacularly destructive moment when a teacher took it upon herself to answer an intimate question for another person.

She wanted to turn him into a dummy, with her as the ventriloquist. There was a person who talked too much in that workshop. She only said seven words, but she talked too much.

When the session was over and the prisoners went back to their daily routine I told the teachers how excited I had been by the class, and how much I wanted to work with these men again. They assured me that it should be possible to arrange, and we agreed to sort out the details by email. But somehow it never happened. The dates I suggested were never quite convenient for them, the prison program wasn't quite flexible enough, the time just couldn't be found. I wondered if they had perhaps been frightened by the raw honesty of the workshop.

But I'll never forget those young men. And I'll never forget that teacher.

In relation to the 'problem' of bullying in schools, it is worth noting that whenever two or more people come together, they'll engage in a transaction to determine the power balance that's going to prevail between them. We could call it a power struggle, although it may be a genteel or concealed one. Once the balance is determined, they will no longer need the same transaction at subsequent meetings, unless one of them is motivated to attempt to change the balance. My favourite example of this is a fictional one, in the opening pages of the Arnold Bennett novel *Grand Babylon Hotel*, where millionaire guest of the hotel, Theodore Racksole, is dining with his daughter in the *salle a manger*. His daughter expresses a wish for nothing but a steak and beer for her meal. The arrogant waiter refuses to lower the tone of the establishment by transmitting such a vulgar order to the chef. Mr Racksole's answer is to excuse himself, leave the room, seek out the owner of the hotel, buy the business from him for £400,000, then place the order for steak and beer – and this time he is successful.[270]

But at Candlebark and Alice Miller, as at many other schools, we have not really seen scenarios where a good-natured, good-humoured, generous child is relentlessly persecuted by other children. Far more frequently, as I argued earlier, children who are allegedly being bullied are children with poor behaviours who are being offered feedback by other kids, but who are unable to accept or process it.

At my schools we tell kids that our most important rule is 'no excluding'. This simply stated concept is well understood by them. If you stopped any Candlebark or Alice Miller student at random and asked them, 'What's the main rule at this school?' they would respond without hesitation. And the rule works very well. No Year 7 kid would dream of telling a Grade 1 child that he or she could not join their game of tag or downball or basketball. But the rule is exploited by students with difficult behaviours who sometimes come to me filled with indignation to complain: 'Jodie and Rudi are excluding me.'

I tell them bluntly: 'But you were so horrible to them on the trampoline, when you kept knocking them over, even after they asked you to stop. Of course they don't want to play with you right now.'

Clarke's account is a consistent and believable one of a deep-seated culture of racism pervading school, community and suburb. Mrs Hird's comments ring disturbingly true. And Niamh Choesang's book generously acknowledges those few people who treated her as a human being, whilst at the same time telling countless stories of cruelty and bullying – usually by teachers or aides. But there is a caveat: we have only one side of their stories. If a child has a lot of unlikeable behaviours, and kids want to 'get back' at him or her, they often seize on anything that is slightly or significantly different about the child and make that the target of their reprisals. This could be red

270 Arnold Bennet, *The Grand Babylon Hotel*, Penguin, Melbourne, 2017.

hair, the child's shape or size, pimples, a lisp . . . it doesn't matter.

Sadly, when Niamh Choesang was finally able to enrol in Year 12 at a 'regular' school instead of the special school she had been attending all her life, she was nineteen years old, but still infantilised by her aide: at the school canteen, for example . . .

Being the age of nineteen, I wasn't exactly health conscious, so usually it would be a jam ball doughnut and a can of coke or a coffee. Well every day I had the same argument with her. After I would tell her what I wanted, she would start.

'Oh Niamh, you can't have that. Why don't you have fruit salad or an egg sandwich instead?'

I thought if I was going to stay awake for the next period (double legal studies, eww) I was going to need a sugar fix, no matter how small.

'Can I please just have what I asked for?' I said, trying to stay calm.

'I don't think that your mother would be happy if she knew what you were eating.'

Breathe Niamh, breathe.

'I know for a fact that she wouldn't give a damn as I am an adult! Can you please just buy what I asked for, as I now only have a few minutes to eat?'

This used to frustrate the hell out of me, because what difference did what I ate make to her? It was my body, if what I ate came with bad consequences then that would be my own fault. I was willing to take that risk.

She would finally buy what I had asked for along with things that I had not, however it took me so long to convince her to buy what I wanted I barely had time to eat it.[271]

Without exception, kids at Candlebark and Alice Miller who have behaved towards others in ways that have caused serious problems

---

271 Niamh Choesang (formerly Niamh Scally), 'I'm Not That Special', pp. 70–71.

have had major difficulties in many areas of their lives. Threats and punishments (even if the punishments are euphemistically labelled 'consequences') achieve little with these children. We can only work with them patiently, over time, to gain their trust, unpack the conversations and incidents that have played out badly, increase their ability to empathise, and teach them better social skills.

This process is usually effective, sometimes surprisingly quickly. It's helped by the fact that other Candlebark and Alice Miller kids are remarkably tolerant and forgiving, and seem to have short memories when it comes to unpleasant exchanges with their peers. I attribute this to two factors. One is the small size of the schools, which does, much as I hate the comparison, have some of the qualities of a family, at least insofar as getting along with others is concerned. If kids at my schools have a falling out, they have to forget it and move on, because, unlike a bigger school, there is no other group they can join: they are 'stuck' with each other.

THE INFLUENCE OF THE STAFF CULTURE

The other factor is the attitude of the staff. Kids in many schools where I have worked are very quick to pick up on which kids are disliked or scorned by teachers, and they imitate the teachers' attitudes towards such unfortunate children.

The best English teacher I ever worked with, Canadian-born John Mazur, was able to transform the lives of unpopular kids by simply hanging out with them himself. Because he was so liked and respected by all the students, who desired to hang out with him too, they had to 'tolerate' the presence of the unpopular kids if they wanted to spend time with John. In the atmosphere John created, the cool kids found that the unpopular kids were actually not so bad – they could be funny, they had opinions, they had ideas – and so they gained respect and status within the school.

The same kind of approach has worked at Candlebark over many years, and seems to be working at Alice Miller (which is still, at the time of writing this, in its childhood), thanks to the men and women employed at the schools. Among the adults, it's not just the teaching staff who matter though. I have seen many schools where some members of the so-called 'ancillary staff' were toxic in their treatment of teachers and students, poisoning the school with negativity and rudeness. The reason for their behaviour was often obvious enough: in these highly hierarchical institutions they were aware that they were likely to be treated disdainfully by the academically qualified members of the teaching staff, and, recognising unconsciously that 'defence is the best method of attack' they attacked ferociously. Office ladies, canteen managers, maintenance men, bus drivers, reception staff, principal's secretaries: I have been in schools where ample evidence existed to indicate that the receptionist was about the most powerful person in the establishment.

In my first week at Geelong Grammar, I moved a water sprinkler so I could start cricket training with the team to which I had been allocated, on the allocated oval at the allocated time. A minute later I saw a florid-faced groundsman – much older than me – marching towards us. His body language and facial expression gave me ample warning that I was in for a classic status battle, so I had time to prepare myself. I let him finish his tirade of abuse at my temerity in turning off the tap without authority, let alone touching the sprinkler, let alone moving it, then, like the preacher in the classic country song 'The Reverend Mr. Black', I 'cut him down like a big oak tree'.[272] It was ugly, but I knew I had to win the battle, otherwise the crowd of twenty thirteen-year-olds watching in fascination would lose all respect for me.

It wasn't until I worked at Timbertop that I found maintenance staff who were generous, intelligent, thoughtful, funny and friendly. One day, reversing a tractor in the machinery shed, I cut clean through a central pillar with a blade that was fitted to the back of the tractor. I hastened to find Doug Galbraith and Laurie Jacob, worried that the

---

272 The Kingston Trio 'The Reverend Mr. Black', *The Kingston Trio No. 16*, Capitol Records, Inc., 1963.

roof of the shed might collapse at any moment. When I told them the bad news, they looked at each other, smiled, and one of them said, 'Weren't we just saying that it was about time we replaced those poles?'

I couldn't believe my luck at working with such good-natured people. I didn't enjoy the same camaraderie at subsequent schools, except at Fitzroy Community School, but happily, the staff at Candlebark and Alice Miller who do the (often unglamorous and usually invisible) administrative work, maintenance, building, cooking and gardening have been, almost without exception, rich contributors to the life of the school, respected, admired, liked and loved by teachers and students.

CHOOSING STAFF

In employing them I use much the same criteria as when employing teachers. The most important thing is that all staff, teachers included, should be adults. I don't mean that they should be over eighteen: I mean that they should have a sense of perspective, an appreciation of relativity, an ability to communicate, and a significant degree of emotional maturity. It's of vital importance to get it right, otherwise carnage results. I think I've stuffed up only a couple of times – with a teacher who, it soon became apparent, was mentally unwell, and two non-teaching staff who were also mentally unwell, but not so easily identifiable.

Thornton Wilder attributes these words to Plato:

Then tell me, O Critias, how will a man choose the ruler that shall rule over him? Will he not choose a man who has first established order in himself, knowing that any decision that has its spring from anger or pride or vanity can be multiplied a thousandfold in its effects upon the citizens?[273]

Schools are not appropriate places for adults with serious emotional

273 Thornton Wilder, *The Skin of Our Teeth*, 1942, Act III.

difficulties to seek healing. Schools have a de facto role, whether wanted or not, as therapeutic communities for children and adolescents. They cannot function simultaneously as therapeutic communities for teachers, who in the 21st century are so often forced into the role of de facto therapists. This role can be, and often is, avoided by teachers, and there may be a kind of wisdom in this avoidance if the teacher feels unsuited to the task. No therapy is better than bad therapy. But regardless of whether teachers accept some responsibility for the emotional lives of their students, emotionally unstable teachers are dangerous, and can damage their vulnerable charges. I suspect many people who apply for positions in schools believe that they can escape from the world by moving into the cloistered environment that some schools might appear to provide. Or they feel that just being with children will be therapeutic. Such people have no understanding of the true nature of schools or children.

Equally, disillusioned or cynical teachers are a danger to the profession, and a danger to their students. I have lost count of the number of job applications I have received over the years that begin with phrases such as 'Burnt out as I am after eleven years teaching in the government system . . .' or 'Having lost all the idealism with which I began my career in teaching, I am turning to your school as my last hope . . .'

I cannot tell you how these letters continue, because I don't read past the first sentence. Much as I sympathise with the frustration and despair of people unable to cope with the destructive leadership and suffocating bureaucracy so frequently encountered in schools and the educational system, I want to hire teachers who have succeeded despite these awful and unfair obstacles.

Talking one day to a good friend who was in her first year as principal of a new progressive school, I asked her: 'What would help you most, as principal, right now?'

She replied: 'Well, it would be good if we could get through a week without a member of staff crying.'

Some resilience, some emotional strength, would seem to be a reasonable expectation of those entering the teaching profession.

I am excited by job applications from people who can prove that they have lived adventurous lives. Currently we have on staff Dr Bettina Lythgoe, a maths teacher who grew up in Argentina, rode a bike through Patagonia at the age of nineteen, hiked across the Andes, did an ice-climbing course in Argentina, then hitched a ride to the Antarctic with the Chilean Navy. She later emigrated to Australia, where she achieved her doctorate in plant physiology and agronomy. She is trilingual, speaking English, Spanish and German. We have a science teacher, Shaun Dennis, who was in the New Zealand Navy until a car load of elderly lady lawn bowlers smashed into him one day as he rode through Dunedin on his motorbike, leaving him badly injured. He re-educated himself to become a graphic designer, and later did a teaching degree. (He's even bilingual, speaking both New Zealand and Australian English.) Another of our science teachers, Daniel Park, was born in South Korea and became a professional golfer before deciding that teaching offered more fulfilment than hitting a small white ball into a hole. One of our primary teachers, Sarah Tacconelli, went to Columbia not knowing a word of Spanish, but started her own canyoning and canoeing company, which she ran successfully for several years. She is known far and wide by her nickname 'Shredder', a sobriquet earned for her ferocious rock-climbing exploits.

Before Candlebark opened I interviewed Wendy Wright, a highly experienced primary teacher, who told me that she and her husband had just spent their wedding anniversary sailing the Gippsland Lakes, and had celebrated their previous anniversary by skiing in Switzerland. At the time of our interview she held a senior position in a school in Thailand. I hired her virtually on the spot.

The school gardener, Martin Barry, pioneered a new approach to property marketing in Australia, starting a nationwide business that dealt with hundreds of real estate agencies. Subsequently he and his son developed a cut-flower farm, airfreighting huge quantities of peonies to Japan. One of our school bus drivers, the late Hanh Tran, was a Vietnamese student who entered Australia on a Colombo scholarship and eventually became head of Radio Australia.

Another teacher, Cameron Kerr, was a ski instructor in Canada, a financial para-planner (whatever that means) in Brisbane, then worked in the Global Corporate Trust Division of the Bank of New York Mellon, in London. He runs half-marathons twice a year, plays competitive tennis at pennant level in Melbourne, and has a two handicap at golf. Yet another, Andy Moffatt, is a psychology graduate from Edinburgh University. 'Formative experiences' (my words) for him included selling licence plates on the phone, pop-riveting luggage trolleys at Heathrow, working as a silver service waiter, hitchhiking from Perth to Darwin to Cairns then Sydney, working at the Royal Bank of Scotland, waitering in Tokyo, and setting up an independent film company specialising in in-house company shoots. He worked as a travel agent for two years before quitting and going on the road again, mostly around Asia, before 'falling into a job' teaching kindergarten and night school in Taiwan. Only then did he do a teaching course, back in Edinburgh.

We have a teacher, Ian da Silva, who built his own energy-efficient environmentally friendly house, then became a consultant to other people wanting to take on similar challenges. We have a Frenchwoman, Dr Christine Mathieu, who has a PhD in anthropology, is one of the world's leading authorities on the histories and cultures of the ethnic minorities along the south-western Sino-Tibetan borderland in China, and is co-author of the bestselling book *Leaving Mother Lake*. She is fluent in English, French, Latin, Spanish and various Chinese dialects. Another teacher, Cathy Snowdon, is a marathon swimmer who counts a relay-crossing of the English Channel among her many achievements. She was in her mid-50s when she and her team swam the Channel. She later attempted a solo crossing of the Channel – and nearly got to the other side!

Sarita Ryan, head of campus at Alice Miller, became a full-time student at a specialist classical ballet school at the age of sixteen, but after leaving school chose Arts/Law at the University of Melbourne. Influenced by a stint of voluntary teaching in India, she switched to education, and spent five years teaching at Candlebark. Like many of our teachers, Sarita eventually left . . . for further adventures. We had one teacher leave because he and some friends bought an old olive mill in Montenegro, which they spent several years restoring and turning into a hostel and cultural centre. Another teacher left to go to a ranch in Oregon that pioneers environmentally friendly methods of farming. Another left to work with kids with severe emotional and other difficulties. Wendy Wright left to teach in Fiji.

Sarita went to Finland to gain her Master of Education and Developmental Studies degree. As part of that course she spent much time in Zambia and Ghana, working with the UN's International Labour Organization. She still found time to perform with dance companies in Europe, at the Edinburgh Fringe Festival for example, where every review of her show rated it 'five stars'.

Yet she returned to us, declining opportunities to study at Cambridge University and the London School of Economics. Similarly, Wendy Wright returned after two wonderful years in Fiji. Scott Hatcher, who went to teach troubled kids, returned after five years of valuable work with them.

As well as looking for teachers who have lived adventurous lives, I look for evidence of creativity. Hence I employed Basil Eliades, an artist who has lectured in education at university level. His commissioned works include the last portrait of Prime Minister Malcolm Fraser before Mr Fraser's death, and a portrait of poet the late Les Murray. He is the author of several books of poetry and a book of short stories, and the creator of *The Men's Deck*, an innovative tool to help men navigate issues of manhood and masculinity. He is an ex-dancer, a violin player, a long-time student of the demanding Korean martial art Tang Soo Tao, and is trilingual, speaking English, French and Swedish.

English and Drama teacher Anne Browning appeared as a performer at theatres like La Mama, the Melbourne Theatre Company, the Queensland Theatre Company, the Playbox Theatre, and the Malthouse, and also directed for the Melbourne Theatre Company.

Music teacher Taran Carter is a well-known Australian composer who has had works commissioned by the Australian Ballet and a number of symphony orchestras. A recent work, *Mixed Precipitation*, for organ and six percussionists, had its world premiere at Melbourne Town Hall in December 2013. Our trilingual chef at Alice Miller, Veronica Galvan, practises and teaches capoeira (Brazilian martial arts). Another music teacher, Anna van Veldhuisen, won an Australia Council Grant for Emerging Artists and a Melbourne Theatre Company award for her score for a Molière production.

For a school, nothing matters more than to have adventurous, creative staff members. People with a zest for life, people who want to explore the world, people who embrace others, people who trust. They are unlikely to be patronising or pompous or contemptuous or destructive when working with anyone, including children and adolescents.

If staff morale is good, a school will function well. If staff morale is poor, nothing, nothing on God's earth, will make the school successful. Morale is always likely to be good when the staff consists of people who are filled with creative energy, who exude positivity, and who are willing to experiment and take risks. Leadership is obviously a critical factor in this. I remember visiting a primary school in Bendigo, years ago. The principal and I set out to cross the playground to get to the library. Recess was just starting. It took us twenty minutes to traverse a hundred metres, because every kid in the place wanted to say hi to the principal, have a chat, tell him what was going on in their lives. I knew I was in a good school.

AN IMPORTANT MEMBER OF THE SCHOOL 'COMMUNITY'

Another member of the Candlebark community has contributed so much to the school that I am embarrassed I haven't paid her a salary. Erica, daughter of teacher Donna Prince and her husband Dave, started coming to school four days a week when she was six months old. What this has meant for our students is described by Donna in an article she wrote for a mothering magazine in 2015:

I have had my students feeding her solids, walking her in the pram and playing with her. I'm saving them from nappy changes! None of them have volunteered for that for some reason! The patience and tenderness my older students show towards Erica is amazing, my students are fantastic people. Kids who don't normally get to hang around with babies have no idea how to act with babies, but hell, I know plenty of adults who have no idea how to be comfortable with a baby. I remember being twelve and being made to sit still between two adults and watched like a hawk when I had my five-minute hold of my baby cousin . . .

My students are responsible, capable and caring. When handing out 'baby' jobs I usually favour the kids who don't have much contact with babies at home. They quickly get over their nervousness. A touching example of this is my crack babysitting crew! We have staff meetings once a week and there are four boys, three in Year seven and one in Grade five, who look after Erica during this time. Last staff meeting I heard a noise and ducked out to investigate. The boys had popped her in the pram and were dancing around her with a full dance routine singing 'Let It Go' from (the movie) 'Frozen'. So very cool. They are amazing babysitters.

So I breastfeed in my classroom as well. This has to be one of the most important benefits of bringing her with me. I have a lovely chair in my room and when I am going to give Erica a feed I just let my students know. Her feeds have mostly happened during recess and lunch anyway, and if they want to hang around they can. I had a lovely discussion with some Grade twos and threes the other day while Erica was having a feed. They were curious as kids are and we just talked about Erica's favourite drinks and food and then they told me all about their Lego party on the weekend. Oh the horror!

I think I am the luckiest Mum/Teacher in the world. I get to bring my baby to work with me which helps me maintain the relationship and the breastfeeding relationship, my classes adore Erica and the other staff members are such a wonderful support. If raising a child takes a village, then I'm pretty stoked about the village I'm in!

I wish to add to this by commenting not on the benefits Erica's presence brings to the school and its students, but to the effect on Erica. She has been fortunate in having wonderful parents, but a lot of kids are in that happy situation. Erica has had something extra. She has had, as Donna says, the advantage of being raised by a village. Her life in this regard is exceptional in 21st-century Western society. It shouldn't be, but it is.

'As a matter of fact, Neill always insisted that Summerhill was first and above all a community and only to a lesser degree a school, which it had to be because the law will not yet allow young people to live in a community unless it calls itself a school and makes certain school-like motions.' So says American teacher John Holt, a fine writer on education, commenting on pioneering British educator A.S. Neill, in his book *Escape from Childhood*.[274]

And what is the result of Erica's time spent in the Candlebark community? Well, I have never seen a happier, more serene child. Erica is charged with positive energy. She is surrounded every day by 170 people who love her, who have her best interests at heart, who involve her in their games and activities. The benefits show in her sociability, her keen interest in life, her obvious delight in her surroundings, her resilience and sense of adventure.

I know Erica is a sample of only one, so therefore not really valid for statistical purposes, but she is the third toddler we have had at Candlebark, and I believe the experience has been valuable for all three. I know all three have benefited the community by being here.

There are two potential lessons in Erica's situation. One, every school should have some babies, for the great benefits that they bring to the students of the school. It's important for teenagers to spend time with babies, infants, toddlers, younger children. Adolescent boys often make great babysitters, especially for little boys. I've seen many disturbed pre-teens and teenagers change completely when given responsibility for a five-year-old. They become gentle and caring, able

---

274 John Holt, *Escape from Childhood,* Penguin, Harmondsworth, 1974, p. 162.

at last to express some tenderness in a culturally acceptable context. They become playful, able to forget about their image, to forget about being cool.

Two, every baby should be raised in a village community of some sort, whether it be a school, a cul-de-sac in a suburb, a retirement home, a country town.

The artificiality of schools, which for centuries now have been taking children and adolescents away from the world and raising them on islands of immaturity, with just a few adults (often ill-chosen and ill-equipped) looking after them, does not attract enough of our attention. The most powerful change we could make to schools is to restructure them so that, demographically speaking at least, they are microcosms of society, rather than institutions that bear little resemblance to the 'real world'.

In doing this, we ought to include the full range of our population, from babies to the elderly. A few places already combine 'senior communities' or nursing homes with childcare centres, kindergartens or schools. In Virginia, United States, an assisted-living facility called Sunrise of Fairfax shares a 7.5 acre campus with Merritt Academy, a private day school for pre-kindergarten to eighth-grade students. Sunrise's website says: 'The arrangement offers residents of our senior living community in Fairfax a unique opportunity to participate in intergenerational programs that truly enrich everyone involved.'[275] In Tasmania, St Michael's Collegiate School, an Anglican girls' school, offers an early learning centre on one of its campuses alongside a home for elderly people. The school describes it as 'Australia's first intergenerational care program providing combined activities for residents of the aged-care facility and children from the Centre.'[276]

We can reasonably expect that there will be benefits to both children and the elderly from this kind of mingling, which has the potential to re-create the world of the village. Again, however, it is important not

---

275 Accessed on the Sunrise website in early 2018. This site is now under development.
276 'St Michael's Collegiate School', Australian Schools Directory, australianschoolsdirectory.com. au/school_print.php?school=4520, accessed 13 March 2019.

to sentimentalise such a scenario. Our students are sometimes quite disconcerted when they visit nursing homes. I remember one child who got a ferocious tongue-lashing from an old lady who accused him of cheating when they played the card game Go Fish.

A campus that includes babies, infants, children, teenagers, adults and old people still excludes one important group: people with severe disabilities. Niamh Choesang's memoir makes clear the dramatic positive differences she found when she went from a special school to a regular high school. But the high school experience was soured when aides from her previous school were hired to look after her. In her view, their attitudes toward people with disabilities were so set in concrete that it was impossible for them to treat her with courtesy and respect.

Christ Church Grammar School in Perth, an Anglican boys' school, is in some ways typical of exclusive, expensive private colleges. But it is remarkable in one respect at least: at the heart of the school, geographically speaking if not metaphorically, is the Peter Moyes Centre, which, in the school's words, 'caters for the learning and developmental needs of boys with low to high support requirements including severe language impairment, autism and Down syndrome as well as intellectual and multiple disabilities'.[277]

As much as is possible, the boys from this centre join the other 1600 students for assemblies, sport, art, music and some specialist classes. They wear the same uniform as other boys, and are proud members of the school community.

---

277 'Peter Moyes Centre', Christ Church Grammar School, shaula.ccgs.wa.edu.au/learning-at-christ-church/academic-enrichment/special-needs-education, accessed 13 March 2019.

13

MAKING BETTER SCHOOLS

If a car is a dud, it doesn't matter how often you respray it, change the tyres, fit spunky new seat covers, it won't go. You can install a reversing camera, BOSE sound system and satellite navigation, but it will continue to sit in your driveway, gathering bird droppings . . .

As a school student, student teacher, teacher and author-in-residence, I have spent more than 50 years bemused, baffled, frustrated and appalled by the blind adherence of governments, bureaucrats and school leaders to a model that is inherently dysfunctional. Changes to the curriculum, the timetable, the architecture, the seating, made and continue to make no substantial difference. Increasing teacher training from two years, to three years, to four; paying teachers more; keeping students at school longer; abolishing streaming or gender segregation or corporal punishment . . . as welcome as some of these measures have been, they can never compensate for the fact that the model is unworkable. For all the talk of excellence/realising your potential/achieving your dreams, schools are still sitting in the driveway, belching out toxic gases.

Recently, when interviewing a woman who wanted to enrol her children at Candlebark, I asked her the obvious question: 'Why choose this school?'

She looked at me with a steady gaze and answered, 'Because the other system is broken.' Then, after a pause, she added: 'It was broken when I went to school, in the 80s, and it's even more broken now.'

After all my years in education, trying to articulate what I thought was wrong with schools, I could only admire the brevity and force of her statement. Yes, the system is broken, and always has been. The problem is pretty easy to identify. The model is based purely on economic grounds, and as soon as we recognise that, we realise why it was never likely to work. As a consequence of the Industrial Revolution, the modern school model was designed to soak up the greatest number of children possible, squash them into the smallest space possible, and assign the fewest number of adults possible to look after them. This got children out of the way, and freed the maximum number of adults to work in the coalmines and factories, thereby adding to the wealth of the industrialists and mine-owners. How could such a model ever succeed in teaching children to be thoughtful, discerning, creative, generous, responsible and mature?

Despite the horror stories about schools that I have recounted, I can say that Candlebark and Alice Miller are successful. The atmosphere of both is energised and positive. The kids are good-natured and welcoming. We do remarkably well in every form of competition with other schools. Our graduates have been spectacularly successful, often in surprising ways. Thumbing through our regional newspaper this morning, I found an article about one of our ex-students. The article began: 'A young Gisborne fashion designer has been rewarded for her hard work. Megan Taylor, 22, was last week named the 2018 inspirational student of the year at Kangan Institute's graduation ceremony and awards night. Ms Taylor has moved on to study for a bachelor's degree after finishing her advanced diploma in fashion design. She suffers from a chronic pain condition known as hypermobility spectrum disorder. "It just adds an extra layer of stuff to deal with throughout the day," she said.'[278]

The fact that the Western model of schooling functions fairly well for many young people, some of the time at least, and does not often result in riots and catastrophe, is a tribute to the good nature of most

---

278 *Sunbury Leader*, April 16, 2019, p. 5.

young people, and the patience and strength of their teachers. Of course, for many other young people it is an unmitigated disaster.

STRIVING FOR SCHOOLING PERFECTION

If we set out to design a perfect school campus I think most people would agree on the essential, tangible elements. Firstly, space, and lots of it. In Australia we are blessed to have the space we do, yet we give more of it to car parks, golf courses, shopping malls and freeways than we do to kids. Many schools with 300 or more students have recreational space equivalent in size to a couple of basketball courts.

Next, we would want interesting buildings, good resources and challenging playgrounds. We would probably also ask for great internet connectivity, an organic garden and a variety of farm animals.

None of this is difficult to achieve. But the fact that schools tick so few of the boxes I've just listed is evidence that our much-vaunted 'caring for children' is as meaningless as mass mailings of Christmas cards from a politician. Forget the mindless bleating of 'children are our future', which has become the mantra of the 21st century. Let's look at the present: why are we so cruel to children? Our actions don't match our rhetoric. We talk a beautiful talk, but we walk a walk of shame.

In 1998, an Australian newspaper published a letter from a lady named Gloria Yates, living in Petrie, Queensland. She wrote 'Our usual caring attitude to juveniles is showing again. Is the press mad? Are all the politicians completely barmy? . . . I have taught children for thirty-four years and am now retired. I can't remember a time when politicians were so much against children . . . I grew up in wartime Britain where children were loved and cared for. God help us all if this child–hating scenario is our blueprint for the future.'[279]

---

279 Gloria Yates, 'Child bashing', *The Australian*, 13 October 1998, referenced in Karen Sampford, 'Identification of Juvenile Offenders: Research Bulletin No 9/98' Queensland Parliamentary Library, 1998, parliament.qld.gov.au/documents/explore/ResearchPublications/researchBulletins/rb0998ks.pdf, accessed 1 April 2014.

Unfortunately, Gloria's concerns, set out so clearly in 1998, are still valid today.

Candlebark, founded in 2005, is 50 minutes from the Melbourne CBD, in 1200 acres of forest, 850 acres of it bought in 1998. It had been operating as a camp for adults and/or children who were deaf or blind or both, and had nine good buildings, including a beautiful double classroom. An imaginative government could have bought it for a school, but no representatives from the Department of Education were glimpsed at the auction.

The buildings have been extended and modified, but remain simple yet attractive; there is an organic garden; there are sheep, pigs, horses, chooks, geese, ducks, goats and a cow called Hettie, who, at age nineteen is working towards her ambition of becoming the world record holder for bovine longevity, hoping to beat Big Bertha, who died in Italy at age 48.

We have 170 students at Candlebark and 200 at Alice Miller – we are small by choice. We could have had 500 at Candlebark alone if we had taken everyone who applied. But we don't screen kids; in fact we take more than our fair share of 'challenging' students.

You could say that we 'fail' with some kids, but that is a relative term, and one difficult to measure. I can think of only four children in fourteen years whose behaviour appeared to deteriorate whilst at Candlebark, but in each of those situations we were dealing with family backgrounds so difficult that we were unable to make a great enough impression upon the parents or the child.

STAYING 'UNBROKEN'

As a general principle, in the face of poor parenting a school cannot succeed. We can ameliorate the behaviour of the child, we can improve his or her resilience, self-control, values, confidence, trust, attitude and work ethic, but ultimately, we will always fail. That's no reason to give up of course: a 5 per cent improvement in a child's emotional health may make the difference between his or her being able to have an enduring relationship or not, between his or her being employable or not. It may significantly reduce the risk that he or she will commit suicide. But for these students, unless they get long-term, skilful, professional help, life will be a painful struggle.

Our worst situations have developed as a result of parents who actively work against the school, subverting what we do. On a number of occasions, we have been baffled as to why parents enrolled their children in a school with which they seem to have little sympathy. For instance, children who have never spent a night away from home, and experience severe distress when separated from their parents, are likely to have a difficult time at a school such as ours, with an active program of camps and excursions. Most of our students will have twenty or more nights a year away from home each year, on trips or sleepovers.

If parents are rigid, controlling and authoritarian, they are unlikely to sympathise with our approach to education.

NANCY

Nancy was a Grade 1 girl whose teacher one day took off her engagement ring to wash some dishes in a sink. When she went to put the ring back on, it had vanished.

We searched everywhere for it, without success. We then turned to the Candlebark parents, asking for help, and explaining how upsetting the loss was for the teacher. We got no immediate results, but a couple of days later the teacher came to me with a strange story. She had been at home, on a Sunday, when Nancy and her mother came walking up the driveway, gave the teacher a bunch of flowers, and expressed their regret for the emotional upset she had experienced. Nancy's mother then added, mysteriously, that she was sure the teacher would get good news soon. On the following Tuesday morning, the ring was found, carefully placed in a conspicuous position near the driver on the floor of the small bus that Nancy caught each day.

Nancy told us strange stories about being abused by her mother, but when we approached the parents they scoffed at the verisimilitude of these reports. They retaliated with strange stories Nancy had told them about being treated badly at school. The parents believed every word of Nancy's accounts. I asked them how it was that we were not to believe Nancy's stories about home but the parents had no problems believing her stories about school. They had no answer to my question, but a couple of weeks later withdrew Nancy from the school.

The TV series *The Naked City*, which ran in the late 1950s and early 1960s, concluded each episode with an anonymous voice intoning the words: 'There are eight million stories in the naked city. This has been one of them.' There are unlikely to be eight million stories in the lives of Candlebark and Alice Miller Schools, but there have certainly been many already, and no doubt there will be many more.

But why is it then that we are not 'broken', to use the word chosen by the mother whom I had interviewed? I have already outlined some reasons, but there are many more. One is simply that we have lots of adults at the schools. An inevitable by-product of the economically driven high ratio of adults to students in most schools is the development of subcultures that are rarely glimpsed by the adults but are often more powerful than the culture the adults claim to be inculcating. The large number of adults employed at Candlebark and Alice Miller makes it easier for us to determine and manage the culture, and makes it harder for disaffected students to succeed in initiating or developing a negative subculture.

Much has been made of research purporting to show that class sizes do not make any difference to students. Unfortunately, this research, including the data most often cited in recent years, from Professor John Hattie of the University of Melbourne in his hugely popular book *Visible Learning*, refers only to academic outcomes, in other words, how well students perform on standardised tests and the like. The data ignores emotional development, social development, spiritual and psychological development. Hattie is honest and explicit about what he explored in the book. In his first chapter, he writes: '[I]t is important from the start to note at least two critical codicils. Of course, there are many outcomes of schooling, such as attitudes, physical outcomes, belongingness, respect, citizenship, and the love of learning. This book focuses on student achievement, and that is a limitation of this review.'[280]

We have small classes and generous staff-to-student ratios because we regard the non-academic aspects of a child's life as having tremendous importance.

KIDS NEED FIRST-HAND EXPERIENCES

In starting Candlebark from scratch I had no complex philosophical treatise on which to rely. I had only a few basic beliefs. The most important of these was that I wanted students to have first-hand experiences. My absolute priority in running Candlebark, and later Alice Miller, was to provide students with a wealth of these.

I had become increasingly concerned by my conversations with young people, which seemed to be more boring with every passing year. Intrigued by this phenomenon, and hastily dismissing the possibility that I might be suffering from ennui, or that I might be the chief contributor of boredom to the conversations, I began to analyse the students' words. It didn't take long to realise that they talked almost exclusively about second-hand and third-hand experiences. Mostly they talked about what they had seen on TV the night before. If they talked about real-life experiences, it was usually about their grandparents' or parents' exploits. I came to the conclusion that these young people had almost no stories of their own. Their lives consisted of coming to school, going home, doing homework, watching TV, having tea, watching more TV, doing more homework, and going to bed. A trip to the mall was an excursion. Their lives were boring, and as a result they were boring.

Recently I watched a 'wonderful' example of 'stunning new technology in education'. An American teacher toured the Large Hadron Collider on the border between France and Switzerland, near Geneva, whilst his students, sitting in a classroom in California, watched in

---

280 John Hattie, *Visible Learning*, Routledge, Oxford and New York, 2009, p. 6

live time and communicated with him. This was supposed to be an advance. The adults have the experience; the students sit on their butts back at school and watch someone else doing stuff.

In 2019, I received a poster from Google advertising 'Google for Education'. It was headed '10 teacher tips to spark classroom learning with G Suite for Education and Chrome Books'. One of the ten tips had the subheading 'Class trips without the bus trips'. The body of the text read: 'Explore the world with Expeditions and immerse your students in one of thousands of virtual reality journeys. Check out the Expedition app.'

Fake experiences cleverly designed to trick students into believing they are having real experiences. Is this the future of education?

People need their own stories. Our stories define us, shape us, enrich us. They help us grow. Stories do not come from watching TV or playing Xbox games or having virtual reality journeys. They come from riding skateboards, climbing trees, making jam, catching a ferry, meeting people, going to Sri Lanka, touring a factory, nursing babies, holding a post for a road surveyor. Too many young people have never seen an echidna nosing its way through the bush, or been to a music festival, or gone abseiling in the Arapiles, or replaced a clutch cable, or ridden a camel.

In starting Candlebark, I also thought it important to counteract the prevailing hysteria that values physical safety above all other considerations. Children can only grow emotionally, socially, spiritually if we step back and let them be adventurous. At my schools, we encourage children to run, jump, roll, climb, ride bikes and skateboards and RipStiks, engage in stick wars and British Bulldog. They play outside without regard to the weather. We are a bit of an outpost against the psychically ill 21st-century adults who wish to wrap children in cotton wool to protect them from physical harm.

Two schools that have a similar approach, and have influenced me strongly, are Fitzroy Community School in Melbourne and Tudor House in Moss Vale, New South Wales. These schools have many outstanding features, but one that strikes me is that, unlike nearly every other primary school in Australia, it is almost impossible to find an overweight student among their enrollees. The students look healthy, because they are engaged in healthy activities every day of their school lives. The same can be said of Candlebark (although, shamefully, not of its principal!).

The unofficial motto of Candlebark and Alice Miller is 'Take risks'. I used to call it our secret motto, but I've talked about it too often for it to be classified as a secret any more. It means 'Be adventurous'. It doesn't mean 'Be reckless'. Usually I add, tokenistically, 'Take care', but all humans, except perhaps some with severe mental disabilities or some who have reached an extreme of self-destructiveness, know to take care. If they don't, a thousand repetitions of 'Take care' will not change their behaviour. It's like the mindless calls of 'Don't fall!' or 'Be careful' to children who are climbing a tree or a set of monkey bars.

Our children get injured, sure, but mostly at home, doing banal things like crossing the room to get food, or playing Monopoly. Despite the daring stuff the students do at school, our rate of significant injuries is extremely low. We have lots of grazes, scratches and bruises, and a very occasional broken bone, but far fewer accidents than other schools of comparable size. I can only put this down to the fact that our kids learn quickly to take care of themselves.

Occasionally we intervene in risk-taking behaviour. I remember a thirteen-year-old student who threw himself around so wildly that he was constantly getting injured. One day I said to him, 'I've got a theory that the reason you keep hurting yourself is because you want to build up an immunity to pain, until you become impervious to it.' I didn't add 'And I reckon it's because you have so much emotional pain inside you, and you're trying to immunise yourself against it.'

He looked at me in shock and stammered: 'You know me so well.'

His behaviour started to change after that conversation. He's now a hardworking, successful builder who is highly respected for his work ethic and strength of character, and the quality of his constructions.

I believe that the harm inflicted on Australian children by the cotton wool approach is crippling, and lifelong. The madness of modern attitudes is found everywhere, but perhaps the United Kingdom leads the world in the insanity stakes. James Williams, a science lecturer who played the role of a housemaster in a British TV reality documentary series called *That'll Teach 'Em*, reported that on the program:

> We had to make the children wear crash helmets and knee pads for the go-kart race – the health and safety advisor insisted on it. Ironically, the only person injured in the race was one of the cameramen, run over by a wayward go-kart when its wheel came off. He wasn't wearing a crash helmet or kneepads . . . once I was asked to comment on a tragic accident that happened in a school. A pupil put an arm through a window at break time. A very nasty cut, but no permanent damage was the result. The parents called for all glass in schools to be safety glass. The local authority, sensibly, said this would cost too much. The parents' response was that the council put cost before children's lives. A great sound bite, but is it really true? I wondered if all the glass in their house was safety glass . . .[281]

In 2009 Britain experienced, and, fortunately, survived the 'Marcus the Lamb' controversy. Marcus was a lamb hand-reared by students at a school in Kent, to help kids learn about the food cycle. As the logical end point in the process, Marcus was slaughtered for his meat, which was not eaten by the kids but was sold so that the school could buy more animals. However, a group of parents campaigned powerfully against the killing of Marcus,[282] and the case became such a cause celebre that eventually the head teacher of the school resigned, after being subjected to vitriolic abuse (she was reinstated in 2010).[283] That strange wailing sound heard in Kent in

281 James Williams, 'Science with a bang', *Times Educational Supplement*, 19 May 2006, tes.com/news/science-bang, accessed 1 April 2019.
282 'Marcus the sheep slaughtered after being raised by schoolchildren', *Guardian*, 15 September 2009, theguardian.com/uk/2009/sep/14/marcus-the-sheep-slaughtered, accessed 1 April 2019.
283 Lucy Cockcroft, 'Head teacher who allowed pupils' "pet sheep" to be slaughtered is reinstated', *The Telegraph*, 3 April 2010, telegraph.co.uk/education/educationnews/7548003/Head-teacher-who-allowed-pupils-pet-sheep-to-be-slaughtered-is-reinstated.html, accessed 1 April 2019.

recent times is the ghost of Beatrix Potter, come from the grave to haunt Marcus's supporters.

Like everyone, I have my mantras, my mottoes . . . my parables. For me, one of the most powerful is a story I was told just before Candlebark opened. It concerned the acquisition of a country campus by a well-known big-city private school, which the school intended to be an adventurous and innovative place for Year 9s, rather like Geelong Grammar's Timbertop. One of the features of the project was that the rural campus was equipped with a fleet of brand-new bikes. When the kids had free time they could go for a ride in and around the quiet little town where the campus was located, or out into the countryside.

However, after the first semester, the school had some concerns, and so decided to restrict the rides to groups of three kids minimum. After the second they added the further restriction that a teacher had to accompany the students. After the third they limited the rides to within the boundaries of the town. After the fourth they said the rides could only happen at weekends. After the fifth they banned bike rides when rain was forecast. After the sixth semester, they sold the bikes.

I'm sure I've got some of the details wrong, but that was the gist of it. And I understand how stuff like that happens – there are various forces that act upon schools like boa constrictors, and whether those forces move slowly or quickly, the relentless pressure they exert has the same eventual, fatal, effect, unless vigorously counteracted.

I am determined we will never 'lock up the bikes', either literally or metaphorically. The effect of the story on me was to make me highly sensitive to any attempts to strangle the spirit of the schools; so much so that I can, as I suggested earlier, become quite feisty when I feel people misunderstand or try to sabotage the adventurous approach we take. Truly is it said that the wanderer's danger is to find comfort, and we do not see it as our job to keep students comfortable. Thus, we have had students hike across the New South Wales border to the top of Kosciuszko then canoe the length of the Snowy River to Bass Strait – a six-week trip. We have had students travel from Broome to Darwin, spending time in Aboriginal communities along the way. We have had them hike the challenging Overland route in Tasmania from Cradle Mountain to Lake St Clair; walk the Great Ocean Track; travel to Italy, to Montenegro, to Tanzania, to Madagascar, to China, to Mongolia, to Albania, to Spain, to Poland, to Germany, to France. Every year we have kids from Foundation onwards doing a four-day camp in first term, which involves a three-hour drive away from home and staying in tents. Parents of Foundation kids can sometimes get nervous about this, but the kids have a wow of a time.

Sometimes we drop students in the forest, three days' walk from the school, and have them hike back. We have five-day bike camps in the Macedon Ranges area every second year, where kids ride a couple of hundred kilometres, staying at a different campsite each night.

They go on canoe trips, skiing trips, abseiling and rock-climbing trips.

But part of our mission is to explore social, political, religious, spiritual, psychological and philosophical ideas with the same courage with which we send kids on five-day bike camps or to canoe the Murray River or to hike the Australian Alps. One of the ways we do this is by engaging with the world whenever and wherever possible. For students at the two schools, the classroom is a convenient meeting point and a useful springboard, but it is not necessarily the place where the most powerful learning happens. So we send groups to the MONA gallery in Hobart, the WOMAD festival in Adelaide, to galleries, museums, live theatre events, dance performances, movies and movie festivals, writers' festivals, parks and zoos and gardens and playgrounds. Like many schools, we take groups to Canberra, to explore places of interest there.

Every student will have at least half a dozen sleepovers a year at school – some will have twenty or more – which may have some educational focus but are often 'just for fun'. As I write this, there is a sleepover at school for the Grade 3s. Two nights ago a motley bunch of kids had a book-reading sleepover . . . just so they could have a few hours of uninterrupted reading. That sleepover was for any kids who wanted to come. Next week Foundation kids and Year 1s will be camping for two nights at Healesville. The Year 7s come back tomorrow night after twelve days in New Zealand, where they've been hiking, rock climbing, ocean kayaking, and doing a *Lord of the Rings* tour.

All of these trips are included in the school fees. Parents are not charged extra for them. We do this partly to reduce administrative costs but also so that parents cannot deny permission on financial grounds for their children to go. It also means that we are not forever nagging parents for further amounts of money.

The only exception to the 'no extra costs' rule is the big Year 9 trip. We run this every year, and it is always of six weeks' duration, with two or three teachers from the school accompanying each group. We do this trip for a number of reasons. The first and obvious one is that we want children to discover new countries, new societies and new cultures, and to overcome the difficulties inevitably encountered in global travel. We do it because we want them to learn to trust the world, to understand that courtesy, friendliness and 'mateship' are not exclusively the province of Australians, but can be found everywhere. But we also do it because we believe that Year 9 is a good time for students to begin to strike out on their own, to move out from under their parents' protective wings. Adolescents who turn on their parents, reject them completely, leave home and have no further contact with them, are in as invidious a position as adolescents who are under the suffocating day-by-day control of suspicious and authoritarian parents. As I noted earlier, members of this latter group are likely to still be living at home when they are 40, lonely, immature, and filled with passive-aggressive feelings.

One of our rules for these trips is that students are not allowed to contact their parents, except with special permission, and parents are not to contact their children. Not surprisingly, some parents fiercely resist the potential loss of control that the six-week odyssey represents. An informal survey of students by teachers one year revealed that 25 per cent of parents were plotting ways to subvert this important aspect of the trip by making secret arrangements with their sons or daughters for direct electronic contact. Remembering the bicycles, I fight the good fight relentlessly with such people.

As a general rule, we do not spend time asking students to reflect on their experiences on hikes or camps or excursions, or to write journal entries about them. We do not ask searching questions like 'What did you learn as a result of this?' or 'How have you changed since the trip?' Adults are not subjected to this kind of interrogation – except in some ghastly workplaces, which should be avoided at all costs – and kids should be likewise exempt. Once the experience is over, it's over. We leave the students to process it consciously and unconsciously, not knowing whether it will change them a little, a lot or not at all.

Gary Younge, in *Another Day in the Death of America*, describes the South Side of Chicago as a place apart, a territory where violence is commonplace. He observes that many of the people who live there stay within the boundaries of the South Side and never go downtown, to the CBD. He quotes a community organiser as suggesting that the ones who do go outside the boundaries are like escapees, with the implication that their lives will be all the better for having gone out into the world.[284]

It doesn't matter whether we are in the South Side of Chicago or South Yarra in Melbourne or the west coast of Tasmania or Westmead in Sydney, the more we can travel, meet new people and have new experiences, the more tolerance, understanding and wisdom we are likely to acquire.

These adventures can only take place if teachers are creative and adventurous in initiating and organising them. As principal, I'm clear on my main role. It's to say *yes*, whenever possible, to everyone who comes into my office. It did not take me many years of working in schools to realise that each of them should have a flag fluttering from the school's tallest point with the word 'NO' emblazoned on it. For this is the secret motto of virtually all schools.

When teacher Donna Prince asked me one day if she could start an Explosions Club at Candlebark, I didn't bother to ask for details, but told her to go right ahead. As a result we have had many exciting

---

284 Younge, *Another Day in the Death of America*, p. 229.

blasts, including pyrotechnic displays. Kids who in the past have not been particularly motivated by attending school are, for obvious reasons, among the keenest to join the Explosions Club.

For some schools, as well as 'NO' a second motto may be appropriate: I remember doing a six-week residency at one of Australia's most famous private all-girls' schools, and being convinced by the end of the first week that they should have a flag fluttering from their flagpole with the word 'SHHHH' prominently displayed. Wherever I went in the school, I heard teachers saying, 'Shhhh, girls, shhhh, be quiet now.' Explosions Club was never going to become a part of their program. The girls were apparently being taught their future roles in life.

Recently I came across some notes I jotted down whilst listening to Michael McGirr, head of Faith and Mission at St Kevin's College Toorak, and author of a number of quirky books including *Snooze: The Lost Art of Sleep*. He had talked about the artificiality of the light in Western society and the unhealthy desire of many people for a culture in which there is no darkness.

I want to provide a natural light for young people, and I absolutely accept that the light will throw a shadow. But, as McGirr said, these days it often feels that the light at the end of the tunnel is the glow of a mobile phone screen. When my wife and I went to Mexico, arriving soon after the Festival of the Dead, we were struck by the way death and images of death, particularly skulls, were woven into the fabric of everyday life – for everybody. This seemed altogether healthier than the typical Western fear and avoidance of death.

One result of our first-hand-experiences approach at the two schools is that our students are bright-eyed and bushy-tailed all day long. At bus stops they stand out from kids from other schools because they are exuberant and lively. They can't wait to get on the bus. In class they are alert and engaged. They have more free time, and hence less class time, than students at conventional schools, but that doesn't hurt them, because as well as being wide awake in class they have a positive attitude, which naturally enough leads to faster learning. I've often taught middle-school maths at Candlebark, and found that we can knock off the syllabus for the whole year in just two or three terms.

TREATING CHILDREN WELL

Above all, we treat children well. Not as equals. Our schools are not particularly democratic. But we treat students with courtesy and generosity. Before starting Candlebark I ran residential writing courses for adults and children. One person I employed as a supervisor for a camp started referring to the students, in their hearing, as 'kiddies'. The age range of the participants was twelve to sixteen.

I understood his reason: he had not long left school himself and was anxious to establish his superiority. But that didn't stop me telling him, after two warnings, that if he used the contemptuous word again, I'd sack him.

The adjective most commonly used by teachers at other schools to describe our graduates is 'mature'. It seems that our students are unafraid to ask questions or take the lead. They treat teachers courteously but warmly, and they show a sophisticated understanding of complex issues. Sometimes, thanks to their parents, they would be like this anyway; sometimes it's a mixture of influences from home and school; sometimes we have done most of the work ourselves.

In 2013, I had an unsolicited letter from a teacher at another school, who had encountered two ex-Candlebark students in one of her classes:

> Aside from Amy being a really lovely girl, as we got in to the swing of the semester she stood out because she is my very favourite thing in a student: a thinker who holds me to task. She asked 'Why' more than almost every other student. 'Why was it that way?' 'Why look with that perspective?' 'Why believe what Thucydides says is true?' And I loved it. This year I am lucky enough to be teaching her again in Philosophy and I also met Bryony in Classical Societies. Bryony, as you know, is another exceptional student.

Having sung their praises I want to clarify; I am not saying that either of them always get everything right or that they are perfect. But both of them are actively involved in their education and take responsibility for when things go right and things go wrong. They think about it and engage with it rather than opening their mouths and waiting for me to spoon feed it to them.

I was determined to strip out from the schooling model everything that could not be justified on sensible grounds. As well, to use a much-overworked expression, I did not want teachers to waste time 'sweating the small stuff'. So many schools are obsessed with students wearing the 'correct' uniform. At the start of the 2018 school year, a Melbourne government high school sent home at least seventeen students for wearing the wrong socks. Another fifteen were given 'all-day internal detentions' for violating the uniform policy of the school.[285] Our solution to these chronic and unproductive confrontations: let's do away with uniform. At a stroke, 20, 30, 40 per cent of the potential conflicts between students and teachers are eliminated.

Report-writing? A waste of time and energy – the involved parents already know how their children are going; the others don't read the reports anyway. Solution: reduce reports to a letter grade, sent out twice a year – the bare minimum to ensure we comply with government regulations. Staff meetings: nearly always a further waste of time and energy. We have one a week.

To cut out the endless chasing of kids and parents for permission slips and money, we require parents to sign a generic form when they enrol their children, giving us permission to take their little darlings anywhere we want, any time we want.

Acting on yet another cue from Fitzroy Community School, we have no staffroom at either Candlebark or Alice Miller, so that contact between teachers and students is maximised. This also reduces

---

285 'Students sent home from school for wearing wrong socks', *The Age*, 6 February 2018, theage. com.au/national/victoria/students-sent-home-from-school-for-wearing-wrong-socks-20180206-p4yzjj.html, accessed 1 April 2019.

the politicking among staff, an activity that can cause considerable damage in many schools. Our staff, almost without exception, embrace experiments, adventures, new ideas. When experts at educational conferences talk earnestly about the difficulties of persuading teachers to be innovative I can (smugly) get out my iPad and play *Crossy Road*.

I wanted the school to be completely mobile, so we have invested a great deal of money acquiring a fleet of buses sufficient to transport the whole student body at the drop of the proverbial hat. Most of the teachers have bus licences. The kids are a delight to take on excursions and camps, and staff frequently remark that taking them off campus doesn't feel like work.

I was aware from my time at Fitzroy Community School that eating together creates a lovely vibe, which helps make the school feel like a warm place. From the start, we have provided morning tea and lunch for all staff and students, every day, and as well we make food available throughout the day. We do not haggle over money in our efforts to make sure the food is outstanding. When the chefs we have employed over the years ask me about the budget for food, I tell them, 'Just get what you need.' We don't buy generic or plain-label brands, even though some of them are of good quality. We buy high-profile brand names, because by doing so we send an implicit message to children that they are respected. They know that we are not palming off cheap stuff on them just because they are kids. We spend about $400,000 a year on food.

TEACHING CREATIVITY . . .?

I haven't made any claims in this discussion that Candlebark and Alice Miller Schools are 'creative'. It's a word that's thrown around freely in recent years, but it's hard to define, and it's a difficult concept to teach, especially when teachers at so many schools are conspicuously lacking in creativity. I think we do help to develop the creative powers of our students, but almost incidentally, by encouraging them, for example, to find their own voices and develop their own identities, in writing, in singing, in painting or potting or sculpting, in drama, in playing musical instruments.

English teacher John Mazur brought the following poem to my attention in the late 1970s. It has been given many different titles over the years, and no one seems to know its origins, but it is popularly supposed to be by a teenage boy who committed suicide a few weeks after writing it. I seem to remember that John called it 'Stiff'. It's very powerful for many adolescents.

He always wanted to explain things
But no one cared
So he drew
Sometimes he would draw and it wasn't anything
He wanted to carve it in stone
Or write it in the sky
He would lie out on the grass
And look up at the sky
And it would be only the sky and him that needed saying
And it was after that
He drew the picture
It was a beautiful picture
He kept it under his pillow
And would let no one see it
And he would look at it every night
And think about it
And when it was dark
And his eyes were closed
He could still see it
And it was all of him
And he loved it
When he started school he brought it with him
Not to show anyone but just to have it with him
Like a friend
It was funny about school
He sat in a square brown desk

Like all the other square brown desks
And he thought it should be red
And his room was a square brown room
Like all the other rooms
And it was tight and close
And stiff
He hated to hold the pencil and chalk
With his arms stiff and his feet flat on the floor
Stiff
With the teacher watching
And watching
The teacher came and smiled at him
She told him to wear a tie
Like all the other boys
He said he didn't like them
And she said it didn't matter
After that they drew
And he drew all yellow
And it was the way he felt about morning
And it was beautiful
The teacher came and smiled at him
'What's this?' she said
'Why don't you draw something like Ken's drawing?
Isn't that beautiful?'
After that his mother bought him a tie
And he always drew airplanes and rocket ships
Like everyone else
And he threw the old picture away
And when he lay out alone and looked out at the sky
It was big and blue and all of everything
But he wasn't anymore
He was square inside and brown
And his hands were stiff
And he was like everyone else
And the things inside him that needed saying
Didn't need it anymore

It had stopped pushing
It was crushed
Stiff
Like everything else.

The difference between a repressive school and one that encourages and nurtures creativity is not that the latter allows students to spend all day hugging trees or scribbling mindlessly on bits of paper . . . or rolling around on the floor. One of the paradoxes of life is that the imposition of limits can actually lead to greater creative expression. It is the nature of the limits that matters. Wearing a tie or 'doing a drawing like Ken's' are limits that are repressive and without merit. They are limits designed to make students as identical as possible. I have sat in an assembly hall of a big private school in Victoria and heard a senior teacher articulating her school's uniform policy with the words: 'There's a reason we call it uniform – it's because we want everyone to look the same.' That was in 2015, not 1955.

But some limits can lead to liberating and delightful outcomes. When I ask students in writing workshops to describe the ocean without using the letter 'a', I know I am far more likely to get something fresh and remarkable than if I give them a blank sheet of paper and ask them to write anything they like, on any topic they like, in any style or genre they want. Brian Eno's famous set of cards known as *Oblique Strategies* – prompting musicians with such phrases as 'Honour thy error as a hidden intention', 'Ask your body', 'Work at a different speed', 'Repetition is a form of change' – incorporate limits that were subsequently used by artists like David Bowie to enhance their music. The brilliance of the bestselling solo jazz album of all time, and bestselling solo piano album of all time, Keith Jarrett's *Köln Concert* (1975),[286] is directly attributable to the limits imposed upon Jarrett

---

286 John Fordham, '50 great moments in jazz: Keith Jarrett's The Köln Concert', *Guardian*, 1 February 2011, theguardian.com/music/musicblog/2011/jan/31/50-great-moments-jazz-keith-jarrett, accessed 10 April 2014.

by the inadequate, defective piano upon which he had to perform.[287]

The anonymous poem 'Stiff' captures the yearning of adolescents for freedom from restrictions, limits and criticism, but the wise adult knows that the young person actually needs something rather less vague. And to develop their creative powers, children and teenagers need support, appreciation, and a warm and positive relationship with their teachers. In particular, most need specific feedback, from people with expertise. In responding to students' writing, I make comments like 'Too many adjectives – one per paragraph is often enough – and even one can be too many', 'Name everything in your story – what did they actually have for breakfast? What was the colour of the bus? How did they pay for the ticket?', 'Too much narrative – maybe break it up with some dialogue?', 'Show, don't tell.'

Sure, the notion of freedom is superficially attractive, but true fulfilment comes from doing outstanding work that has the creator's personality and spirit stamped all over it. Work that is both sophisticated and unique.

In recent years, we have seen a staggering growth in the levels of anxiety among children and parents. This impacts on us every day, and sometimes I feel we run ourselves ragged trying to support anxious children and teenagers, and pacify panicky parents. It's as though we had the epidemic of eating disorders, then the epidemic of self-harming, and now, although those other behaviours are still with us, we have the phenomenon of panic attacks.

If a student is well mentally, problems become manageable, and can be seen in their true light. He or she will be able to cope with everything school and life throws at him or her. If the student is not well mentally, he or she is at grave risk in every imaginable way, and learning will take place with difficulty, and often at a painfully slow pace.

287 Charles Waring, 'How Keith Jarrett Defied The Odds to Record His Solo Masterpiece, "The Köln Concert"', *udiscovermusic*, 24 January 2019, udiscovermusic.com/stories/koln-concert-keith-jarrett, accessed 10 April 2019.

A commonly held belief these days is that by teaching people to be creative we can solve their problems. But tortured minds cannot be comforted by creativity. A million words after writing *Look Homeward, Angel*, Thomas Wolfe was still tormented. After a million notes, Beethoven was not happy; after a million brushstrokes Van Gogh cut off his ear, then committed suicide.

Yet as individuals we are driven to dance, sing, write, play music, act, compose, sculpt, paint. Perhaps it is no more than 'just' a drive, but if so, it is almost as primitive and compelling as the need to breathe and eat and drink. It's possible that the more disturbed our world feels, the more we are compelled to dance, whether with feet or paintbrushes or words.

When a society is fascist and repressive in its nature, it seems that wild and extreme art movements are likely to develop, even if much of such activity is underground or banned from public view by authoritarian regimes. In postwar Japan, for example, the Gutai Group, established by Jiro Yoshihara, found art in the shooting of paint onto a canvas with a cannon and the artist Shozo Shimamoto smashing his way wildly through laminated rice-paper screens. Atsuko Tanaka created *Electric Dress*, made of lightbulbs; Kazuo Shiraga wrestled in mud or hung from ceilings whilst painting with his feet. 'Bid farewell to these hoaxes piled up on the altars and in the palaces, the drawing rooms, and the antique shops ... lock up these corpses in the grave-yards,' Yoshihara wrote in his 1956 *Gutai Manifesto*.[288]

It seems that we have an individual need to express the self, to explore it, to try to define it, probably so that we can connect meaningfully with our inner natures and as well give a sense of ourselves to others. This can be proactive or reactive or both. We have a need to react against oppression and we have a hunger for beauty. All of this is true for the individual, and true for the conglomeration of individuals we call society. The sense that art sustains us, and offers comfort and nourishment, may derive from that.

---

288 Yoshihara, *Gutai Art Manifesto*, 1956.

In this process, art poses at least one problem: how do we find beauty, and perhaps even comfort, in art – for example writing – that is grim, morbid, troubling? Yet this is not so difficult. There is beauty in the dark places. The shadow is as intriguing as the tree. Death is as important as life. Water is vital and beautiful, and so is blood. I find much that moves me, much that is compelling and often noble in every life, no matter what troubling elements it also contains.

If a piece of writing is a beautiful thing in itself, that is enough. If a piece of writing gives a sense of an author striving for truth, that is enough. If a piece of writing is disturbing, I thank the author for having the courage to go to that place and the generosity to take me there too.

THE SCHOOLS WE NEED

So, how can we create genuinely good schools?

Ideally, students should know that they won't be assaulted spiritually, emotionally, mentally, physically . . . by students or by teachers. From teachers, that they will receive a fair hearing, they won't be unfairly convicted and sentenced, they won't be insulted, they will be given the same amount of time and attention and love as the next boy or girl. There will almost certainly be times when they don't feel safe, when things go badly wrong, but that's life, and school should be a place where these situations can be explored, so that learning ensues and progress is made.

Students should have meaningful roles within the school community. If schools must have prefects and captains, every student ought to be given a turn at these positions. Some kids can surprise big-time when allowed the opportunity. In most schools, most students have no meaningful role, and it's one of the reasons they get angrier and angrier at the educational system as they get older. When they in turn become parents and send their own children to school, they will still be angry, and are likely to take that anger out on their children's teachers.

Students need to be taught from the first day that there are many choices in every situation. (Maybe people who kill themselves do so because they think there's only one choice.) If a Grade 1 student has an argument with another student, there are a number of ways for him or her to deal with the matter. Among the options are apologising, mediation, never speaking to the other student again, making a 'victim impact statement' to the other person, bashing the other student up . . . one of the great truths of life is that we are free to do anything we want, as long as we accept the consequences.

Schools would do well to treat students with increased courtesy and respect. The youth worker in a Melbourne shopping mall described on radio how this policy changed the behaviour of teenagers in their centre. When all shopkeepers and retail assistants in the mall were persuaded to start being incredibly nice to the teenagers hanging around there, the vandalism and aggression problems they'd been enduring disappeared almost overnight. The golden rule is to treat young people with the same courtesy as we treat adults. If we don't ask adults to sit on the floor, we shouldn't expect it of children in schools. Their bums are made from the same material as ours. If adults who knock on the staffroom door are not left waiting for long minutes, then children should not be ignored in the way they so often are. If a school allows adults through the main door of the school and into the administration area, then young people should be equally welcome. Children should not be compelled to share their most precious toys with strange kids – adults don't share their precious toys with strange adults.

Schools need to understand the need of young people for physical release, and the emphasis children and teenagers place on competition. At the same time it must be understood that some timid or studious or 'alternative' boys or girls don't feel this way.

SNIFFING OUT A GOOD SCHOOL

So how do parents seeking a good – or even excellent – school for their children get meaningful information to help them make a choice? Well, start by tossing the school's prospectus in the bin. Don't bother reading it. Every prospectus says the same: 'fulfilling individual potential', 'positive, caring atmosphere', 'zero tolerance of bullying', 'extending the gifted and talented' . . . a sea of blah, or, to repeat Don Watson's word, 'clag'.

Also, ignore anything the principal says. These people are better spinners than Shane Warne and Muttiah Muralitharan combined. As a matter of courtesy, prospective parents might have to endure an interview with the principal, but they would be well advised to get it over with as quickly as possible.

And believe me (after all, I'm a principal), life is too short to waste time staring with glazed eyes at the My Schools website. NAPLAN results are statistically unreliable and dangerously misleading. The website itself is morally indefensible.

But there are ways . . .

Before prospective parents bow themselves out of the principal's office, they should request a tour of the school. It's best to ask if some kids can show you around. Of course, the principal will choose the most compliant children available, preferably his/her own son or daughter or, failing that, the school captains. Nevertheless, this doesn't mean you can't get them in a corner at the first opportunity and subject them to intense interrogation.

The killer question to put to them is simply 'What's the worst thing about your school?'

Taken by surprise, even these hand-picked fall guys are likely to gasp out an honest response.

And if the answer reflects badly on the teachers, thank the children kindly, and head for the car park as fast as can decently be managed. Comments like 'Well, some of the teachers are a bit boring . . .', 'The teachers are really mean', 'Mrs Daniels – she's not very fair some-times . . .' simply won't be heard from students in good schools.

The kids' judgements have to be considered in light of the fact that Australian children are on the whole very nice people who will strive to give the best possible account of their school, so you can be sure that even the mildest of these responses conceals a hellhole to which parents should never consider consigning their loved ones.

Students in good schools will reply with positive statements like 'Nothing really, it's heaps better than my last school', or they'll highlight issues so trivial that it's obvious nothing of substance is wrong, like 'I don't like the orange curtains in room 15', or they will mention something that might be considered by many parents a plus, like 'We have to work too hard'.

If they say the school is too strict, it probably is, but of course some parents relish the idea of having their children spend up to thirteen years getting their spirits broken by the peculiar varieties of fascists who are too often found in the teaching profession.

I was fascinated by a conversation I had when teaching at Geelong Grammar. A man 'prominent in public life', as they say, arrived to enrol his son. He confided in me that he had himself been a student at the school, 30 years earlier. Naïvely, I exclaimed, 'You must have loved it, to be sending your son here.'

'No,' he replied, 'I hated every minute of it.'

'But . . . but . . . then why . . .?' I stammered.

'Because I suffered through it, and so can he.'

Ah yes, he probably thought the school was 'character-forming'. And who knows, perhaps he would not have been 'prominent in public life' had he not gone to Geelong Grammar. Perhaps he might have been just, I don't know, a good father.

Almost as helpful as conversations with children about schools are conversations with teachers (but not those in positions of responsibility, whose vested interests weigh too heavily upon them).

Conversations with other parents should be treated with caution, as their views are often based on issues too subjective. If a teacher has, at any time in the previous twelve months, raised the faintest suspicion about the veracity of Angus's story of having his lunch money stolen by a gang of Grade 2 thugs armed with steel bayonets, one or more of Angus's parents may be irredeemably prejudiced against the school.

The other way of evaluating the real worth of a school is to gain access to its two least accessible rooms: the kids' toilets and the staffroom. God forbid parents should even hint that they want to see inside the kids' toilets, unless they want the SWAT squad to be called, and then find their face, or, more accurately, a photographic image of their face, on the front page of the tabloids the next day. But parents can try to arrange for the building to be cordoned off whilst they sneak a look inside. Ideally, they should be greeted by facilities that are sparkling clean, with good-quality toilet paper that will be soft on their little one's bum, and fragrant but environmentally sympathetic soap. Strong doubts about the school should be raised by the sight of a vile and smelly place decorated with crude graffiti that induces instant constipation in all who venture near.

The quality of the lavatory facilities is a good indicator of the regard in which children are held in a school; far better than any number of glossy brochures stuffed with photos carefully calculated and staged to show the gender and ethnic mix the school believes will be most attractive to the customers they want to enrol.

If parents are able to talk their way into the staffroom, they should do so with nostrils quivering and senses on full alert. A drab staffroom populated by dispirited teachers is a red flag. Nothing on the noticeboards but 'Regulations Pursuant to the Act of 1999' and memos pertaining to 'Shoes Purchased for the Purposes of Teaching Physical Education, Tax Deductibility of', plus a few photos of kids with potential anaphylactic reactions? A sink full of unwashed coffee cups? Aggressive notices warning that those who use other people's coffee cups are 'Selfish, and Lack the Right Spirit'?

Forget etiquette, just run for the car park.

When a visitor enters a good staffroom, people will come up and introduce themselves. There'll be bright and lively chatter, and lots of laughter. Children who knock on the door will be treated with courtesy and not left to wait for ten minutes in a cold corridor whilst the teacher they want to see finishes her crossword and has a second cup of International Roast.

The truth about Candlebark and Alice Miller is that everything we do could easily be replicated in other schools and school systems. Yet although we have almost daily visits from educators from all around Australia and overseas, and although they invariably leave singing the praises of our methods, they are very quick to explain why they couldn't possibly change the practices they are currently following – practices that essentially have not changed in more than a hundred years.

Yet we should not despair.

14

CHANGE – IS IT POSSIBLE?

I first saw the 1953 film of Shakespeare's *Julius Caesar* in the early 1960s, and, unlike many, I have to admit, was uninspired by the late Marlon Brando mumbling his way through the movie. But it remains a powerful play, about politics and manipulation and betrayal, with a bit of nobility thrown in. The most famous scene of course is the one where Marc Antony tries to change the mind of the mob. Once Brutus has convinced the crowd that it was a really good idea to assassinate the popular Caesar, Marc Antony has a tough gig on his hands to defend his murdered friend. It would be like Hillary Clinton doing stand-up comedy at the Republican Party National Convention.

However, Antony starts with the irresistible phrase 'Friends, Romans, countrymen, lend me your ears'[289] and never looks back. He speaks so eloquently and movingly about Caesar's great qualities and his love for ordinary Romans that the crowd turns on Brutus.

The scene is famous because it shows how easily public opinion can be reversed. In our world, politicians, advertisers and tabloid media know this, and use shallow and often false arguments to convince people of a particular point of view. I find it amazing that public opinion is so fickle. But, whilst it's unnerving sometimes that a whole society can quickly change its attitude on a topic, I also find it encouraging that the change is often from a negative view of a 'worthy cause' to a positive one.

---

289 William Shakespeare, *Julius Caesar*, Act III, scene ii.

I remember around the year 2000 having the second-hand experience of watching on TV an attempt by the people of a Tasmanian
town to save a stranded whale. One of the rangers organising the
rescue remarked to the camera that only a few years earlier, when
a whale had beached itself in the same area, people from the town
came and carved their initials in the poor creature as it lay dying. He
thought it was extraordinary that in a short space of time they were
now showing such compassion. He also thought it was wonderful. So
did I.

In the 1950s, when I was growing up, nearly all boys were circumcised. In less than a generation that procedure suddenly lost popularity,
except in some Jewish and Islamic families. Most baby boys now begin
their lives without suffering this random and unnecessary intense pain.

People who are same-sex attracted have seen a remarkable change
in community attitudes in the space of a decade or two. Memoirs
like *Against the Law* (1955) by Peter Wildeblood, and *The Naked
Civil Servant* (1968) by Quentin Crisp, detailing the persecution their
authors suffered as a result of their sexuality, could not, we hope, be
written nowadays, although some countries still have a long way to
go – murder of homosexual people by stoning them to death is still
an option for the judiciary to prescribe, in a number of nations.

In 1961, John Howard Griffin published *Black Like Me*, in which
he described his experiences when he used medication to change his
skin colour so that he could pass as a coloured man in the United
States. He told of black people being refused permission to get off
a Greyhound bus at a rest stop so that one desperate man had to
urinate on the floor of the bus, a white man offering $7.50 to procure
a fourteen-year-old black girl for sex, a white man wanting Griffin
to show him his genitals to see whether they matched the salacious
stories he had heard about Afro-American men. He recounted the
story of a job interview with a foreman in an Alabama factory who
calmly explained: 'We're gradually getting you people weeded out
from the better jobs at this plant. We're taking it slow, but we're doing
it. Pretty soon we'll have it so that the only jobs you can get here

are the ones no white man would have . . . We're going to do our damnedest to drive every one of you out of the state.'[290]

Although there is still plenty of racism in the world, huge strides have been made since 1961. As books like Chloe Hooper's *The Tall Man* show, Australia, in its treatment of Indigenous people, continues to be one of the world's laggards. But in my lifetime I have at least witnessed considerable improvement in the respect accorded to Australian Indigenous history and Indigenous culture. Many programs, some on a large scale and some small, have been implemented, in well-motivated attempts to remedy and apologise for past injustices.

We will never again see, in Western countries, the violence that was inflicted on schoolchildren as a matter of course in previous generations. Mrs Lawrence, the Grade 3 teacher at Devonport Primary School for 40 years, caned children, including me, with barely disguised savagery on a daily basis. When my brother volunteered to become a member of the school's lunchtime choir, and one day was talking in the back row during a rehearsal, Mrs Lawrence came up behind him and slashed him so viciously across the back of the legs with a cane that his blood flowed.

We had a test every Friday, covering the week's work, and any child who got fewer than seven marks out of ten for the test was caned automatically. Fridays were not good days for kids with dyslexia, learning difficulties or emotional problems.

In the classroom next door was Mrs Scott, the Grade 4 teacher at Devonport Primary School for 40 years. She taught the same children, from the same background, with the same values and attitudes. She did not use the cane once during her teaching career.

Although many adults cling with almost religious fervour to the clichéd idea that 'children can be so horrible to each other', ignoring the horrors that adults all too frequently inflict on people, schools nowadays are much kinder communities.

Unfortunately some attitudinal changes come too late. Gradually

---

290 John Howard Griffin, *Black Like Me*, Panther, St Albans, 1964, p. 118.

we are starting to recognise the need to conserve the planet and to keep our environment healthy. But the awareness has been too slow coming and, as a result, irreversible damage has been done.

In Queensland, in 1999, farmers heard that they would soon be prevented by the government from clearing their land. They reacted with an orgy of greed and rage, the like of which has seldom been seen. Using bulldozers working in pairs, with heavy chains between them, they cleared an estimated three quarters of a million hectares of forest. Restrictions were eventually brought in, at the end of 2006. However, the Act was watered down by a Liberal government in 2013, allowing the farmers to resume the devastation. The ABC reported that land-clearing rates went from 92,000 hectares in 2010–11 to 266,000 hectares in 2012–13.[291] It quoted a grazier, Nikki Cameron, who defended this behaviour by saying, with breathtaking ignorance and arrogance, 'I think you need to trust the people who are on the land and who have managed the land for many generations.'[292] Barnaby Joyce, from the National Party, was the federal Agriculture Minister at the time. He also defended the farmers' actions, using classic concrete language. If people made the mistake of electing a Labor government, Joyce warned, 'You'll have the state tree police and you'll have the federal tree police.'[293] The president of AgForce Queensland, apparently also an aficionado of concrete language, said, 'We need to stop having silly arguments about trees every time we have an election.'[294]

Queensland parliamentarian Robbie Katter, son of federal politician Bob Katter, spoke of people in Brisbane holding 'fuzzy feelings', which in his view meant they lacked understanding of the desire of Queensland graziers to clear land at a rate equivalent to 100 football

---

291 Quoted in Marty McCarthy, 'Tree clearing', *Landline*, ABC TV, 14 May 2016, abc.net.au/tv/programs/landline/old-site/content/2016/s4462435.htm, accessed 13 March 2019.
292 Quoted in McCarthy, 'Tree clearing'.
293 McCarthy, 'Tree clearing'.
294 Sarah Elks, 'To clear or not to clear: farmers in the dark on new laws', *The Australian*, 29 May 2016, theaustralian.com.au/news/inquirer/to-clear-or-not-to-clear-farmers-in-the-dark-on-new-laws/news-story/a24bfd12faf4057c1a2086f21b140b93, accessed 1 April 2019.

fields every hour ... an image which made more vivid to my sadly limited human brain the amount of destruction wrought by these people. Katter told *The Australian* newspaper: 'We don't impose our views or cultural war and fuzzy feelings on South Brisbane. So we don't appreciate them strongly imposing on our ability to exist up here, to survive out here.'[295]

It seems that in Katter's mind, people who live in cities have no right to hold an opinion about environmental issues. Having been in Singapore whilst Indonesian farmers were holding their traditional annual burn-off, and groping my way through the ash-laden smog, aware that many Singapore people were suffering respiratory ailments as a result of the Indonesian farmers' actions, I would say that city people have every right to respond when farmers act selfishly and destructively. Farmers are, after all, custodians of the land, not owners in the sense that we might be said to own a pair of shoes or a packet of biscuits.

In 2016, a statement signed by 200 scientists described an estimated total of 100 million native birds, reptiles and mammals dying in New South Wales from 1998 to 2005, and an estimated 100 million native animals dying each year in Queensland between 1997 and 1999 as a result of land-clearing operations.[296] The farmers would say that they were doing this for future generations, for their children, and their children's children. They do not seem to realise that their grand-children and great-grandchildren are more likely to curse their names and spit on their graves, for their desecration of the precious land.

To see the devastation wrought in Queensland by the 2019 floods, causing such catastrophes as the drowning of about half a million cattle, is to see one of the consequences of the behaviour of many graziers.

Since the 1960s, much derision has been expressed towards those who hold liberal and progressive views in our society. In the 1950s it

295 Sarah Elks, 'To clear or not to clear'.
296 Richard Kingsford et al., 'Australian's land clearing rate is once again among the highest in the world', *UNSW Newsroom*, 8 July 2016, newsroom.unsw.edu.au/news/science-tech/australia's-land-clearing-rate-once-again-among-highest-world, accessed 1 April 2019.

was convenient to call them Communists, reds, lefties, pinkos. Since then the language has changed to equally contemptuous terms like 'the chardonnay set', 'the latte set', 'armchair socialists', 'greenies', 'the chattering class', 'tree huggers', 'hipsters' and, in Melbourne, 'Brunswick socialists'.

It seems to have gone unnoticed by conservative commentators that on every significant political and social issue in my lifetime the 'chardonnay set' has been correct. Opposition to racial discrimination in the United States and Australia in the 1960s, opposition to the Vietnam War, pursuit of Richard Nixon over the Watergate scandal, opposition to the damming of the Franklin River in Tasmania, opposition to the invasion of Iraq, the promotion of alternative energy to try to reverse environmental damage, advocacy for the humane treatment of animals, opposition to sexual slavery, opposition to the exploitation of workers in the Third World by giant corporations that number their profits in the billions of dollars, demands for those giant corporations to pay their fair share of taxes, opposition to the destruction of the Great Barrier Reef . . . is there any sane person who would argue that these causes have not been entirely worthy?

Instead of the endless denigration of people who hold progressive views, it may be time to recognise and honour them for their courage in consistently taking unpopular stands, maintaining their idealism and integrity in the face of sustained and often vicious attacks, and constantly working for a better world.

Our great challenge, the challenge for all adults but particularly teachers, is to convince children that change for the better is possible and achievable, that their actions can make a difference, and that defeating the forces of ignorance and self-interest – like the Queensland rural lobbyists mentioned earlier – is essential. The title of a 1983 Serbian movie, *How I Was Systematically Destroyed by Idiots*, serves as a useful warning. There is a real risk that we will be destroyed by idiots. Although, as I mentioned earlier, we are all guilty of inflicting damage on the planet on a micro level, nothing comes near the devastation wrought by such self-interested groups as land-clearing farmers from

Queensland and elsewhere, cigarette companies, palm oil producers, certain mining and industrial corporations, and, in Australia in 2019, those who advocate fiercely for coal producers like Adani to be allowed to ruin the landscape so that they can continue to generate pollution on a massive scale.

'The violence that men do not use except subconsciously in defence of a closed mind . . .'[297] We need to recognise violence whenever we encounter it, call it for what it is, and have the courage to resist it. When I see conservative politicians and commentators, red-faced with rage, showering their audience with spittle in their furious denunciations of progressive views and enlightened ideas, clinging to their ignorance like a passenger on the *Titanic* hugging a pillar in the bar and insisting 'The Captain said not to worry; everything's going to be fine', I can only refer to Freud, and speculate on the horrors of the toilet training these people must have endured in infancy. The stubbornness, mean-ness, and compulsive neatness and order that they demand is exactly as Freud described. Their fear of a flood of non-Anglo Saxons spilling into Australia in an uncontrolled mess reminds me of . . . what was it again? It's slipped my mind.

Humans should be humane. We should be able to laugh and cry. It is difficult to imagine many conservative figureheads doing either. If we look at a politician or media commentator and find ourselves unable to picture them laughing or crying, we should deny them access to power. It is difficult to imagine the world's tyrants – Hitler, Kim Jong-il, Pol Pot and Stalin, along with some current world leaders and demagogues – laughing with beautiful delight, or crying with genuine sympathy. For thousands of years sociopaths have been allowed supreme power in many countries, because people who identify their psychopathology and try to oppose them are unable to match the utter ferocity and single-mindedness of their personalities. Instead, they often die – heroically, nobly, self-sacrificingly – but they die. In doing so, they lose, and the world loses.

---

297 Morgan, *The House of Macmillan 1843–1943*, p. 144.

Mature humans are empathetic, imaginative, emotional and insightful. They should be able to understand abstractions. They are thoughtful, which means that they think. They take a careful, calm and considered approach towards the difficulties they encounter, recognising at the same time that their emotions can be important indicators of the direction they should follow.

Mature humans are dishonest, lazy, greedy, cruel and selfish at times. This is because they are human. The modern hankering for 'role models' that 'young people can look up to' is immature and naïve. It assumes that some people are better than others, but there are so many different criteria upon which better and worse can be judged that the concept is meaningless. Anyone who worships, reveres, idolises or even looks up to another person can only hope that they will never learn the full truth about that person, because if they do they are bound to discover that their hero has many flaws. Geniuses are attractive only from a distance. '*Peu d'hommes ont esté admirés par leurs domestiques*' (Few men have been admired by their servants), as Montaigne said.[298] When Darcy's housekeeper praises her master to Elizabeth Bennet in *Pride and Prejudice*, we can be pretty sure that Darcy is a good bloke.

Australia is an exceptionally wealthy and secure country. Yet to walk through a suburban shopping centre or down the main street of any country town is to hear a deafening chorus of cries of poverty and demands for more of everything. People are outraged that the government has not provided better internet access, new croquet lawns, higher payments to people who choose to have children, faster trains, funds for flood victims, grants to cassava farmers, subsidies for importers of condoms, increased prize money for the winners of the Annual Pie Eating Competition . . .

Meanwhile, in countries not far away (as if location were relevant), millions of people are homeless, starving, cold, frightened and dying from illnesses or injuries that could be easily treated were the right medicines, technology, doctors and nurses available.

---

298 Michel de Montaigne, 'Du repentir', *Essais*, 1588, Book III, Chapter 2.

We have a grave responsibility to educate ourselves and our children and grandchildren in our obligations to do more than apply a Band-Aid to a gaping wound, offer more than a jelly bean to a person suffering from malnutrition, give more than a box of tissues to someone who has lost their home in a mudslide.

We are continuing to fail in our moral duty towards our fellow humans.

In our homes and schools, we must do more than teach children and teenagers to be kind and polite to the people with whom they are in contact, to share the birthday cake equally, to dress appropriately, to manage their finances prudently. We must teach them that there is a big world out there, and it is in serious difficulties. Their privileged upbringing carries with it huge obligations.

My hope for Candlebark and Alice Miller Schools is that our students' first-hand experiences, and their exposure to interesting, adventurous adults, will help equip them to revegetate, reforest, regenerate the world. They will do harm, of course, because they are human. I trust them though to commit so many good deeds that the planet will be much the better for the time they spend here. Life can be full of rich delights, and many are found in wild places. But: beware the bulldozers. Their hot breath is getting hotter and closer and louder.

ACKNOWLEDGEMENTS

When I signed with Pan Macmillan for my second ever book, *The Great Gatenby*, I had little idea of what lay ahead. But after a lot of conversations over the phone I found an excuse to go to Sydney, which meant I could ask to meet James Fraser, the publisher at Pan Macmillan.

He invited me to lunch, and I accepted. The day before the meeting I ran into an old friend, Alexander Haege, and I told him what was in store. Alexander knew the restaurants of Sydney, and ran through a quick list, explaining that if I was taken to one restaurant that would suggest the publishers saw me as a long-term literary author, another would mean a commercially viable writer of light fiction, and so on.

I was very impressed, and keen to see what the outcome would be.

The next day I at last met James. He took me to lunch – at the nearest pub, for a counter meal.

Thirty years later I'm Pan Macmillan's longest-serving Australian author. Despite that earthy beginning, it's been a wonderful relationship. They have been professional, adventurous, kind and innovative. I've worked with a long list of exceptional people there, including, in no particular order, James, Roxarne Burns, Jeannine Fowler, Nikki Christer, Ross Gibb, Tracey Cheetham, Simone Bird, Cate Paterson, Phil Lawson, Paul Kenny, Jane Novak, Peter Phillip, Claire Craig, Robin Clark, Julia Stiles, Georgia Douglas, Andrew Farrell, Hayley Crandell and Anna McFarlane.

So I'd like to acknowledge their help in this and every other book of mine that they've published.

Another group which has been of great significance is the teachers with whom I've worked in various schools. I was incredibly lucky to start my career alongside a trio of John Mazur, Bill Montgomery and Scott Sullivan. I learnt more from them than I learnt from any university course or any books I read. Later I had the pleasure of colleagues like Mary Edmonston, Roger Morton, Jenny Clairs, and then had four years with the remarkable Jeremy Madin.

I got involved further down the track with Fitzroy Community School in Melbourne, where the wisdom and generosity of people like Faye Berryman, Jeannette Howden, Tim Berryman and Philip O'Carroll taught me so much.

And then came Candlebark and Alice Miller Schools. The teachers with whom I've had the privilege of working there have been dedicated, full of ideas, willing to try anything that sounds like it might be of value to their students. They also seem notable for their sense of humour, which is a powerful asset in a teacher. I won't mention any of them by name because if I did I'd have to mention virtually all of them, and such a long list would be a bit meaningless, but like many people I am grateful for the ways in which Hartley Mitchell's time and energy have been given to Alice Miller so generously and selflessly, and the fact that Sarita Ryan's leadership of Alice Miller has been so strong, compassionate and whole-hearted.

My brother Sam has always been a good friend – except when we were teenagers maybe!

Finally, Kris Rielly, and Fletcher, Oliver, Wilson, Harry, Charlie and Alexander Tautkus have enriched my life and taught me a lot. Kris's understanding of families has helped immeasurably in the writing of this book.

All of these people and many others have made *The Art of Growing Up* possible, contributing in specific or non-specific ways to it.

Thank you.

SELECTED BIBLIOGRAPHY

Rather than fill an endless number of pages with details of an endless number of books, I'll confine myself to suggesting the following titles for people interested in reading more about education, parenting and life:

Totto-Chan: The Little Girl at the Window by Tetsuko Kuroyanagi. A beautiful book describing an 'alternative' school in Japan. This is a memoir by one of its ex-students, a woman who became a well-known Japanese media personality.

The school was destroyed by fire in the Tokyo air raids in 1945.

Tetsuko Kuroyanagi, *Totto-Chan: The Little Girl at the Window*, Kodansha International, Japan, 2012.

Magister Ludi a.k.a. *The Glass Bead Game* by Hermann Hesse. Everything by Hesse should of course be compulsory reading for everyone, but this is my favourite of his books (along with *Siddhartha*). It is a wonderful dissertation upon education as it could and perhaps should be.

Hermann Hesse, *The Glass Bead Game*, Holt, Rinehart and Winston, Switzerland, 1943.

Risinghill: Death of a Comprehensive School by Leila Berg. Leila Berg wrote in quite a few different genres and it's worth checking out anything she wrote in any of them! But I'd recommend this as the first one on her list to read. It's the story of the life and death of an innovative, progressive, government secondary school in London.

Leila Berg, *Risinghill: Death of a Comprehensive School*, Penguin, London, 1968.

Fitzroy Community School by Philip O'Carroll and Faye Berryman. Pioneers in alternative education in Australia, Philip and Faye have written a detailed history of their remarkable school, and included their philosophy of how schools should be operated. The first chapter is a startling description of how and why most parent-run schools implode. Fitzroy Community School turned 40 in 2016.

Philip O'Carroll and Faye Berryman, *Fitzroy Community School*, Fitzroy Programs, Australia, 2015.

The Drama of being a Child a.k.a. *The Drama of the Gifted Child* by Alice Miller. Again, pretty much anything Alice Miller wrote is worth reading, although sometimes the content can get a bit repetitive. *The Drama of being a Child* is a confronting yet sympathetic exploration of the many ways in which children can be dreadfully damaged by the very people who are primarily responsible for their care.

Alice Miller, *The Drama of the Gifted Child*, Basic Books, USA, 1979.

Indiscretions of a Headmistress by Betty Archdale. Archdale, Headmistress of Sydney Anglican girls' school, Abbotsleigh, was no intellectual, but she was a real personality who did what she thought was right, regardless of the pompous and important people she offended. If you know the politics of Sydney Anglican Diocese, you would enjoy some of her stories, including the one about the local curate who referred 'all through a sermon [at the school] to the Revised Standard Virgin, instead of Revised Standard Version, of the Bible.'

Betty Archdale, *Indiscretions of a Headmistress*, Angus & Robertson, Australia, 1972.

Death at an Early Age by Jonathan Kozol. Kozol is the teacher I've mentioned in *The Art of Growing Up* who was sacked for reading a Langston Hughes poem to his students. This book is a blistering account of some of the many things wrong with the model of schooling which we are following in the Western world.

Here's a piece of writing by one of Kozol's young students, with the original spelling unaltered:

In my school, I see dirty boards and I see papers on the floor. I see an old browken window with a sign on it saying, Do not unlock this window are browken. And I see cracks in the walls and I see old books with ink poured all over them and I see old painting hanging on the wall. I see old alfurbet letter hanging on one nail on the wall. I see a dirty fire exit I see a old closet with supplys for the class. I see pigeons flying all over the school. I see old freght trains throgh the fence of the school yard. I see pictures of countrys hanging on the wall and I see desks with wrighting all over the top of the desks and insited of the desk.

Jonathan Kozol, *Death at an Early Age: The Destruction of the Hearts and Minds of Negro Children in the Boston Public Schools*, Penguin, New York, 1967 and 1985, (first published 1967).

Anton Makarenko: His Life and His Work in Education by Anton Makarenko. (Note that different people spell his surname in different

ways.) This book can be downloaded at marxists.org/reference/
archive/makarenko/works/life-and-work.pdf

Makarenko was a big fan of Maxim Gorky, and Gorky actually
visited the 'colony' which Makarenko created in Russia for young
criminals, orphans and homeless kids. Here's a sample from the book;
a man remembering how he was taken out of jail by Makarenko, to
go to the 'colony':

'Good,' Makarenko said, and turned to the governor. 'So we can go
straight from here?'

'Yes, go along,' the governor said. 'Now mind, Kalabalin . . .'

'Please don't, everything will be alright,' Makarenko interrupted.
'Goodbye. Come along, Semyon.'

I love that exchange between Makarenko and the governor; where
Makarenko cuts the governor off immediately, knowing full well that
the man is about to launch into a pious sermon to Kalabalin on how
'he'd better be careful and behave himself properly or else . . .'

Little moments can count for a lot.

Anton Makarenko, *The Road to Life*, quoted in Kumarin,
Anton Makarenko

Impro and *Impro for Storytellers* by Keith Johnstone. These books are
not specifically about education or teaching, but they were hugely
influential for me. Johnstone is one of those geniuses who can take
what we knew unconsciously and teach it to us so that it becomes
part of our conscious understanding.

Keith Johnstone, *Impro*, Faber & Faber, London, 1979.
Keith Johnstone, *Impro for Storytellers*, Routledge, London, 1999.

Homer Lane and the Little Commonwealth by E.T. Bazeley. Homer Lane established a farm community, a 'reformatory', for fifty or so young criminals in the English countryside, in 1914. His approach was unorthodox but highly successful. A.S. Neill referred to Homer Lane as 'the most influential factor' in his life. Sadly, the Little Commonwealth was killed off by several things, including dissension within the Committee which governed it, and an accusation by a teenage girl of some sort of sexual misconduct by Lane. It seems likely that the accusation was baseless, but it did result in the Commonwealth closing.

E.T. Bazeley, *Homer Lane and the Little Commonwealth*,
Allen & Unwin, London, 1928.

Dibs in Search of Self by Virginia Axline. An account, taken from recorded play therapy sessions with a boy who is aged five when we first meet him. He is considered 'mentally retarded' by his mother, and his paediatrician has asked 'Mentally retarded? Psychotic? Brain-damaged? Who can get close enough to find out what makes him tick?' The book is a deeply moving account which offers profound insights to the development of a young child.

Virginia M. Axline, *Dibs in Search of Self*, Penguin Press, Melbourne, 1990.

South of Darkness

My name, then, is Barnaby Fletch. To the best of my knowledge I have no middle name and cannot say of whom I am the son, or of whom my father's father's father was the son. Alas, my origins are shrouded in mystery...

Thirteen-year-old Barnaby Fletch is a bag-and-bones orphan in London in the late 1700s.

Barnaby lives on his wits and ill-gotten gains, on streets seething with the press of the throng and shadowed by sinister figures. Life is a precarious business.

When he hears of a paradise on the other side of the world – a place called Botany Bay – he decides to commit a crime and get himself transported to a new life, a better life. To succeed, he must survive the trials of Newgate Prison, the stinking hull of a prison ship and the unknown terrors of a journey across the world.

And Botany Bay is far from the paradise Barnaby has imagined. When his past and present suddenly collide, he is soon fleeing for his life – once again.

A riveting story of courage, hope and extraordinary adventure.

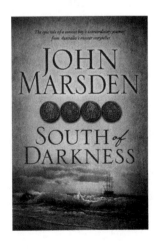

Tomorrow, When the War Began

Ellie and her friends leave home one quiet morning, wave goodbye to their parents, and head up into the hills to camp for a while; seven teenagers filling in time during school holidays.

The world is about to change forever. Their lives will never be the same again.

Would you fight? Would you give up everything? Would you sacrifice even life itself?

Tomorrow, When the War Began asks the biggest questions you will ever have to answer.

'The reader is unwittingly flung headlong and gasping into the plot . . . the images created are so vivid that they stay with you long after the book is reluctantly closed on the final page'
MELBOURNE HERALD-SUN

'. . . a story to be read at full pelt–I could not put it down–and then returned to, for a second and third more thoughtful savouring'
AUSTRALIAN BOOKSELLER & PUBLISHER

'. . . an enlightening book about growing up and discovering who you are'
SUNDAY TELEGRAPH

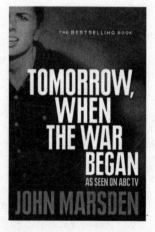

The Dead of the Night

Hell is still the safest place on earth.

When you've run out of choices, you've only got yourself.

As war rages, as the enemy closes in, as Ellie and her friends fight for their lives, they are left with nothing.

Nothing but courage, spirit and pride.

The Dead of the Night is the second volume in the award-winning Tomorrow series.

'John Marsden's *The Dead of the Night* is one of those rare sequels that sustains the standard of its predecessor, for adult devotees as well as discerning teenagers'
THE WEEKEND AUSTRALIAN

'This is a can't put down read–the reader must know what happens next'
SUN-HERALD

'. . . this sequel on its own is a fantastic book, but teamed with *Tomorrow, When the War Began*, is simply outstanding . . . it rates five stars'
HOBART MERCURY

'. . . tense and dramatic . . . crackles with suspense'
CANBERRA CHRONICLE

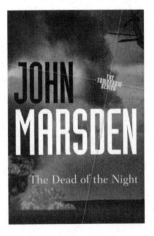

The Third Day, the Frost

Live for what you believe in . . .
Die fighting for it.

The third day comes a frost . . . a killing frost.

The enemy spreads across the land, cold and relentless. They invade. They destroy. They kill.

Only the heroism of Ellie and her friends can stop them.

When hot courage meets icy death, who will win through?

In 2000, The Third Day, the Frost won Germany's Buxtuhede Bulle for the best book in the world for young people published in the previous two years.

'This is real Day of the Jackal stuff and, if you want action, adventure and heart-stopping danger, *The Third Day, the Frost* delivers'
SYDNEY MORNING HERALD

'. . . a high octane adventure . . . unputdownable'
AUSTRALIAN BOOK REVIEW

'. . . tense, exciting and, most importantly, realistic, I wish I could read this series again for the first time'
SUN–HERALD

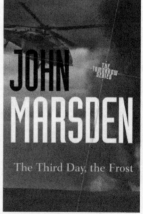

Darkness, Be My Friend

Nowhere to run, one place left to hide.

Darkness is the friend and enemy of those who hunt by night. And for those who hunt by night there can be a darkness of the soul, a darkness of the heart. Ellie has to defeat an inner darkness if she is to defeat the outer one. This is the engrossing story of her brave and bold struggle.

'. . . another enthralling tale of survival from one of the country's best-loved children's authors'
MERCURY

'A tale of gripping intensity and blinding fear, it will have your adrenaline rushing, your head pumping, the blood roaring in your ears and your fingernails bitten down to the quick'
QUEENSLAND TIMES

'This is a book that is hard to put down . . . it's gripping in its intensity and its intrigue. It's Marsden at his best!'
GEELONG ADVERTISER

'. . . check your heart rate as you read'
THE AGE

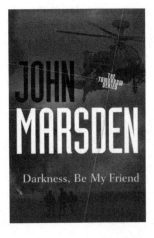

Burning for Revenge

The world is on fire. The world of Ellie and her friends has been set alight and is in flames. No-one will come out of it unscathed.

Burning for Revenge is scorching: the hottest book you'll ever read.

A sensational novel from the series that has transfixed millions of readers worldwide.

'Once started, this book is hard to put down. It should carry a warning "Don't start it at night unless you are an insomniac"'
THE CATHOLIC WEEKLY

'You will not be able to put this down until the last page has been turned–and even then you will be left breathless, thirsting for more!'
QUEENSLAND TIMES

'. . . if you pick up this book to dip in you'll find that you are galloping along with the narrative, unable to extricate yourself until those final words'
AUSTRALIAN BOOK REVIEW

'As addictive as the earlier books in the series and guaranteed to attract even more readers'
ILLAWARRA MERCURY

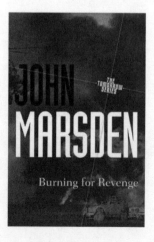

The Night is for Hunting

Hunting and being hunted.

Sometimes life seems to offer nothing more than a chase to the death.

The fight to survive has never been fiercer.

But as they wage war, Ellie and her friends still find time for other things: friendship . . . loyalty . . . even Christmas.

If only they can withstand another night.

The Night is for Hunting is the sixth volume in the award-winning *Tomorrow* series.

'. . . elevation of adventure literature to heights that are only achieved once or twice in a generation'
SFSITE.COM

'It is without a doubt the best series for younger readers that an Australian writer has ever produced'
DAILY ADVERTISER

'Adventure in a world where the characters must fight and survive–a powerful mixture and a tale very well told. The Night is for Hunting is another winner by this top-selling author who knows how to write for young people and what makes them tick'
GEELONG ADVERTISER

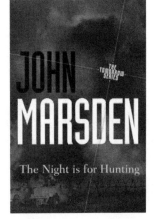

The Other Side of Dawn

This is a story of courage and adventure, of a tiny group of teenagers engaged in a struggle in which everything is at stake: their families, their friends, their countries, their lives. For them, there can be no turning back, no surrender. Too much rests on their shoulders, too many lives are at stake. They must go on . . . to life, to death, to the unknown.

You will never forget the brave hearts of Ellie and Homer and their friends.

A sensational novel from the series that has transfixed millions of readers worldwide.

'I feel, now that I have finished the series, something is missing. I wish I'd never read the series, so that I could discover it all now'
SARAH LAIN, UNITED KINGDOM

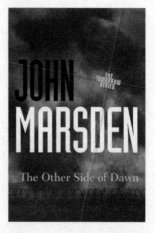